palgrave advances in
continental political thought

Palgrave Advances

Titles include:

Michele M. Betsill, Kathryn Hochstetler and Dimitris Stevis (*editors*)
INTERNATIONAL ENVIRONMENTAL POLITICS

Terrell Carver and James Martin (*editors*)
CONTINENTAL POLITICAL THOUGHT

Michelle Cini and Angela K. Bourne (*editors*)
EUROPEAN UNION STUDIES

Jeffrey Haynes (*editor*)
DEVELOPMENT STUDIES

Palgrave Advances
Series Standing Order ISBN 1–4039–3512–2 (Hardback) 1–4039–3513–0 (Paperback)
(*outside North America only*)

You can receive future titles in this series as they are published by placing a standing order. Please contact your bookseller or, in the case of difficulty, write to us at the address below with your name and address, the title of the series and the ISBN quoted above.

Customer Services Department, Macmillan Distribution Ltd, Houndmills, Basingstoke, Hampshire RG21 6XS, England

palgrave advances in continental political thought

edited by

terrell carver
professor of political theory
university of bristol

and

james martin
senior lecturer in politics
goldsmiths college
university of london

palgrave
macmillan

First published 2006 by
PALGRAVE MACMILLAN
Houndmills, Basingstoke, Hampshire RG21 6XS and
175 Fifth Avenue, New York, N.Y. 10010
Companies and representatives throughout the world

PALGRAVE MACMILLAN is the global academic imprint of the Palgrave
Macmillan division of St Martin's Press LLC and of Palgrave Macmillan Ltd.
Macmillan® is a registered trademark in the United States,
United Kingdom and other countries. Palgrave is a registered
trademark in the European Union and other countries.

ISBN-13   978–1–4039–0367–9 hardback
ISBN-10   1–4039–0367–0 hardback
ISBN-13   978–1–4039–0368–6 paperback
ISBN-10   1–4039–0368–9 paperback

This book is printed on paper suitable for recycling and
made from fully managed and sustained forest sources.

A catalogue record for this book is available from the British Library.

Library of Congress Cataloging-in-Publication Data
Palgrave advances in continental political thought / edited by Terrell Carver &
James Martin.
    p. cm. — (Palgrave advances)
Includes bibliographical references and index.
ISBN 1–4039–0367–0 (cloth) — ISBN 1–4039–0368–9 (pbk.)
    1. Political science—Europe—History. I. Carver, Terrell. II. Martin, James,
1968– III. Series.

JA84.E9P35 2005
320'.092'24—dc22
                                                                    2005051477

10 9   8   7   6   5   4   3   2
15 14 13 12 11 10 09 08 07 06

Printed and bound in Great Britain by
Antony Rowe Ltd, Chippenham and Eastbourne

contents

introduction

terrell carver and james martin

What is Continental Political Thought? What relevance does it have for us today? The term 'Continental' has something of a bad reputation. In a very descriptive sense, it refers us, geographically speaking, to Continental Europe; but in so doing, it brings with it a number of meanings that might prejudice us against it and our understanding of its value and relevance.

Think, for a moment, of European history and culture. Two major wars in the last century, a recent history of revolutions and authoritarian dictatorships, imperial domination and genocide. Hardly a recommendation for sober political dialogue! Or consider European cinema: movies commonly believed to be self-consciously 'arty', sometimes disturbingly erotic, intellectually profound and, as a consequence of all this, rather difficult to comprehend. Unlike Hollywood movies – think of the annual 'blockbuster' – which typically leave us in no doubt who the good guys are and why they should win, we often leave a European film uncertain as to whether we really got the message at all.

Political theories, of course, are not movies. But they occupy some of the same classifications we employ to divide up our tastes in popular culture. As with the movies, we tend to come to theories with a number of expectations and presumptions. More often than not, we find these confirmed when we enter into the world of the theoretical text. Thus 'Continental Political Thought' may well conjure up a number of characters making profound and complex statements in beautiful yet fraught European contexts. We might, if we follow the subtitles or the commentaries, 'get the story' these texts are telling … up to a point. All too soon, however, we find ourselves unsettled by their strange use of language, elliptical style and, frankly, odd attitude towards the world. It is highly likely that we will emerge wondering whether perhaps the oddness of the ideas presented to us isn't in some way a masquerade or

1

fraud, a deliberate and pretentious overstatement to make what in the end is only a small point.

Like European cinema, Continental political ideas have been accused of precisely these crimes. Unlike the Anglo-American tradition of thought, with which they are commonly contrasted, Continental ideas are routinely derided for being too 'poetic', needlessly convoluted and hence dangerously removed from 'common sense' and the needs of everyday life. Or, at least, that is what we often hear. But, like any good movie, if we are prepared to set aside for a moment our initial prejudices and spend some more time considering what is being said, we will find there is more there than our initial reactions lead us to believe. If we enter into their spirit and consider their enduring value or contemporary resonances, we may find ourselves transformed, or at very least *in*formed, in a way we hadn't expected.

The purpose of this book is to serve as an accessible guide to the political thought of key thinkers in the Continental tradition and, in particular, to make clear the continuing relevance of his or her ideas. Each chapter focuses on an individual thinker, sketches the major elements of their ideas and indicates why and how they remain relevant to theorising politics today. But what *is* the Continental tradition? By way of an introduction to the collection, we shall dwell for the moment on answering precisely that question.

political theory ... the continental way?

In gathering together under one name a number of individuals who thought and wrote within the geographical boundaries of Continental Europe, are we implying there is a distinctive *way* of theorising politics that can be called 'Continental'? In a (perhaps very Continental) sense yes but, also, no. Use of the term 'Continental' only began in the twentieth century, long after many of the thinkers listed under that category lived and died. Nor is it the only term we might use to distinguish these thinkers. Other terms might be 'European' or perhaps more technical descriptors such as 'idealist' or 'anti-empiricist'. However, these alternatives cover either too many or only some of the thinkers and schools of thought examined here. 'Continental' is an inclusive term but also suggests a broad tradition, extending beyond the characteristic features of any one set of thinkers or indeed any specific geographical setting. In so doing, however, it loses the precision it would have if it referred merely to one school of thought and becomes instead a generic, if sometimes very vague, marker of commonality. Let us consider the central strands of that commonality.

An original theme of Continental thought is widely agreed to be a critical reaction against the Enlightenment, the movement of ideas which first emerged in Europe in the seventeenth century and reached its height in the eighteenth, driven by the belief that reason – rational thought untainted by blind prejudice and tradition – enables us to grasp the material and social world objectively. Such a view, expounded in scientific 'discoveries' and statements such as those of Isaac Newton and Francis Bacon, and in the philosophy of René Descartes, underscored a belief in the progress of human society that could be brought by human knowledge. Only rational thought, it was believed, permitted us to grasp the principles that govern material and social life with any certainty, whether this be through empirical observation or by methodical, reasoned enquiry. Truths could not be accepted simply on the basis of assertion or 'revelation'. The political implications of this radical mode of thinking are obvious: religious and traditional forms of authority were placed in doubt, their intrinsic veracity questioned and the obligation to obey them without question was undermined. Thus the Enlightenment set in motion a new cultural expectation that truth and moral value be accountable to reason. These ideas played no small part in preparing the way for the democratic revolutions in America (1776) and France (1789) which renounced the authority of monarchy and demanded that government be founded on the rights of individuals to liberty, free from the burden of hereditary hierarchy.

For a variety of reasons, however, many Continental thinkers found this aspiration to be hugely overstated. Few rejected outright the possibilities opened up by the use of reason critically to evaluate the human condition independently of religious dogma or interference, nor did they entirely dispute the advantages of political systems that sustained the individual freedom and the rights of citizens to hold their rulers to account. But whilst the advantages of rational knowledge and rational political organisation were not in themselves disputed, nor were they uncritically embraced. For Continental thinkers – because they were following in the wake of David Hume's scepticism about the ability of reason to grasp the world fully, and because they were living through the profound disruptions brought by political and economic change – the epistemological claims of modern scientific understanding and the political demands for individual freedom were themselves open to doubt and critical reflection, such that neither could be assumed to command automatic assent. For many thinkers, then, the claims of reason and the case for free political orders had yet to be properly made. It is precisely this critical, but not dismissive, philosophical and political attitude that sits at the basis of the Continental tradition as we know it today.

The reaction to Enlightenment rationalism and to the dangers of social and political systems premised on the freedom of citizens marks a central point of difference with the other dominant strand of thought in the West (one also defined by its geographical location), Anglo-American thought. In crude terms, Anglo-American thought is believed to have inherited a much more positive view of the possibilities engendered by reason and the virtuous character of liberal institutions. By contrast with the Continentals, this tradition has underscored the ability of rational subjects to grasp the world through the use of scientific techniques and empirical analysis, uncovering its law-like nature and enabling science to further the cause of human progress through the elimination of obstacles to knowledge and freedom. The 'analytical' style of philosophical reasoning, with its careful attention to logic, the pitfalls of contradiction and the coherence of ordinary language exemplifies well this approach. It is perhaps no surprise that this tradition owes its name to the two countries – the US and the UK – where the parliamentary democratic form of government and liberal-capitalist societies have been most stable and enduring.

But this crude distinction between Continental and Anglo-American traditions hides a much more complex reality. Like the distinction between Hollywood and European cinema, it certainly tells us something about *some* of the preoccupations of its proponents, but that only really scratches the surface. First of all, it would be wrong simply to bundle together all the thinkers in this volume (and the wider Continental tradition) and separate them off from another, sweeping category of Anglo-Americans, as if these were both homogeneous groups who all agreed that they were part of a common tradition, especially one opposed to the other. What are now called Continental and Anglo-American thinkers have been as much associated with each other as they have differed. Ideas and theories from one camp have often been, and still are, appropriated by the other. Thus Continental ideas and political theories are easily found in America and Britain (for example, the work of Michel Foucault and Jacques Derrida), and Anglo-American theories are widely disseminated and taken up in Continental Europe (for example, the work of J.L. Austin and John Rawls).

Second, even where the philosophical orientation has differed, similar political themes have often prevailed amongst both traditions. Continental thinkers have been concerned with the nature of freedom and justice, the role and function of the state and power, the place of morality in a secular political system, and so forth. In this they do not always differ radically from the Anglo-American tradition. Like thinkers in Britain and America, Continentals have themselves adopted political positions that range from the deeply reactionary and conservative to liberal, socialist and revolutionary. Sharing similar forms of the modern economy and political institutions, it will come as no surprise that similar political attitudes have dominated.

If we take these reservations into account, can we say there is *any* kind of tradition of Continental political theory? Despite the blurred boundaries between the traditions, it *is* possible to indicate a number of preoccupations that delineate it. In doing so, however, it might be best to understand 'tradition' not like some kind of fixed, ritualistic form of repetition but more like a genre of cinema, that is, an ensemble of different but thematically related texts and practices, sometimes dealing in issues encountered in other genres but in a novel way, sometimes developing new themes entirely but from a common starting point. Just as we shouldn't expect each film in a genre of cinema to share exactly the same preoccupations and styles, neither do the varieties of political thought. And yet there will be family resemblances, reactions to shared experiences and phases of history, common tropes and ways of establishing the audience's perspective. It is these, frequently subtle, commonalities that permit us to talk of a 'tradition' of political thought without reducing it simply to a shared geographical origin. These common themes and styles allow the Continental tradition to be taken up outside of the Continent itself and modified in light of different experiences and national traditions, and yet remain broadly within a Continental camp.

What are the themes and styles common to the Continental tradition of political thought? As we have suggested, a critical reaction to Enlightenment rationalism is at the root of this tradition. As a consequence, Continental thinkers have tended to dispute the idea of the rational subject as the foundation of knowledge and the source of social and political order. Instead, the individual subject has been understood to be bound up with the world rather than radically autonomous from it. This has led to a strong sense of the historicity of reason. In some instances, the individual subject has been seen as secondary to a higher order of subjectivity – such as 'World Spirit' or social class – rather than as a freely independent and sovereign individual. Continental thinkers, therefore, have been more sceptical about the possibility of developing a knowledge of politics based exclusively on the point of view of the individual and so have sought to conceptualise politics as a process that attends to society in a more inclusive sense.

Often, in fact, Continental thought has spurned the common sense of the individual and demanded a more philosophically challenging approach to politics, one that looks beyond the ordinary understanding of individuals and seeks to grasp the 'totality' or uncomfortable 'truth' of society in a more profound way. This has frequently led to the charge of philosophical obscurity and metaphysical confusion. There is certainly something in this charge, but it also misses the point: namely, that to grasp the world of politics it is necessary to climb out of the perspective of the isolated, rationally calculating individual and to think through the connections between different subjects across time and space. Inevitably, this takes us out of the comfortable position of the reasoning subject and demands that we occupy a view that makes that individual subject seem only part of the story.

It follows from this critical view of the rational subject that, whilst the objects and themes of Continental Political Thought have been similar to other traditions, it has viewed these without the assumption that political institutions should be entirely premised on satisfying the needs of 'the individual' or even individuals. If rational subjectivity is not the starting point for thought, then supporting individual freedom cannot be the sole concern in theorising political life. For subjects to be brought together under common institutions, other *preconditions* must be met. Thus Continental thinkers have been preoccupied with delineating the wider preconditions for institutions to work, such as economic equality, common cultural dispositions and attitudes, conceptions of politics, power and self-hood, and so on. Very often this has involved a polemical approach to other theories and beliefs which are viewed as distorting our picture of how we might live together. Whether in support of liberal, socialist or any other kind of society, Continental thinkers have explored their political preferences by interrogating the limitations of other theories. In particular, the Continental tradition has pointed to the limitations of liberal forms of government and society, not always in order to reject them but, rather, to highlight the need for a deeper understanding of the nature of, for example, order, community or freedom which is thought to be lacking in the outlook of liberalism's less critical defenders. Without greater theoretical understanding of these aspects of politics, it is argued, political life will be undermined.

In summary, we might say that Continental Political Thought has self-consciously asserted the importance of *theorising* itself as part of the construction of a satisfactory public life. Unless we think differently about how we live together and what the preconditions are for this shared life, politics will always remain in some sense alien to us. In suggesting that political order is incomplete without this theoretical comprehension, however, Continental thinkers have been accused not only of being too literary (or too metaphysical) but also of failing to adopt a neutral, 'scientific' stance towards their object of enquiry. If the political world requires theory to complete its formation, then isn't the theorist him or herself assuming a superior, perhaps elitist position akin to Plato's philosopher kings? Undoubtedly this is one danger of the Continental approach, which is routinely accused of being intellectualistic and self-glorifying for those who adopt its vocabulary. But it is not a necessary consequence, nor is it entirely exclusive to the Continental tradition. As this book seeks to demonstrate, the insights of Continental Political Thought – even those at its most metaphysical and 'dangerous' – have been utilised in a more democratic age for a plurality of purposes without succumbing to the (purported) self-aggrandising qualities of its originators.

More justly, we might say that the Continental tradition reminds us that not only does politics need its thinkers, but that, in many if not all respects, politics *is* a form of thinking. This demands that we rise to the challenge and subject ourselves and our preferences to the most rigorous and, sometimes, abstract form of critical theoretical enquiry. The implication here – and it is an implication that remains constantly open to debate – is that critical theoretical reflection yields a politics – and a citizenry – that is equal to the challenges of the age.

doing the continental ...

While the structure of this book may appear roughly chronological, there is really no intention here of presuming that a tradition has 'unfolded' or developed through a chain of thinkers, each in dialogue with the previous one(s) in some special way, and in turn rather mysteriously passing 'the torch' to the (generally unknown, or often unexpected) next one in line. Rather, and in keeping with the Continental genre of doing political philosophy, as outlined above, each chapter contains other thinkers already present in the other chapters. This is because each chapter is written, not from the historical point of view, because from that point of view, successive thinkers in the book do not yet exist, in most cases, and so could not then feature in the discussion, except through the 'magic' of the metempsychosis that intellectual historians so often deploy. Instead these chapters represent a synchronic set of conversations and debates crafted by our 20 distinguished contributors. Each chapter delivers 'the basics' in terms of biography and context through which the author, featured in the chapter, is made known to the reader. After that, however, and working through his or her concerns and thoughts, each author then develops an ideas- and issues-based discussion. This allows elaboration, say, of Spinoza's views on religion in conjunction with the later views of Marx and Nietzsche (though neither had a reputation as a Spinoza scholar or commentator), and also with those of Althusser and Deleuze (who did). Thus each contributor's task was not to lay out his or her author in relation to a presumed tradition, nor to stick strictly to the author's thought in his or her own conception and context, but rather to show how political thought *can be done* from the author's major texts. While brief summaries (below) do little justice to the quality of this work in political philosophy, they are a guide to the contributor's philosophical interests and an invitation for readers to tackle what intrigues them, and then work from there to other chapters, as the contributor's citations, and the reader's interests, suggest. In addition to a reading list of references, each chapter also concludes with a short guide to further reading, as does this introduction.

Any selection of 'Continental' thinkers in an ascribed tradition in political philosophy will be both defective and selective. Rather than limit our contributors to short formulaic entries, and rather than create a spurious encyclopaedic impression of 'coverage', we have instead aligned the volume from the poststructuralist and postmodern perspective taking in the very latest theoretical engagements in political philosophy (that is, the seven chapters comprising the 'postmoderns'), and worked through their major interlocutors, inspirations and foils in the twentieth century (the 'moderns'). The same principle then applied to selecting the 'classics' as necessary precursors, though of course this rough scheme of periodisation in no way excludes the 'Postmoderns' engaging the 'Classics' directly (as noted above, in their engagement with Spinoza). The choice of thinker throughout the book was also somewhat driven by the editors' determination to secure contributions from some of the liveliest and most challenging minds in political philosophy today, offering neither obeisance to seniority nor worship of youth (nor, indeed, national or geographical preference). We have encouraged our contributors to put their own ideas and predilections to the fore in organising, composing and arguing through the problems that make political philosophy the stimulating and topical study that it is.

In Chapter 1 Caroline Williams outlines Spinoza's radical monism and attack on religion, and discusses their anti-Cartesian appeal for structuralists and poststructuralists, comparing his critique of anthropomorphism in conceptions of God with the work of Marx and Nietzsche. Spinoza's refusal to countenance a break between nature and culture puts him outside the social contract theorisations of Enlightenment thinkers. This Continental philosophical position has made him a major interlocutor for Althusser in constructing an anti-humanist account of ideology, and for post-Althusserian reflections on liberation, mass politics and democracy.

Chapter 2 on Kant, by Howard Williams, aligns Kant's transcendental (rather than empiricist) philosophical system with the contemporary work of John Rawls, in which reason is deployed independently of experience to solve fundamental problems in politics, and the contemporary thesis in international relations of the 'democratic peace', initiated by Michael Doyle and extended by Francis Fukuyama. As a rationalist Kant was seeking to encompass the knowing subject and the known world in one totality, making him an important reference point in Continental attempts to think through commonplace philosophical dualisms and to expose an uncritical linkage between science, knowledge and sensory experience.

Kant's most thoroughly Continental critic was Hegel, Anthony Burns' subject in Chapter 3. Burns draws out Hegel's alignment with Spinoza's monism and pantheism, albeit reinterpreted within a dynamic and historical scheme. French poststructuralists came to Hegel via Marx, and took the former severely to task for his (alleged) reliance on binary oppositions and his metaphysical essentialism. Burns looks ahead to a reappropriation of Hegel as a mediator between extreme social constructionism, in which individuals have no generative or moral 'essence' constraining them, and an 'essentialist realism', in which 'humanity' derives from something natural or conceptual that can be known.

Marx, in Chapter 4, emerges in Bradley J. Macdonald's account as a powerful force in reconceptualising the terms of engagement between philosophical thinking and the political, social and economic world as a global phenomenon. Critique, praxis and emancipation are a crucial trilogy through which a trio of 'moderns' have articulated their philosophical and political concerns: Gramsci, Lukács and Althusser. However abstruse the postmodern 'turn' in political philosophy may seem to be, Marx is very much a 'presence', or in Derrida's words, 'there is no future without Marx'.

Gordon A. Babst presents Nietzsche in Chapter 5 as the gleeful and irreverent philosopher whose exuberance in rejecting all previous philosophical traditions has aligned him at least emotionally with postmodern thinkers, and stylistically with their aphorisms and abhorrence of systems. Nietzsche's thought is thus balanced between an overwhelming scepticism and relativism (to the individual perspective) and an affirmation of life that ran quite counter to conventional understandings of both religion and democracy. Arguably he and Marx represent an important twin commonality in terms of critique and challenge through which 'Postmoderns' have self-consciously articulated their political and philosophical concerns.

As Edward Wingenbach indicates in Chapter 6, Heidegger is the central 'modern' philosopher in the Continental tradition. His explicatory and hermeneutic approach to meaning, and to the larger issues of 'being', present a stark contrast with the spare propositions and (supposed) analytical clarity espoused by the empiricist, positivist and logical schools cultivated more readily in the English-speaking philosophical world. Heidegger's meditations on the complexities of human consciousness and self-reflective experience raise highly political issues of truth, knowledge, subjectivity and method that set the terms for all succeeding philosophers in this volume. Even if the thinkers themselves do not engage with Heidegger directly, the debates surrounding the thinkers and the issues that they raise proceed on terrain that Heidegger established.

Chapter 7 on Gadamer, by Keith Spence, continues the Heideggerian theme of self-consciously philosophical interrogation of classic philosophers with respect to meaning, interpretation and understanding. This is pursued through a method and style that embraces complexity in a way that came to centre language, as well as meaning, within 'postmodern' conceptions of subjectivity, identity and agency. Contrary to reductive and analytical philosophical approaches that bracket off important areas of experience, both individual and collective, Gadamer's work highlights a tension between truth and any method, such as philosophies of science (especially positivism), that claimed to establish and exhaust truth in any definitive sense. From this the 'postmodern' concept of the 'excess' (in meaning, and in life) is but a very small step.

Chapter 8, by Renato Cristi, takes up Schmitt, whose work has been revived as a major influence in certain areas of 'postmodern' political thought. Along with Heidegger he was identified with the Nazi Party, and this biographical circumstance has delayed and coloured his reception as a philosopher. While in some ways Schmitt argued for a reassertion of Hegel's political scheme and values, calling for a strong state to preserve order, and a framework of supportive civil and ethical associations within this sovereign structure, his major theme was 'the concept of the political', pursued in contradistinction to what he perceived to be liberal individualist (and anti-state) principles that posed a constant, corrosive threat to order and stability. His quasi-theological and emotionally dichotomising 'friend and enemy' distinction plays a role in deep-seated 'postmodern' explorations and critiques of mechanistic, economistic and optimistic conceptions of human subjectivity deployed within twentieth-century liberalisms.

Gramsci, in James Martin's Chapter 9, represents a curious nexus in political thought, working and writing as an activist, moving Marxism away from an 'orthodox' philosophical purity, opening the way to a 'postmodern' examination of ideas, culture, mythology, experience and subjectivity within a view that was nonetheless focused on class, exploitation, inequality and democracy. His concept of 'hegemony', or ideological leadership (of one group, class or state over another), opened the way to complex considerations of history, tradition and culture in political change, including tactics, frustrations, coalitions and calculations. How far Marxism can be stretched to accommodate this perspective, and indeed, the extent to which Marx's writings themselves can be separated from Marxism, have opened up post-Marxism as a 'Postmodern' preoccupation.

Chapter 10 takes up a similarly problematic figure, Lukács. Timothy Hall argues that he has suffered unwarranted critical neglect. Unlike Gramsci, Lukács wrote his major works for publication, and has therefore left a hermeneutic problem for his readers, in that he revised 'orthodox' Marxism within what appears to be Marxist terminology. Lukács' reworking of classic themes, such as 'historical materialism', now emerges in a post-Marxist (if not postmodern) perspective as a critique of ahistorical theories of development that have persisted within 'orthodox' Marxism (and its mirroring commentaries, both critical and sympathetic) within the anti-Continental, 'analytical' tradition. As the author of an anti-reductive, anti-representational and anti-transcendental social theory, rooted in concepts of shared meaning and political activism, Lukács will be revisited and revitalised within 'postmodern' philosophical enquiries into the exigencies of contemporary politics.

Arendt, as discussed in Chapter 11 by Roy T. Tsao, was a student and disciple of Heidegger whose writings mark a significant mid-century 'Continental' engagement with 'classics' of the tradition (Kant, Hegel, Marx), intertwined with lengthy philosophical engagements with current political issues, such as imperialism, nationalism, revolution and (famously) totalitarianism. Having fled the Nazis to the US in 1941, Arendt represents an important link between the 'Continental' tradition, particularly in linking politics with philosophical analyses of human subjectivity (see her discussions of 'alienation', 'natality' and the 'work/labour' distinction), and the new global struggle between American power and the communist regimes through which Cold War politics was framed. Arendt prefigures current 'postmodern' political concerns with terror, 'fundamentalisms' and acute ethical dilemmas in war and its aftermath, where philosophical views on truth and justice cannot be prised apart from questions of power.

Althusser, the subject of Benjamin Arditi's Chapter 12, is an idiosyncratic commentator on Marx and associate in a French structuralist philosophical school from which crucial thinkers, such as Lacan and Derrida, eventually did the most to create 'postmodernism' as a contemporary intellectual phenomenon. Althusser's quest to produce a structuralist, 'scientific' Marx by establishing an 'epistemological break' (in text and thought) was widely followed in global Marxist circles, as was his work to link philosophy with action via the concept of 'ideological state apparatuses'. Remarkably Althusser drew on Freudian concepts to criticise Hegel's dialectic, as it was understood within the Marxist tradition, and he linked his structuralist philosophical presumptions with the work of Spinoza. In this framework the relationship between ideology, as a feature of society (linked to, but not reducible to, the economy), and the human subject (via the concept of 'interpellation') became problematic in a way that engaged the 'Continental' tradition in developing a poststructuralist political theory.

In the final chapter on the 'moderns' Lasse Thomassen engages with the living philosopher Jürgen Habermas, presenting him as a powerful successor to Kant in terms of his rationalism and transcendental methods, and in terms of his preoccupations with morality, ethics and international peace. Yet with his position as chief successor to the influential latter-day Marxism of the Frankfurt School, and his attention to plural perspectives on truth within the 'linguistic turn', Habermas thus straddles the Continental and analytical traditions in a unique way. Against 'postmodern' thinkers he argues the case for rationality derived from deliberative consensus, and thus links his thought very powerfully with contemporary theories of deliberative democracy.

The opening 'postmoderns' essay is Chapter 14 on Lacan, by Kirsten Campbell. Lacan's revision of Freudian psychoanalysis reflects the 'linguistic turn' so important since the 1960s and 1970s. In this development language plays a crucial role in constituting the human subject, and in that way its properties constrain and empower us. Lacan's conceptualisation of language as a symbolic structure has been extremely influential, and his work was an acknowledged influence on Baudrillard, Derrida, Deleuze, Foucault and Žižek. It helped to further postmodern scepticism concerning stable structures of meaning, understanding and identity that were formerly said 'to secure' the political subject and indeed politics as a field of human activity.

Chapter 15, by Dimitrios E. Akrivoulis, presents a contrasting figure in French intellectual life, Ricoeur, who worked within the Heideggerian hermeneutic tradition rather than within structuralism derived from Lévi-Strauss. While his philosophical anthropology had little to do with psychoanalysis, the centrality of language in his work, and the links with Marx (rather than with Marxism), have made him an important figure in the strand of current political philosophy that focuses on discourse and the power of symbolic schemes. Through these conceptual schemes past/present/future are constructed as shared 'imaginaries'. Time itself is not a structuring feature of the political world in this conception, but rather a feature of the narratives through which politics is enacted.

Foucault is the subject of Andrew Barry's Chapter 16. While his interests were in history and sociology, and in particular in the way that the social and physical sciences have transformed life, culture and politics since the late seventeenth century (rather than in philosophy, psychoanalysis or politics), Foucault has nonetheless had a huge influence on 'postmodern' thinking about the human subject, the political regime and fundamental philosophical conceptions of truth and knowledge. This is all the more surprising, given the apparently causal empiricism and historicism of the historical explorations and reflections that constitute his work on sexuality, the body and social institutions and practices, for example, prisons, madness and 'governmentality'.

The philosopher Derrida is evoked in Michael Dillon's Chapter 17, in which he recounts how he came to read Derrida and how this process affected his own intellect and life. Dillon's text mirrors Derrida's fascination with the linguistic surface of written communication, and this makes reading an active process through which meaning and political import are constructed, rather than received. Deconstruction is thus a close or heightened engagement with a text where the limits of the sayable and knowable are tested. Derrida's exploration of the 'metaphysics of presence' shows how what is said 'to be', through language, is always haunted by what is to-come, and is thus necessarily unstable. So also is the subjectivity through which this language is constructed, a conception reflected in his theorisation of democracy as a politics of friendship and hospitality.

In Chapter 18 Nathan Widder presents the political philosophy of Deleuze as an analysis and critique of the centrality of identity in political thought and practice. Drawing on both Lacan and Foucault, and following in the Hegelian tradition of disarticulating identity into history, culture and discourse (rather than naturalising it as human 'individual' needs and interests), Deleuze challenges the very logical structure of oppositions through which all meaning, including that of any terms of identity, has been constructed through a determinate instance and its 'other' or opposite. Deleuze follows a Lacanian logic through which otherness can never be adequate to securing a determinate identity, and he performs a Nietzschean reversal of Platonism that makes logical categories into ghostly simulacra (rather than 'realities'). Deleuzean politics is thus fine grained, oriented to acts of will in 'segments' of resistance at a 'molecular' level.

Chapter 19, by Timothy W. Luke, re-evaluates the work of Baudrillard, the French 'postmodernist', arguing that his aphoristic style and nihilistic tone have prejudiced his critical reception. While drawing on the 'classics' of the Continental tradition, Baudrillard was a pioneer of a new philosophical anthropology through which he challenged conventional accounts of culture, history, taste, production, value and method. His world of simulation and hyperreality stakes out the importance of science fiction in any political imaginary that challenges the power-driven 'realities' of contemporary politics. Arguing that in a capitalist global 'present' where information and entertainment merge in commercial simulations of 'the real', Baudrillard undermined conventional notions of representation and truth, reality and fantasy, production and exploitation. Rather than understanding the internet in conventional analytical and political terms, Baudrillard reversed this in a quintessentially 'postmodern' way.

Glyn Daly, in Chapter 20, explains how, starting from a background in psychoanalysis, Žižek has engaged such 'postmodern' preoccupations as cyberspace, film and fiction. In doing so he constructs challenging critiques of liberal theories, yet politically he argues for transcendentalism and universalism that thinkers in the Foucaultian tradition have decisively rejected. He also validates the human subject as a concept within psychoanalytic discourse. Žižek's thought emphasises the way that human thought and action are situated in realities that are delusional consistencies (and of course always inconsistent with each other). Thus politics does not comprise stable individuals and determinate events within some given 'real' that constitutes their context. Contrary to conventional politics, in which substantial change is constantly and neurotically avoided, Žižek presents a politics of miraculous disruption, risk and passion that gives the lie to the charge that all 'postmodern' thought is cynical.

In conclusion these 20 chapters showcase current work in political philosophy that draws on a 'Continental' tradition, itself a complex palimpsest of conversational texts through which the authors featured in each chapter have encountered one another's ideas. While the list could certainly be extended, this introduction has demonstrated, we hope, a coherence in inspiration, focus and method that is distinctively 'Continental'. English-speaking readers in particular will find evident and useful contrasts when they look over the corresponding 'classics' and 'moderns' of the liberal empiricist tradition. We hope, in presenting this book, that the challenges will be productive ones.

further reading

Critchley, S. (2002). *Continental Philosophy: A very short introduction*. Oxford: Oxford University Press.

Simons, J. (2005) *Critical Political Theory*. Edinburgh: Edinburgh University Press.

West, D. (1996) *An Introduction to Continental Philosophy*. Cambridge: Polity Press.

part i
'classics'

1
baruch de spinoza
caroline williams

The writings of Baruch de Spinoza (1632–1677) have occupied a somewhat marginal position in the history of political thought. His political works have rarely been included in contemporary anthologies of the subject, although this has been less the case in the earlier part of the twentieth century. It is almost as if the name of Spinoza has been erased from the canon, or remains concealed between the twin figures of Machiavelli and Hobbes. Yet Spinoza was one of the key harbingers of political modernity. His *Tractatus Theologico Politicus* (*TTP*), the only work to be published during his own lifetime, and considered by many of his contemporaries to be a subversive political tract, presented the freedom and power of the individual as the most important political goal. In the view of many political philosophers, it is the first statement of liberal democracy. Studied closely by Marx in his early years and a significant influence upon Rousseau's *Social Contract*, the clandestinely published *TTP* was read far and wide throughout Europe (see Israel, 2001). The silence surrounding Spinoza's position and recognition in modern political thought is thus an uncomfortable one, given this history, but it is slowly finding a new voice. In recent years Spinoza scholars have begun to weave together the political writings with the much more widely read *Ethics*. They have come to see the essential inter-relation between the two and the resources and challenges held there for a radical political theory. Spinoza's rejection of a conception of the individual subject as a sovereign being *imperium in imperio*, his account of the affective ties that always influence the form of the social bond between subjects, and his emphasis upon the nurturing of joyful affects for a life of freedom and action, each contribute to his vision of politics. This kind of reading shows how Spinoza's account of the physics of bodies and the figure of the multitude prevents any straightforward incorporation of his thought into liberal political philosophy. This chapter will first situate Spinoza and his writings in his own time and introduce the central elements of his philosophy. Only then may the radical potentiality of Spinoza's thought and its challenge to politics and philosophy be posed.

the heresy of spinoza

Spinoza's name was tainted from the very beginning. His parents were Sephardic Jews from Portugal who settled in the more liberal Netherlands, where Spinoza was born in 1632. Such Jews were known as Marranos, and were so called because they had forcibly converted to Christianity after the Spanish Inquisition. As a result they maintained a curious mixture of the two religions and lived a largely secretive religious life. Spinoza grew up within a relatively orthodox Jewish community in Amsterdam. He soon became associated with the more progressive circle within its members who debated the two central issues of the day, namely whether philosophy should remain the handmaiden of theology, forever subordinated to the claims of divine reason, and whether the new sciences (represented in radical form at the time by Cartesianism) could be brought to bear upon theological explanations of the world. The distinct claims of science, theology and philosophy would later be synthesised in the secular Enlightenment philosophy of Kant and Hegel, but it is to Spinoza's philosophy that one must turn to find some of its first articulations and its most radical formulation.

Spinoza paid for his commitment to free thinking at the age of 23 (and before the publication of any of his philosophical and political works) with a *cherem*, an official excommunication from the Jewish community. Such a curse required that the community no longer converse with, read the works of, nor trade with the 'Godless' philosopher. Thus Spinoza was forced into a solitary life of thinking, taking up the profession of lens grinder to make a living and assisted by a small stipend provided by his friend, Van Enden. It would be a mistake however to assume that the excommunication was enforced absolutely. Spinoza and his circle still met regularly, and parts of the unpublished *Ethics* were read and distributed among them. Spinoza was also visited by some of the leading thinkers of his time, including Leibniz and Oldenburg, the first secretary of the Royal Society of London, who was responsible for publishing the works of Robert Boyle. Spinoza's letters are also a richly informative source of the discussions surrounding his work as well as providing us with some of the deepest criticisms of Spinoza's ethico-political perspective made by his contemporaries. The picture they give us is of a man immersed in the life and issues of his time rather than living in isolation from them, writing a philosophy that would be marked as a 'savage anomaly', to use Antonio Negri's enigmatic phrase, for centuries to come. It is a philosophy that perhaps finds some of its most sensitive readers in our time.

Spinoza published only one work during his life: the *Tractatus Theologico Politicus* in 1670. Spinoza's other major works, the unfinished *Tractatus Politicus* (*TP*) and the *Ethics*, were published posthumously, along with his early *Short Treatise on God and Man*, the *Treatise on the Emendation of the Intellect*, and a largely expository work (conceived from a series of lessons on Descartes given by Spinoza) entitled *Principles of Cartesian Philosophy*, to which was appended Spinoza's own *Metaphysical Thoughts*. For Spinoza scholars, the latter three works form part of the pre-*Ethics* writings where Spinoza experimented with some of the key ideas that were to form the basis of the *Ethics*. This work, described by Jonathan Bennett (1984) as Spinoza's 'one indisputable masterpiece', has sometimes been viewed as a self-contained text without the trails leading to and from the political works of his lifetime.

The *Ethics*, however, has a complex history. Written over a 15-year period, the genesis of this work was broken up by Spinoza's writing of the *TTP* and his turn towards a more explicit theorisation of the space of politics. Some writers have suggested that it is precisely here that Spinoza sought to present, in a more popular and accessible form, the geometric arguments of the *Ethics* (for example, Curley, 1990) and any reader of both texts will notice how the *TTP* brings many of the formulations of the *Ethics* to bear upon the political world. It would be a rather narrow approach to view the *Ethics* simply as an ethical work, because the novelty of Spinoza's approach is in bringing together previously differentiated spheres of knowledge. It contains a theory of nature and man's virtue in relation to it, a psychology of the passions and their relation to human action and freedom, as well as a sketch of Spinoza's political theory and an indication of its place within his system as a whole. The *Ethics* is a work on many different levels, and in its maturation and distinct rhythms of development we find the course of man's collective liberation, as well as his understanding of the world and the causes that underlie it. What then are the central principles of Spinoza's philosophy that proved so exceptional to his time and generated the *cherem* against him?

from god to world

By far the most daring aspect of Spinoza's philosophy is his radical monism. Spinoza rejects the idea that there exists in the world a plurality of substances, of which God is only one, a divine substance distinct from, and beyond the human world of relations accidental to their nature. Unlike Descartes, for example, Spinoza refuses to countenance any dualism between human and celestial orders of being, as well as any dualism between mind and body. There is only one substance, God, with an infinite power of existence. This substance is perpetually expressed through an infinity of attributes, of which thought and extension are but two. Each attribute expresses the eternal and infinite essence that is God, which is the cause of itself, as well as the cause of all being and expressions of reality. Since everything in reality expresses and is a part of this infinite essence, Spinoza writes of God as identical with nature itself. Hence the equation of *Deus, sive Natura* ('God, or Nature') that was to result in so much ambiguity and discussion regarding the theological ground of Spinoza's thought and his apparent atheism. It is the richness and metaphysical novelty of this knot between God and world, existence and power, that has produced such huge diversity within interpretations of Spinoza over the centuries (for a summary, see Moreau, 1996).

The implications of this radical association of God and Nature are far reaching. Spinoza sweeps away the idea of a transcendent God who creates the world, as well as that of a hierarchical chain of being from God to human existence. The passage from God to the realm of concrete life can involve no degradation or loss of power for the latter, because Spinoza's substance (that is, God, or Nature) *lives through* what happens in nature and is its constitutive, productive power. When Spinoza writes about God or Nature being self-caused, as well as the cause of all things, he qualifies this in an important sense by distinguishing between an *immanent* and a *transitive* cause (*Ethics*, Part I, Proposition 18). Since God is not prior to what he creates, he can no longer be designated as its transitive cause distinct from his effects. Instead we must understand Spinoza's use of the term 'immanent cause' as indicating a kind of indwelling cause, a perpetual generation and production of life that cannot be viewed simply as an effect of God's actions or motives. God is not the Creator; rather, as nature itself, God is the principle of creation and becoming in the world.

This idea of substance and its attributes opens the first part of the *Ethics*, which then proceeds to develop an account of the mind and its possible freedom from servitude and superstition, together with a theory of truth and a human understanding of eternity. The opening definitions of the work concerning God could have only outraged the ecclesiastics and religious thinkers amongst Spinoza's contemporaries, by whom he would be branded an atheist. The *Tractatus Theologico Politicus*, through which much of this perspective was initially received, directly challenged the legitimacy of the revelatory power of the scriptures. The bible became, in Spinoza's hands, just like any other literary work, and it was to be interpreted as the adventures of the imagination. In this way, the *TTP* could be seen as an exploration of imagination as the 'theologico-political figure of reality' (Negri, 1991, p. 89), and it is through what we will call here the 'analytic of the imaginary' that contemporary political thinkers such as Étienne Balibar and Louis Althusser would later read Spinoza.

The central message of the *TTP* asserted the power of reason above superstition and religious ritual. Spinoza's aim was to dispel the mists of superstition that through the imagination also shrouds man's reason. Like Epicurus and Machiavelli before, and Marx and Nietzsche after, Spinoza argued that religion invests us with irrational hopes and fears, grounding these fluctuating emotions in religious rites and beliefs governed solely by

superstition. At the same time, individuals invest God with anthropomorphic characteristics, so that he may become vengeful or benign, cruel or virtuous. Irrational belief in God's will and actions comes to take the place of a more rational understanding of our place in nature. We tend to mistake reality for the way our imagination is affected (*Ethics*, Part I, Appendix). This attack on religion is arguably far more damaging than the demystifying strategies of Marx or Nietzsche, as Spinoza takes his argument right to the heart of biblical exegesis, claiming that Moses could not have written the Torah in its entirety since it relates the latter's death, as well as describing places that bore a different name in his time. Religious prophets, he argued, had no supernatural powers; this horizon of prophecy was nothing more than the horizon of human imagination. It was the way in which the passions tied individuals together as a collectivity, in other words the *imaginary* basis of human sociability and community, that Spinoza sought to understand in the *Ethics*. What were its causes and how could knowledge of it transform such a condition of servitude and superstition?

body and mind, passion and action

For a fuller account of the philosophical underpinnings of the movements of mind, body and imagination we must return to the *Ethics*, as it is here that Spinoza continues his challenge to the emerging Cartesianism that became paradigmatic of modern philosophy. It is this aspect of his thought that was also later appropriated in the anti-humanist arguments of some structuralists and poststructuralists. Spinoza develops his position in direct contrast to Descartes. Mind and body are not distinct substances with their own realities, and the body and passions are not subservient to the rationality of mind. Instead both must be conceived as two intricately interwoven expressions or configurations of the *same* human form. Mind, for Spinoza, is only an *idea of the body* perceived under the attribute of thought rather than extension. Thus, Spinoza writes that 'the mind does not know itself except insofar as it perceives ideas and affections of the body' (*Ethics*, Part II, Proposition 23). In other words, mind cannot be severed from its relation to the body, as it can for Descartes. It should rather be conceived as 'thinking body', because each of its ideas has its source in images regarding the affective state of the body.

Part III of the *Ethics*, entitled '*De Affectibus*' or 'Concerning the Origin and Nature of the Affects', forms the basis for an investigation into the physics of bodies and the various intensities of emotions or passions that accompany them. When in the Preface to Part III Spinoza writes of considering 'human actions and appetites just as if it were an investigation of lines, planes, or bodies', his objective is not just to treat the passions in geometric style, but also to consider them according to the causes that shape and determine them. Like the Stoics before him, Spinoza viewed the passions as natural things that follow the common laws of nature (see James, 1993), and like every other part of nature, individuals strive to persevere in being, to maintain and affirm their existence and power. Spinoza calls this primary, active mobility at the heart of what it means to exist, *conatus*. The *conatus* involves both the body and the mind; in relation to the former we may speak of appetite, and to the latter, will. What we understand by consciousness is not the act of thinking *per se* but a mind conscious of its own desire or *conatus* (*Ethics*, Part III, Proposition 9, Scholium).

There are three primary primitive affects that appear to mobilise and dispose the individual to act: desire, joy and sadness. However, Spinoza shows that it is the precise density and strength with which desire or *cupiditas* combines with the other primary affects that determines the shape and intensity of the resulting passion. Thus he presents a full medley of passions or affections that are derived from these three, from hatred, anger and despair, to love, hope and gratitude (see *Ethics*, Part III, Definitions of the Emotions). The primary affects, then, are *transitive states* through which bodies pass, and they may involve increases or decreases in our power to act, depending upon the kind of affection or passion they engender. The more the body's power is hindered and diminished by passions deriving from sadness, the more our very existence is consumed by external things for which we have no understanding. How can we come to experience joyful affects? Or to put this in other words, how can we arrive at an understanding of the natural causes underlying our actions? For Spinoza, it is this understanding that signifies our rational grasp of the laws of necessity and brings us closest to what he calls in Part V of the *Ethics* an 'intellectual love of God'.

These are not just the questions of the sage or the philosopher as so many commentators have implied – Spinoza cannot easily be characterised as elitist. This entire economy of the passions, which anticipates psychoanalysis by more than 200 years, rests on a relational ontology. It is this profoundly social ontology that has been developed by contemporary readers, for whom Spinoza's analysis of human sociability is an important aspect, tied as it is to the form and movement of the political. Spinoza's perspective is far from psychological egoism and philosophical atomism (see, for example, Balibar, 1997; Collier, 1999; Ravven, 1998). The body can never be distinct and self-contained; it is always made up of the traces and residues of many memories, interactions and events. The body is 'worked up' not through solitary experiences but as part of an interactive, trans-individual process. This, of course, makes the kind of social relation between individuals, and the ethico-political arrangements that help shape our experience, of great importance. 'Citizens are not born but made', Spinoza writes in the unfinished *Tractatus Politicus* (ch. V, para. 2), and they may be manipulated to fear the sovereign power of the state or monarch (as Hobbes also understood), just as they may also learn to coexist in friendship and mutuality, to live according to the common will and to be guided as if by one mind (as Rousseau likewise articulated). Might we not situate Spinoza's politics, the detail and complexity of which we have yet to examine, as it appears to stand, that is, between the social contract theory of Hobbes and Rousseau?

It will be argued here that to interpret Spinoza within the bounds of social contract theory is to restrict the openings presented by his political philosophy. Whilst Spinoza discusses the human condition within the state of nature as one of man's natural right, which always extends as far as his power, the natural human condition is not one marked by terror and fear of others giving rise, as it does in Hobbes, to the constant threat of war. Spinoza's refusal to contaminate natural right with ideas of juridical or moral right certainly appears Hobbesian, but for the former thinker the identity of right and power transcends mere individual right to embrace the whole of nature. For Spinoza, the equation of right and power is, as C.E. Vaughan writes, 'a speculative principle which unravels the secret of the whole universe' (Vaughan, 1925, p. 68). It is derived not from any state of nature doctrine but from the primary principle of his philosophy: *Deus, sive Natura*. Since, as we noted above, the power of nature is identical with the power of God, every thing in nature acts according to its natural determinations, whatever its individual disposition and moral implication (see *TTP*, ch. XVI; Spinoza, 1985, Letters 19 and 21 to Blyenbergh; Negri, 1991, pp. 108–13).

Ultimately for Vaughan, this leaves Spinoza without a theory of obligation or moral duty and hence vulnerable to precisely those charges levelled toward Hobbes, namely that his system leads straight to despotism and tyranny (Vaughan, 1925, p. 122). In relation to Rousseau, the parallel, for some commentators, seems more immediate (Eckstein, 1944; Smith, 1997, ch. 5). Just as Rousseau proposes the total alienation of each in the community (1993, bk. 1, ch. 6), so Spinoza suggests that when 'each transfers the whole of his power to society, ... [it] is called a democracy, which can be defined as the universal union of all men that has the supreme power to do all that it can' (*TTP*, ch. XVI).

The very terms of discussion here appear to cast Spinoza within the mould of social contract theory, oscillating between Hobbes and Rousseau. His political philosophy does not belong here, however, because it subverts so many of the key concepts of social contract theory. Given the elaboration of Spinoza's naturalism above, it is clear that there can be no absolute break between nature and culture, just as there is no original essence or capacity to be associated with the human being, beyond that of the *conatus*, the power to persevere, to become (a perspective that appears to bring Spinoza closer to Nietzsche than to Hobbes). By the time Spinoza, in his last years, embarked upon the *Tractatus Politicus*, reference to a state of nature concept had disappeared (Balibar, 1998, p. 62). If we understand Spinoza's metaphysics as inseparable from his politics, then the absolute transfer of right to the state is inconceivable. The power of nature and its expression through the *conatus* in the finite mode of human existence is inalienable. It is not a power that can be domesticated absolutely as law (*potesta*). It is a power of becoming and constitution (*potentia*), one that subverts the transcendence of nature by society and culture, and is disruptive of every claim to contain the power of individuals. It is for this reason that Spinoza is often regarded as a political realist, concerned not with the conditions of legitimacy of the emerging modern state, but with the complex production and reproduction of power that ceaselessly modifies the political terrain. His interest is in the *formation* of individuality (as the people, community, individuals, nation), specifically with 'how it is constituted, how it tries to preserve its own form, how it is composed according to relations of agreement and disagreement or of activity and passivity' (Balibar, 1997, p. 227). To consider the resources for politics presented by Spinoza's philosophy, our attention will return once again to his philosophical anthropology: to the analytics of the passions, the constitution of imagination in political life and to the kind of politics best suited to Spinoza's metaphysics. It is precisely these aspects of Spinoza's thought that have engendered the contemporary interest in his radical politics and its relevance today.

thinking the political in the shadow of spinoza

In a letter to Hugh Boxel regarding the existence of spectres and ghosts, Spinoza indicates three of the thinkers who remain close to him: Democritus, Epicurus and Lucretius (Spinoza, 1985, Letter 56). Spinoza finds in these thinkers the first elements of a materialist account of the universe, and, in particular, a search for the natural causes of celestial events (see also Strauss, 1965). It is with Democritus and Epicurus (thinkers who were also read closely by Nietzsche) that Spinoza begins to think about the power of the imagination and the way in which superstitious belief stems from fear and a lack of knowledge of natural causes. When Louis Althusser in his final writings returned to reflect upon Spinoza's conception of imagination and its relation to the affective experience of subjectivity, he writes of finding there not only 'the matrix of every possible theory of ideology' but also resources to think 'the materiality of its very existence' (Althusser, 1998, pp. 7, 10).

Althusser had already claimed, in his *Essays in Self-Criticism* of 1973, that his project to establish a Marxist science that rejected all subjectivist, historicist and empiricist modes of thinking had been misunderstood. He was not a structural Marxist engaged in an analysis of the formal, law-like properties of a society. His Marxism had been supplemented in an important way by his 'detour via Spinoza' (Althusser, 1973, p. 134). It was to Spinoza rather than Marx that Althusser turned in order to theorise the function of ideology. Thus: 'Spinoza refused to treat ideology as a simple error, or as naked ignorance, because it based the system of this imaginary phenomenon on the relation of men to the world "expressed" by the state of their bodies' (Althusser, 1973, p. 136). In his influential 1972 essay 'Ideology and Ideological State Apparatuses', Althusser presented ideology as the mechanism that, through material practices and symbolic rituals, as well as a belief system, interpellates individuals as particular kinds of social subjects. These practices and rituals work to tame and discipline subjects, normalising and subjecting the body to certain regimes of thought and action, as Foucault would later explore with great effect. However, they also work on an affective level via specific modes of identification and imitation.

In the *Ethics* (Part IV, Proposition 27), itself composed after the *TTP* was written, Spinoza analyses this mechanism through what he calls the *affectum imitatio* (the imitation of the affects). Every individual is constituted by a process of imaginary identifications, or *affectum imitatio*, which communicate affects via the images each individual has of others with whom they agree or disagree in temperament and outlook. These images may be shared ones, but they can also be profoundly *ambivalent* ones, generating vacillating emotions of love and hate in individuals dependent on their own specific projections regarding similarity and difference. The imagination has a critical relation to the affects; it is the vehicle that activates ideas and images in the mind regarding the state of the body. The discussion above regarding the relation between body and mind has already presented the latter as an *idea* of the body. It is only through imagination that the mind can have the body as its object. Since the body is part of a relational ontology and always already socialised, the imagination is the result of the intermingling, binding of many bodies with a multiplicity of affects and passions. In short, it is collective and somewhat anonymous in structure.

Spinoza's account of the imagination and its affective relations clearly presages Marxist account of ideology's unconscious operations and effects. It was this dimension of Spinoza's thought, in theoretical alliance with Lacan's notion of the imaginary, that was to prove so productive to Althusser's explorations of the concept. Since we are composed of imaginative communications of image and affect, every human community, as Freud also knew so well, must rely upon such mechanisms of identification and recognition. In Althusser's own presentation however, the creative power of imagination appeared foreclosed. Many of Althusser's strongest critics were to find an absence of agency and a heavy weight of determinancy within his account of ideology. Through readings of Althusser in particular, the anti-humanist perspective that we can associate with Spinoza's rejection of individual sovereignty and free will came to represent falsely the death of the subject (see Williams, 2001, Introduction and ch. 2).

Such a conclusion to the Althusserian *corpus* remains rather one-sided. Althusser continued to think in the shadow of Spinoza, even if he did not fully develop the implications of this thinking for his account of ideology. In his posthumously published autobiography, Althusser, like Deleuze (1990), thinks through Spinoza's speculation that 'nobody yet has determined the limits of the body's capabilities: that is, nobody has yet learned from experience what the body can and cannot do, without being determined by the mind, solely from the laws of its own nature in so far as it is considered as corporeal' (*Ethics*, Part III, Proposition 2, Scholium). This regard for the body and its powers, and for the interconnections between the nature of the body and a knowledge of the causes, order and connection of things, is clear in Althusser's final reflections:

> That one can liberate and recompose one's own body, formerly fragmented and dead in the servitude of an imaginary and, therefore, slavelike subjectivity, and take from this the means to think liberation freely and strongly, therefore, to think properly with one's own body, in one's own body, by one's own body, better: that *to live within the thought of the conatus of one's own body was quite simply to think within the freedom and the power of thought*. (Althusser, 1998, p. 13)

The conclusions here are no doubt lacking a political framework, but we do find Althusser considering, through a Spinozist perspective, the idea of the liberation and recomposition of the subject beyond the servitude of the imaginary. We must turn to those contemporaries of Althusser, in particular Balibar and Negri, for an effort to think through the collective dimension of this project of liberation, and to find in Spinoza not only a philosophy of the future but an attempt to theorise the affective foundations of democratic life.

democracy, power and the multitude

Was the core of Spinoza's political thought democratic? This question has provoked a rich discussion within Spinoza studies, given that only four sections of the chapter devoted to democracy in the *Tractatus Politicus* were written at the time of his death in 1677. Some scholars claim that the defence of democracy in the *TTP* gives way to a preference for aristocracy in the *TP* (see, for example, Prokhovnik, 1997); others that Spinoza's experience of the savage death of the brothers De Witt at the hands of a mob highlighted the unpredictable and inconstant nature of the masses that left them unfit for self-rule (see Feuer, 1963, p. 138). Others still argue that democracy can best be understood as a *tendency* within any political regime, that is, 'the "truth" of every political order, in relation to which the internal consistency, causes and ultimate tendencies of their constitutions can be assessed' (Balibar, 1998, p. 33). Despite this controversy, the precise contours of which will not be developed here (see Further Reading), insofar as Spinoza's contribution to the history of political thought is documented, he is often viewed as the first liberal democrat. His advocacy of freedom of speech and opinion and his emphasis on democracy as the *optima respublica* are viewed as the main indicators of this (Feuer, 1963; Smith, 1997). Any state that wishes to guarantee its own stability must allow the free expression of (particularly religious) thought. It follows that a state that creates ideological closure by requiring that all citizens think in the same way will tend towards self-destruction. The purpose of the state, then, appears to be to guarantee freedom. At the same time, the stability of the state *requires* the support of its citizens. We can make greater sense of Spinoza's observations here if they are considered in the context of his account of democracy.

In the *TTP* (ch. XVI) Spinoza describes democracy as the most natural regime, because it is the political form that best approximates the individual's natural state where right and power coexist. Democracy is also the political state where man's natural sociability may thrive. Not only is there 'no single thing in Nature which is more useful to man than a man who lives under the guidance of reason' (*Ethics*, Part IV, Proposition 35, Corollary 1), but the more man shares things in common, the greater is his power of acting. If Spinoza's political philosophy is redemptive in its goal to increase reason, virtue, power and knowledge in the citizen, then this form of liberation of the self is inseparable from a collective liberation, that is, from an increase in the power and freedom of others (see also Montag, 1999, Preface). To understand Spinoza's ethico-political project as a therapeutic exercise of pure intelligence or a journey of self-mastery is an asceticist and ultimately elitist reading of his political philosophy. Such a characterisation ignores the masses as the potent political force that underscores Spinoza's relational ontology and his account of the power of bodies.

The readings of both Balibar and Negri confront this apparent tension in Spinoza's writings between individual and collective by claiming that his thought is truly subversive, precisely because it poses the question of the *multitudo* as a potent political force. In an essay entitled 'Spinoza, the Anti-Orwell: The Fear of the Masses', Balibar (1994) nevertheless argues that Spinoza's adoption of the 'standpoint of the masses' is a rather ambivalent one. This, he argues, is due to two important reasons.

First, there is an ambivalence regarding the possible elimination of psychic conflict and the neutralisation of the passions. Spinoza's theorisation of *affectum imitatio* (discussed above) recognises that since men are subject to the passions, they are often pulled in different directions (Part IV, Proposition 37, Scholium 2). At the level of collective life, these fluctuations and vacillations of affect (for example, between fear and hope, happiness and despair) can make the masses a sometimes unpredictable force, guided more by what may generate recognition and coherence in world view than by that which may bring about a preponderance of joyful affects. This in part accounts for Spinoza's view regarding obedience in a democracy (that one may obey out of free choice or out of fear).

Second, there is an ambivalence surrounding Spinoza's attitude towards the masses, which is far from consistent. In the *TTP*, it is the multitude (as ignorant *vulgas* or crowd) who are viewed as most receptive to superstitious belief in miracles and least likely to act according to reason. A significant shift takes place in the later *TP*, however, where Spinoza focuses on the political *power* of the multitude, a power that may not be recognised as equivalent to political right but is nonetheless decisive. Thus: 'The right [*Jus*] of the state ... is determined by the power [*potentia*] not of each individual but of the multitude' (cited in Montag, 1999, p. 25). The 'fear of the masses' in Balibar's title refers then to the fear that the masses experience, as well as to the fear that they inspire in the political order. Political systems that exclude the masses, preferring to maintain them in a state of ignorance, are unlikely to remain peaceful regimes, but will merely provoke their indignation and possible rebellion.

Antonio Negri's (1991) powerful reading of Spinoza in *The Savage Anomaly* presents the imagination as 'the primary, exclusive metaphysical problem' of his thought. Since imagination is composed of the multiplicity of affects that bind the social body in one way or another, one can understand the multitude only in relation to this schema. The strategic political role of the imagination *may* be negative insofar as it ties individuals to relations of servitude by persuading them that the state embodies their freedom. The ontological function of imagination, however, is wholly positive: it produces particular determinations of being and its reconstitution underlies every transformation in the relations between bodies. Spinoza is not just a political realist when he shows how a stable polity based on virtue and the common good can be achieved both by knowledge (utilising reason) and by affective imitation (that is, disciplining and manipulating the passions). His thought also reveals, as Balibar is also aware, a dynamic mobility between real and imaginary relations: 'Every real city is always founded simultaneously on both an active genesis and a passive genesis: on a "free" ... rational agreement, on the one hand, and an imaginary agreement whose intrinsic ambivalence supposes the existence of a constraint, on the other' (Balibar, 1998, p. 112). It is then through the imagination that the collective body is composed and decomposed; the imagination always has a political content. It is not for conservative reasons that Spinoza (like Machiavelli in the *Discorsi*) argues that every political system, whatever its form, must be an 'affective regime' and adapt to the existing symbols and habits of thought of a people if it wishes to be stable.

Balibar's and Negri's attention to the affective foundations of democracy present the concept as having certain real limits. Since it is linked to the ambiguity of the passions, democracy risks being destroyed from within. A paradigm case of this would be the totalitarianism that inheres in democracy, as discussed by Claude Lefort (1988). It is for this reason that Balibar prefers the term *democratisation*. He suggests that democracy is a *tendency* in Spinoza's thought that functions as an index of a regime's consciousness of its own internal elements and the extent of their democratic (and affective) incorporation. Thus when Spinoza discusses the problem of (in)stability in monarchy and aristocracy, caused mainly by abuses of power by the rulers, it is via the introduction of democratic principles (for example, the establishment of a representative council in a monarchy, variations and extensions in the qualifying right for aristocracy) that the order is preserved. Democracy conceived as a political *regime*, however, will always remain aporetic in structure. This is because the visceral antagonism at the heart of the political cannot be neutralised or contained completely. Since reason will always traverse the passions, and the latter will be implicated in any account of political life, democracy will remain riven by internal conflict, discord and possible decomposition as affects derived from sadness (for example, intolerance, envy and fear) cause it to stagnate. There is an *ethical imperative* attached to this tension. Through the cultivating of passions derived from joyful affects (for example, tolerance, friendship, *pietas*) democracy can remain responsive to otherness and the singular whilst still being subject to the risks of political closure.

A good example of a suppressed political conflict, arguably one of the most glaring contradictions of Spinoza's philosophy, is the exclusion of women from citizenship. The relations of dependency and natural difference that, for Spinoza, characterise relations between the sexes, disqualify women from voting and holding office (see *TP*, ch. XI, final paragraph). That woman's participation be rejected due to her *imbecilitas*, with few exceptions, is reflective of the construction of sexual difference within modern philosophy. It is nonetheless incompatible with Spinoza's own characterisation of nature and the place of the human within it, as well as being antithetical to his view of the entwinement of mind and body, passion and action, reason and imagination.

To introduce sexual difference into the realm of the political is to encounter once again the circulation of affects *between* individuals, and to recognise that we are first and foremost passionate bodies constructed trans-individually. To enable a particular difference to thrive and develop requires that what we have called here the figure of the multitude be held in abeyance, hence enabling the question: what *kind* of relation between the sexes may be imagined? To think in the shadow of Spinoza allows us to utilise certain parts of his philosophy in creative ways to think about the present. Spinoza is not a legislator but an interpreter, to utilise Zygmunt Bauman's formulation. His political thought is not a closed circle that explains the past. It constituted a strategic intervention in his own time and, in our own time, Spinoza's thought continues to offer many tools for thinking about the affective dynamic of the political. The interpretations of Spinoza considered here may have identified an aporia at the heart of his thought but it is by working through the aporetic structure of his thinking that some of its more radical formulations have been developed.

further reading

For a general account of Spinoza's thought within scepticism see R. Popkin, *The History of Scepticism from Erasmus to Spinoza* (University of California Press, 1979). For an interesting study of Spinoza's Marrano heritage as well as his relation to modern philosophy, see Y. Yovel, *Spinoza and Other Heretics*, 2 vols (Princeton University Press, 1992); for other intellectual antecedents of Spinoza's political thought, see Strauss (1965). The structure, argument and main themes of the *Ethics* are dealt with in an accessible and wide-ranging manner by G. Lloyd in *Spinoza and the Ethics* (Routledge, 1996), and a discussion of each of the main concepts and ideas in Spinoza's thought is presented in G. Deleuze, *Spinoza: Practical Philosophy* (City Lights Books, 1988). For a general account of Spinoza's political philosophy, see in particular S. Rosen 'Benedict Spinoza', in *History of Political Philosophy*, 3rd edn, ed. R. Cropsey and L. Strauss (Chicago University Press, 1987), and R. McShea, *The Political Philosophy of Spinoza* (Columbia University Press, 1968). Readers interested in the ontology of the affects may consult Deleuze's challenging and inspiring work *Expressionism in Philosophy: Spinoza* (Zone Books, 1990), but for a reading that develops the full political implications of, and a theory of imagination in, Spinoza's writings, they should turn to Negri (1991). This book situates Spinoza in Dutch politics, considers the genesis of Spinoza's thought, and assesses him critically against figures such as Hobbes, Rousseau, Kant and Hegel. G. Lloyd and M. Gatens (1999) is an excellent text that explores Spinoza's concept of imagination in a metaphysical and political context and points to the ways in which his thought exceeds the liberal paradigm. Balibar (1998) is a fine effort to think through Spinoza's philosophy as a political anthropology, and his essay 'Spinoza, The Anti-Orwell' (1994) is a key essay for discussions surrounding Spinoza's account of the multitude. Finally Montag and Stolze (1997) collects key influential political essays and extracts by French and Italian scholars and indicates the breadth and creativity present in contemporary Spinoza studies.

references

Althusser, L. (1973) *Essays in Self-Criticism*, trans. G. Lock. London: New Left Books.

Athusser, L. (1998) 'The Only Materialist Tradition, Part 1: Spinoza' in *The New Spinoza*, ed. W. Montag and T. Stolze, pp. 3–19. Minneapolis, MN: University of Minnesota Press.

Balibar, É. (1994) 'Spinoza, The Anti-Orwell: The Fear of the Masses', in *Masses, Classes, Ideas: Studies on Politics and Philosophy Before and After Marx*, pp. 3–37. London: Routledge.

Balibar, É (1997) 'Spinoza: From Individuality to Transindividuality', in *Mededelingen vanwege het Spinozahuis*, pp. 3–36. Delft: Eburon.

Balibar, É. (1998) *Spinoza and Politics*, trans. P. Snowdon, intro. W. Montag. London: Verso Books.

Bennett, J. (1984) *A Study of Spinoza's Ethics*. Indianapolis, IN: Hackett.

Collier, A. (1999) 'The Materiality of Morals: Mind, Body and Interests in Spinoza's *Ethics*', *Studia Spinozana* 7: 69–93.

Curley, E. (1990) 'Notes on a Neglected Masterpiece (II): The *Theological-Political Treatise* as a Prolegomenon to the *Ethics*', in *Central Themes in Modern Philosophy*, ed. J.A. Cover and M. Kulstad. Indianapolis, IN: Hackett.

Deleuze, G. (1990) *Expressionism in Philosophy: Spinoza*, trans. M. Joughin. New York: Zone Books.

Eckstein, W. (1944) 'Rousseau and Spinoza', *Journal of the History of Ideas* 5: 259–91.

Feuer, L.S. (1963) *Spinoza and the Rise of Liberalism*. Westport, CT: Greenwood Press.

Israel, J. (2001) *Radical Enlightenment: Philosophy and the Making of Modernity 1650–1750*. Oxford: Oxford University Press.

James, S. (1993) 'Spinoza the Stoic', in *The Rise of Modern Philosophy: The Tension between the New and Traditional Philosophies from Machiavelli to Leibniz*, ed. T. Honderich. Oxford: Clarendon Press.

Lefort, C. (1988) *Democracy and Political Theory*, trans. D. Macey. Cambridge: Polity Press.

Lloyd, G. and Gatens, M. (1999) *Collective Imaginings: Spinoza, Past and Present*. London: Routledge.

Montag, W. (1999) *Bodies, Masses, Power: Spinoza and his Contemporaries*. London: Verso Books.

Montag, W. and Stolze, T. (1997) *The New Spinoza*. Minneapolis, MN: University of Minnesota Press.

Moreau, F. (1996) 'Spinoza's Reception and Influence', in *The Cambridge Companion to Spinoza*, ed. D. Garrett, pp. 408–33. Cambridge: Cambridge University Press.

Negri, A. (1991) *The Savage Anomaly: The Power of Spinoza's Metaphysics and Politics*, trans. M. Hardt. Minneapolis, MN: University of Minnesota Press.

Prokhovnik, R. (1997) 'From Democracy to Aristocracy: Spinoza, Reason and Politics', *History of European Ideas* 23: 105–15.

Ravven, H. (1998) 'Spinoza's Individualism Reconsidered: Some Lessons from the Treatise on God, Man and his Well-Being', *Iyyun, The Jerusalem Quarterly* 47: 265–92.

Rousseau, J.-J. (1993) *The Social Contract and the Discourses*, trans. and ed. G.D.H. Cole. London: Dent.

Smith, S. (1997) *Spinoza, Liberalism and the Question of Jewish Identity*. New Haven, CT: Yale University Press.

Spinoza, B. (1992) *Ethics*, trans. S. Shirley. Indianapolis, IN: Hackett.

Spinoza, B. (1958) *The Political Works*, ed. and trans. A.G. Wernham. Oxford: Oxford University Press.

Spinoza, B. (1985) *Collected Works of Spinoza*, Vol. 1, ed. and trans. E. Curley. Princeton, NJ: Princeton University Press.

Strauss, L. (1965) *Spinoza's Critique of Religion*, trans. E.M. Sinclair. New York: Schocken Books.

Vaughan, C.E. (1925) *Studies in the History of Political Philosophy Before and After Rousseau*, Vol. 1. Manchester: Manchester University Press.

Williams, C. (2001) *Contemporary French Philosophy: Modernity and the Persistence of the Subject*. London: Athlone.

2
immanuel kant
howard williams

Kant was born on 22 April 1724 in Königsberg, now Kaliningrad. He never left his native city. By all accounts the furthest he ever travelled from the port was 60 miles or so when he became tutor to a household in a nearby town (Kuehn, 2001, p. 97). Immanuel was not himself a healthy child and survived his youth only with great good fortune. Throughout his long life Kant was understandably greatly preoccupied by his health and in his period of renown turned down offers of academic appointments outside Königsberg, often on the grounds of ill health.

By all accounts his 'Pietist' parents Johann and Anna Kant were the most devout and Christian of parents. Pietism was a radical Protestant movement, similar to and greatly influenced by English puritanism. It played a significant role in the development of modern Prussia, providing that society with an ethos of industriousness, discipline and reverence that suited an enterprising but absolutist regime. The experience of his mother's early death must clearly have developed in him a spirit of independence and self-reliance that was cruelly enhanced when his father died in 1746 when Kant was still a student.

Kant enrolled at Königsberg University in 1740 when he was only 16. At university it seems likely that he may have studied physics and philosophy as his main subjects, although it is also possible that it may have been medicine (Gulyga, 1977, p. 23). It is clear that under the influence of his teachers, particularly Martin Knutzen, Kant's main love became philosophy (Kuehn, 2001, p. 79). It was only with the greatest difficulty that Kant was able to embark upon an academic career. For many years he lived in great poverty, alleviated only by his elevation to a chair in philosophy at the university in 1770. Although he was deeply devoted to his philosophical studies, he was not a recluse. Evidence of Kant's cosmopolitanism is that amongst his favourite guests and closest friends were two English merchants, Joseph Green and Thomas Motherby. Apparently Kant is reported to have read every page of his *Critique of Pure Reason* first out loud to Green before committing himself to its arguments (Kuehn, 2001, p. 240). Kant very much liked the company of women and accounted for his single status with the view that when he 'needed a woman he could not have supported one, and when he was able to support one he no longer needed one' (Gulyga, 1977, p. 75).

Although Kant's life was on the whole that of a quiet, reserved academic, he did in his later years draw the attention of the authorities. In particular he ran into difficulties with the censor in the early 1790s over his writings on religion. Under Frederick the Great (1740–86) Prussia had enjoyed a remarkable degree of religious toleration. However, under Frederick's successor, Frederick William II, the atmosphere changed. Kant wished to draw out the implications of his critical philosophy for religion in a book that was to appear under the title *Religion within the Boundaries of Mere Reason*. When he attempted to publish the work in serial fashion in a number of journals the censors thwarted him, and when the second edition of the book appeared in 1794 things came to a head. Kant was ordered by the King to stop publishing on religious issues. He duly complied whilst the King was alive but returned to writing on religious questions in 1797 upon the King's death (Kant, 1998b, p. xxxii). By this time Kant's religious and political thinking was completely at odds with the orthodoxy of the times in Prussia. He was known for his enlightened views and enthusiastic support for republican principles in France. Although far from being an advocate of revolution Kant nonetheless looked forward to radical political changes both within and outside his own country.

the copernican revolution

Kant's political philosophy is an integral part of his philosophy as a whole, in particular of his practical or moral philosophy. This philosophy represents an extraordinarily ambitious undertaking. Kant himself designated it *critical philosophy* and conceived it as a critique of all previous metaphysics. He regarded his mature philosophical system as in many respects wholly novel, so there are no significant precursors we can draw upon to explain his thinking. Kant likened the impact of his own critical philosophy upon metaphysics to the revolution brought about in astronomy by Copernicus' heliocentric theory. Just as Copernicus had put the science of the heavens on a firm footing by regarding the sun, instead of the earth, as the centre of the universe, so Kant saw himself providing philosophy with a more secure basis by putting the human subject at its centre and not the outside world. Kant advanced this novel view in *The Critique of Pure Reason* (1781 [1998a]) and presented its implications for moral philosophy in *The Groundwork to the Metaphysic of Morals* (1785 [1996]) and *The Critique of Practical Reason* (1787 [1996]). It was to be a decade later before he was able to present in a systematic form its implications for political philosophy in *The Metaphysics of Morals* (1797 [1996]), but he published perhaps his best-known work on politics, *Perpetual Peace*, two years prior to that (1795 [1996]).

Kant has become a figure of central importance in present moral and political theory on two grounds, representing two key lines of interpretation. The first is that Kant has been associated with the reconstruction of political theory that has taken place through the work of John Rawls. Rawls draws heavily on Kant in presenting his theories of justice (as a version of moral constructivism). Vital to the idea of justice as fairness is an ideal of consistent, internally coherent and reasonable behaviour that acts as a measure of right action. This measure is established, insofar as possible, without regard to any particular circumstances. Kant's moral philosophy has been crucial to Rawls in doing this, as Rawls draws upon Kant's account of practical reason. This is reason directed towards the principles or maxims that we hold in acting. Kant's moral philosophy is based on the idea that it is possible to draw up coherent rules of conduct for rational beings. These rules are constructed by our moral consciousness itself and not drawn from any other source (Rawls, 1996, p. 100). Several of Rawls' former students, including Thomas Hill and Onora O'Neill, have impressively developed this line of argument, applying it to moral and political issues of the day. The second line of interpretation is the one that has identified Kant with the 'democratic peace' thesis. This thesis, first advanced in its contemporary form by Michael Doyle, argues that the spread of liberal-democratic political systems throughout the world will ultimately bring harmonious and peaceful international relations. Doyle, in two widely-cited articles (1983), follows closely the arguments of Kant's *Perpetual Peace*, and uses empirical evidence to demonstrate that the positive developments Kant had anticipated were taking place. This thesis was extended and reinforced by Francis Fukuyama's (1992) influential writings on the 'end of history'. In the late 1990s the discussion of this peace thesis played a key part in international relations thinking. Fukuyama has gone on to defend the pertinence of the theory even after the events of September 11, 2001. Side by side with these prominent attempts to use aspects of Kant's practical philosophy to produce a political and international theory relevant to our times there has also developed – perhaps as equally significant – a body of Kant scholarship that pays close attention to the precise arguments of his political writings in order to draw out their implications for contemporary politics. Some of this scholarship is reflected in the further reading below. It is generally characterised by an attempt to determine what kind of liberal politics Kant supports: interventionist or non-interventionist at the national level; and at the international level, state-centred or cosmopolitan.

Kant referred to his philosophy as a Copernican revolution because he wanted to draw attention to the way in which our knowledge has its origin just as much in our self-awareness as in the outside world. Here he saw himself as taking a middle path between the system-building rationalism of philosophers like Leibniz and Wolff and the common sense empiricism of Locke and Hume. The rationalists were seeking to encompass the outside world and the subject in one totality, whereas the empiricists were seeking to distinguish our knowledge of the outside world from the impact of our cognitive faculties upon it. However, in Kant's view, there is no 'outside world' without the contribution that our cognitive faculties (our thinking abilities) make towards its construction. These cognitive faculties shape the objects we perceive through our senses. There is indeed an external stimulus that brings these objects into our awareness in the first place, but we cannot know that in its purity. We can know objects only as they are formed by our self-awareness. Kant refers to a thing that is part of our ordinary experience, and so already structured by our peculiar kind of self-awareness, as a *phenomenon*, and a thing that is taken apart from our mode of self-awareness as a *noumenon*. A key thesis of Kant's *Critique of Pure Reason* is that we can only know a thing of the first kind, and we cannot know the latter kind of thing in itself. He uses this thesis to demonstrate that previous metaphysics, driven by the dynamics of pure reason, was fundamentally in error, because it assumed that it was possible to know things in themselves. According to Kant, there are strict limits to human knowledge. Natural science works insofar as its practitioners regard the knowledge they put forward in the form of laws as applying to things only insofar as they appear in our experience. We can know things only as they appear to our senses and understanding. We cannot go beyond those senses and understanding to state that we have knowledge of an absolute reality. This for Kant was the drawback of previous metaphysics. Philosophers like Spinoza, Wolff and Leibniz believed that in their systems they were depicting an ultimate reality. Under the influence of the British empiricists John Locke and David Hume, Kant was highly sceptical of such views.

Although the outcome of Kant's critical philosophy was to put severe limits on what we might know, the implications of this Copernican revolution for practical philosophy were highly positive. While in theoretical philosophy Kant believed he had to reign in the demands of reason, in practical philosophy he believed that reason could have the widest possible scope. Reason in its practical use should seek to transcend experience. Kant argued this because practical philosophy appeals to the human individual as an intelligent being. An intelligent being is one that is capable of recognising the requirements of reason and seeks to implement them in action.

Kant, taking a step that is characteristically modernist, reverses the traditional hierarchical relationship between theoretical and practical reason. The theory–praxis problem is a nucleus around which political philosophy has revolved. For example, Marx's more radical prioritising of practice – including within practice what Kant explicitly excludes, revolutionary practice – overshadowed both politics and political theory for a large part of the twentieth century. Within international relations the struggle between realists and idealists rested on the efficacy of practice (understood in a Kantian sense) in altering the age-old behaviour of the human race. Since classical times it had been customary to accord theoretical reason, as the contemplation of the world, a higher level of significance than practice, as the attempt to act in the world. Plato's and Aristotle's elevation of contemplation above practice, consolidated through the Christian tradition, had dominated philosophy up to Kant's day. This tendency to prioritise theory was, if anything, aided by the successful development of natural science in the early modern period. Scientists like Galileo and Newton appeared to have conclusively demonstrated the advantage of the purely theoretical outlook, but Kant turned inward in the face of the apparently worldly success of science. The limits he saw to the employment of theoretical reason led him to find what he regards as an altogether more promising outlet for reason in setting out the principles for rational human action. The totality that reason seeks has for Kant its sole legitimate outlet in moral – and by extension – political philosophy. This reversal of traditional hierarchy was to reverberate in political thought throughout the modern period.

political philosophy as practical philosophy

Political philosophy for Kant is part of practical or moral philosophy. This implies that not only is Kant's political outlook derived from his Copernican revolution in philosophy but also that it is dependent on his overall approach to morality. Just as the *Critique of Pure Reason* is a key text in determining Kant's view of metaphysics as a whole, so his *Groundwork to the Metaphysics of Morals* is a foundational text for his political philosophy, later published in systematic form in the *Metaphysics of Morals*. In the *Groundwork* Kant presents his notion of the categorical imperative that governs autonomous or ethical human behaviour. There are very many ways in which the categorical imperative can be put, but there are two aspects that stand out. First of all, the categorical imperative requires that we act only in accordance with rules that can be universalised (or generalised). We have to imagine what it would be like if everyone adopted the same maxims as ourselves in acting. Secondly, the categorical imperative requires that we treat others never simply as means but always also as ends. This second dimension demands that we never deal with others in an exploitative manner. We should regard all other individuals as an end in themselves (just as we should regard ourselves). These moral ideals underlie the whole of Kant's practical philosophy. In terms of political philosophy Kant is concerned to outline a view of social and political arrangements in which each person is accorded liberty and is considered of equal moral worth to others.

Kant developed and presented his political philosophy at an extraordinarily tumultuous time. He had given indications of what his political position might be in several articles, published in the *Berlinische Monatsschrift*, edited by a progressive friend, Johann Biester, and also in passing in the three *Critiques*.

His essays on 'Idea for a Universal History' and 'What is Enlightenment?' (1784 [1991]) represent significant examples of the former. However, his main writings on politics appeared in the period of the French Revolution and its aftermath. Clearly by this time Kant was a well-known intellectual figure in Prussia, and his views on matters of public concern were followed with great interest. Although not asked like Burke to comment directly on the French Revolution by prominent participants in those events, Kant was in a similar situation in that his anticipated (wise) advice was awaited with great eagerness by the reading public. Kant was already in a precarious public position in Prussia even before he began to publish on disputed questions connected with the Revolution. Kant nonetheless went ahead with his programme of publications on political issues in the shadow of the epoch-making events in France and the staunch opposition of his own rulers to the principles brought to the fore by those events. In doing this Kant showed the greatest courage and extraordinary tact in presenting to the German public a political philosophy true to many of the main principles of the new French Republic and at the same time compatible with obedience as loyal subjects of the Prussian state.

In his political writings Kant presents himself as a principled republican, opposed to the persistence of the enlightened absolutist sovereignty of monarchs. The first definitive article of *Perpetual Peace* requires that 'the civil constitution in every state shall be republican' (Kant, 1996, p. 322). There are two key aspects to a republican constitution. The first aspect is that those who make the laws in society are not at the same time those individuals who carry them out. For Kant there has to be a clear separation of powers between the legislature and the executive. Anyone who is in the position to have a hand in doing both will be unable to avoid the temptation of showing favour to themselves in the framing or the execution of the law. Secondly, Kant requires that the people's representatives should make the laws. This is highly significant for him since he believes that individual citizens should be able to regard laws as emanating from their own wills. This they will do only if they think they have a part in shaping them. Kant was an opponent of direct democracy. He did not think that the people as a whole should shape the laws, and certainly they should not then go on to administer the laws themselves.

Kant presents his ideas on citizenship in the essay 'On the Common Saying: That may be correct in theory but it does not apply in Practice'. The key terms against which citizenship should be measured are: freedom, equality and independence. The essay was published in 1793, one of the most eventful years in the French Revolution. Kant's formulation no doubt reflects the impact of the key ideas of the revolution: liberty, equality and fraternity. Interestingly, the key term for Kant in his own triad is that of independence, the term that substitutes for the ideal of fraternal solidarity expressed by the revolutionaries. Kant's concept of freedom mirrors the ideal of the American and French revolutions in requiring that each should be free to seek happiness in the way they see fit (Kant, 1996, p. 291). As human beings we are innately free but this freedom carries with it an acceptance of the possibility of legal coercion when we step beyond the law. Kant's concept of equality is somewhat more circumscribed than what the more radical politicians of these times may have demanded since it focuses upon equality before the law. Kant is not looking for complete material equality in society. Indeed he sees it as a bad thing, but rather recommends equality of opportunity: 'every member of a commonwealth must be allowed to attain any level of rank within it (that can belong to him as a subject) to which his talent, his industry and his luck can take him' (Kant, 1996, p. 293). The pronoun 'him' that appears in this quotation denotes a limitation of Kant's political philosophy, in that he does not accord equal rights to women. Although in keeping with supposed Enlightened opinion in his time Kant's attitude to women represents a justifiable point of criticism of his thinking. Though many female commentators have found stimulating and worthy aspects to Kant's account of the female role in society (Schott, 1997), there are nevertheless several respects in which Kant's account stands in stark contrast to the universality of his moral philosophy. At the core of Kant's vision of healthy republican society is the independent citizen who votes for the representatives that determine the laws on his behalf and engages in open scholarly and literary debate about the issues of the day. Women (along with men who are not their own masters) are excluded from this category. They belong to the ranks of passive citizens who enjoy the same standing in relation to the operation of the laws as all other citizens but play no direct part in shaping them. Kant has a participatory view of the political process. He favours a popular model of sovereignty over an absolutist one, but he is very selective about who should belong to the popular element. Democracy in its classical sense does not attract Kant in the same manner as republicanism.

Direct democracy in Kant's view would allow individuals to specify the law in their own case. The people (or, inevitably a select part of it) would favour themselves. Any genuine form of ruling has, therefore, to be representative. The separation of powers extends not only to the separation of the legislature from the executive but also to the judiciary. Trial by jury denotes the separation of the judicial power from the other two. The executive may well appoint the judges but the people themselves through their representatives determine the verdict of guilty or innocent (Kant, 1996, p. 460). Kant sees the relationship amongst these three powers as one of subordination, in other words, no one can usurp the power of another in their particular sphere. The legislative body is sovereign since it represents the united will of the people so that the ruler or executive body is subject to its laws and can be removed (but not punished), should it lose the legislature's confidence.

Thus the main message of Kant's political philosophy was at odds with the absolute power of the Prussian crown. Yet Kant did not regard this philosophy as hostile to his own rulers. He absolutely rejected any attempts to remove the king from office through resistance or rebellion (Kant, 1979, p. 155). He differs from Hobbes, not about the latter's rejection of the right of resistance of the subject to the sovereign, but rather about his rejection of any right of criticism (Williams, 2003). Kant argued that the only correct way of bringing about political change (guided by well-informed public debate) was from the top downwards, rather than from the bottom up.

republicanism and cosmopolitanism

Kant's *Perpetual Peace* (1795) stands comparison with Machiavelli's *The Prince* (1516) as one of the most important short books in the history of political thought. *Towards Perpetual Peace*, as the title reads literally, is not to be interpreted as a utopian political tract but rather as the most biting criticism of the realist tradition in politics, represented at its best by Machiavelli and Hobbes. *Perpetual Peace* continues many of the themes that we have outlined above. At the heart of Kant's vision of a settled world order is the idea that all political constitutions should ultimately be republican. As with domestic politics Kant believes that we can only enjoy a peaceful international society if we recognise and subscribe to moral ideas that make it possible. Just as property can be founded only if we draw on the *a priori* ideas of an original community of property and a social contract, so we can have a harmonious world civil society only if we accept and deploy similar moral ideals. For Kant this is no imaginative flight of fantasy. The fruits of civilisation will never remain secure if we do not accept certain regulative ideals of international society. Everyone wishes to flourish in order to acquire wealth and property in their own way, but this can be achieved in a lasting way only if we recognise in practice certain principles that we all know to be correct in theory. Here there is a parallel with Kant's pure moral philosophy. We can all potentially act against the requirements of the categorical imperative, but all human individuals – as rational beings – must nonetheless recognise its force.

There is therefore a satirical edge to *Perpetual Peace*. Kant acknowledges the power of realist arguments in politics and notes that they are deeply entrenched in everyday life, diplomacy and relations amongst rulers. However he believes that if they are consistently pursued they undermine themselves. Cynicism about politics in the long term, he thinks, is untenable. As he seeks to show in the section of the book devoted to the 'Guarantee of Perpetual Peace', the long, untamed, competitive course of world history and politics may legitimately be seen as having beneficial effects. Even war can be seen as contributing to this process both by encouraging sacrifice and nobility in individuals and by forcing individuals to live under the protection of law within a state (Kant, 1996, pp. 334–5). The hostility and conflict amongst states also obliges the human race to work towards its own improvement. The concrete proposals he puts forward in *Perpetual Peace* are intended to enhance this effect. They are rules that are implicit in the existence (and, above all of the persistence) of human society on this planet.

The republican constitution advocated in the first definitive article is the sole kind of political arrangement that is compatible with the freedom, equality and independence of human individuals. For us to act freely in society we must be subject to possible legal coercion. We have to regard ourselves as co-authors of the laws that so regulate us. This is possible only under a republican constitution where our representatives make the law. Because those legislators are the sovereign power it is the kind of state where war is least likely because those who have to pay the price for war – both in terms of financing it through taxes and by providing the armed combatants – are those who make the final decision on waging war.

Kant does not envisage bringing about lasting peace by doing away with the state. He sees the state as a vital staging-post in creating a worldwide civil society. Historically it is only within nation-states that the rule of law has been established. But we must not be satisfied with this position. We have to move on from the civil society established within the state by the social contract to an international civil society also implicit within the social contract. The second definitive article of *Perpetual Peace* is concerned with this vital step. It is important to be aware that it is not the state that is the main target of Kant's critique in this article but rather international law. As Kant puts it, 'The law of nations should be based upon a federalism of free states' (Kant, 1996, p. 325). Here Kant is not advocating that states give up their independence immediately and merge with like-minded states but rather that their leaders should understand the legal relations amongst states as resting upon a community of states. Existing international law is both admired and resented by Kant. He admires it because, however deficient it may be, it nonetheless recognises the need and aspiration for relations amongst states to be regulated by law. At the same time he resents it very much because it rests too firmly on the notion of the complete and arbitrary independence of states. The starkest evidence of this wilful independence is the apparent right in existing international law of states to go to war. Kant regards the notion of a 'just war' as self-contradictory, and he mocks the international law theorists Grotius, Pufendorf and Vattel as 'sorry comforters' for their defence of the idea. Thus a vital step forward in the search for international peace will be made if the rulers of states see their legal relations, not as based on presumptions of hostility, but rather on ones of community.

The third definitive article of *Perpetual Peace* aims at a similar transformation in our thinking about world politics. This is an article that all individuals as well as the rulers of states can adopt. This article requires that 'cosmopolitan right should be limited to conditions of universal hospitality' (Kant, 1996, p. 328). At first sight this seems an innocuous requirement, but it has far-reaching implications for the way in which states treat non-subjects and individuals treat the inhabitants of other territories. This principle involves a far-reaching critique of imperialism and colonialism; it also implies that refugees should be treated humanely, for they have done nothing wrong in arriving within our territories. Every human individual throughout the world has the right not to be a guest within another territory but has the right to visit (Kant, 1996, p. 329). As the earth is not an infinite space spreading in all directions, but rather a globe and so bounded, there is always the chance that the paths of two individuals may cross. So we have to inhabit the earth as a common home where we can expect not to be treated by others always as an enemy. We have to see this relationship from two sides, not only from the standpoint of ourselves coming across another individual (and not wanting to be treated badly) but also from the standpoint of another coming across us (and also not wanting to be taken advantage of). Kant therefore implicitly condemns the European practice in relation to other inhabitants of the globe of subduing nations, taking hold of their property and territory. He praises in this context the actions of the Japanese and the Chinese in thoroughly restricting the access of Europeans to their territories. The cosmopolitan right of hospitality can be deduced from the notion of public right in general. Members of the human race can only realise their innate freedom on this assumption.

The six preliminary articles are also not simply utopian precepts but elements of a working system of international peace. They flow from the aim of creating and retaining a civil society. Let us take the most apparently utopian of these preliminary articles: the one that rules out standing armies. Permanent professional armies presuppose the permanent possibility of war. The rulers of states have to be committed in principle to de-professionalising armies because to regard another as an instrument of war is to dehumanise them and at the same time to create a continuous threat to other nations. Kant is not saying here that states should not be prepared to defend themselves, for he supports the idea of citizens' armies, but rather he supports a frame of mind that regards war eventually eliminable. Without this frame of mind, civil society becomes unsustainable.

From *Perpetual Peace* we can see that Kant has a major programme of political change. The question arises: how does he see this change from an anarchical world society, with regimes varying from the republican to the autocratic, to a peaceful world civil society where there are only republics? The short answer is that this should take place through reform from the top down. It is a task for political leaders to transform the principles and institutions upon which their polities are based and with that their international policies towards the ideal. The realist political leader may simply scorn such a programme as moral idealism. For this reason Kant pays a great deal of attention to demonstrating how politics and morality cannot conflict with one another. Hence he rejects a purely prudential (interest-driven) manner of determining political policy and instead argues for a politics based on principle. He argues against a solely prudential politics on two grounds. First, he argues that it leads to internally inconsistent policies. Machiavellian political leaders find themselves at one time advocating a certain policy wholly without reservation and under other circumstances they will be equally as forceful in opposing it. Second, he argues that no political leader can be sufficiently well informed about the development of events always to support the policy that will produce the best consequences. It is only with a moral policy that a political leader can be confident. Political leaders are not justified in believing that moral policies will always lead to success but they are justified in believing that they are only correct ones to follow. For Kant, politics must always bend the 'knee before right' (1996: 347).

a world state or simply a loose federation of sovereign states?

It is a matter of controversy how Kant sees the development of the kind of worldwide federation of states that should underpin international law. In his international writings he gives hints both in the direction of a possible future world state and in the direction of a very loose federation driven by several or one exemplary republican state (Cavallar, 1999, p. 113). Kant seems to believe that we should not lose sight of the eventual possibility of one world state, but for the foreseeable future we should be content with an approximation towards this ideal through an ever-expanding federation of free states – which are either already republican or slowly modifying themselves towards this condition. An immediate move to a world state seems to Kant to be unwise because of the vast territories over which it would reign and the impossibility of linking them up coherently. In Kant's day the time for information and goods to travel from continent to continent was so long that he could only envisage confusion arising from an attempt at global political unification. However, as the ultimate ideal is one worldwide civil society Kant thinks that we need to retain a notion of possible political unity that would go side by side with it. In the short term, however, he thinks the best way to work towards world peace is for like-minded states to federate loosely, never forcing other states into the fold but seeking always to persuade them of its advantages. Here Kant's political philosophy is driven by *a priori* considerations. The human condition as that of the only rational being on earth requires for its preservation that we should form a worldwide civil society with a common political arrangement. We can never obscure totally or wish away this rational (*a priori*) requirement. It is then a matter of judgement for the leaders of each state, who always retain the right to be autonomous, as to how this condition (which is theoretically necessary) should be realised in the world.

Kant answers positively the question: is the human race capable of improving? However, he does not argue for its empirical inevitability. As one of the best-known representatives of the Enlightenment, twentieth-century postmodernist writers have subjected Kant to a great deal of criticism. He is often taken by these thinkers as an archetypical example of the philosopher who relies on a historical metanarrative of progress. In this respect it is true to say that an account of progress grows out of Kant's philosophy, but this is in a subtle and complex sense that is often missed by postmodernist critics. The lynchpin of Kant's philosophy is not this hypothesis about progress but rather his account of human freedom. For Kant humans are the kinds of beings that act on principle. They are, in other words, consciously able to set themselves goals. These goals are not given to us by nature but arise from our unique role as the sole finite representatives of rational nature. Reason for Kant is through the human individual present in nature. But it is not realised in nature. Reason can only be realised progressively by the human race as a whole. Thus Kant's metanarrative about progress does not point to a fact, but rather to a set of goals. If we are to act freely we have to act as though progress does occur. The proper realisation of human freedom requires a worldwide civil society. Perpetual peace is implicit in human autonomy.

further reading

The best and most recent biography of Kant in English is Kuehn (2001); see also Gulyga (1977). For surveys and critical discussions of his social and political thought, see Williams (1983), Mulholland (1990), Wood (1999), Guyer (2000) and Flikschuh (2000), which situates Kant's political thinking within contemporary debates sparked by John Rawls in political theory. For critical discussions of the international dimensions of Kant's political thought, see Cavallar (1999), Williams (2003) and Doyle (1983), which advanced the 'liberal democratic peace thesis'. Baron (1995) is a very lively defence of Kantian morality; for a key book on Kant's philosophy of history see Anderson-Gold (2001). Kaufman (1999) considers carefully what Kant's political thinking might imply for social policy, Kneller and Axinn (1998) present essays on current implications of Kant's thought, and Schott (1997) collects essays on Kant in relation to women and feminist concerns.

references

Anderson-Gold, S. (2001) *Unnecessary Evil. History and Moral Progress in the Philosophy of Immanuel Kant.* Cardiff: University of Wales Press.

Baron, M. (1995) *Kantian Ethics Almost Without Apology.* Ithaca, NY: Cornell University Press.

Cavallar, G. (1999) *Kant and the Theory and Practice of International Right.* Cardiff: University of Wales Press.

Doyle, M. (1983) 'Kant, Liberal Legacies, and Foreign Affairs: Parts 1 & 2', *Philosophy and Public Affairs* 12: 205–35 and 12: 1151–63.

Flikschuh, K. (2000) *Kant and Modern Political Philosophy.* Cambridge: Cambridge University Press.

Fukuyama, F. (1992) *The End of History and the Last Man.* London: Penguin.

Gulyga, A. (1977) *Immanuel Kant.* Frankfurt am Main: Suhrkamp.

Guyer, P. (2000) *Kant on Freedom, Law, and Happiness.* New York: Cambridge University Press.

Kant, I. (1979) *The Conflict of the Faculties*, trans. and ed. M.J. Gregor. New York: Abaris Books.

Kant, I. (1991) *Kant's Political Writings*, trans. H. Nisbet and ed. H. Reiss. Cambridge: Cambridge University Press.

Kant, I. (1996) *Practical Philosophy*, trans. and ed. M.J. Gregor. Cambridge: Cambridge University Press.

Kant, I. (1998a) *The Critique of Pure Reason*, trans. and ed. P. Guyer and A. Wood. Cambridge: Cambridge University Press.

Kant, I. (1998b) *Religion within the Boundaries of Mere Reason*, trans. and ed. A. Wood and G. di Giovanni. Cambridge: Cambridge University Press.

Kaufman, A. (1999) *Welfare in the Kantian State*. Oxford: Oxford University Press.

Kneller, J. and Axinn, S. (eds) (1998) *Autonomy and Community: Readings in Contemporary Kantian Social Philosophy*. Albany, NY: State University of New York Press.

Kuehn, M. (2001) *Kant: A Biography*. Cambridge: Cambridge University Press.

Mulholland, L.A. (1990) *Kant's System of Rights*. New York and Oxford: Columbia University Press.

Rawls, J. (1996) *Political Liberalism*. New York: Columbia University Press.

Schott, R.M. (1997) *Feminist Interpretations of Immanuel Kant*. University Park, PA: Pennsylvania State University Press.

Williams, H.L. (2003) *Kant's Critique of Hobbes: Sovereignty and Cosmopolitanism*. Cardiff: University of Wales Press.

Williams, H.L. (1983) *Kant's Political Philosophy*. Oxford: Blackwell.

Wood, A. (1999) *Kant's Ethical Thought*. New York: Cambridge University Press.

3
g.w.f. hegel
anthony burns

Georg Wilhelm Friedrich Hegel (1770–1831) was a German philosopher whose life spanned the last third of the eighteenth and the first third of the nineteenth centuries. For Western Europe this was a period of great commercial expansion, combined, especially in England, with industrial revolution. Politically, European history at this time was dominated by the French Revolution of 1789, and hence also by the growth and development of the modern state and its eventual transition into the liberal democratic state of today. Hegel was greatly interested in the significance of the revolution for the German states and especially for Prussia where, at the end of his life, he taught philosophy at the University of Berlin.

Hegel is a major figure in the history of political thought, someone whose views have a significance, not simply for the study of German history and politics at the time of the French Revolution, but for anyone who wishes to develop an understanding of European or even world history from the time of the ancient Greeks to the present. One of Hegel's concerns is that of tracing the significance of great turning points in that history, such as the transition from a premodern to a modern society that occurred in Europe from about the sixteenth century onwards. Hegel's political thought is sometimes seen as being representative of the standpoint of modernity, and, for this very reason, as now out of date. There are, however, those who feel that Hegel's ideas are still relevant for our understanding of political problems today. From this point of view, whether one agrees or disagrees with Hegel, one cannot afford to ignore him. Despite the limitations imposed by the historical context within which they were written, Hegel's ideas continue to possess a wider significance at the beginning of a new millennium.

hegel on philosophy and metaphysics

Hegel's philosophy may be summarised in terms of three basic principles: idealism, monism and teleology. Hegel is a philosophical idealist who challenges the common sense understanding of the nature of reality. According to Hegel, common sense tells us that reality is composed of a multiplicity of material or physical objects that exist separately from one another and from the knowing subject. It also tells us that we can derive knowledge of reality through the senses. From this point of view, things appear to us as they truly are in reality. Hegel argues that we cannot rely on the senses, which sometimes deceive us. However, he rejects scepticism, the view that knowledge of reality is not possible.

According to Hegel, it is possible for us to develop knowledge *of* reality because reality is conceptual, or a form of thought. Hegel is not an idealist because he thinks that reality subsists only in the mind or consciousness of the knowing subject, a doctrine that he calls 'subjective idealism' (Hegel, 1975, pp. 70, 73–4, 188). Rather, he is an idealist because he believes that it is only concepts that are truly real. In Hegel's terminology, this is a form of 'objective idealism' or 'absolute idealism' (Hegel, 1975, pp. 52, 73, 140, 223). Like Plato, Hegel associates reality with entities that are timeless and universal. Those things which are real do not exist in time and space and do not change or decay (Hegel, 1975, pp. 33–7). It is, however, only ideas or concepts that possess these features. It follows from this that physical objects are not real. For both Plato and Hegel, the world of physical objects is the world of appearances. This is how the entities that are real appear to us through our senses (Hegel, 1975, pp. 33–7, 67, 73, 140, 186–8, 223).

Hegel distinguishes between the appearance of an individual thing and its essence. He subscribes idiosyncratically to the doctrine known as essentialism (Hegel, 1975, pp. 162–6). According to this view, all individual things have an essential nature. Hegel identifies this with the conceptual reality that underpins their appearance. In his view, understanding reality involves grasping its essential nature. The features that are associated with the essence of a thing are encapsulated in the definition of its concept.

In Hegel's opinion all individual things have a complex structure. They are concrete unities of two component elements, an underlying reality or essence, on the one hand, and a corresponding appearance or existence, on the other. Philosophy must take each of these aspects into account. It must see an individual thing as a combination of a universal with a particular (Hegel, 1975, pp. 39–40, 226–7). For Hegel, to look at things in this way is to consider them in their actuality (Hegel, 1975, pp. 200–2, 226). He maintains that concepts or essences are not transcendent but immanent entities. They subsist and necessarily manifest themselves in and through the individual existent things that inhabit the world of appearances (Hegel, 1975, pp. 19–22, 33–7, 62, 73, 78, 95, 113–15, 120, 163, 166, 174, 184–90, 204–7, 223–8, 244–5).

According to Hegel, common sense tells us that individual things or substances are isolated and separated from one another. Hegel follows Spinoza in rejecting this view. He maintains that all things must be thought of dialectically, as being necessarily related to each other, because they are component parts of some greater totality or whole (Hegel, 1975, pp. 15, 52–3, 78, 115–21, 191). Spinoza defines the concept of substance with reference to that of independent self-subsistence. From this point of view, a substance is by definition some thing which is the cause of itself and which is not caused by any other thing. It follows from this definition that for Spinoza there could only be *one* substance, namely the universe as a whole. Hegel refers to this as the absolute (Hegel, 1975, pp. 40, 69, 123–7, 223; 1977, pp. 9–12, 46–8). Both Hegel and Spinoza associate the idea of a being that is self-subsistent, or the cause of itself, with the notion of God. Consequently, in their view, God and the one substance are the same thing. This is so, because by definition the concept of the universe covers everything that there is, from which it follows that there could not be anything outside of the universe that might be said to be a creator or the cause of it.

Like that of Spinoza, Hegel's philosophy is therefore a form of pantheism. It is a philosophy that sees God in all things and all things in God. Every individual thing or object, from this point of view, is but a specific form or manifestation of God. In a sense, therefore, each individual thing *is* God, or an aspect of the divine presence that dwells immanently within all things. It follows from this that just as for Spinoza there can only be one substance, so also for Hegel there can only be *one* concept (*Begriff*). Hegel refers to this as *the* Concept (Hegel, 1975, pp. 110, 223).

It is impossible to understand Hegel's philosophy without acknowledging his debt to Spinoza (Hegel, 1974, p. 283). However, Hegel is critical of certain aspects of Spinozism. Unlike Spinoza, Hegel tends to view all actual things dynamically or historically. One of his criticisms of Spinoza is the fact that Spinoza's philosophy lacks this dimension. Hegel insists that we must think of the one substance that is God as undergoing a process of change and development through time, in and through history. His understanding of change is teleological. All processes of change progress towards some final end point or goal.

Like Aristotle, Hegel thinks of all actual things as having a life like that of natural organisms. They have a period of infancy, one of maturity and one of old age. In the course of their development they become at the end explicitly what, at the beginning they *were* implicitly or potentially. Hegel uses the word 'idea' in a technical sense to refer to those features of a thing that it possesses when it has fully actualised its potential. Hence just as for Hegel there is only one Concept, so also there is just one idea, which Hegel refers to as *the* Idea or the Absolute Idea (Hegel, 1975, pp. 214, 265, 274–9, 292–3).

We have seen that Hegel maintains that all individual things are appearances of just one underlying reality, which is the concept of that thing. This also applies to Hegel's understanding of the self or subject. There are very many particular selves, one for every individual human being. Each one of these is an existent entity. As such it is an appearance of just one underlying reality, namely the concept of the self or subject (Hegel, 1975, p. 38). For Hegel, then, there can be just one Self and one Subject. Hegel refers to this as the absolute Self or Subject, which again is God (Hegel, 1975, p. 85). It is this that manifests itself in a particular form in every individual human being. Again, therefore, each individual self *is* God, in one of God's many different manifestations.

Unlike Spinoza, for Hegel the one substance may be thought of as analogous to a human being. It is a Person possessing a subjective mind or consciousness (Hegel, 1975, p. 98). This *one* Person grows and develops over time, in and through the history of the world. It actualises its potential and moves from a state of immediate consciousness to, ultimately, one of mature self-consciousness. Another of Hegel's criticisms of Spinoza is that he does not think of the one substance as a developing self-conscious subject (Hegel, 1975, pp. 82, 213–15; 1977, pp. 9–10).

hegel and the history of philosophy

Hegel sees the history of philosophy as a process of development towards a correct understanding of the actual world and of the true nature of reality, at the end of which things appear to the knowing subject as they really are in themselves, and what he refers to as absolute knowledge relating to the one Idea is finally achieved (Hegel, 1977, pp. 479–93). It follows from the above that when the subjective mind of any individual human being develops a true understanding of reality, what this amounts to is that it is God who has developed such an understanding of himself. This must be so, because, for Hegel, there is only one thing or substance. Hence the entity that is the subject of knowledge is identical with the entity which it knows – the object of knowledge (Hegel, 1975, p. 292). The consciousness that an individual human being has of the reality which it knows, therefore, is nothing other than the consciousness which God as the subject of knowledge has of himself as the only possible object of knowledge. It is the self-consciousness of God.

For Hegel the history of philosophy involves the growth and development of both the consciousness and the self-consciousness of God, a process which culminates in his own philosophical system. Hegel believes that it is only in and through his own philosophy that God has finally become fully aware of the fundamental truth, that what appears to be an external world subsisting independently of mind or spirit is in fact not so. Hegel associates all earlier philosophising with alienation: the separation of mind or consciousness, or the knowing subject, from the object of knowledge, and the failure to appreciate that this object is in essence identical with itself (Hegel, 1975, p. 261; 1977, p. 10). For Hegel, the task of philosophy is to overcome this alienation. It is this process of development which Hegel outlines in his *Phenomenology of Spirit* (1807).

From Hegel's point of view, the history of philosophy is an odyssey. It is a quest, the outcome of which is that, as in the case of the development of an individual human being from youth to old age, mind or spirit is finally reconciled both with itself and with the world around it, because the world no longer appears alien to it. Hegel's philosophical system is also therefore, as Hegel himself acknowledges, a theodicy. As is the case with religion and mythology its aim, by other means, is to 'justify the ways of God to man' (Hegel, 1953, p. 18; 1975, p. 209).

hegel's political thought

Hegel's political thought is an application of these metaphysical principles to questions of politics and law (Hegel, 1979, pp. 10–12, 20, 34, 137, 140, 155, 160, 175, 225, 283). It is also a theoretical justification for constitutional government, specifically constitutional monarchy (Hegel, 1979, pp. 176, 288–9). For Hegel the principle of all constitutional government is that of the rule of law. In his view, we can consider individual laws, constitutions and the states with which they are associated as being concrete entities or actualities. They are combinations of a universal with a particular. The universal in question is the concept of what it is for something to be a law, a constitution, or a state. This concept encapsulates the essential nature and hence the rational basis of all laws, all constitutions and of all states. As such, it is necessarily associated with the most fundamental principles of natural right or law. In part one of the *Philosophy of Right* Hegel refers to these as the principles of abstract right (Hegel, 1979, pp. 37–74). The particular features with which this universal is associated when it is incorporated into positive laws are contingent and historical. They can and do differ legitimately from constitution to constitution, and from state to state (Hegel, 1979, p. 146). As actualities, the positive laws of an individual constitution or state, whether these are statute laws or customary laws handed down by ancient tradition, constitute a specific form of manifestation, or a specific appearance, of the underlying essence which is the concept of right or law. Hegel associates the concept of right or law with the principle of reciprocal freedom, a principle that he considers to be the most important principle of justice, understood as a non-distributive normative principle (Hegel, 1979, pp. 32–3, 160, 225).

Hegel's political thought is best seen as an attempt to steer a middle course between two extremes. According to the first, we can accept what is without seeking to defend it by rational argument, for example by appealing to tradition, to religion, or to mythology. Alternatively, according to the second, we could engage in abstract philosophical speculation about questions of right or what ought to be. However if we do this then it is likely that, like the revolutionaries of 1789, we will be completely at odds with the existing social and political order. In Hegel's opinion, this second approach to politics is other-worldly and utopian (Hegel, 1979, p. 10). It is an approach which Hegel explicitly associates with the rebelliousness of youth, and which he contrasts with the wisdom of the elderly (Hegel, 1953, pp. 35–6; 1975, pp. 115, 291; 1979, pp. 133–4). Hegel rejects the idea that we could construct a rational or abstract blueprint of an ideal society which is necessarily supra-historical and then use it critically to evaluate existing constitutions, thereby finding them unjust or irrational in their entirety.

Hegel's own approach involves the idea that, at a time when the existing social and political order is under threat because of the example set by the French Revolution, we can no longer rely on outmoded forms of legitimation to preserve it. In the modern age of Enlightenment or the 'age of reason', instead of tradition, mythology or religion, only philosophy can provide a rational justification for the status quo. For Hegel, rather than seek to replace existing constitutions in their entirety, the most important political task of his day is a twofold one. On the one hand it is necessary to codify existing constitutions so that the rationality that is already to be found within them will become clearer (Hegel, 1979, pp. 16, 134–6, 138–9, 144–5, 159, 271–3). On the other hand, so as to preserve them, it is necessary that we reform existing constitutions so that they move closer to the principle of constitutional monarchy. The model we should employ to guide such modernising reforms is the French Revolution, suitably interpreted. It is this that in the latest stage of world historical development provides us with our understanding of the Idea of the state.

history and politics

Hegel's views on politics are informed by his philosophy of history. This contrasts the political thought of pre-modern societies, especially ancient Athens, with that of Rome and of modern European society, which Hegel associates with the classical liberalism of the seventeenth and eighteenth centuries. According to Hegel, the most important source of social and political integration in premodern societies was not the power of coercive law but virtue or the sense of duty. It was the consensus that existed around their commitment to shared ethical values and a shared political identity. Hegel argues that the transition from premodern to modern society is associated with a tendency for traditional communities of this kind to be replaced by a new kind of society and a new principle of social integration. Modern societies, Hegel maintains, are nothing more than an aggregation of isolated, self-interested individuals, or social atoms. These individuals are weakly integrated into society, possess no strong sense of political identity or shared ethical values, and have no strong sense of duty. Consequently, modern society needs to be regulated or policed by the coercive apparatus of a bureaucratic state (Hegel, 1953, pp. 289, 294–5, 308–9, 315–17, 320).

According to Hegel, premodern society might be seen as based on the principle of community without liberty, whereas modern society is based on the contrasting principle of liberty without community. As against each of these Hegel calls for the creation of new kind of political order, a revived form of ethical life appropriate for the modern era, in which both the principle of community and that of individual liberty would be respected. One of the most important principles of social integration in this society will, once again, be that of moral consensus. Hegel envisages a society in which individuals will voluntarily consent to carry out the duties associated with their station in life as members of particular social institutions. These are the duties which they owe to the state, in the broad sense in which Hegel sometimes employs this term, that is to say the ethical community of which they are members (Hegel, 1953, p. 37; 1979, pp. 107, 162). Hegel argues that this will require the revival or the strengthening of corporate groups, or of intermediate associations between the individual and the narrow bureaucratic state, each of which will have a dual function. On the one hand, it will protect the individual and individual liberty from the intrusions of the state in the narrow sense, the state whose principal function is to make and enforce laws. On the other hand, it will inculcate the right values in its individual citizens, thereby educating them and integrating them into the wider community, whilst at the same time regulating their conduct by promoting the development of the sense of duty within them (Hegel, 1979, pp. 106–7, 163).

Unlike the states of our own day, the type of state that Hegel considers to be modern at the beginning of the nineteenth century is neither liberal nor democratic. It is not liberal because Hegel is strongly critical of the limitations of classical liberalism, especially the excessive individualism of its version of the doctrine of natural rights and the social contract theory of the state based upon this (Hegel, 1953, p. 452; 1979, pp. 71, 156, 242, 266–7). In Hegel's view, classical liberalism does not attach sufficient importance to the claims that the community, society as a whole, or the state in the broad sense, can legitimately make on the individual. It attaches too much importance, not to the value of liberty as such, for Hegel himself is committed to this same value, but rather to a particular understanding of the concept of liberty, namely the idea that liberty is simply a matter of the individuals being able to do what they want or choose to do with their own lives and property, no matter what the implications of this might be for society as a whole.

In short, Hegel rejects what is usually referred to as the negative view of liberty (Hegel, 1979, pp. 22, 27–8, 206, 227, 259–60). Against this, Hegel endorses the positive view (Hegel, 1953, p. 50; 1979, pp. 22, 230, 260). On this view, the liberty of the individual is associated with rights that are sustained by law. For Hegel, however, there can be no rights without duties (Hegel, 1979, pp. 29, 280). The concept of liberty properly understood, therefore, is associated with that of obedience to the laws, not of the bureaucratic state as such, but rather of the historical community of which one happens to be a member, and with performing the duties associated with one's station in that community.

This view of liberty is not sufficiently individualistic to meet the requirements of classical liberalism. The state that Hegel recommends is not a democratic state, either. Hegel is a paternalist. He defends the principle of aristocracy, or of rule by the best. In the *Philosophy of Right* the task of legislation, especially the codification of existing customary laws, is given to the bureaucracy, which Hegel assumes, can be relied upon to rule wisely and justly in the universal interest of society as a whole (Hegel, 1979, p. 132). The monarch in Hegel's *Rechtstaat* merely provides a rubber stamp for their decisions. The most Hegel is prepared to concede here is a limited involvement by representatives of 'the people', the purpose of which is again an educational one, to explain to citizens why it is their duty to obey the law (Hegel, 1953, pp. 57, 61–2; 1979, pp. 33, 130, 156–7, 175, 182–3, 186, 195–6, 198, 200–5, 227, 292–5).

hegel's influence and his relevance today

Hegel's influence on Marx and Marxism generally is well known (Burns and Fraser, 2000; Poster, 1975). So far as his contemporary relevance is concerned, it is his reception in poststructuralism and postmodernism in late-twentieth-century France which is most significant (Browning, 1999; Butler, 1999; Gutting, 2001; Kelly, 1992; Sherman, 1999; Williams, 1998). Hegel's political thought is a justification of the modern nation-state at a time when such a state did not yet exist in Germany. Since then, of course, times have changed. This has led French theorists like Jean François Lyotard to argue that we are now living in a radically different type of society in a postmodern world (Lyotard, 1984). It is argued that the most significant feature of contemporary politics is the rise and decline of the nation-state as the basic unit of politics in the most advanced societies of the West during the nineteenth and twentieth centuries, a decline associated with globalisation. From this point of view, the nation-state has been eroded both from above and below. It has been eroded from above by the development of international supra-state organisations that carry out what are evidently political functions. This has weakened the 'state' side of the nation-state equation by undermining its sovereignty. It has been eroded from below because globalisation is associated with an increased differentiation and fragmentation of society. This has weakened the 'nation' side of the nation-state equation. It has undermined the nation as a unified cohesive unit, the members of whom possess a shared political identity and shared moral and cultural values – the very basis for what Hegel refers to as ethical life in his *Philosophy of Right*.

Today we are living in a pluralistic, multicultural society, and no adequate approach to politics can ignore this fact. There is therefore a need today to rethink one's understanding of the very nature of politics in a postmodern world (Grillo, 1999; Hutcheon, 2003; Rengger, 1995; White, 1991). From this point of view, Hegel's political thought is tainted by the modernist assumptions with which it is historically associated. Its alleged statism, or its overriding emphasis on the political importance of the nation-state and the duties owed to it, combined with its alleged intolerance of individual differences and social diversity cannot, it is argued, help anyone to understand the politics of today.

According to Hegel's critics, one of the main reasons for this is the inadequate philosophy upon which his political thought is based. This philosophy has been subjected to severe criticism, especially in France, by advocates of poststructuralism, inspired by the writings of Nietzsche (Schrift, 1995). In poststructuralist philosophy this critique often involves a rejection of 'binary oppositions', for example, the distinction between the appearances of things and their underlying essence, which are held to be central not just to Hegel's philosophy but to the entire Western philosophical tradition (Howarth, 2000, pp. 36–7; Schrift, 1995, pp. 15–17; Young, 1990, p. 99). For poststructuralists there are no essences and no conceptual reality underpinning the appearances of things. Hence there can be no metaphysics as this is traditionally understood. Postructuralists endorse Nietzsche's judgement that 'the apparent world', the world directly accessible by the senses, 'is the only one' (Nietzsche, 1968, p. 36). In their view, because of his essentialism, Hegel privileges the principle of identity or sameness over that of difference and attaches no importance to the features that make things the unique individuals that they are. Moreover, this alleged tendency in Hegel's metaphysics is reflected in his ethical and political thought (Young, 1990, pp. 97–9). Here also, his critics point out, Hegel employs the outmoded language of essentialism, more specifically of humanism, a language which assumes that all individuals, no matter what differences there are between them, nevertheless share the same common humanity (Hegel, 1979, pp. 134, 169).

Poststructuralists object to this for two reasons. First, they argue that humanity for Hegel is merely an abstract category. Hence it follows that Hegel's philosophy can attach no value to particular features like race or gender which make individual human beings unique. Second, they reject humanism because in their view the features which are claimed by humanists to be common to all human beings are invariably not so. Although humanists intend to talk generically about 'man' as a species, or in Hegel's case Man with a capital 'M', what they actually talk about is invariably men, or the male of the species. Thus, it is argued, humanism inevitably excludes certain categories of people, especially women.

So far as ethics is concerned, the tendency of poststructuralist thought today is to respond to the criticism that a doctrine inspired by Nietzsche's philosophy can have no ethic at all by attempting to develop an ethics of difference based on the principle of respect for the other simply as an other. Here others ought to be valued not, as Hegel argues, because they are similar to oneself in certain respects, having to do with a shared human essence, but precisely because they are different. The injunction of this new ethic is that we respect others, not *despite* the differences that exist between us, but *because* of those differences. The inspiration for this approach to ethics is the work of Emmanuel Levinas (Bauman, 1993; Caygill, 2001; Challier, 2001; Critchley, 1999a; 1999b; Hand, 1996; Squires, 1993).

According to poststructuralists, in the advanced societies of the West today the most important kind of politics is identity politics. This involves the ascription of social identity to particular individuals (Benhabib, 1996; Calhoun, 1994; Grillo, 1999; Laclau, 1994; Young, 1990). Identity politics has little to do with the legislative activities of a nation-state, or with politics as this is traditionally understood. Rather it has to do with the institutions of society and with social roles, for example those associated with gender differentiation, and with the duties that are attached to them (Benhabib, 1992; Butler, 1990; Butler and Scott, 1992). Social identities are associated with classificatory labels and hence also with a particular language or discourse (Howarth, 2000). The central claim made by poststructuralists is that one's identity as a self or as a subject is entirely socially constructed, and for this very reason is open to contestation and change. Consistently with their Nietzschean rejection of metaphysics generally, poststructuralists argue that there is no essential or universal self that underpins the particular self that is constructed by society, or the self as it appears to the world. It has been suggested that Foucault's proclamation relating to the 'death of the subject', analogous to Nietzsche's proclamation of the 'death of God', is best thought of as a criticism, along these lines, not of Descartes and of the Cartesian notion of the subject (Calhoun, 1994, p. 10), but specifically of the notion of the 'absolute Subject' in Hegel's *Phenomenology of Spirit* (Butler, 1999, p. 175; Macey, 1993, p. 169). On this view, the social construction of the self, or the ascription of social identities to specific individuals, necessarily involves the exercise of power, which is inherent in all social relationships. The purpose of identity politics is to unmask this exercise of power by exposing the politics that is involved in the process of identity construction. The suggestion is, therefore, that precisely because of his essentialism, his humanism, and his blindness to gender differences, all of which are associated with a discourse endorsing traditional social roles, and all of which imply a rejection of the view that identity is a contestable social construction, Hegel is unable to assist in the theorisation of this most important dimension of politics today (Hutchings, 2003; Jagentowicz Mills, 1996).

At least some of these criticisms of Hegel are unjustified. First, so far as his alleged statism is concerned, it should again be noted that Hegel distinguishes between a broad and a narrow sense of the concept of the state (Hegel, 1979, pp. 163, 364–5). It is true that Hegel spends some time discussing the state in the narrow bureaucratic sense of the term. However, the relevant section of the *Philosophy of Right* takes up just one section of part three of this work. Hegel spends as much if not more time discussing the relationship which exists between this bureaucratic state and the various institutions which constitute society as a whole, the state in the broadest possible sense of the term, the sphere of ethical life (Hegel, 1979, pp. 105–6). Moreover, the view that Hegel's political thought is totalitarian because it completely subordinates the individual to the narrow bureaucratic state is clearly false. Hegel's corporatism aims at protecting individuals from this bureaucratic state by placing a variety of intermediate social institutions between them (Hegel, 1979, pp. 153–4, 163). Hegel does consider the wider ethical community, or the state in the broad sense, as a totality or whole which is greater than the sum of its individual parts, the corporate groups that constitute it, but this view does not involve a rejection of the values of plurality or diversity. All that it involves is a recognition by Hegel that if the wider social order is to be maintained, then, underlying this healthy diversity, there must be at least *some* principle of social cohesion or integration, at least some moral consensus, and at least some shared values, based on the principle of their common humanity, which all of these groups hold in common. For without this the coercive power of the bureaucratic state would not be sufficient to restrain the process of ongoing social fragmentation and the inevitable conflicts between different groups which would arise in consequence of it. In a world in which religious fundamentalism and associated political extremism are on the increase, Hegel's political thought might be construed as implying a sensible call, on humanitarian grounds, for self-restraint and toleration of the differences which exist between the various individuals and groups which constitute multicultural society today.

Second, Hegel's philosophy is not a binary philosophy, as his poststructuralist critics claim, but a ternary one. It is true that Hegel distinguishes between the essence of an individual thing and its appearance, and that he does in some sense attach more importance to the former than he does to the latter. Nevertheless he also insists that each of these concepts can only be understood in relation to a third concept, that of actuality. Considered from the standpoint of its actuality, the appearance of an individual thing is just as important as its underlying essence, for without that appearance the thing in question could not *be* actual (Hegel, 1975, pp. 189, 198, 272). Similarly, the concepts of universal and particular are each related to a third concept, that of individuality (Hegel, 1975, pp. 226–9; 1979, pp. 175, 279), and the concepts of identity and difference are each related to a third concept, that of identity-in-difference (Hegel, 1975, pp. 120–1, 152, 167–8, 171, 180, 228). For Hegel each of these ternary categorisations is a way of emphasising the importance of the very thing that poststructuralists accuse him of ignoring, namely the particular characteristics which make an individual thing the unique entity which it is, and which differentiate it from other things (Hegel, 1975, p. 198). In the case of human beings, Hegel attaches importance to every feature of an individual self or subject, even those which he considers to be contingent features, such as race or gender, although he does not of course consider these to be as important as the universal and necessary features which he associates with the essence or concept of the self and with our shared humanity. Moreover, a logical implication of Hegel's view that these features are contingent is that this aspect of an individual self, the particular manner in which it appears to the world, must be an historical or sociological construct (Hegel, 1979, pp. 23, 127, 133–4, 169, 235, 268–9, 271). In my view, then, this poststructuralist criticism of Hegel is based either on a misrepresentation or on a misunderstanding of one of the fundamental principles of Hegel's metaphysics.

Finally, Hegel also has an interest in identity politics, which is evidently not a postmodern (or even a modern) phenomenon (Calhoun, 1994, pp. 9–10, 23). There are two reasons for thinking this. The first has to do with the broad thrust of Hegel's political thought, the point of which is to persuade his readers that they should accept their allotted station in life together with the attendant duties associated with it, in other words the particular social identity which has been ascribed to them by the hierarchical institutions of their own society. It is true that Hegel's intention is to justify these institutions, and hence also existing social inequalities, which he considers to be compatible with his humanism and his belief in the equal worth of all human beings (Hegel, 1979, pp. 130, 237). Nevertheless, it does not seem inappropriate to call this a form of identity politics. The second reason is Hegel's discussion of the master–slave relation and the ascription of these identities to particular individuals as the outcome of a 'struggle for recognition' in the *Phenomenology of Spirit* (Hegel, 1977, pp. 111–19), which has been so influential in twentieth-century French philosophy (Butler, 1999; Gutting, 2001; Kelly, 1992; Poster, 1975; Sherman, 1999; Williams, 1998). A lot of research is currently being done in this area, and it is perhaps this aspect of Hegel's political thought which is currently the most discussed (Fraser, 1999; Fraser and Honneth, 2003; Lash and Featherstone, 2001; Taylor, 1994; Thompson, 2005; Williams, 1998). It is not difficult to see how this section of the *Phenomenology*, suitably interpreted, could be related to identity politics in general, and to feminist political thought in particular. Simone de Beauvoir's assertion that Hegel's treatment of 'the relation of master to slave' applies 'much better to the relation of man and woman' is noteworthy in this regard (de Beauvoir, 1981, pp. 96–7).

We have seen that one reason why poststructuralists reject Hegel's version of identity politics is because of Hegel's humanism. In my view, however, this is a strength and not a weakness. One of the most important current tasks for political theorists is to respond to poststructuralism by developing a new humanism which is neither sexist nor ethnocentrist and which values the plurality and diversity of contemporary society. Hegel's efforts to mediate between essentialist realism on the one hand and extreme social constructionism on the other could assist in this task. It is this more than anything else which establishes the continued importance of Hegel's philosophy today.

further reading

For a study of Hegel's *Phenomenology*, see Stern (2002), and for the *Philosophy of Right*, see Knowles (2002). For Hegel on history, see McCarney (1998). Hegel and twentieth-century France are discussed in Baugh (2003), Butler (1999), Kelly (1992), Roth (1988), Sherman (1999) and Williams (1998). For the encounter between Hegel and postmodernism, see Browning (1999). Hegel and feminism are considered in Hutchings (2003) and Jagentowicz Mills (1996).

references

Baugh, B. (2003) *French Hegel: From Surrealism to Postmodernism.* London: Routledge.
Bauman, Z. (1993) *Postmodern Ethics.* Oxford: Blackwell.
Benhabib, S. (1992) *Situating the Self: Gender, Community and Postmodernism in Contemporary Ethics.* Cambridge: Polity Press.
Benhabib, S. (ed.) (1996) *Democracy and Difference: Contesting the Boundaries of the Political.* Princeton, NJ: Princeton University Press.
Browning, G.K. (1999) 'Lyotard's Hegel and the Dialectic of Modernity', in *Hegel and the History of Political Philosophy*, ed. G.K. Browning, pp. 118–27. London: Macmillan.
Burns, T. and Fraser, I. (eds) (2000) *The Hegel–Marx Connection.* London: Palgrave.
Butler, J. (1990) *Gender Trouble: Feminism and the Subversion of Identity.* New York: Routledge.
Butler, J. (1999 [1987]) *Subjects of Desire: Hegelian Reflections in Twentieth Century France.* New York: Columbia University Press.
Butler, J. and Scott, J.W. (1992) *Feminists Theorize the Political.* London: Routledge.
Calhoun, C. (1994) 'Social Theory and the Politics of Identity', in *Social Theory and the Politics of Identity*, ed. C. Calhoun, pp. 9–36. Oxford: Blackwell.
Caygill, H. (2001) *Levinas and the Political.* London: Routledge.
Challier, C. (2001) *What Ought I to Do? Morality in Kant and Levinas.* Ithaca, NY and London: Cornell University Press.
Critchley, S. (1999a) *Ethics-Politics-Subjectivity: Essays on Derrida, Levinas and Contemporary French Thought.* London: Verso.
Critchley, S. (1999b [1992]) *An Ethics of Deconstruction: Derrida and Levinas*, 2nd edn. Oxford: Blackwell.
de Beauvoir, S. (1981 [1949]) *The Second Sex.* Harmondsworth: Penguin.
Fraser, N. (1999) *Adding Insult to Injury: Social Justice and the Politics of Recognition*, ed. K. Olsen. London: Verso.
Fraser, N. and Honneth, A. (2003) *Redistribution or Recognition? A Philosophical Exchange.* London: Verso.
Grillo, R. (1999) *Pluralism and the Politics of Difference.* Oxford: Oxford University Press.
Gutting, G. (2001) *French Philosophy in the Twentieth Century.* Cambridge: Cambridge University Press.
Hand, S. (1996) *Facing the Other: The Ethics of Emmanuel Levinas.* London: Curzon.
Hegel, G.W.F. (1953) *Lectures on the Philosophy of History*, trans. J. Sibree. New York: Dover.
Hegel, G.W.F. (1974) *Lectures on the History of Philosophy*, Vol. III, trans. E.S. Haldane and F.H. Simpson. London: Routledge.
Hegel, G.W.F. (1975) *Logic: Being Part One of the Encyclopaedia of the Philosophical Sciences*, trans. W. Wallace. Oxford: Oxford University Press.

Hegel, G.W.F. (1977) *Phenomenology of Spirit*, trans. A.V. Miller. Oxford: Clarendon Press.

Hegel, G.W.F. (1979) *The Philosophy of Right*, trans. T.M. Knox. Oxford: Oxford University Press.

Howarth, D. (2000) *Discourse*. Buckingham and Philadelphia: Open University Press.

Hutcheon, L. (2003) *The Politics of Postmodernism*, 2nd edn. London: Routledge.

Hutchings, K. (2003) *Hegel and Feminist Philosophy*. Cambridge: Polity Press.

Jagentowicz Mills, P. (ed.) (1996) *Feminist Interpretations of G.W.F. Hegel*. University Park, PA: Pennsylvania State University Press.

Kelly, M. (1992) *Hegel in France*. Birmingham: Birmingham Modern Languages Publications.

Knowles, D. (2002) *The Routledge Philosophy Guidebook to Hegel's Philosophy of Right*. London: Routledge.

Laclau, E. (ed.) (1994) *The Making of Political Identity*. London: Verso.

Lash, S. and Featherstone, M. (eds) (2001) *Recognition and Difference: Theory, Culture and Society*, 18: 2–3.

Lyotard, J.-F. (1984) *The Postmodern Condition: A Report on Knowledge*. Manchester: Manchester University Press.

Macey, D. (1993) *The Lives of Michel Foucault*. London: Vintage Books.

McCarney, J. (1998) *The Routledge Philosophy Guidebook to Hegel on History*. London: Routledge.

Nietzsche, F. (1968) *The Twilight of the Idols: or How to Philosophize with a Hammer*, trans. R.J. Hollingdale. Harmondsworth: Penguin.

Poster, M. (1975) 'The Hegel Renaissance', in *Existenial Marxism in Postwar France: From Sartre to Althusser*, ed. M. Poster, pp. 3–35. Princeton, NJ: Princeton University Press.

Rengger, N.J. (1995) *Political Theory, Modernity and Postmodernity*. Oxford: Blackwell.

Roth, M.S. (1988) *Knowing and History: Appropriations of Hegel in Twentieth Century France*. Ithaca, NY: Cornell University Press.

Schrift, A.D. (1995) *Nietzsche's French Legacy: A Genealogy of Poststructuralism*. London: Routledge.

Sherman, D. (1999) 'The Denial of the Self: The Repudiation of Hegelian Self-Consciousness in Recent European Thought', in *Hegel's Phenomenology of Self-Consciousness*, ed. L. Rauch and D. Sherman, pp. 163–222. Albany, NY: SUNY Press.

Squires, J. (ed.) (1993) *Principled Positions: Postmodernism and the Rediscovery of Value*. London: Lawrence & Wishart.

Stern, R. (2002) *The Routledge Philosophy Guidebook to Hegel's Phenomenology of Spirit*. London: Routledge.

Taylor, C. (1994) 'Multiculturalism and the Politics of Recognition', in *Multiculturalism: Examining the Politics of Recognition*, ed. A. Guttman, pp. 25–73. Princeton, NJ: Princeton University Press.

Thompson, S. (2005 forthcoming) *The Political Theory of Recognition: A Critical Introduction*. Cambridge: Polity Press.

White, S.K. (1991) *Political Theory and Postmodernism*. Cambridge: Cambridge University Press.

Williams, R.R. (1998) 'Recent Views of Recognition and the Question of Ethics', in *Hegel's Ethics of Recognition*, ed. R.R. Williams, pp. 364–412. Berkeley, CA: University of California Press.

Young, I.M. (1990) *Justice and the Politics of Difference*. Princeton, NJ: Princeton University Press.

4
karl marx

bradley j. macdonald

The philosophy of Karl Marx (1818–1883) is intimately political, having been written to bring about changes in the political world. As he famously argued in *Theses on Feuerbach* (1845): 'The philosophers have only *interpreted* the world, in various ways; the point is to *change* it' (Marx, 1977c, p. 423). Such a political intention is represented in Marx's lifelong journalistic work; his activism in the Communist Correspondence Committee, the Communist League (for which Marx and Engels wrote the famous *Manifesto of the Communist Party* [1848]); and, of course, his founding role in the International Workingmen's Association. Moreover, even in his most 'philosophical' and/or 'economic' modes of writing, Marx always assumed there were intimate links between the most arcane economic or philosophical discussions and their political role in the struggles of the working classes. Indeed, in an interview in the New York *World* in 1871, Marx clearly traced the relation of his theory to the political struggles associated with the working class:

> It is hardly likely … that we could hope to prosper in our way against capital if we derived our tactics, say, from the political economy of Mill. He has traced one kind of relationship between labour and capital. We hope to show that it is possible to establish another. (Marx, 1974, p. 399)

What does such a practical political horizon to Marx's *oeuvre* do for our understanding of his political theory? In what way does such an ideological dimension offer insights into Marx's unique contribution to the study of politics? Ultimately, I would argue that such a horizon initiates an important articulation of the political within (and by) his writing, one that infuses Marx's position with a self-reflective deconstructive orientation, as well as inaugurating perceptive discussions of more traditional political subjects associated with the nature of the state, political action, and political knowledge.

critique, praxis, emancipation

Following the recent argument by Simon Critchley (2002) on the character of Continental philosophy, we are drawn to the way in which this tradition attempts to offer wisdom about how to lead a good life, rather than a value-neutral science about how the social and political world works. Not all theorists within this tradition shied away from the attribution of 'science' to their theory. Indeed, Marx saw his own analyses as linked in some way to the scientific apprehension of social reality, but clearly not in the positivist and/or neo-Popperian ways articulated in the Anglo-American tradition (for a perceptive discussion of this issue, see Carver, 1975). In terms of the political theory of Marx, this Continental character has been implicitly or explicitly conveyed by labelling his theory 'critical theory', 'critical' (as opposed to 'scientific'), or as an exemplar of a 'critical social science' more specifically (see, for example, Fay, 1986; Gouldner, 1980; Marcuse, 1964). As Critchley further clarifies, in the Continental tradition the goal of wisdom is productively enacted, in some way or another, through the discursive constellation of 'critique', 'praxis' and 'emancipation' (2002, pp. 54–74). Of course, any astute reader of Marx will see this triptych of concepts and discursive strategies – critique, praxis and emancipation – to be central to his theory in general. Let us explore how these concepts and discursive strategies help flesh out Marx's political theory.

critique

Marx always saw his theory as critique (as evidenced in the title of many of his works; most famously, of course, in his crowning achievement in political economy, *Capital: A critique of political economy* [1867–94]), a deconstructive/ reconstructive practice associated with uncovering the social and political conditions and consequences tied to prevailing ideas, beliefs, and practices (be they associated with, for example, Hegelian and/or Young Hegelian philosophy, bourgeois political economy, nineteenth-century socialist and communist theories, or the capitalist life-world more generally). In these contexts, to critique is to render what seems natural, universal and common sense as ultimately problematic, socially produced and thus potentially limited in scope, constantly in the process of transformation, and, in turn, a context open to human intervention. In terms of received ideas and beliefs, Marx's notion of critique has been rendered famously as 'ideology critique' and is guided by the words Marx (with Engels) used in *The German Ideology* (1845–46), one of the first works (while never published in his lifetime) that lays out Marx's unique 'materialist' conception of history:

For each new class which puts itself in the place of one ruling before it, is compelled, merely in order to carry through its aim, to represent its interest as the common interest of all members of society, put in an ideal form; it will give its ideas the form of universality, and represent them as the only rational, universally valid ones. (Marx and Engels, 1947, pp. 40–1)

The key point in this analysis, of course, is to clarify the way seemingly universal values, beliefs, ideas, and so forth, are actually intimately associated with the practical interests of class actors, and thereby, in the context of a particular class hegemony, represent the values, beliefs, and ideas of their very domination over other social groups. Again, from *The German Ideology*:

The ideas of the ruling class are in every epoch the ruling ideas: i.e. the class, which is the ruling material force of society, is at the same time its ruling intellectual force ... The ruling ideas are nothing more than the ideal expression of the dominant material relationships grasped as ideas; hence of the relationships which make the one class the ruling one, therefore the ideas of its dominance. (Marx and Engels, 1947, p. 39)

Obviously, such comments have initiated interpretative conundrums within Marx studies over their exact meaning, a meaning ultimately related to what Marx meant by his conception of history more generally, and his understanding of ideology more specifically. But whatever our ultimate interpretation of Marx's position in this respect, such comments show him to be clearly arguing that such discourses must be viewed in their relationship to material factors surrounding economic production, particularly the class interests and struggles involved in that realm.

Moreover, as noted previously, Marx was also keenly aware of the way in which everyday social practices presented themselves as something mystical, displaying a character that obfuscated their true nature. Thus, in Marx's earliest sustained foray into economic analysis, *The Economic and Philosophical Manuscripts* (1844), we are treated to his famous discussion of 'estranged labour' in which he notes that, under conditions of capitalist private property, commodities (including human labour) become things that seem to have a life of their own, ultimately confronting the individual as something distantly related to the purposes of human sustenance and life, and becoming the very embodiment of one's supreme denigration as a human being. As Marx clarified:

[I]t is clear that ... the more the worker exerts himself in his work, the more powerful the alien, objective world becomes which he brings into being over against himself, the poorer he and his inner world become, and the less they belong to him. It is the same in religion. The more man puts into God, the less he retains in himself. The worker places his life in the object; but now it no longer belongs to him, but to the object. (Marx, 1977a, p. 324)

In Marx's later, mature writings, of course, such a condition is related to how, under the unfettered functioning of capitalism, the more workers produce the less they receive in wages. Literally, the worker becomes increasingly impoverished as capitalist production increases, given, partially at least, the consequent development of technology and the subsequent deskilling of labour Marx assumed would develop. Yet, at this early stage in his thought there is something else going on as well. Importantly, he is also making a more philosophical, indeed somewhat metaphysical, claim concerning how the human constitution of outside powers (be they God or money or commodities) inevitably robs them of their unique potential as humans. Indeed, as clearly indicated within this passage, Marx's notion of critique drew early sustenance from the critique of religion developed by the Young Hegelians, particularly Ludwig Feuerbach. While Feuerbach argued that belief in God was an expression of human beings taking their defining potentialities (which are rendered by Feuerbach, and by Marx in his works before 1845, as 'species being') and alienating them into a separate reality, Marx argued that religion was more specifically an '*expression* of real suffering and a protest against real suffering' (Marx, 1977b, p. 244). As Marx continues from his 'Introduction' to *A Contribution to the Critique of Hegel's Philosophy of Right* (1844): 'Thus the criticism of heaven turns into the criticism of earth, the *criticism of religion* into the *criticism of law* and the *criticism of theology* into the *criticism of politics*' (Marx, 1977b, pp. 245–6). As would become completely clear beginning in 1845, Marx's 'criticism of politics' would ultimately translate into a criticism of one's material existence, particularly the economic mode of production that underlies and defines, in some fashion, the very politics that one confronts.

This masking, ideological function inhering within social reality itself is also represented in Marx's mature economic writings. In Marx's section on the 'The Fetishism of the Commodity and its Secret' in *Capital*, Vol. 1 (1867), he argues that, given developed modes of exchange under capitalist production, 'the social relationships between producers', that is, the historically and contingently constituted economic relations that individuals find themselves within and act out, 'take on a form of a social relation between the products of labour' (Marx, 1976, p. 164). Thus Marx argues that we confront the socially produced reality of the fetishism of commodities (that is, as in anthropological studies, a situation in which something which is humanly created takes on a life of its own, expressing powers and characteristics as if they were intrinsic qualities associated with the object itself). Indeed, if anything, Marx's discussion of the intrinsic conditions of exploitation under capitalism in this work – uncovered via an analysis of the twofold character of commodities (that is, use-value and exchange-value and their corresponding forms of labour – concrete and abstract), and articulated in the important concept of surplus value – is an elaborate attempt to find underneath the mystical shell of capitalism the true character of this economic mode of production. In this critique, Marx uncovered the way in which the capitalist lifeworld presents the exchange between the worker and the capitalist in the labour market as free and equal exchange, thereby obfuscating the relations of power (within the production process itself) associated with exploitation, that is, the production relationships in which the worker produces more value than is paid in wages, such 'surplus value' being appropriated by the capitalist. Of course, even here, part of the task of Marx's critique of the capitalist lifeworld is to uncover the contingent social relationships (particularly the relationships of dependence and dominance that abound within the economic mode of production) that give rise to seemingly natural, thing-like structures of everyday life. This not only allows one to move from the appearance of the everyday world we confront to a conceptualisation of its historical constitution and character; it also allows us to understand more clearly the role that humans collectively hold in constituting this social reality, and thereby it elucidates the potentiality for radical social transformation, indeed, the possibility for human emancipation.

praxis

The concept of praxis ('practice', or as Marx noted in the *Theses on Feuerbach*, 'sensuous human activity' [Marx, 1977c, p. 421]) is clearly central to Marx's theoretical position in two interrelated ways: it is integral to Marx's methodological position overall; and, it signifies more specifically the agency–structure nexus. First, praxis, as embedded and exhibited in the human world of social and economic life, is the ultimate conceptual focus and, dare we say, 'explanatory variable' of all of Marx's work. Thus Marx felt compelled when confronted by his intellectual cohorts the Young Hegelians, for example, to criticise their position for being overly focused on the supposed efficacy of ideas and consciousness at the expense of factors within the material life in which individuals find themselves. In the process of critiquing the Young Hegelians, Marx (with Engels) sets out the defining way in which the analysis of material life will be the basis of his approach:

> In direct contrast to German philosophy which descends from heaven to earth, here we ascend from earth to heaven ... We set out from the real, active men, and on the basis of their real life process we demonstrate the development of the ideological reflexes and echoes of this life-process. The phantoms formed in the human brain are also necessarily sublimates of their material life-process, which is empirically verifiable and bound to material premises. (Marx and Engels, 1947, p. 14)

Famously, Marx succinctly articulated this position in the fourth paragraph of his 'Preface' to *A Contribution to the Critique of Political Economy* (1859). Briefly, as in *The German Ideology*, Marx (1996c, pp. 159–60) claims in the 'Preface' that his position does not, like German philosophy in its Hegelian and Young Hegelian guises, assume that consciousness determines social existence, but rather the opposite. One's social existence is further specified as the mutually constitutive interplay between the 'material productive forces' (for example, technology, technological skills and know-how) and the 'relations of production' (the latter is considered by Marx to be the 'economic structure of society', and is represented legally as 'property relations' but which can be more specifically defined, as noted above, as economic relationships of dependence and dominance). Arising from this economic foundation are the legal, political, religious, philosophical, in short, 'ideological' practices associated with that society. Importantly, as Marx noted, when there ensues a contradiction between the productive forces and the relations of production within the economic foundation (that is, when these relations of production no longer help to engender these productive forces, but become 'fetters' to their further development), then 'an epoch of social revolution commences', in which new relations of production arise to take on the further development of the productive forces. From such economic transformations come other transformations associated with 'the whole colossal superstructure' associated with 'ideological' practices. As articulated thusly, Marx's 'materialist' position is indeed quite provocative, as well as clear. Yet one must be careful here: such supposed clarity (expressed in a seemingly universalist and value-neutral voice) has led to overly simplified characterisations of Marx's position, in which it is argued, for example, that Marx's claims in these passages are really functionalist explanatory arguments, ones that can be ultimately reduced to a form of technological determinism (see the now classic interpretation in Cohen, 1978). The problems with such an interpretation come out nicely in exploring the second use Marx makes of the concept of praxis.

Second, for Marx the concept of praxis also reflects the process of how individuals are both the agents *and* constructs of social practices more generally. If one were to rely strictly on the reading of the Preface of 1859 we just laid out, one would be hard pressed to see the role of human agency in historical transformations, let alone of class struggles more specifically (and, as we know from the first sentence in section I of the *Manifesto of the Communist Party* – 'The history of all society up to now is the history of class struggles' [Marx and Engels, 1996, p. 1] – the role of class struggle is central to Marx's understanding of history). Indeed, in the Preface Marx seems to talk as if human action is merely a consequence of larger structural shifts in the economic mode of production. Yet of course this is not really the case. As Marx argued in *The Eighteenth Brumaire of Louis Bonaparte* (1852): 'Men make their own history, but they do not make it just as they please in circumstances they choose for themselves; rather they make it in present circumstances, given and inherited' (Marx, 1996b, p. 32). Indeed, in the *Eighteenth Brumaire* – as well as in Marx's other historical analyses, like the earlier *The Class Struggles in France* (1850) and the later *The Civil War in France* (1871) – Marx explores the intricate way that economic developments create opportunities for class actors to enter onto the historical stage, in the process elucidating the contingency of political action, and, in turn, the importance of a bounded human agency in history. Moreover, in the historical intricacies of Marx's narrative in the *Eighteenth Brumaire*, in which he lays out the class infighting and power struggles within the French bourgeoisie that ultimately led to the autocratic rule of Louis Bonaparte, we are offered a rather interesting, indeed penetrating, display of the 'slippages' his theory allows for seemingly purely political and cultural factors to explain the particular developments he discusses in detail. In this way, Marx's historical writings offer wonderful counterpoints to reductionist portrayals of his theory, portrayals in which economic conditions always overdetermine political and cultural developments, and in which, in general, structure always trumps agency. Whether Marx intended these 'slippages' to be displayed, or they appear behind his back, so to speak, is unclear. What is clear, I would argue, is that one can read such discursive deterritorialisations rather readily in this type of work by Marx (see Macdonald, 2003).

Earlier, in the *Theses on Feuerbach*, Marx argued that what distinguished his position from that of both idealism and Feuerbachian materialism is the emphasis he gave to what we would call, in contemporary social science parlance, the agency–structure interplay. That is, a 'new materialism' (like Marx's) must be able to articulate not only the way in which structures bound and determine human life, but also the way in which concerted human action transforms those very structures. And, moreover, as humans transform their social conditions they inevitably initiate transformations within themselves. Marx called such an interplay '*revolutionary practice*' (Marx, 1977c, p. 422).

emancipation

Marx's focus on revolutionary practice is not just a philosophical and/or empirical claim about the way in which our social world operates. It is something a bit more. For, if anything, Marx's intention was to write and theorise so as to help the cause of human emancipation. To do so, humans must be aware not only of the nature of the social conditions under which they exist, but also that such conditions are continually open to human intervention, and can thus be transformed through collective action. If critique allows one to uncover the contingently produced character of seemingly naturalised social phenomena, and the concept of praxis settles the region from which such a character emanates and on which subsequent transformations must occur, emancipation is the process by which human beings overcome their historically constituted self-limitations and strive truly to objectify and institute practices that will allow for the full flowering of human potentialities. Of course, given Marx's conception of history, emancipation must come from fundamentally transforming the economic conditions of human life. That is, critique must become (and *be*) praxis. As Marx averred in his 'Introduction' to *A Contribution to the Critique of Hegel's Philosophy of Right*:

> Clearly the weapon of criticism cannot replace the criticism of weapons, and material force must be overthrown by material force. But theory also becomes a material force once it has gripped the masses. Theory is capable of gripping the masses when it demonstrates *ad hominem*, and it demonstrates *ad hominem* as soon as it becomes radical. To be radical is to grasp things by the root. But for man the root is man himself. (Marx, 1977b, p. 251)

For those who still wish to interpret Marx's conception of the theory–practice nexus, only intimated above, as replicating Plato's conception of the rule of philosopher-kings (where specialised knowledge allows unmitigated rule by these individuals over those who will be forced to be free and just), or its contemporary caricature in Lenin's conception of the vanguard party, they have fundamentally misread Marx. As a certain type of 'materialist', Marx argued that his theory (his critique, his emphasis on material practice, and his conception of emancipation) only arises because there is a demonstrable agent whose practices clearly signify and represent his ideas, and whose political actions are already expressing these discourses. Of course, for Marx this agent was the industrial working class under capitalism. Moreover, the emancipation of the working class must be work of the working class itself, not of any intellectual sect which sees history in the interests of that class. Historically speaking, working class activists were already articulating a critique of capitalism in terms of how the capitalist robbed the 'fruits of their labour' (as the Anglo-Irish working-class activist Bronterre O'Brien put it in 1833), and were also already proclaiming, in one form or another, that the resolution of their problems lay within the institution of socialism and/or communism. So in this respect, aspects of Marx's theory were neither radically new nor distant from actual working-class discourses. What differentiated his vision of communism from these earlier articulations were two arguments. The first was that communism was to be an important outgrowth of the very capitalist system that was exploiting humanity in the modern West, a quantitative outgrowth that would ultimately imply a qualitative transformation of current structures. As Marx (with Engels) argued in *The Manifesto*, the bourgeoisie (and thus capitalism) has played a 'most revolutionary role in history' (Marx and Engels, 1996, p. 3). What Marx meant, of course, is that capitalism has engendered incredible technological developments within the productive forces of human society, and was thus a necessary stage in humanity's movement toward communism, the latter being an economic system premised upon such technology and guided, as Marx noted in *Critique of the Gotha Programme* (1875), by the principle 'from each according to his abilities, to each according to his needs!' (Marx, 1996d, p. 215).

Second, and maybe more importantly, the coming into being of communism would be the result of the concerted political effort of the majority of individuals, the working class. In his own political activities, and expressed consistently in his writings, Marx was adamant that only the working class (that is, those who owned nothing except their ability to labour, which they sold on the market for a wage or salary) could bring about the revolutionary changes that would transition human society toward communism. In schematic form, Marx saw that the very developments associated with capitalism would create the conditions for working-class revolutionary consciousness: not only would the spread of liberal democracy attached to capitalism provide an outlet for the development of ideas and political strategies necessary for emancipatory political action, but the very structural movements toward concentration and, what we now call, globalisation created a shared political culture for the development of international working-class revolutionary politics.

articulating the political: theory, class struggle, writing

Of course, Marx's articulation of 'critique', 'praxis' and 'emancipation' – the way in which each of these concepts and/or discursive strategies opens up Marx's unique horizon for understanding politics – shows why he is considered such an important thinker within the Continental tradition. If anything, Marx's particular rendering is an excellent example of the way in which these concepts and/or discursive strategies can be effectively and productively integrated together to form a systematic appraisal of human society (though of course he not is not the only one). Yet are there other aspects to the political represented and displayed in Marx's theory that are not clearly evident in the above rendering? What do his writing and theory, taken formally and substantively, say about the nature of the political? In what way, if at all, is the political expressed in Marx's work that may actually seem counter-intuitive to more conventional renderings?

Earlier, we noted that Marx assumed that his theory was intended to change the world. That is, Marx assumed that his whole theoretical discourse was intimately attached to the contingent political struggles transpiring during the time in which he was writing, struggles linked, for him at least, to the working class. Importantly, such a position – if unravelled in terms of its assumptions and implications – actually raises interesting issues about how we are to interpret Marx's theory, and, importantly, how we are to evaluate its relevance for political struggles today. In *Theses on Feuerbach*, Marx noted the following about the nature of theory in general, and, by implication, of his own theory: 'All mysteries which lead theory to mysticism find their rational solution in human practice and in the comprehension of this practice' (Marx, 1977c, p. 423). Now, aside from reasserting the importance of the notion of praxis to his understanding of the nature of social life, what this statement elucidates is also Marx's engagement with political and historical contingency in his materialist conception. What seems to be implied here is a constant reappraisal of one's theory, making sure that anytime one's theory becomes questioned by new social and political 'mysteries', and thereby becomes a form of 'mysticism' (that is, something which no longer has connections to real powers and attributes in our world), one can find the solution in a renewed comprehension of 'human practice', and, in turn, a renewal of one's theoretical armour. In this respect, Marx's theoretical orientation allows for the constant deconstruction of one's theoretical tools and concepts. As Jacques Derrida put it in *Specters of Marx* about this unique political dimension to Marx's theory:

> Who has ever called for the transformation to come of his own theses? Not only view of some progressive enrichment of knowledge, but so as to take into account there, another account, the effects of rupture and restructuration? And so as to incorporate in advance, beyond any possible programming, the unpredictability of new knowledge, new techniques, and new political givens? (Derrida, 1994, p. 13)

Whether we agree with other facets of Derrida's strange and diffuse text on Marx, we should follow Derrida in seeing that Marx's theoretical position, in relation to his own thought, initiates and enables – whether intentionally or not – an interesting discourse on the very contingency, historicity, and, in turn, *politics*, of theory itself.

If the 'political' (as historicity and contingency) is articulated in Marx's rendering of the nature of theory, it also has more clear, indeed commonsense, portrayals that should be explored. Obviously, as noted earlier, one of the hallmarks of Marx's theoretical position is its resolute emphasis on the role of class struggle in defining human history. Conventionally, such a position has taken two directions, which have important resonances on things political. First, if economic classes are the defining agents within human history, then particular political structures established during different periods are actually instruments of the dominant class's hegemony (or, as Marx and Engels argued in relation to the capitalist period in *The Manifesto*: 'The power of the modern state is merely a device for administering the common affairs of the whole bourgeois class' [Marx and Engels, 1996: 3]). This argument clearly provides an important way for understanding what we conventionally call 'politics' by always asking us to interpret the class interests and strategies behind seemingly neutral, supposedly independent, state structures. Of course, as may seem apparent, what such a claim actually means is unclear, and, given its interest for social and political theorists, has led to avid debates within Marx studies over the last 30 years (for a critical overview of this debate, see Barrow, 1994). Second, when discussing the struggle for power between the bourgeoisie and the working class under capitalism, there is usually an assumption that the very political trajectory of the working class is overdetermined by developments within the capitalist mode of production, and thereby, strangely, such a trajectory reflects the project of the bourgeoisie. I say strangely only because, as is well known from the narrative laid out in *The Manifesto*, it is due to the supposed intended developments of capitalist production (which reflect the economic interests of the bourgeoisie) that the material conditions arise for the growth of working-class political consciousness, and, in turn, the ensuing gradual movement toward communism (see Marx and Engels, 1996, pp. 8–10). Thus a certain Marxian understanding of the revolutionary project of the working class is that of a sorcerer's apprentice, an unintended destructive force (from the position of the capitalist class at least) tied to inherent transformations within capitalism itself.

Yet if we were to stay only on this conventional plane of understanding the political resonances of Marx's emphasis on class struggle, we miss other interesting conceptualisations that arise within his theory. One particularly interesting element relates to what we have just been saying about the working-class political project. While we may interpret working-class politicisation as a response to, or outgrowth of, capitalist restructuration and development, there are also indications, particularly in Marx's *Grundrisse* (1857–58), that he also perceived the working class's irreducible independence from, and antagonism to, the capitalist class. As rendered in Antonio Negri's work (for example, *Marx Beyond Marx* [1991]), we can see that Marx also argued that the working class, in its struggles against capital, actually is the driving motor force behind capitalist restructuration. Thus, what appears to be the unfolding of seemingly objectivist capitalist economic laws is actually an intimately political response to continued antagonism from the working class. That is, what Marx seems to be saying (if we are to accept Negri's interpretation) is that what appears to be a strictly economic logic is actually resolutely political: it is motivated by the struggle for power between the working class and capital. In this sense, the political (as worker's antagonism) always comes before the economic, always provides a force that (de)structures and (de)stabilises capitalist development. And, importantly, this implies that there are no political guarantees in history, only contingent struggles that give, at most, *a posteriori* assurances to one's actions.

Yet, we have not quite finished our exploration of the political in Marx. If we looked at the way that Marx rendered the politics of theory and the multifaceted contingencies of class struggle, we have only hinted at the discursive politics he initiates *by and through his writing*. That is, following in the footsteps of poststructuralist understandings of discourse and language, we want also to look at how Marx's very language enacts particular political objects and subjectivities (within author and reader alike). Derrida's aforementioned *Specters of Marx* is an example of this type of analysis, if for some a rather extreme, even problematical, one. For what Derrida attempts to do is to use Marx's discussion of the 'specter of communism' in the opening remarks of the *Manifesto* to initiate and enact a critical reading of 'spectrality' associated with

Marx and Marxism's relevance today. For Derrida, of course, the point is not to link such figurations to Marx's intentions, but to use them to explore a new politics that inheres within, but is also constitutively outside, the tradition that Marx initiates in his work (indeed, it is the very tension between that which is intended and that which questions those very intentions that constitutes the true nature of 'inheritance' for Derrida). In a similar vein, though exhibiting more attentiveness to what Marx actually says in his theory, the recent work of Carver (1998) has also attempted to emphasise the figural and rhetorical politics of Marx's writings. If Derrida draws upon the figure of the 'specter' to unravel a politics within (and against) Marx, Carver does a wonderfully productive reading of Marx's use of the vampire metaphor in *Capital*, both to clarify important concepts within this notoriously difficult work and to render the way in which Marx used such figures and metaphors to position the reader politically (Carver, 1998, pp. 7–23). Overall, then, to understand this aspect of Marx's articulation of the political is to delve into the intricacies of Marx's literary tropes, metaphors, metonyms and figurations.

marx in the twenty-first century

[N]o future without Marx, without the memory and the inheritance of Marx: in any case of a certain Marx, of his genius, of at least one of his spirits. For this will be our hypothesis or rather our bias: *there is more than one of them, there must be more than one of them.* (Derrida, 1994, p. 13)

What I hope is clear in the foregoing discussion of Marx's political theory are the ways in which Marx is still relevant for theorists in our own theoretical and political context, one that is, to be sure, different from Marx's. Ultimately, the reason that Marx speaks to us today is that his theory still engages fundamental aspects to our social world. That is, Marx's unerring interrogation of the capitalist lifeworld continues to provide important critical insights into our condition, and still inspires new discourses about where we will be going in the future. In this respect, Marx's critique of alienated labour, his conceptualisation of the problematic consequences of the dominance of commodity fetishism in our lifeworld (which Georg Lukács [1971] would later render as 'reification' and Guy Debord [1983] would encapsulate in his conception of the 'society of the spectacle'), and his claim concerning the inevitable capturing of the state apparatus under capitalism by the capitalist class, all still ring true, and are showing signs of life and evocation in the many anti-capitalist struggles that are emerging in our century, of which the anti-World Trade Organization/globalism political discourses represent only one important manifestation.

If anything, such different articulations of the political within Marx's theory show the incredible richness of his ideas for contemporary theorists. While one could argue that these different layers of Marx's political discourse – from the clear political intentions that inform his whole theory to the intricacies of his textual politics to the literal use of this concept by political actors struggling against current capitalist injustices – are actually competing, even contradictory, and therefore must be expunged to offer the contemporary reader a univocal voice on the nature of politics, I would argue the exact opposite. It is only because we can discern such divergent – seemingly contesting and contrasting – positions (be they intended by Marx or not) that his ideas can be a living presence in our present theoretical and political world. Indeed, one would hope that, if Marx were alive today and confronted with the clarion call for univocality in his own theory, he would respond, as he supposedly did in a similar way to a well-meaning follower of his ideas: 'If that is what you want with my theory, then I am not a Marxist!'

further reading

Of Marx's works listed below, the most significant for his understanding of politics and the political are *The German Ideology, Manifesto of the Communist Party, The Eighteenth Brumaire of Louis Bonaparte, The Civil War in France*, and, *Capital*, Vol. I. Among the extensive secondary literature on Marx, Barrow (1994) does a rich critical analysis of Marx's and, later, Marxism's characterisation of the state. Gouldner (1980) explores productively the tension between critique and science within Marx's work. Derrida (1994) and Carver (1998) enact the 'postmodern' within Marx's thought, with surprising results. For one of the best overall collections of essays on all facets of Marx's thought, consult *The Cambridge Companion to Marx*, ed. T. Carver (Cambridge: Cambridge University Press, 1991).

references

Barrow, C. (1994) *Critical Theories of the State: Marxist, neo-Marxist, post-Marxist*. Madison, WI: University of Wisconsin Press.

Carver, T. (1975) Editor's Preface to Marx's 'Introduction' (1857) to the *Grundrisse der Kritik der politischen Okonomie*, in *Karl Marx: Texts on method*, ed. T. Carver, pp. 3–45. New York: Barnes and Noble Books.

Carver, T. (1998) *The Postmodern Marx*. Manchester: Manchester University Press.

Cohen, G.A. (1978) *Karl Marx's Theory of History: A defence*. Oxford: Oxford University Press.

Critchley, S. (2002) *Continental Philosophy: A very short introduction*. Oxford: Oxford University Press.

Debord, G. (1983) *Society of the Spectacle*. Detroit: Black and Red Books.

Derrida, J. (1994) *Specters of Marx: The state of the debt, the work of mourning, and the new international*, trans. P. Kamuf. New York: Routledge.

Fay, B. (1986) *Critical Social Science: Liberation and its limits*. Ithaca, NY: Cornell University Press.

Gouldner, A. (1980) *The Two Marxisms: Contradictions and anomalies in the development of theory*. Oxford: Oxford University Press.

Lukács, G. (1971) *History and Class Consciousness*, trans. R. Livingstone. Cambridge, MA: MIT Press.

Macdonald, B. (2003) 'Inaugurating Heterodoxy: Marx's *Eighteenth Brumaire* and the "limit-experience" of class struggle', *Strategies: Journal of theory, culture, and politics* 16(1): 65–75.

Marcuse, H. (1964) *One-Dimensional Man: Studies in the ideology of advanced societies.* Boston: Beacon Press.

Marx, K. (1974) 'The Curtain Raised' [1871], in *Karl Marx: Political Writings*, Vol. 3, *The First International and After*, ed. D. Fernbach. New York: Vintage Books.

Marx, K. (1976) *Capital: A critique of political economy*, Vol. 1 [1867], trans. B. Fowkes. Harmondsworth: Penguin Books.

Marx, K. (1977a) *Economic and Philosophical Manuscripts* [1844], in *Karl Marx: Early writings*, trans. R. Livingstone and G. Benton. Harmondsworth: Penguin Books.

Marx, K. (1977b) 'Introduction' [1844] to *A Contribution to the Critique of Hegel's Philosophy of Right*, in *Karl Marx: Early writings*, trans. R. Livingstone and G. Benton. Harmondsworth: Penguin Books.

Marx, K. (1977c) *Theses on Feuerbach* [1845], in Appendix to *Karl Marx: Early writings*, trans. R. Livingstone and G. Benton. Harmondsworth: Penguin Books.

Marx, K. (1996b) *The Eighteenth Brumaire of Louis Bonaparte* [1852], in *Marx: Later political writings*, ed. and trans. T. Carver. Cambridge: Cambridge University Press.

Marx, K. (1996c) 'Preface' [1859] to *A Contribution to a Critique of Political Economy*, in *Marx: Later political writings*, ed. and trans. T. Carver. Cambridge: Cambridge University Press.

Marx, K. (1996d) *Critique of the Gotha Programme* [1875], in *Marx: Later political writings*, ed. and trans. T. Carver. Cambridge: Cambridge University Press.

Marx, K. and Engels, F. (1947) *The German Ideology* [1845–46], ed. R. Pascal. New York: International Publishers.

Marx, K. and Engels, F. (1996) *Manifesto of the Communist Party* [1848], in *Marx: Later political writings*, ed. and trans. T. Carver. Cambridge: Cambridge University Press.

Negri, A. (1991) *Marx Beyond Marx: Lessons on the Grundrisse*, trans. H. Cleaver, M. Ryan, and M. Viano. Brooklyn, NY: Autonomedia.

5

friedrich nietzsche

gordon a. babst

Friedrich Wilhelm Nietzsche (1844–1900) was an irreverent philosopher, one who openly disdained his intellectual inheritance, and gleefully promoted an interrogation of standards of value long-since entrenched in the West. His writings were regarded as controversial as soon as they appeared, and were gradually viewed as important because of his attention to topics such as Enlightenment reason, morality in the classical and Christian traditions, power, knowledge, and the nature of the good life. Nietzsche's views on those and other issues, and his exuberant rejection of all entrenched orthodoxies, have led some to regard him as the last modern thinker, or first postmodern thinker (Koelb, 1990; Robinson, 1999; Owen, 1994). Interestingly, Nietzsche has not been regarded as a political thinker, or his works as inherently political, until fairly recently (Warren, 1988; Ansell-Pearson, 1991, 1994; Hunt, 1991; Hatab, 1995; Owen, 1995). Earlier would-be political interpretations of Nietzsche were not so positive in their approach. Nietzsche, 'in fact, did not hold any of the standard political ideologies ... he was not interested in the same questions to which the standard ideologies are answers' (Hunt, 1991, p. 26). However, his thinking is regarded now as political because it focuses critical attention on issues such as how to organise society so as to make possible the best life for humankind, and how to fashion power relations that work best to that end. This chapter presents three politically relevant and interrelated aspects of Nietzsche's philosophy, all of which concern selfhood and how an individual might live and judge a joyful human life that is rational and free.

Nietzsche did not theorise the state, or prioritise it when he discussed political phenomena – quite the contrary. He demoted the state in human affairs in favour of culture, which he feared was becoming increasingly sterile the more liberal and democratic it grew, as he remarks in one of his earliest works. Nietzsche is commenting here on the vulnerability of art and great, noble undertakings in democratic states:

> But if the custom of democratic suffrage and numerical majorities be transferred to the realm of art, and the artist put on his defense before the court of aesthetic dilettanti, you may take your oath on his condemnation ... They are connoisseurs of art primarily because they wish to kill art ... For they do not want greatness to arise. (Nietzsche, 1957 [1874], pp. 16, 17)

Nietzsche proposed that the purpose of the state is to safeguard and promote the health and vibrancy of a nation's culture. Lest the state be antagonistic to culture, it must recede into the background, its role being to enable as much as possible the plasticity he saw inherent in the nature of man and human culture.

In this chapter I offer a context for Nietzsche's thought, and address the political import of his perspectivism in knowledge, which is perhaps where he has had his most influence on succeeding thinkers. I also discuss his doctrines of 'Will to Power' and the 'Overman' [*Übermensch*], and offer some concluding thoughts on Nietzsche and politics. Nietzsche's perspectivism would appear purely relativistic, were it not for these doctrines that reflect an affirmation of life, though on novel terms.

the context of nietzsche's thought

'My time has not yet come, some are born posthumously' (Nietzsche, 1979 [1888], p. 39). In the quotation below, and elsewhere, Nietzsche's assessment of the culture of modernity was prescient, a characteristic of which he was obviously aware:

> Today one can see coming into existence the culture of a society of which *commerce* is as much the soul as personal contest was with the ancient Greeks and as war, victory and justice were for the Romans. The man engaged in commerce understands how to appraise everything without having made it, and to appraise it *according to the needs of the consumer*, not according to his own needs ... This type of appraisal he applies instinctively and all the time: he applies it to everything ... This becomes the character of an entire culture, thought through in the minutest and subtlest detail and imprinted in every will and every faculty. (Nietzsche, 1982 [1881], Aphorism 197, p. 175)

Although Nietzsche was born into a pious family at Röcken, near Leipzig in Prussian Saxony, religion quickly grew stale for the young man, who from an early age focused his most trenchant criticisms on Christian teaching. He forthrightly suggested that joy was quotidian, to be found in this life and on this earth. Nietzsche found the 'pious illusion' that the Christian religion offered merely useful in social terms, because it restrained the uncourageous from acting on their destructive impulses:

> A religion that, of all the hours of man's life, thinks the last the most important, that has prophesied the end of earthly life and condemned all creatures to live in the fifth act of a tragedy, may call forth the subtlest and noblest powers of man; but it is an enemy to all new planting, to all bold attempts or free aspirations. (Nietzsche, 1957 [1874], pp. 42, 49)

For those few who dare to act on their drive towards self-actualisation or greatness, Christian moral teaching can set no real limits. Nietzsche himself was one who never felt the need for even the illusion of piety, as he recounts in his bizarre, purported autobiography *Ecce Homo*:

> I have never reflected on questions that are none – I have not squandered myself. – I have, for example, no experience of actual *religious* difficulties. I am entirely at a loss to know to what extent I ought to have felt 'sinful'. I likewise lack a reliable criterion of a pang of conscience: from what one hears of it, a pang of conscience does not seem to me anything respectable … 'God', 'immortality of the soul', 'redemption', 'the Beyond', all of them concepts to which I have given no attention and no time, not even as a child – perhaps I was never childish enough for it? (Nietzsche, 1979 [1888], pp. vii, 21)

Nietzsche lived through what one might regard as the high water mark of modern faith in progress through the application of the scientific method to human problems, an activity at one with Enlightenment reason. Nietzsche quickly became extremely sceptical of such optimism and rejected it as unwarranted. The generally enthusiastic reception all over Europe given to industrialisation, urbanisation and, especially, democratisation – whether driven by liberal practices, or inspired by socialist ideals – was not shared by Nietzsche, who regarded the practice of life for Europeans as becoming, instead, increasingly commercial, vulgar and counterfeit.

Nietzsche eschewed the vaunted autonomy of liberal theory, for example, as phony and enfeebling because it lacked an ideal-affirming life for the individual, despite its rampant individualism. Liberal democratisation for Nietzsche was enforcing mediocrity, levelling humanity downward and so preventing a sincerity and generosity of spirit that he associated with greatness. Indeed, that mediocrity was so successful because the people it produced were skilled at evading the project of self-fashioning. They may well have believed that they were freely choosing to let the state provide them with ideals of behaviour and a shared understanding of values, but in so doing they were only alienating themselves from becoming what they could be because they never arrived at values through their own critical efforts (Hunt, 1991, p. 36). Instead, people should be framing their own values for themselves, values grounded in the exigencies of living in a human community.

Nietzsche, however, is not an authority on the workings of capitalism and its intersection with politics, society and culture, because, unlike Karl Marx, he seems to have had little focus on the economic restructuring of society that took place in the nineteenth century. Nietzsche seemed to hold, for example, that democracy, not capitalism, was to blame for the modern malaise of individual choice. Today we are more likely to attribute to consumerism the false sense of empowerment that comes through choosing which mass-produced item to buy, or which lifestyle to copy. Nietzsche described democracy in these terms:

> Parliamentarianism, that is to say, public permission to choose between five political opinions, flatters those many who like to *appear* independent and individual and like to fight for their opinions. In the last resort, however, it is a matter of indifference whether the herd is commanded an opinion or allowed five opinions. – He who deviates from the five opinions and steps aside always has the whole herd against him. (Nietzsche, *The Gay Science* [1882], in 1977, p. 267)

In another essay, 'What is Noble?', he criticised democracy for its 'intermarriage of masters and slaves', arguing instead for an order of rank among human beings (Nietzsche 1966 [1886], p. 208). Nietzsche was by no means a systematic thinker, and his works reflect a philosopher troubled by many things, often reaching for a metaphorical or poetic description when rational analysis seemed unable to put the point.

perspectivism in knowledge

Nietzsche thoroughly distrusted Enlightenment reason and its apparent promise to present reality as it actually exists through dispassionate, objective knowledge cleansed of any contaminating elements. Enlightenment rationalism, for Nietzsche, was disturbing, because it seems to remove the human subject from the activity of acquiring knowledge, in actuality a far more personal and interpretative process than 'objectivity' seemed to allow. Nietzsche regarded the typical Enlightenment stance on reason and knowledge as a deception, more an act of self-congratulation. In his view this rationalism masked a denial of life that has characterised the Western tradition, resulting in ambiguous if not sham progress. 'There is no pre-established harmony between the furtherance of truth and the well-being of mankind', he wrote (Nietzsche, *Human, All Too Human* [1878], in 1977, p. 198).

Nietzsche's understanding of the activity of knowing is commonly labelled *perspectivism*, because it centres the knowing subject, within which are a host of character traits, ambitions, reactions to the events of life, and so on. This is a view that the subject legitimately filters what is taken in through the knowing activity. Nietzsche unambiguously endorses perspectivism:

> From now on, my dear philosophers, let us beware of the dangerous old conceptual fable which posited a 'pure, will-less, painless, timeless knowing subject', let us beware of the tentacles of such contradictory concepts as 'pure reason', 'absolute spirituality', 'knowledge in itself'; – for these always ask us to imagine an eye which it is impossible to imagine, an eye which supposedly looks out in no particular direction, an eye which supposedly either restrains or altogether lacks the active powers of interpretation which first make seeing into seeing something – for here, then, a nonsense and non-concept is demanded of the eye. Perspectival seeing is the *only* kind of seeing there is, perspectival 'knowing' the *only* kind of 'knowing'; and the *more* feelings about a matter which we allow to come to expression, the *more* eyes, different eyes through which we are able to view this same matter, the more complete our 'conception' of it, our 'objectivity' will be. But to eliminate the will completely, to suspend the feelings altogether, even assuming that we could do so; what? Would this not amount to the *castration* of the intellect? (Nietzsche, 1996 [1887], pp. 98–9)

Any philosophy that takes for its goal the elimination, to the greatest possible extent, of subjectivity in the activity of knowing, simply misses the only thing that can be important about knowing in the first place. For Nietzsche this was what knowing does to enhance the life of the person or society involved. If subjectivity were eliminated, philosophers beginning with Plato would have expunged their personalities from their work, and would instead have tried to abstract from their philosophical activity something more 'real' that was 'out there somewhere'. Nietzsche argued that the 'task is rather to bring to light what we *must ever love and honour* and what no subsequent enlightenment can take away: great individual human beings' (Nietzsche, 1962 [1894], p. 24).

For Nietzsche the grammar of language is misleading. It promotes a fiction that the quintessentially human is in the subjects who know something, rather than in the sensual individuals who will what they feel. In his characteristic way Nietzsche undermines the traditional reverence for reason, and its restrictions on what thoughts it is possible to have:

> All that philosophers have handled for thousands of years have been concept-mummies; nothing real escaped their grasp alive. When these honorable idolaters of concepts worship something, they kill it and stuff it; they threaten the life of everything they worship. Death, change, old

age, as well as procreation and growth, are to their minds objections –
even refutations ... Let us be philosophers! Let us be mummies! Let us
represent monotono-theism by adopting the expression of the gravedigger!
And above all, away with the body, this wretched *idée fixe* of the senses,
disfigured by all the fallacies of logic, refuted, even impossible, although it
is impudent enough to behave as if it were real! ... 'Reason' is the cause of
our falsification of the testimony of the senses ... We enter a realm of crude
fetishism when we summon before consciousness the basic presuppositions
of the metaphysics of language, in plain talk, the presuppositions of reason.
Everywhere it sees a doer and doing ... 'Reason' in language – oh, what an
old deceptive female she is! I am afraid we are not rid of God because we
still have faith in grammar. (Nietzsche, *Twilight of the Idols* [1889], in 1977,
pp. 479, 480, 482–3)

Nietzsche disdained philosophy because it discounted subjectivity and
favoured objectivity, so expressing a 'Will to Truth'. He located this longstanding
practice in the way that philosophers have fallen prey to linguistic traps
that foster the mistaken view that there is a subject–object relationship in
which the object is fixed so that the 'knower' can apprehend its true, essential
features. According to Nietzsche:

a thought comes when 'it' wishes, and not when 'I' wish, so that it is a
falsification of the facts of the case to say that the subject 'I' is the condition
of the predicate 'think'... even the 'it' contains an *interpretation* of the
process, and does not belong to the process itself. (Nietzsche, 1966 [1886],
p. 24)

And further to this theme:

[T]here is no 'being' behind doing, acting, becoming; 'the doer' is merely
a fiction imposed on the doing – the doing itself is everything. (Nietzsche,
1996 [1887], p. 28)

Nietzsche believed that this move first appeared when the ancient philosopher
Parmenides, in a moment as 'un-Greek as no other', felt himself 'seized by
that icy tremor of abstraction', which he describes as follows:

Experience nowhere offered him being as he imagined it, but he concluded
its existence from the fact that he was able to think it. This is a conclusion
which rests on the assumption that we have an organ of knowledge which
reaches into the essence of things and is independent of experience ... It is
absolutely impossible for a subject to see or have insight into something
while leaving itself out of the picture, so impossible that knowing and being

are the most opposite of all spheres. (Nietzsche, 1962 [1894], pp. 69–70, 81–2, 83)

In demolishing the basis in language of received wisdom, and in his assumption that he was thus making a contribution to the project of living more honestly and ethically, Nietzsche foreshadows the thinking of Ludwig Wittgenstein. Wittgenstein suggested that language users were similarly subject to certain deceptions. These were promulgated by the grammar of language itself (positing a 'knower' and 'known'), as well as by the view that knowledge and practice in ethics arises from specialised knowledge of logic and language. For Wittgenstein, ethics was not about facts, nor was it a matter of truth expressible through language (Barrett, 1991).

For Nietzsche, philosophy did not originally prioritise objectivity in knowledge, not least because it did not originally prioritise knowledge. Rather, in its original stages, philosophy prioritised life and the world in which we live and encounter others engaged in activity or struggle:

The Greeks … were the very opposite of realists, in that they believed only in the reality of men and gods, looking upon all of nature as but a disguise, a masquerade, or a metamorphosis of these god-men. Man for them was the truth and the core of all things; everything else was but semblance and the play of illusion. For this reason they found it unbelievably difficult to comprehend concepts as such. Herein they were the exact opposite of modern man. (Nietzsche, 1962 [1894], p. 41)

A better understanding of philosophy, one moored to the lives of people, would be to regard it as a well-formed reflection on what is noble. This would entail reflecting on the events shared by a community. That community would have to be alive to itself and would enhance its grasp of itself through this activity. This activity would be one best performed by individuals expressing a 'Will to Power' in the company of others. It would never be final.

What we ought to retain from the best of philosophy is not its content, but its characteristic mode of enquiry, one that cannot be separated from interaction with a community. To regard any incidental finding in philosophy, even in the best philosophy or, worse, to apprehend such a finding in abstraction, is to believe in a myth. This myth is facilitated by the grammar of language and is as unnatural to the thinking of the distant past, as it is second nature for us today. Nietzsche's view that we are better off forgetting about some supposedly truthful text in philosophy foreshadows Jacques Derrida's stance on the nature of any text, or, perhaps better put, the lack of anything in a text, which, when correctly grasped by the reader, unlocks a truth. The only truth is the one we are living, not the one we are living for, be it some abstract wisdom from the past, or a belief in a mythical life yet to come.

The political import of Nietzsche's perspectivism in knowledge is multifaceted, but must include a denial of teleological notions regarding the purpose of human life, whether grounded in religious views or in scientific or social scientific 'knowledge'. Nietzsche rejected both a quasi-religious view of human history proceeding through stages and animated by some Hegelian spirit, as well as the views of Darwin or Marx that history unfolds in patterns, despite their emphasis on material struggle. All of these views foundered on the same shoals: a woefully misguided attempt to impose a final determination on life in a human community. Whether religious/mythical or scientific, the move is much the same, according to Nietzsche. It is a move that denies to living persons the joy of spontaneous self-fashioning, which takes place according to the changing standards of excellence in any given community. This move attempts to sequence in advance the timeframes of human culture. Nietzsche believes this disempowers ordinary human beings and takes away their agency, ultimately sapping culture of its vitality. Of course, this move may be welcomed by those unaware of its import, as it is a move to govern what is mysterious, if not a threat, to life, society or the world. Moreover, this move is performed by someone or by some group of people, perhaps over generations, who thereby amass power through providing this (supposedly) valuable service. Thus the meek herd of humanity is seduced into compliance by making them believe in their weakness as a strength, and suggesting to them that the strong are 'evil'. Therefore for Nietzsche this is a move that must be resisted:

> To demand of strength that it should *not* express itself as strength, that it should *not* be a will to overcome, overthrow, dominate ... makes as little sense as to demand of weakness that it should express itself as strength ... It is only through the seduction of language (and through the fundamental errors of reason petrified in it) ... that it can appear otherwise. (Nietzsche, 1996 [1887], p. 29)

In a word, the liberal state, repository of the power of the submissive, was for Nietzsche simply a secularised version of Christianity, and science was the secularised version of the 'Will to Truth', an attempt at transcending the limitations of this world. Nietzsche wonders, why this desire to transcend? To what need is it a response? Why desire to know all there is to know about a sanitised realm of absolutes? Nietzsche believed that such desires were rooted in an unhealthy, fearful denial of worldliness and, specifically, of a world in which it is necessary to struggle against opponents. Nietzsche theorised the 'Will to Power' and the 'Overman' as antidotes both to the sway of conventional morality and to the power of its standard-bearers (for example, priests, public officials). He deplored the *ressentiment* (or repressed vengefulness) of the submissive, whose strength in numbers thinly veiled their lack of power.

'will to power' as a political concept

Zarathustra has seen many lands and many peoples: thus he has discovered the good and evil of many peoples. Zarathustra has found no greater power on earth than good and evil. No people could live without evaluating: but if it wishes to maintain itself it must not evaluate as its neighbour evaluates. Much that seemed good to one people seemed shame and disgrace to another: thus I found. I found much that was called evil in one place was in another decked with purple honours. One neighbour never understood another: his soul was always amazed at his neighbour's madness and wickedness. A table of values hangs over every people. Behold, it is the table of its overcomings; behold, it is the voice of its will to power ... Truly, my brothers, if you only knew a people's need and land and sky and neighbour, you could surely divine the law of its overcomings, and why it is upon this ladder that it mounts towards its hope. (Nietzsche, *Thus Spoke Zarathustra* [1883], in 1977, pp. 223–4)

Nietzsche's concept of 'Will to Power' offers us a new and different perspective from which to view ourselves, one based in subjective human agency in the context of a world that we create in order to enhance that agency. '[L]ife simply *is* will to power' (Nietzsche, 1966 [1886], p. 203). This way of living is a project at first only the few will be strong enough to undertake. The weak do not undertake self-fashioning through 'Will to Power', because they remain spellbound by conventional morality and ways of understanding reality. They will not challenge the claims to objectivity and certainty made by those whom tradition empowers to be in moral or political authority.

Those who fear to launch a new interpretation of the world, or to create the world anew, suffer from slave morality, according to Nietzsche, as he puts it in one of the most penetrating analyses of human civilization ever written, *On the Genealogy of Morals*. By contrast, those who dare to assert their claim that power, not knowledge, is the only thing of worth in itself, belong to a different class, that of the 'Overman', a concept discussed in the next section. Because slaves say 'yes' to received wisdom and culture, and 'no' to innovation, especially in the area of morals, they are unable to offer humanity at large a new interpretation of its condition, or to create themselves so as to be a model for others. By themselves they cannot lift the state of human culture, or give us a 'glimpse of a man who justifies *mankind* ... a reason to retain *faith in mankind!*' (Nietzsche, 1996 [1887], p. 28).

It is sometimes said that Nietzsche urges on us a nihilism, which is to will nothing, or a moral nihilism, which would be to will that there were no morals. Neither of these is true, as the 'Will to Power' is, firstly, a *will* that wills and judges itself and what is necessary, though on its own terms, given the death of God, and the eclipse of the old standards of right and wrong. It is God, and the old standards of right and wrong, Nietzsche suggests, that are the real nihilistic temptations (Nietzsche, 1996 [1887], p. 136). The 'Will to Power' expresses the strong desire for life, affirming it and the struggles with deaths it entails. Though according to the good and evil of conventional standards, this may be to will nothing of value. For Nietzsche, by contrast, it opens up a whole new vista for humanity:

> The greatest recent event – that 'God is dead', that belief in the Christian God has become unbelievable – is already beginning to cast its first shadows over Europe ... Do we perhaps still stand too much within the *immediate consequences* of this event – and these immediate consequences, its consequences for *us*, are, conversely from what one could expect, in no way sad and darkening but, rather, like a new, hard to describe kind of light, happiness, alleviation, encouragement, dawn ...We philosophers and 'free spirits' in fact feel at the news that the 'old God is dead' as if illumined by a new dawn; our heart overflows with gratitude ... at last the horizon seems to us again free, even if it is not bright, at last our ships can put out again, no matter what the danger, every daring venture of knowledge is again permitted, the sea, *our* sea again lies there open before us, perhaps there has never yet been such an 'open sea'. (Nietzsche, *The Gay Science* [1887], in 1977, pp. 208–10)

Of course, by explicitly rejecting Christian moral standards, and, even more scandalously, suggesting that they had always thwarted the emergence of the best in human will, Nietzsche opened himself up to the charge of being an immoralist – a charge he welcomed: 'I am proud to possess this word which sets me off against the whole of humanity. No one has yet felt Christian morality as *beneath* him' (Nietzsche, 1979 [1888], p. 101). It was his view that if pious posers and their intellectual champions were labelling him their enemy, then he must be on the right track:

> Today, as we have entered into the reverse movement and we immoralists are trying with all our strength to take the concept of guilt and the concept of punishment out of the world again, and to cleanse psychology, history, nature, and social institutions and sanctions of them, there is in our eyes no more radical opposition than that of the theologians, who continue with the concept of a 'moral world-order' to infect the innocence of becoming by means of 'punishment' and 'guilt'. Christianity is a metaphysics of the hangman. (Nietzsche, *Twilight of the Idols* [1889], in 1977, p. 500)

An important political implication of Nietzsche's concept 'Will to Power' is that convention, religion and the 'objective' pursuit of truth are redescribed as instruments whereby weak, small people hold in line those who would be great human beings and make humanity worth belonging to.

Unfortunately, the political interpretation of Nietzsche's concept of 'Will to Power' given here is *not* the one most associated with him, at least until fairly recently, namely, the view that his thought was congenial to the National Socialist (Nazi) movement that came to power in Germany in the 1930s. It is this concept of 'Will to Power', perhaps more than any other in the Nietzschean *corpus*, that led to his posthumous association with the Nazis and with fascist thought. Indeed, Nietzsche's book *The Will to Power*, based on his notes, was published only after his death by his sister. It is believed that these notes were edited by her to fit in with her own interpretation of his life and works, and to serve her anti-Semitic political purposes. Douglas Smith, who introduces Nietzsche's *On the Genealogy of Morals*, remarks that in fact Nietzsche 'vehemently opposed organized anti-Semitism, which he regarded as a production of vulgar *ressentiment*' ('Introduction' in Nietzsche, 1996 [1887], p. xxvi). Nietzsche himself found German or Prussian nationalism in the Bismarckian mode, as well as contemporary anti-Semitism, offensive, and an abuse of the people (Kaufmann, 'Peoples and Fatherlands', in Nietzsche, 1966 [1886], pp. 188–9). In contrast to wilful misinterpretations, Nietzsche actually *praised* the Jews of Germany:

> I have not met a German yet who was well disposed toward the Jews; and however unconditionally all the cautious and politically-minded repudiated anti-Semitism, even this caution and policy are not directed against the species of this feeling itself but only against its dangerous immoderation, especially against the insipid and shameful expression of this immoderate feeling – about this, one should not deceive oneself ... The Jews, however, are beyond doubt the strongest, toughest, and purest race now living in Europe; they know how to prevail under the worst conditions (even better than under favorable conditions), by means of virtues that today one would like to mark as vices – thanks above all to a resolute faith that need not be ashamed before 'modern ideas'. (Nietzsche 1966 [1886], p. 187)

The 'Will to Power' thus expresses a human ability to come alive to oneself and to create the values one wishes to live by, not fearing the company of others who, too, would do the same, and who would work towards the end of a self-actualised humanity. The state is not the site of the 'Will to Power', nor does it, fascist or Nazi illusions to the contrary, provide the ideals for which people ought to strive. The state has no will, only an individual does, and only an individual can will an improvement in the character and quality of humanity.

the doctrine of the 'overman'

Let us therefore *limit* ourselves to the purification of our opinions and evaluations and to the *creation of our own new tables of values* ... We, however, *want to be those who are* – the new, the unique, the incomparable, those who give themselves their own law, those who create themselves! (Nietzsche, *The Gay Science* [1882], in 1977, p. 237)

And Zarathustra spoke thus to the people: *I teach you the superman.* Man is something that should be overcome. What have you done to overcome him? (Nietzsche, *Thus Spoke Zarathustra* [1883], in 1977, p. 237)

Nietzsche's perspectivism in knowledge and his concept of 'Will to Power' are related to his doctrine of the 'Overman'. This is because of their centrality to his life-affirming individualism, and, in turn, to the political organisation of a society that best facilitates the way a genuine individual could live well in the company of others. However, Nietzsche argues that not everyone is capable of the prerequisite: an overcoming of oneself that allows the 'Will to Power' to take hold, so that one enters a new world without the baggage of the past.

The 'Overman' is a creative artist, one who has endured self-overcoming, and who is now fashioning his greatest work, the self, as an expression of a 'Will to Power', unfettered by foolish things that either subdue others or merely vex them. What the 'Overman' must first overcome, however, is a habitual, ingrained manner of making judgements about oneself, values, and the world. This revaluation of values, a critical look at the value of values, will lead the 'Overman' to a thoroughgoing refutation of all that Western civilisation holds dear. Nietzsche believed that this would begin with an overcoming of the dichotomy 'good and evil' that falsely and restrictively structures all our judgements. On that score he wrote:

Strange madness of moral judgments! When man possesses the feeling of power he feels and calls himself *good*: and it is precisely then that the others upon whom he has to *discharge* his power feel and call him *evil*! (Nietzsche, 1982 [1881], Aphorism 189, p. 111)

Good and evil, in reality, are twin aspects of the same system of making judgements, a system that reflects a distant historical reversal of values, when the weak co-opted the strong through praising the qualities that they, models of 'slave morality', exemplified, such as meekness, moderation and obedience to authority rooted in the dichotomy 'good and evil'.

The 'Overman', by contrast, gathers strength and chooses self-affirmation, transcending the moral system based on good and evil, and now making judgements that reflect humanity at its purest. This is a model individual with ideals to struggle for, or against, but always authentic, never derived. The 'Overman' embraces the struggle checked by centuries of adherence to a system of moral valuation based on good and evil. For the 'Overman' this is a necessary struggle that cannot be won by one person for another. Life depends on self-preservation and on a struggle through which an earnest individual casts off childish moralities and embraces the self that dares to stand against the world, in solitude, if need be.

Put differently, humanity must be won, and it can only be won through the 'Will to Power' – through passion, not reason, and through struggle against the violence done to humanity by unworthy ideals. The 'Overman' is able to struggle, ultimately on behalf of a self-actualised humanity, because the 'Overman' alone can direct the will through a self-imposed discipline. Nietzsche finds this quality of character lacking in ordinary people, who understand only discipline and punishment based on authority handed down through Christian moral teaching, now enshrined in the Church's successor, the state. The 'Overman' is not a threat to others, unless they try to fetter him, instead of challenging him to debate, while holding as provisional their own most cherished dogmas. Nietzsche's views on autonomy and rational engagement with politics can now be read on analogy with those of J.S. Mill, rather than with anyone or any movement of the far right (Owen, 1995).

Having secured a moral grounding, the 'Overman' does not need anything from others; what is more, the 'Overman' is able to place justice on a different footing – generosity. The 'Overman' is capable of generosity, of leading people, by example, out of the modern version of Plato's 'cave', where ignorance, small-mindedness and impotence rule (Hunt, 1991, pp. 94–6). Shocking ordinary people and challenging their misconceptions and prejudices, especially those based in judgements of good and evil, the 'Overman' models a freedom won against the struggles that life presents. Freedom is the reward, inaccessible to those who do not win themselves away from what they have become, due to the degenerate society they find themselves in. For Nietzsche, liberal democratic society is a model of degeneracy, because it promises a placid, untroubled life to those who remain obedient to its moral code, pursuing their prefabricated notions of the good life, free from suffering.

In Nietzsche's view, a reborn humanity, a human culture wrought with a nobility of purpose for all humanity, will not recoil from the existential *Angst* that faces it, but will instead create new values and meanings attuned to sensual living. The 'Overman' has overcome the despair of modernity that lies hidden under the veneer of 'objective' knowledge, resisting the false comforts of religion and a morality that encourages meekness. Following through the analogy with Plato's philosopher-king, who emerges from and returns to the cave, the 'Overman' dares a revaluation of values so that we can be sure we understand that by which we live, and in the light of which we choose. The 'Overman' dares to act alone, as an individual, through willing and acting in the world in freedom, displaying this possibility for others who are prepared for it.

concluding thoughts on nietzsche

Nietzsche suggests that there is no reason to regard the 'Overman' as cruel, or the 'Will to Power' as debasing, because judgements of that kind betray a system of morality unsuited to the task of maximising our responsibility for who we become, and because this valuation of values does not help us to organise our thoughts differently and to make new ones possible. A Nietzschean polity would invite the contributions of genuine free-thinking individuals and would modify current democratic practice. At present the mass of citizens view their freedom as freedom from politics, unaware of the consequences. Because they do not create a political regime inspired by individuals who have overcome the straitjackets of modern presumptions and moralities, they suffer consequences for their personal liberty. Citizens in the Nietzschean polity, by contrast, would be empowered to improve themselves, unafraid to laugh at their missteps and would be full of encouragement for the best in each other. They would experience themselves as their most important life's work, rather than fashioning themselves and their society as they have learned to do, simply re-enacting what they have inherited and then mistaking this for a great accomplishment. It is important to read Nietzsche today for the insight he provides into envisioning a political regime which is not founded on the certainty of any epistemological or ethical convictions, yet which is successful because it genuinely trusts in individuals and in humanity itself. It does not need authoritarian structures that minister to the fears and anxieties that encumber individuals in even the most liberal of regimes, preventing them from living the best life together in a fully human community.

further reading

Of Nietzsche's works listed below, the most significant sources regarding his understanding of humanity in the modern era and the implications this has for political theory are *On the Genealogy of Morals* and *The Use and Abuse of History*. The two edited collections, *A Nietzsche Reader* and *The Portable Nietzsche*, as well as his purported autobiography *Ecce Homo: how one becomes what one is*, are philosophically very rewarding. Ansell-Pearson (1991) represents a good introduction to Nietzsche, and Hunt (1991) focuses on justice and virtue. Warren (1988) stands as the classic rediscovery of Nietzsche in political thought, rescuing his reputation from spurious associations with Nazism.

references

Ansell-Pearson, K. (1991) *Nietzsche contra Rousseau: a study of Nietzsche's moral and political thought*. Cambridge: Cambridge University Press.

Ansell-Pearson, K. (1994) *An Introduction to Nietzsche as a Political Thinker*. Cambridge: Cambridge University Press.

Barrett, C. (1991) *Wittgenstein on Ethics and Religious Belief*. Oxford: Blackwell.

Hatab, L.J. (1995) *A Nietzschean Defense of Democracy: an experiment in postmodern politics*. Chicago: Open Court.

Hunt, L.H. (1991) *Nietzsche and the Origin of Virtue*. London: Routledge.

Koelb, C. (ed.) (1990) *Nietzsche as Postmodernist: essays pro and con*. Albany, NY: State University of New York Press.

Nietzsche, F. (1957) *The Use and Abuse of History* [1874], trans. A. Collins. New York: Macmillan.

Nietzsche, F. (1962) *Philosophy in the Tragic Age of the Greeks* [1894 mss], trans. Marianne Cowan. Washington: Regnery Gateway.

Nietzsche, F. (1966) *Beyond Good and Evil: prelude to a philosophy of the future* [1886], trans. Walter Kaufmann. New York: Vintage/Random House.

Nietzsche, F. (1977) *A Nietzsche Reader*, trans. R.J. Hollingdale. London: Penguin.

Nietzsche, F. (1979) *Ecce Homo: how one becomes what one is* [1888], trans. R.J. Hollingdale. London: Penguin.

Nietzsche, F. (1982) *Daybreak: thoughts on the prejudices of morality* [1881], trans. R.J. Hollingdale. Cambridge: Cambridge University Press.

Nietzsche, F. (1996) *On the Genealogy of Morals* [1887], trans. D. Smith. Oxford: Oxford University Press.

Owen, D. (1994) *Maturity and Modernity: Nietzsche, Weber, Foucault, and the ambivalence of reason*. London: Routledge.

Owen, D. (1995) *Nietzsche, Politics and Modernity*. London: Sage.

Robinson, D. (1999) *Nietzsche and Postmodernism*. Cambridge: Icon Books.

Warren, M. (1988) *Nietzsche and Political Thought*. Cambridge: Cambridge University Press.

part ii
'moderns'

6

martin heidegger

edward wingenbach

Martin Heidegger was born in 1889, near the Black Forest of southern Germany. As a student he studied theology and philosophy at the University of Freiburg, where Edmund Husserl served as his mentor. Later, while teaching at the University of Marburg, he produced *Being and Time* (1927), the work that earned him Husserl's chair at Freiburg in 1928, and in 1933 he became Rector. During this period and until 1945 Heidegger was a member of the Nazi party, an affiliation he never explained or recanted. Major figures who studied with Heidegger include Leo Strauss, Hannah Arendt, Karl Löwith, Hans-Georg Gadamer, Emmanuel Levinas and Herbert Marcuse. His legacy for political theory emerges most clearly in the deconstructive approach of Jacques Derrida and the genealogical method of Michel Foucault, each of whom represents a distinct aspect of Heidegger's thought. He died in 1976.

heidegger's thought: 'being and time' and the meaning of politics

The argument developed in *Being and Time* is central to both Heidegger's thought and an understanding of twentieth-century Continental tradition. *Being and Time* evokes and demarcates an approach to meaning and to our understanding of existence, forming the foundation for all later Heideggerian investigations. I select the verbs 'evoke' and 'demarcate' carefully, as Heidegger's text proceeds more by way of provocative phenomenological reflection in an ever-expanding circle of clarity than by way of traditional argument. Heidegger's phenomenological method involves a careful analysis of our experience of everyday life, as our everyday existence provides the only sure access to the meaning of Being. Meaning manifests in our everyday experiences, so an investigation such as the one Heidegger proposes might begin anywhere, as all aspects of everyday experience offer potential routes to develop an understanding of Being. Given Heidegger's method and the objectives of this guide, I will address only a few of the implications of *Being and Time* for political thought, and in the process hope to elucidate the more general importance of Heidegger's approach to thinking.

The question of the meaning of Being animates *Being and Time*, a question at once utterly apolitical and ultimately at the core of politics. How, Heidegger wonders, might we even pose the question? His answer: we must examine the experiencing of existence as given to the only being that questions meaning, namely us. We cannot pose the meaning of Being as a question to be investigated apart from our being, as to do so is to already propose an answer, an answer lacking justification or grounds. Being may be a thing external to us, but that conclusion may only emerge from a phenomenological investigation of our own being (which Heidegger names *Dasein*, or 'being-there'), one uncommenced in Western metaphysics. To the extent we understand our being in an average and vague way, we merely assert 'the traditional theories and opinions about being in such a way that these theories, as the source of the prevailing understanding, remain hidden' (Heidegger, 1996, p. 4).

In this sense the situated character of *Dasein* constitutes *Dasein*'s being and thus its meaning. We find ourselves already immersed in meanings and theories of which we are neither author nor chooser, caught up in a world given both to us and by us, a phenomenon Heidegger describes as 'thrownness'. The structures of meaning providing us our possibilities for existence are our world, and these possibilities define *Dasein*: '*Dasein* is always its possibilities' (Heidegger, 1996, p. 40). The meaning of our being in everyday understanding is thus provided to us by the prevailing understandings of our particular existence (Heidegger terms this 'ontic'), and these prevailing understandings constitute our being-in-the-world. Even unreflective *Dasein* must understand the world in some way, and this understanding determines rather than discovers the meaning of *Dasein*'s being. Heidegger writes, 'Understanding of being is itself a determination of being of *Dasein*' (Heidegger, 1996, p. 10). *Dasein*'s understanding is a constitutive practice that both structures and reveals itself, 'in which constantly exercised understanding understands itself' (Gadamer, 1989, p. 266).

Heidegger's analysis of how *Dasein* relates to its world reveals with more clarity the connection between *Dasein*'s engagement in understanding and the way in which that understanding obscures the actual character of existence. He begins with things, which we relate to as either *zuhanden* (handiness or ready-to-hand) or *vorhanden* (objectively present or present-at-hand). Initially we experience things in the world as immediately available, handy to our use. When we write with a pen or drink from a mug we do not consider the status of the thing in use nor do we separate its being from our own. Such things are simply closed to us and, in the moments of use, part of our being.

The meaning of our world is made accessible to us in its use. When, however, the pen dries up or the mug leaks, we contemplate them as objects with a presence apart from our own, as external to our own being and a problem to be solved.

On Heidegger's account, the objective presence of other beings in our world always derives from the initial encounter in use. The insight is simple but acute. The meaning of things 'in themselves' emanates not from their independent status as things with meaning but from *Dasein*'s projection of meaning in its usage of the things. Thus, 'To expose what is merely objectively present, cognition must penetrate beyond things at hand being taken care of' (Heidegger, 1996, p. 66). The meaning of beings within *Dasein*'s world, and thus the meaning of that world itself, emerges only in *Dasein*'s engagement with them. *Dasein* is not an objective thing among other objective things; rather, the world and beings within it are disclosed by *Dasein* as relevant things with meaning.

Here Heidegger's major question, what is the meaning of Being, separates a bit from the concerns of the political theorist. Heidegger exposes the constitution of the meaning of the everyday world by *Dasein*'s understanding in order to identify how, precisely, to ask his question. His ultimate concern lies not with the everyday being of *Dasein* but with the meaning of Being itself, the Being that makes possible the meaning of beings in the world. He calls this pursuit '*fundamental ontology*, from which alone all other ontologies can originate', and asserts that this ontology 'must be sought in the existential analysis of *Dasein*' (Heidegger, 1996, p. 11). Only in this context does Heidegger's concern for authenticity develop. Authentic *Dasein* grasps its own possibilities within its thrownness, and in such a moment of vision finds itself able to grasp the possibilities that define its situation. Authenticity, however, neither separates *Dasein* from others nor provides it with control over its world. It is a mode of being of a *Dasein* situated in a world already disclosed to it by others, a mode revealing how thrownness defines *Dasein*'s finite possibilities. This finitude of authentic *Dasein* permits Heidegger to locate his ontological access to the meaning of Being, but it is not and should not be read as a prescription for how to live. Authentic *Dasein* is not an ideal state of being, and no *Dasein* could ever live 'in authenticity'. Whether Heidegger succeeds in his ontological task is of little concern to political theory, as political inquiry may be transformed by the profound insights generated almost incidentally by the existential analysis of *Dasein*, understood as a being-in-the-world that understandingly discloses the meanings and possibilities available within that world. Among many possible approaches to Heidegger's political implications, three are explicated below.

being-with, the individual and the political

Dasein always finds itself already in a world, a world of meanings structured by our understanding prior to that understanding being made explicit. *Dasein*'s own understanding of its own being, then, is also structured by the world in which it finds itself: 'Initially and for the most part, *Dasein* is taken in by its world' (Heidegger, 1996, p. 107). It seems obvious that this world is one that includes other beings with the same character of *Dasein*, and that we encounter these other *Daseins* within this world. Yet here we confront a puzzle. If the world is given to us within and by our understandings of it, and other *Daseins* also engage the world in a similar fashion, what is the ground upon which we 'encounter' other *Daseins*? Heidegger's answer is that we do not. The world we find ourselves within is the world constituted for and by us with other *Daseins*, both historically and in our current projections of understanding. My *Dasein* only has meaning insofar as it emerges from the being-together of *Dasein* (Heidegger names this *Mit-Dasein*). *Mit-Dasein* is primordial, and the experience of *Dasein* as its own (authentic; in German *eigentlich* or ownmost-like) derives from our inescapable condition as being-with-others.

Elaborating this insight, Heidegger introduces the often misinterpreted concept of the 'They' (*das Man*). In our average, everyday existence, we relate to the world as at hand for us and find our own *Dasein* as it emerges within the context of use. In those actions, we do not explicitly separate our being from that of others, unless doing so intentionally. As a result, 'The "others" does not mean everybody else but me – those from whom the I distinguishes itself. They are, rather, those from whom one mostly does *not* distinguish oneself, those among whom one is, too' (Heidegger, 1996, p. 111). Neither an I nor an isolated subject, *Dasein* experiences itself as an I because the They, understood here as the average understanding of meaning projected by *Mit-Dasein*, sets up the world that way. *Dasein* is produced by the They and can only understand its relationship to the world in an understanding disclosed with others. This description is neither totalitarian nor absolute; depending on how *Mit-Dasein* has disclosed the world in which we find ourselves, we may be able to experience the meaning of our *Dasein* in various ways or in only one.

Thus two important points emerge. First, the being of *Dasein*, even when most authentic (ownmost), is always primordially a being-with-others; we cannot escape or avoid the influences, judgements and interpretations of the other *Daseins* with whom the world is constituted. Second, this being-with may open or close the range of possibilities available to *Dasein* and thus the range of control we have over our lives. When the average understanding of the *Mit-Dasein* dominates, expressed as the They, the range of possibilities of meaning contracts, and may even make the constitutive character of understanding impossible to perceive. Heidegger makes both points clear in the following:

The They is an existential and belongs as a primordial phenomenon to the positive constitution of Dasein. It itself has, in turn, various possibilities of concretation in accordance with *Dasein*. The extent to which its dominance becomes penetrating and explicit may change historically. (Heidegger, 1996, p. 121)

Dasein's possibilities for meaning, and thus something like freedom, expand or contract along with the historical limitations of the They.

If every *Dasein*'s authentic understanding of its own Being emerges, by definition, out of a more primordial *Mit-Dasein*, how should Heidegger's concern about the They be understood? Clearly, *Dasein* cannot 'escape' *Mit-Dasein*, and the desire to do so would obscure rather than clarify authentic understanding. The danger presented to *Dasein* by the They emerges from the variability of its explicit dominance. Consider, for example, the fear of majority tyranny articulated by John Stuart Mill. The majority in democratic societies, he asserts, is most dangerous not merely because it controls the legislature but because it tends to 'prevent the formation of any individuality not in harmony with its ways, and compel all characters to fashion themselves upon the model of its own' (Mill, 1974, p. 63). At its worst, what Heidegger might call its most penetrating and dominating, the members of democratic societies conform to its vision of human existence without any reflection at all. Mill hopes to develop institutional protections mitigating this tendency toward social tyranny; such protections should enlarge the range of personal development by protecting individuals from direct interference or increasing their capacity to resist the dominance of the public. Heidegger would recognise Mill's aim as an attempt to transform the character of the They (in this case, the democratic public), and thus transform the range of possibilities available to any particular *Dasein*. We cannot escape the They, understood as the lived experience of *Mit-Dasein*, but we may find it easier to mediate its influence and engage it intentionally if we are aware of its shaping influence, and such awareness depends precisely on the range of understandings available to us in the world disclosed to us by *Mit-Dasein*. If we cannot recognise the extent to which we are caught up in the meanings disclosed by the They (with us), we cannot see the manner in which we produce our own entrapment. Note, importantly, that this entrapment cannot be considered an inevitable consequence of the analysis of *Mit-Dasein*, but simply one possible manifestation of *Mit-Dasein*'s average understanding of the world, and as such it is subject to transformation.

Heidegger's analysis of the They helps elucidate some odd tensions in contemporary political forms. Democracy in its liberal manifestation celebrates individualism and self creation, yet seems to generate little more than superficially diverse versions of conformity. Successful individuals devote their life to disclosing their 'selves' in ever more particular and precise variations, experiencing their own being as an end, and thus alienated even from the mysterious 'thing' doing the work on the 'self'. *Dasein* caught in this manifestation of *Mit-Dasein*'s average understanding rarely will glimpse the penetration of the They. Worse, when it does glimpse this domination, its only responses (become autonomous, individuate more, resist) simply reinforce the underlying dynamic. Michel Foucault, in both *Discipline and Punish* and the first volume of *The History of Sexuality*, describes these processes in slightly different ways, as well as the transformative possibilities latent within them. More gloomily, Guy DeBord's *Society of the Spectacle* portrays the closure of possibilities as almost irresistible, where every moment of insight spawns a new option for 'individuation'. An alternative account, best depicted in Hannah Arendt's *The Origins of Totalitarianism*, encourages conformity through terror, reinforced by mass enthusiasm. Totalitarian practices model explicitly the penetrating dominance of the They; but its very effectiveness as an exemplar reveals the limits of its danger. The incitement to individuate characteristics of capitalist democracy poses greater dangers precisely because it is so much more difficult to discern.

the truth of the world

The dominance of the They provides a model for understanding the disclosure of truth more generally. Heidegger's notion of world depends upon discourse, understood not merely as language but as the constellation of potential meanings out of which language emerges. He distinguishes the structures of meaning constituted by discourse, which he calls world, from the meaningless substance out of which and upon which world projects, which he names 'earth' or the '*es gibt*' (see 'The Origin of the Work of Art', Heidegger, 1977b). The truth of the world is uncovered in *Mit-Dasein*'s discourse, and these truths are revealed to *Dasein* as variously open to re-appropriation and interpretation.

It is at this level that the framing of politics occurs. While the options for action of *Dasein* are constrained by the They, the possibilities of the They are in turn restricted by the world. The political decisions of individuals reflect the larger context of communal political expectations, which are in turn governed by the conceptual possibilities available within the background assumptions about what the political encompasses. Significantly, each seemingly discreet level of disclosure informs and is in turn informed by the others. This universe of conceptual possibilities frames or bounds the meanings available, rendering some dominant and obvious, others more difficult to discern, and still others opaque or even unimaginable. The limitations of the framing of the world only maintain themselves as disclosed in turn by particular *Dasein* projecting within the established discourse of *Mit-Dasein*; transformations at any level shift the range of possibilities available at all the others, as world, they and 'self' are all continually disclosed together in an ongoing temporal process.

Nevertheless, a significant danger emerges here. While the meaning of the world, and thus the background assumptions constitutive of the political, are always disclosed in an active process of projective understanding, this world may be disclosed in a way that covers over or obscures the very character of that process. Heidegger's well-known critique of technology offers one such account. Technology refers not to the use and operation of machines but to an ethos toward the world that views all relations in terms of cause and effect, efficient production, and instrumental value. Technological disclosure reveals a world of discrete objects associated by relations of causation and manipulated towards some end. The purpose of the world is to be rendered useful for us, where useful involves the efficient satisfaction of needs. In such a world, all knowing is discovery, and all meaning is calculable. Ultimately humanity discloses itself in the same terms as this world, discovering its own being as pure instrumentality as well. Finally, Heidegger asserts, 'the illusion comes to prevail that everything man encounters exists only insofar as it is his construct' (Heidegger, 1977a, p. 308). But the technological frame dismisses fabrication as meaningless, a mere function to serve further efficiency without value of its own. And thus the technological frame arrives at nihilism: all the world is constructed by us, and therefore lacks any meaning; as the creators of a meaningless world we, too, are meaningless. We thus encounter only and everywhere ourselves in our meaningless existence. At this point, what possibilities for transformation still exist?

Any political approach or theoretical claim dependent upon the discovery of the truth of the world or human nature commits a significant error. Such approaches ignore the historical and emergent character of the meaning of truth; the meaning of reality is our common project, disclosed by our actions. When we come to view truth as something to be discovered 'out there' we subjugate ourselves to our own creations. Ontologically, we cannot discover truths, only disclose them, and in the act of disclosing, assert them. To premise politics upon nature or truth subordinates *Dasein*'s disclosive potential to its own disclosure.

history, meaning, politics

The assertion that the world appears in the understanding of *Mit-Dasein* is likely to strike novice readers as odd, if not impossible. Heidegger asserts not that everything is constructed by us as if by the gods, but simply that the meaning and significance of things in our common world emanate from what we might call a referential context. This context both emerges from and concurrently gives shape to the fundamentally interpretive activity of existence. *Dasein*, he writes, '*is* as an understanding potentiality-for-being ...' (Heidegger, 1996, p. 213). This analysis of the existence of *Dasein* in its everydayness reveals the ontological truth that the essence of Dasein's being is time. *Dasein*, as potentiality-for-being, always exists as its own future, always discloses to itself the possibilities it has resolved to involve itself with already. As temporal, *Dasein* can never exist 'in the present', for the present is always to come and has already passed. *Dasein*'s future stretches out of its past, and the present simply describes the continual anticipation of possibilities disclosed in the future and made available by the past.

The temporal co-projecting of the meaning of the world in its possibilities reflects the situation or 'thrownness' of *Dasein*. The projection of meaning, always emerging from the prior situation, should be conceived as a temporal event stretching back as far as human consciousness. At every moment in time *Dasein* has always found itself within limited possibilities, curtailed both by the finitude of death and the bounds of discourse. Heidegger calls the overall situation (thrownness within a range of possibilities) of *Dasein* within a temporal horizon 'heritage', and the limited possibilities within which finite *Dasein* operates 'fate' (see Heidegger, 1996, section 74). *Dasein* cannot escape its fate or step outside its heritage, as the very possibility to do so must already present itself as a possibility within that fate; the desire both to overcome our fate and succumb willingly must already be available within the heritage of the *Dasein* so inclined. Lastly, and most controversially, the fate of *Dasein* must be linked to that of the *Mit-Dasein* within which *Dasein* always already exists. Heidegger claims that, 'if fateful Dasein essentially exists as being-in-the-world as being-with-others, its occurrence is an occurrence-with and is determined as *destiny*' (Heidegger, 1996, p. 352).

The use of concepts like fate, destiny, and heritage contribute to the tendency of some scholars to interpret Heidegger's work is either deterministic or fascist, as the common meanings of such terms imply the powerlessness of the individual agent and the predominance of the national or social identity. Yet neither is the case. To be limited by tradition does not imply our choices are subject solely to historical causation. To see fate as the origin of choices need not demand submission to a role, nor compel us to 'accomplish' a destiny. *Dasein*, disclosing the world meaningfully with others, is both the source and subject of its heritage, and thus controls its own destiny. History, understood as a living process, circumscribes the range of meaningful disclosure at a given moment. But each disclosure of possibilities transforms, often subtly, our understanding of the meaning of our world, and thus tradition transforms as well. The point is important, and easily missed. *Dasein* always engages its own history and that engagement either transforms or conserves the traditions out of which meaning springs. Political action is structured by the possibilities available, and political activity reflects these historical limitations.

The distinction between politics (*la politique*) and the political (*le politique*), so central to much of contemporary Continental political thought, begins to emerge in this insight. If, following Philippe Lacoue-Labarthe and Claude Lefort, we posit a distinction between everyday policy (politics) and the background conditions legitimising and structuring the regime within which policy struggles take place (the political), we find that the political shapes and confines politics. Should we desire significant change in politics, we must direct our attention to the transformation of the political, as it serves as the boundary for conceivable policy outcomes. As the political expands, so does the range of policy options, and as the political contracts, policy narrows. Heidegger's account of heritage and fate offer a similar though less restrictive understanding of politics. Our everyday political activities are structured by the possibilities made available within a tradition. Only certain possibilities may be conceived. Yet at each moment tradition is constituted again, transformed in some way, and new possibilities may surface. This claim does not imply that heritage or tradition *will* be transformed; under particular enframings *Mit-Dasein* may reconstitute the same destiny over and over. The point, however, is politically promising. In every community, the background structures of the political regime require the constant and active institution of these very structures. Cornelius Castoriadis articulates this dynamic quite well: 'Thus society [the political] is always self-instituting – but for almost the whole of human history this fact of the self-institution has been veiled by the very institutions of society itself' (Castoriadis, 1997, p. 333).

The political implications of Heidegger's analysis of history carry the same equivocal promise as his analysis of the They: both are primordial aspects of our being, under certain conditions both may manifest in such a fashion that we are largely cut off from our own authentic possibilities for freedom, and both always and unavoidably carry with them the potential for their own transformation. We are both author of and prey to the They, as we are the author of and prey to our fateful destiny. With the proper awareness of these structures of our everyday being we open up a promising potential for political theory, both as analysis and praxis.

heidegger's method: examining the problem of agency and social construction

Heidegger's thought, as illustrated above, provides insight into the constitution and limitations of politics understood broadly. But his approach also yields specific insights when deployed as a method within political theory debates. In this section, Heidegger's approach is applied to an important problem in traditional liberal theory in order to demonstrate the value of his method for political thought.

Liberal freedom tends to be conceptualised as an ability to generate values and exert control over objects without control by external influences, at least where that influence is determinative. As accounts of the social construction of subjectivity gain purchase in contemporary liberal theory, this central premise requires reconceptualisation. Liberal politics is premised upon the freedom of agents to engage in choices for which they alone hold ultimate responsibility; a recognition that the agent always finds itself enmeshed within a social context, and thus agent's beliefs do not arise *ex nihilo*, renders the claim of autonomous freedom problematic. One unsustainable response might be to deny social influence altogether. More sophisticated liberals recognise the fact of social construction while asserting the ability of the subject to constitute itself actively and consciously. For the self-consciously constituted liberal subject, the problem of freedom becomes the problem of independence: how does one establish an area of autonomy where nature, history, and the social world do not *wholly* determine the actions of an agent? In either case, liberal theory is left with a choice: assert the capacity to cause without prior causation, thus preserving the ideal of responsibility while at the same time ignoring obvious social facts, or accept the reality of social influence, thus imperilling either freedom or responsibility. The former asserts independent agency at the cost of radical self-deception, while the latter offers the liberal subject only despair about the impossibility of its aspirations. Heidegger's work in his lecture on *The Essence of Human Freedom* offers a way to preserve the strong form of responsibility while also asserting some meaningful theory of causation.

Heidegger describes liberal freedom in its negative version as 'a relationship of non-dependence of one thing on another' (Heidegger, 2002, p. 7). Yet a relationship of non-dependence nevertheless presumes a prior relationship. The constitution of meaning always already presumes a connection between the meaning emerging and the non-meaning against which it emerges (see Heidegger, 1969, pp. 23–41). We cannot ask about freedom from something without already recognising in the question itself that the prior relationship exists, and will continue to exist. Once free, I will be free only in relation to the thing I am free from; should that from which I am free cease to exist, so will my freedom from it. What liberal theory terms negative freedom represents the temporal experience of *becoming* free, in an everyday or practical sense:

> Breaking free, casting off fetters, overcoming constrictive forces and powers, must be a fundamental human experience, by which freedom, understood negatively, comes clearly into the light of knowledge. (Heidegger, 2002, p. 15)

The experience of freedom is the experience of escaping from that which we encounter as a restriction. The corollary experience is a desire for complete escape from control. This analysis reveals freedom as 'the essence of relationship' between positive and negative freedom (Heidegger, 2002, p. 8). Positive freedom provides the ground upon which negative freedom operates, since positive freedom does not mean escaping from something but 'determining one's own action purely through oneself' (Heidegger, 2002, p. 15). In short, positive freedom entails the authentic action of a self actively choosing within the constraints that serve as the condition of all possibility of the being of such a self.

The language of constraint appears, at least initially, to concede the central problem articulated above. If all actions of a subject occur within and against a network of social construction, how can free actions be distinguished from conditioned ones? Theories of freedom tend to associate spontaneity with autonomy, implying that the spontaneous, uncaused character of actions guarantee their freedom. If an act is uncaused – spontaneous – it must be autonomous. If spontaneity is impossible, autonomy must be as well, rendering freedom of any sort untenable. Heidegger, transforming Kant, distinguishes the two: 'Absolute spontaneity is the faculty of the self-origination of a state; autonomy is the self-legislation of a rational will' (Heidegger, 2002, p. 18). Autonomy needs no warrant from spontaneity, as a self can will an action regardless of the action's originality. Spontaneity represents far too high an aspiration; as with art, radical and constant originality is an impossible and largely undesirable standard.

If the distinction holds, most subjects will rarely, if ever, experience spontaneity, but most can and will experience autonomy. If we accept the definition of positive freedom as the sense of authentic choosing within constraints, then positive freedom resembles autonomy. Insofar as the problem of determinism depends upon an understanding of freedom as essentially uncaused, the distinction between spontaneity and autonomy resolves the problem, reserving uncaused actions for the absolute spontaneity of extraordinary circumstances.

Nevertheless, the dilemma of causation remains. Autonomous choosing where the will affects no unanticipated or unconstrained outcome appears hollow, and provides a theory of freedom consistent with social construction but effectively meaningless. Freedom means nothing where choices are genuine but effects uncaused or at least uninfluenced by the choice. On this point it is important to distinguish degrees of causation. The idea of freedom, in its purest form, resembles spontaneity, 'unconditioned causality' (Heidegger, 2002, p. 184). Such a rarified understanding of freedom ignores the more limited yet meaningful practical experience of freedom:

> The reality of freedom is *not an objective reality … The factuality corresponding to the idea of freedom is that of praxis.* We experience the reality of freedom in practical will-governed action. *Freedom possesses practical reality …* (Heidegger, 2002, p. 185, italics in original)

Heidegger distinguishes between practical and ideal causality in order to argue that the practical reality of causation survives the loss of the ideal of spontaneous causation. Praxis does lead to effect, and actions do have consequences not previously determined by an earlier cause or construction. Insofar as the will of a particular subject determines a particular outcome, autonomy exists. And since, as we have seen, construction of a delimited horizon does not lead to identical subjects, the 'will is not determined *a priori* independently of experience, i.e., it is not purely determined will' (Heidegger, 2002, p. 188).

Again one might object that this solution is insufficient to solve the puzzle of freedom, particularly the dilemma of responsibility. Why, if praxis simply permits a subject to indulge a taste for variety within a horizon of limited options, should subjects take freedom seriously? Particularly given the pain, anxiety, and difficulty the experience of freedom seems to entail? Why grasp the slim reed of the 'not purely determined will'? Heidegger's answer seems to be that we cannot do otherwise unless we lose our will entirely. Will, he argues, 'is the capacity to determine one's causality, to determine oneself in one's causation' (Heidegger, 2002, p. 188). Hence willing, however constrained, expresses the essence of a subject's distinct identity or personality. The autonomous subject wills distinct causations within the history and horizon of meaning in which they always already find themselves. It is in the process of willing, developing 'representations of the desired effect', that we find ourselves acting in authentic freedom (Heidegger, 2002, p. 188).

These desired effects emerge from the fact that 'what is distinctive to man is his personality, the essence of which is self-responsibility' (Heidegger, 2002, p. 187). In each and every case of willing, the subject chooses, and must choose, to will something. This willing involves the response of a self to particular conditions, a response that might be other than it was for different personalities. The will is therefore both not determined and an expression of responsibility, where responsibility involves the act of responding in a way identifiably connected to a subject (understood precisely as a situated *Dasein* that, though constituted as *Dasein* by and with others, finds itself in its own distinct relation to historical possibility). In other words, responsibility emerges in the relations of willed causation demanded by the experience of everyday living; insofar as we will, we are already susceptible to responsibility. The fact that the relations of responsible causation occur non-spontaneously within a horizon of possibilities does not deliver this responsibility over to insignificance.

Both free willing and the responsibility it entails might be rendered meaningless if the distinct personality of each subject is itself merely an artifact of other causes. If willing reflects utterly predictable, completely constituted, and over determined choices then no causation, however small, obtains, and thus no freedom is possible. Heidegger's theory provides a powerful rejoinder:

> The essence of the person is this self-responsibility: to bind oneself to oneself, but not egotistically, i.e., not in relation to the accidental 'I.' To be in the mode of self-responsibility, to answer only to the essence of one's self. To give this priority in everything, to will the ought of pure willing. (Heidegger, 2002, p. 199)

The distinction articulated here between oneself and the 'accidental I' provides the key. The 'accidental I' should be understood as the inauthentic subject lost amongst the chatter of the present, unable to contemplate and choose among possible options because every choice seems already made or obviously correct. Such a subject essentially has no self. The 'essence of one's self' emerges (notice, the essence of self is a process, not a static object) only through the intentional willing of responsibility.

Hence the authentic self engages causation, in two distinct ways. First, the self must be capable of willing an end or outcome (praxis). All subjects, authentic and responsible or inauthentic and accidental, demonstrate this capacity. Second, the self must will the specific end of engaging the world *as a self*, binding oneself to one's own distinctiveness. Authentic freedom, expressed in the second type of willing, thus permits a subject to both recognise the process and limits of social construction and engage in non-determined, meaningful freedom.

Authentic freedom, as understood in Heidegger's theory, is not susceptible to the paralysing and disempowering conflict between construction and autonomy so common to the liberal understanding of freedom. For liberalism, the issue of freedom becomes more difficult as the constructed character of social agents becomes clearer. A constructed subject, if constructed to desire freedom in the traditional sense, finds itself with a dilemma. Either one can accept social construction and engage the process actively, or one can deny it and assert unconditioned freedom. The former risks the internalisation of external norms and thus oppression. As a result, subjects begin to see freedom as an impossibility. The latter risks even worse outcomes, since the subject may feel itself to be free, an uncaused causer, in a manner wholly inconsistent with the actual reality of the operation of social norms and the constitution of subjectivity. In short: alienation or pathology.

Heidegger offers a promising alternative. His approach evades the constructed/autonomous distinction, revealing freedom as constrained but not determined. To the extent all subjects engage in willed causation, all subjects possess the capacity for freedom. The real issue of freedom involves the character of the willing. Those subjects who ignore or abdicate their participation in and subjugation to the processes of social constitution will, inevitably, act without meaningful freedom. They will feel free and act predictably, at least within horizons of meaning disclosed for them by the They. Yet their freedom, in this case, is a freedom of perpetuating existence through behaviours, actions and thoughts identified as familiar to the self, where familiarity of identity masks the possibilities for real choice or will. On the other hand, those subjects who engage the process of self-construction as an activity of will, where choices and actions emerge from a context that is both constrained and constructed but also uniquely and essentially mine, will experience freedom as a meaningful activity and find it worth defending. Heidegger shows how *Dasein*'s engagement with the process of construction increasingly creates a social space from which we can will to cause outcomes not already determined. As we direct our positive freedom toward our self and the world, we may even come to experience negative freedom by reshaping the relationship between will and context. Thus Heidegger's account of authentic freedom, an account that could be repeated from a variety of core political concepts, demonstrates how his analysis of meaning permits significant engagement with the ontological possibilities that frame the meaning of Being and thus the possibilities for political action.

further reading

Of Heidegger's works listed below the most significant is *Being and Time* (1996), and it should be read if at all possible. Gelven's Commentary (1989) provides outstanding guidance and summary. *Basic Writings* (1977) contain most of Heidegger's major essays. For those seeking an accessible and relatively accurate overview of Heidegger's philosophy, Collins's *Introducing Heidegger* (1999) provides both. In the secondary literature, Dallmayr's *Twilight of Subjectivity* (1981) remains the best expression of Heidegger's implications for politics, and *The Other Heidegger* (1993) elucidates further. De Beistegui's *Heidegger and the Political* (1997) offers a somewhat different account of the role of the political within Heidegger's philosophy, while Caputo's indictment of Heidegger's potential fascism in *Demythologizing Heidegger* (1993) offers a balanced critique. For external commentary on Heidegger's thought *The Cambridge Companion to Heidegger* (1993) and *Feminist Interpretations of Martin Heidegger* (2001) provide a good mix of critical views by knowledgeable authors. Finally, Derrida's *Specters of Marx* (1994), though not directly about Heidegger, represents an outstanding demonstration of the use of his approach to generate political insights.

references

Caputo, J.D. (1993) *Demythologizing Heidegger*. Bloomington, IN: Indiana University Press.

Castoriadis, C. (1997) 'Radical Imagination and the Social Instituting Imaginary', in *The Castoriadis Reader*, ed. David Ames Curtis, pp. 319–37. Oxford: Blackwell.

Collins, J. and Selina, H. (1999) *Introducing Heidegger*. Cambridge: Icon Books.

Dallmayr, F. (1981) *Twilight of Subjectivity: Contributions to a post-individualist theory politics*. Amherst, MA: University Of Massachusetts Press.

Dallmayr, F. (1993) *The Other Heidegger*. Ithaca, NY: Cornell University Press.

De Beistegui, M. (1997). *Heidegger and the Political*. New York: Routledge.

Derrida, J. (1994) *Specters of Marx: The state of the debt, the work of mourning, and the new international*. New York: Routledge.

Gadamer, H.-G. (1989) *Truth and Method*, trans. J. Weinsheimer and D.G. Marshall. NY: Crossroad.

Gelven, M. (1989) *A Commentary on Heidegger's Being and Time*. Dekalb, IL: Northern Illinois University Press.

Guignon, C. (ed.) (1993) *The Cambridge Companion to Heidegger*. Cambridge: Cambridge University Press.

Heidegger, M. (1969) *Identity and Difference*, trans. J. Stambaugh. Chicago: University of Chicago Press.

Heidegger, M. (1977a) 'The Question Concerning Technology', in *Basic Writings*, ed. D.F. Krell, pp. 283–318. San Francisco, CA: Harper & Row.

Heidegger, M. (1977b) 'The Origin of the Work of Art', in *Basic Writings*, ed. D.F. Krell, pp. 91–112. San Francisco, CA: Harper & Row.

Heidegger, M. (1977c) 'What is Metaphysics?' in *Basic Writings*, ed. D.F. Krell, pp. 143–88. San Francisco CA: Harper and Row.

Heidegger, M. (1996) *Being and Time: A translation of Sein und Zeit*, trans. J. Stambaugh. Albany, NY: SUNY Press.

Heidegger, M. (2002) *The Essence of Human Freedom*, trans. T. Sadler. New York: Continuum.

Holland, N.J. and Huntington, P. (2001) *Feminist Interpretations of Martin Heidegger*. University Park, PA: Pennsylvania State University Press.

Mill, John Stuart (1974) *On Liberty*. London: Penguin Books.

7
hans-georg gadamer
keith spence

Hans-Georg Gadamer (1900–2002) was born in Marburg, Germany and died in the course of his 103rd year in Heidelberg. For over 80 of those years he was active as a philosopher of unusual breadth and consistency. Gadamer's interests encompassed a historical range from the pre-Socratic to the postmodern, and spanned the full range of the humanities, including poetry, aesthetics, philology and theology, as well as philosophical and political thought. This variety is complemented by an equally noteworthy continuity of form and approach. Gadamer's favoured literary form was the short essay, which he produced in abundance and which provide the basis of his many works, the most significant of which is his canonical *Truth and Method*. Regardless of the complexity of the subject under discussion, these essays are typically marked by a distinct clarity of expression and conversational tone. Their clarity is partly attributable to the origins of many of the pieces, which were typically first presented as lectures, but is also a testament to Gadamer's determination to make his work as accessible as possible to as wide an audience as possible. In this ambition Gadamer's work departs from that of many Continental philosophers, whose writing self-consciously seeks to breach the boundaries of grammar and vocabulary in search of novel forms of thought and expression that are ostensibly less conventional or restrictive than those complying with prevailing linguistic norms. Gadamer's subtle clarity is also a mark of his lifelong preoccupation with questions of meaning, interpretation and understanding (*verstehen*), issues that his work helped to re-establish in the second half of the twentieth century as decisively important throughout the human sciences and beyond.

The following discussion begins with a short biographical outline focusing on the politically crucial period of Nazi rule in Germany and the complexities of Gadamer's relationship with his intellectual mentor, Martin Heidegger. Four principal themes characteristic of Gadamer's thought are then considered in turn: the universality of interpretation for all human understanding; the finite and historically conditioned character of that understanding; the recovery of prejudice and tradition within philosophical thought; and finally, the centrality of dialogue and the fusion of interpretative horizons in the formation of meaning. The account of these themes offers at best a fragmentary introduction to Gadamer's work, but does point to its primary political implications and addresses two of the most prominent sets of debates undertaken by Gadamer, one with the critical theorist, Jürgen Habermas, and the other with the godfather of deconstruction, Jacques Derrida.

The questions and thematics raised by Gadamer's work and the dialogues it provoked continue to exert influence, sometimes in covert and implicit forms, throughout many areas of contemporary political thought, and the concluding section of this chapter identifies aspects of this legacy and its continuing significance. Gadamer's patient, exegetical, interpretative approach always seeks to open out rather than foreclose debate in questions of politics as much as any other area. When questioned, Gadamer identified himself as a liberal in political matters, but beyond this general categorisation, there is no readily available political theory or doctrine to which the label 'Gadamerian' can be applied. His influence is instead apparent in the way that the interpretative or *hermeneutical* practices that he advocated have become pervasive throughout the discipline, as has the critical *ethos* of dialogical engagement and opposition to dogma and doctrine in all of its forms that Gadamer made manifest throughout his life and work.

a politicised life

Gadamer, the son of a University chemist, determined from early in life that his academic interests resided in the library rather than the laboratory. His initial work on Plato was completed at Marburg in 1922 under the guidance of the Kantian philosopher Paul Natorp, who introduced Gadamer to the work of Martin Heidegger. The impact of Heidegger's thought on Gadamer was immediate and irrevocable. Between 1923 and 1928 Heidegger held a chair in philosophy at Marburg, during which time Gadamer worked as his assistant and student whilst completing his second doctorate, or *Habilitationsschrift*. Gadamer was far from alone in finding the Heidegger effect to be an 'intoxicating' one (Gadamer, 1994, p. 62), and the introduction to *Truth and Method* recorded the 'impulse received from Heidegger' as the standard by which Gadamer wished his work to be judged (Gadamer, 2000, p. xxv). Subsequent appreciations (for example, Gadamer, 1994, pp. 15–18, 61–7, 113–16) similarly recall how Heidegger's thought remained the animating source to which Gadamer continually returned. He was, however, never a slavish disciple of Heidegger, and even in late writings was careful to distinguish points of difference between them (for example, Gadamer, 1998, p. 201). The relationship between the two was therefore consistent in terms of both personal loyalty and intellectual engagement.

The critical nature of their connection is significant because Heidegger was, infamously, a public supporter of Nazism during his short period (1933–35) as *Rektor* of Freiburg University, and subsequently never offered a clear public account – or recantation – of his views and actions. This silence, combined with the difficulty and apparent anti-humanism of his works, prompted widespread debate concerning the relationship between Heidegger's thought and politics that crystallised into two broad positions (Rockmore, 1992; Wolin, 1993). Those who admire Heidegger's philosophy tend to regard his political activities of the 1930s as evidence of poor judgement and worse character that are not connected with either the content or the significance of his philosophy. Against this view it is claimed that Heidegger's thought was more deeply implicated with and shaped by his Nazism, and that those influenced by him are in consequence tainted by a subterranean totalitarian influence (Lilla, 2002; Wolin, 2001).

During the latter stages of Gadamer's life the 'Heidegger question' was reignited in Germany by Victor Farias' *Heidegger and Nazism* (1989), a biography that exposed the depths of Heidegger's anti-Semitism and the near-comical obeisance with which he sought to promote himself as the philosopher-king of Nazism. This prompted renewed interest in the responsibilities of intellectuals in general, and of those who prospered within the University system between 1933 and 1945 in particular. In this climate of opinion Gadamer's 'war record' – he moved to Kiel in 1934 before taking up professorships at Marburg (1937) and Leipzig (1939) – was inevitably scrutinised in detail. It had been previously accepted that Gadamer, who never joined the Nazi party, had distanced himself from politics during the period. This presumption was challenged by a new generation of researchers more concerned than their predecessors had been to expose and confront the secret histories of the recent past.

Gadamer offered a vigorous defence of his decision to remain in Germany, and against charges that he was complicit with and tacitly benefited from Nazi rule (Wolin, 2000). As the published version of his radio interview on the subject (Gadamer, 2000, pp. 115ff.) announced, in his experience 'the real Nazis had no interest in us at all'. Under examination, however, details of his conduct did emerge that demand consideration in the context of two sets of political debates. The first concerns Gadamer's relation to the politics of that time, and the second concerns the politics surrounding the reception and interpretation of his work as a whole.

In 1933 Gadamer was a signatory to a pro-Nazi Teachers' Proclamation, and he voluntarily attended an indoctrination programme for academics in 1936. For Gadamer those actions, although unpalatable, were unavoidable if he was to avoid involuntary emigration or worse. His motto during the Nazi period was that 'this too will pass' (Gadamer, 2000, p. 127), and he found solace in classical studies and in the hope that Germany would ultimately emerge from the catastrophe of Nazism. More controversially, in 1941 Gadamer travelled to occupied Paris where he delivered a talk on the German nationalist thinker Herder to an audience of French prisoners of war. He later acknowledged that this visit could be 'misconstrued', but insisted that the trip was not politically motivated. Instead he travelled at the invitation of a friend he wished to visit, and because 'it was a good chance to see Paris' (Palmer, 2002, p. 473). Retrospectively this trip does appear to have involved an error of judgement. The extent to which a misguided journey and lecture that apparently included a subtle jibe at the expense of the Nazi regime (Palmer, 2002, p. 474) constitutes complicity with it is, however, eminently debatable.

These inconclusive and arguably trivial accommodations need to be located in the wider context of the twelve-year Nazi period, during which Gadamer attained his first full position at Kiel, a highly pro-Nazi University. Gadamer's appointment there was as the replacement for the Jewish philosopher Richard Kroner, but he maintained that he had not sought to exploit or tacitly condone the prevailing anti-Semitism in order to advance his own career. Indeed, he accepted the position with Kroner's knowledge and support, and the two resumed a longstanding friendship after the war. At Kiel and elsewhere, however, he had no option but to work with colleagues who were publicly and avowedly pro-Nazi, and his attitude towards them was considered and revealing. '[O]ne saw', said Gadamer,

> what would happen to those who did not cooperate. I mean the pressure was intense. I do not claim any moral qualities for this, only political ... I was just a little more clever [than those who made concessions, such as joining the Nazi party] ... in taking seriously as colleagues those who were Nazis but who were at the same time genuine, rational scholars; avoiding, of course, political conversation. (Gadamer, 2000, p. 129)

This bifurcation between the deranged politics of Nazism and 'rational scholarship' cuts through a good deal of the ambiguity surrounding Gadamer's actions. By imposing a strong distinction between the rational and the pathological upon his dealings with colleagues, he distinguished questions of personality from those of philosophy. This was not simply a pragmatic convenience that allowed him to survive through desperate times in Germany. It was the mode of his principled detachment from the politics of Nazism and its adherents. The want of documentary evidence and coherent argument is no more likely in future to inhibit the rush to judgement of those imagining a link between the character and thought of Heidegger and those who drew inspiration from him than it has been in the past. Before participating in this rush, it is therefore appropriate to recall that Gadamer, perhaps more than any other associate, was aware of the nature of Heidegger's character and its connection with his calamitous political and personal failings. But he was also fully aware of the depth and insight of Heidegger's thought and, unlike many later critics, intellectually capable of separating the rational from the irrational and keeping the domains distinct.

The extent of Gadamer's political 'cleverness' was recognised at the end of World War II, when the Soviet occupying forces made him *Rektor* of Leipzig University (within East Germany prior to the reunification of 1990), a position that would not have been entrusted to anyone suspected of connection with the Nazi regime. He instituted the revival of the University in straitened circumstances, but had little more sympathy for Soviet Communism than he had had for National Socialism. In 1947 he seized the opportunity to return west to Frankfurt. Two years later he made the final move of his career to the Chair in Philosophy at Heidelberg, and there he embarked upon his most philosophically productive period (see Schmidt, 2002, pp. 7–11). The material that comprised *Truth and Method* was assembled during the 1950s, and its appearance in 1960 was followed by numerous essays and collections, most notably those translated as *Philosophical Hermeneutics* (1976), *Reason in the Age of Science* (1981) and *Hermeneutics, Religion and Ethics* (1999). These and other works drawn from Gadamer's ten volumes of collected works in German extend and refine the positions advanced in *Truth and Method* whilst remaining within the interpretative framework that it defines. In so doing, as Jean Grondin (2003, p. 15) has commented, 'a work which was originally modest thus became gigantic, and no friend of hermeneutic thought will complain'.

gadamer's hermeneutics: themes and debates

The originally modest work alluded to by Grondin was an historical survey of interpretative methodologies within the human sciences. The text that appeared in 1960 as *Truth and Method* is, as both its title and depth indicate, considerably more ambitious. Its three principal divisions deal in turn with truth in the experience of art, in the act of understanding within the human sciences and within language, and in the medium of understanding and experience. In following this course, Gadamer offers a dense account of history, aesthetics and interpretation within philosophy from his own distinctive phenomenological and existential standpoint. In the plainest terms, Gadamer sought to grasp or comprehend the subject matter – the phenomena – of philosophy as they arise and are experienced by self-consciousness in a direct and unmediated form. Rather than conforming to *a priori* explanatory criteria or standards of proof, phenomenology presents itself as an elementary and descriptive practice rather than a theoretically predetermined one. The existential aspect of his thought complements and supports this, as Gadamer insists on the temporally finite and historically conditioned character of the human situation. Identifying these standpoints is helpful because they allow Gadamer to be located and distinguished from alternative formulations (for example, transcendental, Christian and Sartrean; see Friedman, 1999) of phenomenology and existentialism to which his thought cannot be readily assimilated.

The historical, aesthetic and interpretative structure of *Truth and Method* is laden with detail drawn from studies of classical, medieval, romantic and modern thought. This results in a text that resolutely defies summary, and rather than attempting to do so some core themes will merely be suggested here. The first question concerns the very title of the work. As Gadamer clarified in a subsequent 'Afterword', it was explicitly not his purpose to provide a methodology that would lead to truth claims and underwrite them. Rather, the title directs the reader to the tension (Gadamer, 2000, p. 555) between truth and method, and the inadequacy of any method that claims to establish and exhaust truth definitively. This argument is directed most fiercely against scientific and positivist conceptions of truth, which were in the ascendant during the period of its composition. Following Heidegger's lead, for Gadamer the scientific model of truth is a derivative and secondary one that takes for granted the existence and human significance of the phenomena in question (be they concrete objects or abstract concepts). The question of truth properly concerns the disclosure or unconcealment of these meanings and their grounding in commonplace activities of dialogue, interpretation, understanding, agreement and disputation. It is not therefore a self-evident property of propositions and principles that is underwritten and verified by the application of the 'correct' philosophical method. Truth, for Gadamer, concerns how matters are revealed and produced as meaningful phenomena in the course of human affairs, so rather than *Truth and Method*, either 'Meaning and Method' or 'Meaning against Method' are arguably more apposite renderings of the German title, *Wahrheit und Methode*.

Within this account of truth Gadamer does not refute or deny the usefulness of scientific methodologies, but rather establishes their location and limits within particular disciplines, and with that the unsustainable nature of claims to universality advanced on their behalf. Despite their differences, the same is equally so with the humanities, no particular area of which can legitimately claim a monopoly on truth, either. *Truth and Method* poses the question 'how is understanding possible' in any and all situations, and Gadamer's response accords priority neither to politics, physics nor to any other discipline. This is because, for Gadamer, 'understanding is not just one of the various possible behaviours of the subject but the mode of [its] being ... the nature of the thing itself makes the movement of understanding comprehensive and universal' (Gadamer, 2000, p. xxx). Rather than any particular cognitive method or epistemic practice, understanding is not only universal but, as the 'mode of being', it is what constitutes human existence in and experience of the world.

As a phenomenologist, the universality accorded to understanding is concrete and substantive. It cannot be achieved through abstract reasoning or formal logic that, as with methodological claims to truth, are derived from understanding rather than foundational for it. This is encapsulated in Gadamer's claim that '[b]eing that can be understood is language' (Gadamer, 2000, p. 474). Just as the problem of understanding is universal, so is its medium of resolution. 'Understanding is language bound' (Gadamer, 1976, p. 15) and as such is always specific and situated in historical time and space. The hermeneutical task is not simply a passive one of understanding the world as it is encountered and inherited in linguistic forms that precede and exceed us. It is also an active one, inspired by Aristotelian conceptions of practice (*praxis*), activity (*ergon*), wisdom (*phronesis*) and judgement (*synesis*), and of engagement in 'infinite dialogue' with other languages, interpretations and forms of life, 'in the direction of the truth that we are' (Gadamer, 1976, p. 15).

These closely related claims about understanding and language, and the limits of scientific method, are superficially uncomplicated, but Gadamer's use of them to underpin his ontological claims regarding the nature of human existence is far-reaching. Notably, the critique of 'scientism' is also a critique of the Enlightenment aspiration to transparency in knowledge and to domination of the world, and of the ever-increasing scope exerted by modes of reasoning constructed according to that ambition. To the last, Gadamer called attention to the 'destructive powers that technology has placed in human hands', and to the 'critical recovery ... required for us to bring about a new equilibrium between nature and culture' (Gadamer, 1998, p. 205). This critical recovery does not involve the Luddite repudiation of science, but rather its 'demythologisation' (Gadamer, 1981, p. 150) within the hermeneutical problematic. This response to the question of technology is provocative because it challenges science not merely instrumentally (that is, in terms of risks and exploitation) but also on its own terms as a mode of reason and knowledge. Instead of apocalyptically condemning technology and its consequences (as Heidegger, for example, tended to do), Gadamer invites reflection on alternative understandings (such as those of the Greeks, and of Eastern civilisations), in contrast to the reification of the scientific within modern Western culture. Gadamer's standpoint thereby places the status and inevitability of the social, political and technological orders shaped by the Enlightenment in question in terms of understanding as well as consequences.

It is characteristic – indeed, a characteristic frustration – that Gadamer opens out these expansive questions without offering more than the outline of a response to them. Amongst the reasons for this apparent reticence is his insistence on the finite nature of understanding. This is most evident in Gadamer's treatment of two aspects of language and understanding, those of prejudice and tradition. Languages are immense and diffuse structures of meanings, identities and differences. Acquiring a language is a process of immersion in which habits of thought, assumption and response are adopted pre-critically. The activity of interpretation and understanding relies upon this immersion and familiarity. Indeed, without it we would be unable to understand at all, which leads to Gadamer's claim that '[i]t is not so much our judgements as our prejudices that constitute our being' (Gadamer, 1976, p. 9). The 'experimental fervor' (Gadamer, 2000, p. 276) of the Enlightenment serves to discredit prejudice by privileging pure or unconditioned reason. Part of Gadamer's task in *Truth and Method* was to rehabilitate it, along with the corollary notion of tradition.

To write in praise of prejudice is to invite misunderstanding insofar as it is commonly associated with irrational bias, intemperate opinion or the intention to mislead or dissemble. Gadamer's deployment of the term needs therefore to be distinguished from these formulations. For Gadamer's hermeneutics, prejudice invokes those prejudgements or pre-understandings that, as participants within languages, we bring to activities of dialogue and interpretation. It is the vast assemblage of typically unarticulated understandings that, borne by language, are present and inform the conduct of any linguistic interchange. Rather than being arbitrary and irrational, prejudice is the form in which language as a historical medium conveys and makes manifest tradition and its authority upon judgement.

> Our historical consciousness is always filled with a variety of voices in which the echo of the past is heard ... this constitutes the nature of the tradition in which we want to share ... in it we have, as it were, a new experience of history whenever the past resounds in a new voice. (Gadamer, 2000, p. 284)

Traditions and their meanings are therefore both formative and active elements of the conversations that we undertake in search of understanding. When we search for meanings in a text or work of art, for example, we (often unconsciously) incorporate and respond to previous interpretations. In so doing we do not obliterate or overwrite those meanings, but rather add to them and, as it were, extend by our contributions the 'effective history' (Gadamer, 2000, p. 300f.) of the artefact in question. Likewise, when we study a text or a work of pictorial art we do not simply absorb the imagery or the marks on the page. We also evaluate and respond to the history of the piece, to previous accounts of its meanings and effects, and so on. The meanings of historical texts, of canonical authors, and of iconic images are thereby continually evolving and accreting. In the course of this process new understandings are ventured and contested, the originality and impact (or otherwise) of which are inseparable from the histories of which they become a part.

Meaning and understanding are, therefore, historical 'all the way down', and there is no non-linguistic or extra-historical standard against which an interpretation can be judged. This, it should be noted, is not a simplistic form of linguistic idealism or relativism that denies the existence of an external world or allows that any interpretation is valid irrespective of its context or provenance. It is rather a claim that the disclosure of human significance is, and can only be, linguistic and historical in form. An historical consciousness sensitive to the temporal development and sedimentation of its meanings is not moribund, reactionary or arbitrary in form. This, in an era of unthinking modernisation and the fetishisation of the new, is by no means a banal observation.

Of the critical debates occasioned by *Truth and Method*, the most enduring are those that Gadamer conducted with the leading 'second generation' critical theorist (and former assistant to Theodor Adorno) Jürgen Habermas (Habermas, 1977; Nicholson, 1991; Warnke, 1987, ch. 4). Although Habermas was appreciative of Gadamer's work, his critique centred upon its apparently limited critical resources. Gadamer's hermeneutics are deemed deficient insofar as the reliance upon tradition and prejudice accepts the authority and effect of the judgements of the past upon the present, and is thereby unable to generate the forms of critical and emancipatory knowledge, in particular regarding the effects of power, that became central to Habermas' neo-Kantian theory of communicative action (Habermas, 1984, 1987). From Habermas' standpoint Gadamer offers refined interpretations of the world, but is unable to change it. Neither of the protagonists emerged decisively ascendant from their debates, but it is apposite here to offer some remarks upon its course.

For Gadamer neither prejudice nor tradition is beyond examination. Hermeneutical reflection is self-conscious about both its own historicity (Gadamer, 2000, p. 299) and its prejudices, which are opened up and placed in question in the course of understanding. This, as we have seen, is an active practice rather than a matter of passive reception, and prejudgements can be erroneous or misleading. Rather than being ossified, traditions are always interpreted and understood in the course of ongoing dialogue. It is in keeping with Gadamer's outlook that there is, however, no method or measure beyond the course of interpretation itself to determine which particular judgements are accurate and which misleading. Such determinations are often a matter of time, as 'local and limited prejudices die away, but allow those that bring about genuine understanding to emerge clearly as such' (Gadamer, 2000, p. 298). Tradition and the authority that it conveys in the form of prejudgement are always open to interpretation and scrutiny, with judgement on and correction of them a part of the unfolding, historical and situated hermeneutical process itself.

Openness to criticism and reformulation is therefore immanent throughout both the theory and practice of Gadamer's hermeneutics, but the notion of critical standard or rational procedure that stands outside of language and history in the rationalistic form of a universal principle or Archimedean point of view is a quixotic one. No responsible hermeneutics, as Gadamer repeatedly avows, can claim the last word and impose closure upon discussion (Gadamer, 2000, p. 579; 1998, p. 211). Indeed, the Enlightenment, which (for example in Kant's critical philosophy) took just such a transparent and unconditioned rationality as its basis, is itself a process that is bound up with, responds to and carries forward rich traditions of thought in virtually every domain and discipline of enquiry. Drawing inspiration from Aristotle rather than Kant, Gadamer identifies himself within a different tradition from that of Habermas, but the thought of both is conditioned by their responses to these varied inheritances. In challenging Gadamer, Habermas inadvertently demonstrated the inevitability and universality of the interpretive challenges that he seeks to undermine. Over the course of his career Habermas has progressively recognised this, accommodating interpretative judgement within his theorisation of the 'lifeworld' to the point where, in the judgement of Michael Theunisson (1999, p. 255), 'he relies on Gadamer's hermeneutics to such an extent that he undermines his own critique of Gadamer's position'.

One area where Gadamer is vulnerable to criticism is in the generous presuppositions he makes about those engaged in the pursuit of understanding. The orientation towards understanding and agreement that is a requirement of participants distinguishes his approach as a hermeneutics of trust and agreement rather than of post-Nietzschean suspicion, manipulation and the will to power. This question of trust leads to the final Gadamerian theme to be considered here, that of the fusion of horizons (Gadamer, 2000, p. 306f.) in the formation of understanding.

A hermeneutical situation is a dialogical and intersubjective encounter between interlocutors whose prejudgements constitute horizons of meaning that establish the limits of their understanding. These horizons are not, however, fixed. They are 'always in question because we are continually having to test all of our prejudices' (Gadamer, 2000, p. 306), and the achievement of understanding involves a fusion and supersession (p. 307) of these boundaries. This refiguration of prejudgements occurs in and through language itself. It is not a merging of viewpoints, nor a convenient convergence of opinions. Rather, when a genuine event of understanding occurs, 'what emerges in its truth is the logos, which is neither mine nor yours ... it [dialectic] is the art of forming concepts through working out their common meaning' (Gadamer, 2000, p. 368). The outcome of the hermeneutical encounter is therefore a transformation where 'the fusion of horizons that takes place in understanding is actually the achievement of language' (Gadamer, 2000, p. 378). This might involve, for example, the formation of a new viewpoint and the articulation of its assumptions and conditions, perhaps expressed in a new vocabulary or interpreted from within a shared and transformed horizon of prejudgements.

The apparent abstraction of this formulation is belied by its connection with the notion that 'being that can be understood is language'. The fusion of horizons affords the possibility of new perspectives and vocabularies that are as political as they are philosophical or aesthetic. Gadamer's own studies have for the most part focused on German literary figures such as Hölderlin, Rilke and Celan. This is far from accidental, as such poets operated at the cutting edge of language, located within genres and traditions yet always forging new meanings and ways with language that, at their most effective, exemplify the fusion of horizons sought by Gadamer. In a related vein, transitions in political understanding are typically also accompanied by such changes. In cases of revolution, for example, the transformation of subject into citizen can be part of a wholesale reformulation of political and cultural vocabularies and attendant social and institutional relationships. Similarly, understandings forged in the course of dialogues concerning the claims for recognition of the marginalised, discriminated and dispossessed change not just language, but the assumptions and meanings of the social world constituted by it. The politics of identity and culture is therefore always also a politics of language and interpretation (Taylor, 1994).

The weakness alluded to above is that successful achievement of the fusion anticipated by Gadamer can never be guaranteed, even in apparently propitious circumstances. This was the case with a second set of dialogues in which Gadamer participated with Jacques Derrida, one of the founders of deconstruction and a philosopher who, like Gadamer, is deeply indebted to Heidegger. Potentially, at least, their discussions afforded the possibility of insight and understanding, but what actually transpired was a refusal of engagement on the part of Derrida, whose contributions concerned readings of Nietzsche and Heidegger (Dostal, 2002, pp. 27–8) that evaded rather than engaged in dialogue. Whether he was acting out of irony or bad faith is impossible to say, but Derrida certainly declined the opportunity to place his own prejudgements in question. This led Gadamer (1998, pp. 61–2) subsequently to question 'whether Derrida is capable of engaging in a genuine conversation'. Intentionally or otherwise, he did succeed in revealing the limits and dependencies of Gadamer's approach that are exposed whenever the risks and opportunities of hermeneutic understanding are refused.

gadamer's enduring presence

It is inevitable that all but a few fundamental issues arising from Gadamer's life and work are omitted from this discussion. The political possibilities disclosed by his work on language, tradition, judgement and understanding are not diminished by this brevity. The same can be said of Gadamer's continuing influence throughout the human sciences. *Truth and Method* was initially received by its Anglophone audience primarily as a treatise on literary interpretation (for example, Weinsheimer 1985), but the ongoing breakdown of the Continental/analytical distinction in philosophy has facilitated the development of Gadamer's influence through phenomenology and critical theory into mainstream debates within social and political theory. As Gianni Vattimo (1988, p. 399) observed, in the wake of Gadamer's work hermeneutics became 'the common idiom of both philosophy and culture'.

Gadamer's influence is in this sense subtly present, though often in an implicit rather then fully acknowledged form, throughout the abundant political discourses addressing questions of interpretation, deliberation, dialogue and contestation.

Most prominently, Gadamer is accorded a central role within Richard Rorty's attempt to replace the epistemological tradition of 'systematic philosophy' with a culture that promotes ironic and edifying self-creation rather than foundational models of truth (Rorty, 1979, p. 358f.). Within such a culture, philosophy takes on a distinctly Gadamerian form as the 'conversation of mankind' (Rorty, 1979, p. 389). Rorty's neo-pragmatist dismissal of truth, and inclination to efface every conceptual boundary he encounters, sits ill with Gadamer's invocation of concepts, categories and distinctions throughout philosophy and its history. His notion of the conversation of mankind as an unending one – with no termination point or final vocabulary – is, however, in keeping with Gadamer's insistence on the perennially open character and ethos of the hermeneutical endeavour.

Gadamer's reluctance prematurely to foreclose dialogue by offering definitive pronouncements naturally extended to contemporary political issues, and it is this commitment to questioning and its pursuit that marks out his politics as liberal and constitutional in form. This is confirmed, for example, in his insistence on the role of the *polis* as 'the whole of our external social being' and the location of collective action and common life (Gadamer, 1999, p. 32). The place accorded to the *polis* here, as with Gadamer's preferred vocabulary of *praxis*, *ergon* and *phronesis*, is drawn from Aristotle. Politics, as a form of practical philosophy, is a part of and predicated on the Aristotelian virtues and ethical practices of wisdom and judgement (Gadamer, 1999, p. 147f.). As we have seen, Gadamer criticises aspects of Enlightenment thought associated with the valorisation of science and instrumental reasoning, and in this regard his political orientation towards 'social being' emerges in opposition to the individualism and atomisation that is characteristic of modern Western societies. This aspect of his thought has strong affinities with the communitarian critique of liberal political theory (Mulhall and Swift, 1997), within which the elaboration of tradition, narrative and interpretation by Charles Taylor (1989, 1994) and Alasdair MacIntyre (1985, 2002) are profoundly influenced by Gadamer.

For political thought Gadamer's presence is therefore evident throughout debates surrounding critical theory, deconstruction, pragmatism and communitarianism. His account of the conditions and limits of understanding does not admit ready or easy resolutions to the perennial problems of political order and power, and constantly calls into question the prejudices of Enlightenment and its cultural formations. This ethos of dialogue and cultivation is manifest throughout his work, as it was in his life. In his insistence that the tasks of interpretation are unending, Gadamer's hermeneutics is a valuable foil to rationalistic theories that attempt to contribute to political theory by bringing the discipline to a premature close, and against alternative imperatives that dissolve political understanding in unexamined ideological prejudice, conceptual indeterminacy, suspicion or mistrust.

further reading

Of Gadamer's works listed below the most significant is of course *Truth and Method*. The essays on the scope and universality of interpretation collected in *Philosophical Hermeneutics* are also especially noteworthy. Gadamer's commitment to dialogue is well represented by the interviews collected in *Gadamer in Conversation*, which also serves as a valuable overview of his life and work. Amongst the extensive secondary literature, Warnke (1987) includes discussions of Gadamer's debate with Habermas and his appropriation by Rorty. Grondin (2003) offers a more comprehensive reading. In addition to several politically oriented essays, Dostal's (2002) *Companion* contains an extensive bibliography of primary and secondary sources.

references

Dostal, R. (2002) 'Gadamer: The man and his work', in *The Cambridge Companion to Gadamer*, ed. R. Dostal, pp. 13–35. Cambridge: Cambridge University Press.
Farias, V. (1989) *Heidegger and Nazism*. Philadelphia, PA: Temple University Press.
Friedman, M. (ed.) (1999) *The Worlds of Existentialism*. London: Prometheus Books.
Gadamer, H-G. (1976) *Philosophical Hermeneutics*, trans. and ed. D. Linge. Berkeley, CA: University of California Press.
Gadamer, H-G. (1981) *Reason in the Age of Science*, trans. F.G. Lawrence. Cambridge, MA and London: MIT Press.
Gadamer, H-G. (1994) *Heidegger's Ways*, trans. J.W. Stanley. Albany, NY: SUNY Press.
Gadamer, H-G. (1998) 'Dialogues in Capri', in *Religion*, ed. J. Derrida and G. Vattimo, pp. 200–11. Cambridge: Polity Press.
Gadamer, H-G. (1999) *Hermeneutics, Religion and Ethics*, trans. J. Weinsheimer. New Haven, CT: Yale University Press.
Gadamer, H-G. (2000) *Truth and Method*, 2nd edn, trans. J. Weinsheimer and D.G. Marshall. London: Continuum.
Gadamer, H-G. (2002) *Gadamer in Conversation*, ed R.E. Palmer. New Haven, CT: Yale University Press.
Grondin, J. (2003) *The Philosophy of Gadamer*. Bucks: Acumen Press.
Habermas, J. (1977) 'A Review of Gadamer's *Truth and Method*', in *Understanding and Social Enquiry*, ed. F. Dallmayr and T. McCarthy, pp. 335–63. Notre Dame, IN: University of Notre Dame Press.
Habermas, J. (1984) *The Theory of Communicative Action*, Vol. 1: *Reason and the Rationalization of Society*, trans. T. McCarthy. Cambridge, Polity Press.
Habermas, J. (1987) *The Theory of Communicative Action*, Vol. 2: *Lifeworld and System: A critique of functionalist reason*, trans. T. McCarthy. Cambridge: Polity Press.
Lilla, M. (2002) *The Reckless Mind: Intellectuals in politics*. New York: NYRB Books.
MacIntyre, A. (1985) *After Virtue*, 2nd edn. London: Duckworth.
MacIntyre, A. (2002) 'On Not Having the Last Word: Thoughts on our debts to Gadamer', in *Gadamer's Century: Essays in honour of Hans-Georg Gadamer*, ed. J. Malpas, U. Arnswald and J. Kertscher, pp. 173–94. Cambridge, MA, and London: MIT Press.

Mulhall, S. and Swift, A. (1997) *Liberals and Communitarians*, 2nd edn. Oxford: Blackwell.

Nicholson, G. (1991) 'Answers to Critical Theory', in *Gadamer and Hermeneutics*, ed. H.J. Silverman, pp. 151–62. London: Routledge.

Palmer, R.E. (2002) 'A Response to Richard Wolin on Gadamer and the Nazis', *International Journal of Philosophical Studies* 10: 467–82.

Rockmore, T. (1992) *On Heidegger's Nazism and Philosophy*. Berkeley, CA: University of California Press.

Rorty, R. (1979) *Philosophy and the Mirror of Nature*. Princeton, NJ: Princeton University Press.

Schmidt, L. (2002) 'Hans-Georg Gadamer: A biographical sketch', in *Gadamer's Century: Essays in honour of Hans-Georg Gadamer*, ed. J. Malpas, U. Arnswald and J. Kertscher, pp. 1–13. Cambridge, MA and London: MIT Press.

Taylor, C. (1989) *Sources of the Self*. Cambridge: Cambridge University Press.

Taylor, C. (1994) *Multiculturalism and the Politics of Recognition*, expanded edn., ed. A. Gutmann. Princeton, NJ: Princeton University Press.

Theunisson, M. (1999) 'Society and History: A critique of critical theory', in *Habermas: A critical reader*, ed. Peter Dews, pp. 241–71. Oxford, Polity Press.

Vattimo, G. (1988) 'Hermeneutics as *Koine*', *Theory, Culture and Society* 5: 399–408.

Warnke, G. (1987) *Gadamer: Hermeneutics, tradition and reason*. Cambridge: Polity Press.

Weinsheimer, J.C. (1985) *Gadamer's Hermeneutics: A reading of Truth and Method*. New Haven, CT: Yale University Press.

Wolin, R. (1993) (ed.) *The Heidegger Controversy: A critical reader*. Cambridge, MA: MIT Press.

Wolin, R. (2000) 'Nazism and the Complicities of Hans-Georg Gadamer', *The New Republic* (15 May): 25–45.

Wolin, R. (2001) *Heidegger's Children*. Princeton, NJ: Princeton University Press.

8

carl schmitt

renato cristi

Carl Schmitt (1888–1985), born in Plettenberg, Sauerland, was one of twentieth-century Germany's most influential minds. A distinguished constitutional jurist who taught law in Bonn (1922–28), Berlin (1928–45) and Cologne (1933), his counsel was sought by right-wing politicians during the Weimar Republic. His authoritarian views helped consolidate Hindenburg's presidential regime in 1930. Expressing those same authoritarian views, he publicly defended the legitimacy of the Nazi revolution in March 1933, and then joined the party weeks later. As a constitutional adviser to Göring, he was rewarded with important official appointments. In 1936, after suffering persecution at the hands of the SS, he was forced to resign, but retained his academic privileges. After the war, he was jailed for a year as a security threat by the US military authorities, and later detained as a possible defendant by the Nuremberg tribunal. After his release in 1947, he refused to sign a de-Nazification certificate, claiming that he had drunk the Nazi bacillus, but had not been infected. Schmitt was not allowed to teach but continued to exercise a lasting influence within Germany's conservative circles. In comfortable retirement (a group of entrepreneurs set up a special account, called *Academia Moralis*, on his behalf), he endeavoured to clear his intellectual work from charges of anti-Semitism and doctrinaire complicity with the Nazis.

the conservative counter-revolutionary

Schmitt's extraordinary intellectual activity extended beyond the confines of constitutional law and legal theory. *Political Romanticism*, published in 1919, was his entry into political theory at a time when his country lay defeated and faced revolutionary upheavals. His aim was to bolster a conservative reaction by denying political romantics like Adam Müller and Friedrich Schlegel genuine conservative credentials. He sought to offset their inability to make commitments by favouring the resolute counter-revolutionary stand of de Maistre, Bonald and Gentz, all of whom 'took sides against the French Revolution' (1986, p. 122). With company like that he was heartened to take sides against the German democratic revolution. What characterised those Catholic counter-revolutionaries was their ability to decide politically, to confront the *either–or* head on. Schmitt's critique of political romanticism was the point of departure for his ensuing critique of liberalism. In his view, the romantic distrust for state and authority matched the liberal disposition that favours discussion, consent and the rule of law.

The intellectual task attempted by Schmitt after the promulgation of the Weimar constitution on 11 August 1919 was a bid to assert the juridical import of political notions like sovereignty, emergencies and dictatorship. These could find a place within the overtly liberal temper of the Weimar constitution. Accordingly, in his *Die Diktatur* (first published 1921), he exposed the real proportions of its Article 48. In his view, that article could accommodate either a commissarial or an absolute dictatorial role for the *Reichspräsident*, interpreted as 'bearer of constituent power' (1928, p. 202). This and other ambiguities within Weimar's constitutional design were not at all unexpected. They were part of an attempt to accommodate a 'combination of a sovereign and a commissarial dictatorship' (1928, p. 203).

Schmitt explained this uneasy adjustment as the confluence of two distinct elements: a liberal element that stressed the protection of individuals by assuring a sanctuary for their immunities and privileges, and a political element that rested on the constituent power (*pouvoir constituant*) of the people and allowed the formation of a strong state. Since a democratic *volonté générale* could override and render superfluous inalienable human rights (1928, p. 140), there was a need to distinguish between liberalism and 'the political'. A strong authoritarian state contradicted the spirit of liberalism that saw in it a threat to individual freedom. The self-imposed task assumed by Schmitt was to bring to light the tensions that lay beneath Weimar's placid liberal facade. It was one thing to recognise the sovereign rights of individuals and quite another thing to sanction the attribution of broad unlimited powers to the executive authority, powers that could even configure an absolute dictatorship. If conceived as an outlet for the constituent power, the *Reichspräsident* could be empowered to go beyond the limits set by the constitution. Schmitt sought to bring out this repressed aspect of the constitution in order to graft onto it his own counter-revolutionary programme.

The notion of sovereign dictatorship manifested Schmitt's desire to keep alive the monarchical principle, inaugurated by the French *Charte* of 14 June 1814 and the Congress of Vienna, and key to the 1871 Imperial Constitution destroyed by the German revolution. This principle allowed the monarch, as subject of constituent power, to stand above the constitution. While the function of a commissarial dictator was the preservation of the constitutional order, the aim of a sovereign dictator was to protect the constitution, or to eliminate 'the whole existing order' and to generate a new constitution. Here resided 'the meaning of the *pouvoir constituant*' (1928, p. 137).

In accordance with this line of thought, his *Political Theology* (first published 1922) explored the notion of sovereignty, so maligned by liberal thinkers and rescued from oblivion by the Catholic counter-revolutionaries. 'De Maistre spoke with particular fondness of sovereignty, which essentially meant decision' (1985a, p. 55). The foundations of a legal order rested on a transcendent source: a subject who could decide politically. Sovereignty secured the unity of the state, which could then generate a system of law. Liberal theorists reversed this order of generation. According to Kelsen, a supreme underived *Grundnorm* grounded a legal order, the central point of which was the sovereign state. There was no transcendent subject of constituent power, no *natura naturans*, no eminent legislator to which the state's highest authority could be traced. 'The basis for the validity of a norm is only a norm' (1985a, p. 19). According to Schmitt, 'Kelsen solved the problem of sovereignty by negating it ... This [was] in fact the old liberal negation of the state ...' (1985a, p. 21).

Schmitt recalled the year 1848, when the notion of authority was invoked by Donoso Cortés, 'one of the foremost representatives of decisionist thinking and a Catholic philosopher of the state' (1985a, p. 51), to justify his call for a dictatorship of the sword to offset the dictatorship of the dagger. Donoso realised that the monarchical principle had perished and that the forces of absolutism could not resist the challenge of an adversary who made similar absolutist demands. The *pouvoir constituant* claimed by monarchs had been regained by the people. Donoso observed how liberalism had unsuccessfully tried to mediate in this battle between political theists and atheists. 'According to Donoso Cortés, it is characteristic of bourgeois liberalism not to decide in this battle but instead to begin a discussion' (1985a, p. 59). Liberals evaded a decision and engaged in endless parliamentary discussions. For Donoso, 'there was thus only one solution: dictatorship' (1985a, p. 52).

A plea for a strong executive state not hamstrung by constitutional niceties was the one theme that stood out in Schmitt's early Weimar production. This theme marked the conceptual continuity of his entire intellectual production. To be strong a state needed to assert its sovereignty, its executive authority and unity, so as not to yield to the fractious temperament of civil society, the site of pluralism and liberal dissolution.

complexio oppositorum: authority and freedom

In 1923, Schmitt published *The Crisis of Parliamentary Democracy* to explain how contemporary parliamentarism had strayed away from nineteenth-century liberal ideals. As practised in the Weimar Republic, parliamentarism had 'lost its moral and intellectual foundation and only remain[ed] standing through sheer mechanical perseverance as an empty apparatus' (1985b, p. 21). Surprisingly, Schmitt joined the chorus of those who sought the reform of parliamentary practice, rather than the one calling for its demise. Deviating from his counter-revolutionary stance, Schmitt now appeared to promote a reform of parliamentary life, and for this he proposed an enquiry into the philosophical principles. The parliamentary institution had been defiled by the prevalence of democratic ideals. By opening the door to democracy, the Weimar constitution had introduced an ambiguity which had eroded parliamentary practices and weakened the executive state. Parliaments were no longer places of rational discussion. Deputies were not bound only to their conscience and free from the instructions of the electoral group they represented. Also, parliaments had ceased to be, if they ever were, open to public scrutiny. Deliberations that were supposed to be public, as required by the constitution, were in fact shrouded in secrecy.

This book marked a turning point in the development of Schmitt's thought. He now realised that liberal demands were not necessarily conjoined with democracy. Liberalism was not a *political* imperative and so its demands could be confined within the *social* sphere. This allowed for the configuration of a liberal civil society and a conservative political state. Schmitt attained this more pliant understanding of liberalism through a recast view of Catholicism. The universalism inherited from Roman imperialism allowed the Church to adjust its solemn course through history and weather continually changing circumstances. In his essay *Römischer Katholizismus und politische Form* (1st edn 1923), the uncompromising counterrevolutionary adopted a more nuanced position. Schmitt appeared no longer concerned with the Church's infallibility or its authoritarian inflexibility. On the contrary, he deflected the charge made by those who accused it of 'unlimited opportunism' and celebrated its 'marvelous elasticity' (1925, p. 6). The Church supported, and in turn denounced, liberals and democrats, republicans and legitimists, and even socialists. Tocqueville and Donoso Cortés were both devout Catholics (1925, p. 10). Political regimes were mere forms which the power of Catholicism used to its own advantage.

According to Schmitt, conservatism faced two menacing opponents: Russian communism and Western liberalism. One might argue that 'great Catholics saw liberalism as a far worse enemy' (1925, p. 52). But he urged the Church to take sides with Western European liberalism. Just as in the nineteenth century the Church 'was more akin to Mazzini than to the atheistic socialism of Bakunin' (1925, p. 53); now it should support liberalism in the name of European civilisation. Schmitt's accommodation with liberalism was brokered by his perception of the Church's flexible conservatism.

Proof of Schmitt's own liberal accommodation was his endorsement of the Weimar constitutional regime in 1924. He now disassociated the role of the *Reichspräsident* from that of the sovereign prince demanded by the monarchical principle. Alongside the constitutional division of powers, the monarchical principle determined that there should always be a residual state power, a power that could 'never be encompassed without residue by the constitutional rules' (1924, p. 236). The German Imperial constitution of 1871 acknowledged the *plenitudo potestatis* of monarchs, by means of which they could modify the constitution by decree. According to Schmitt, the *Reichspräsident*, in spite of the decisionist temper recognised by Article 48, could not be understood as a bearer of the monarchical principle. But giving up on a sovereign dictator did not hinder Schmitt from trying to turn the *Reichspräsident* into a commmissarial dictator.

Schmitt's accommodation to liberal constitutionalism had affinities with Hegel's conservative liberalism. Like Hegel, Schmitt bolstered the authority of a conservative state while attempting to preserve the autonomy of civil society. The freedom of individuals, exercised in the context of an unalloyed market economy, demanded a strong state. Schmitt's rapprochement to the Weimar system was not without caveats. So long as the possibility of a dictatorship of the proletariat remained in place, he would retain his option for a dictatorship of the opposite sign. With this insurance policy in his back pocket, he felt encouraged to affirm an intellectual allegiance to Weimar's constitutional system. In 1925, he expressed this acceptance in no uncertain terms. 'Today the revolutionary situation that lasted between November 1918 and February 1919 is over; the sovereign dictatorship of a constituent national assembly does no longer exist. For seven years now the Weimar constitution is valid in Germany' (1926, p. 27). Like Gentz, he too could also assume a more liberal attitude as long as he could free himself from the fear of revolution.

the constitution of authoritarian liberalism

'The constitution of the modern civil *Rechtsstaat* is always a mixed constitution' (1965, p. 200). This statement in Schmitt's *Verfassungslehre* (1st edn 1928) was the axis on which turned the whole argument of the book. By opting for a constitutional *status mixtus* Schmitt forswore his earlier advocacy of political absolutism. But the *Verfassungslehre* deviated significantly from the ideal constitution envisaged by liberalism. The liberal ideal (but not liberal reality) maintained a critical and negative view with respect to the political and severely limited the sovereignty of the state. 'The tendency of the liberal rule of law is to repress the political ...' (1965, p. 41). By contrast, Schmitt incorporated political and liberal elements side by side. 'The constitutions of present-day liberal states are always composed of two elements; on the one hand, rule of law principles for the protection of bourgeois freedom *against* the state, and on the other hand, the political element from which the proper state-form is to be derived' (1965, p. 41).

Schmitt was committed to proving that principles arising from opposed traditions of thought could still be blended in a viable working manner.

Genuine harmonisation required that each of the principles in the mixture be given fair recognition and that a proper balance be struck between them. The *Verfassungslehre* might then be seen as a *modus vivendi*, where liberal principles were embraced by this unforgiving critic of liberalism. But Schmitt's incorporation of liberal principles did not appear to be insincere or contrived. The *Verfassungslehre* brokered a genuine philosophical *rapprochement*, which was set out in three consecutive moments.

1. The first constitutional *status mixtus* assembled liberal and political elements. 'The liberal rule of law constitution is a mixed constitution in the sense that it blends a liberal element, in itself closed and independent, and a political formal element' (1965, p. 202). The liberal element was defined by the rule of law, or *Rechtsstaat*, which demanded 'the protection of citizens from the abuse of state power' (1965, p. 126). The political element was meant to secure the unity of the state. This unifying element could adopt different forms: monarchy, aristocracy and democracy. The juxtaposition of liberal elements and any of these political forms produced the relativisation of the latter. Absolute monarchy became constitutionally limited monarchy; absolute democracy, constitutional democracy.
2. The liberal rule of law determined that the political element ought not itself to remain unblended. Neither a fully actualised monarchy nor a fully actualised democracy, but a mixture of these political forms should be conjoined with the rule of law. Schmitt's constitutional paradigm contained a balanced mixture of the democratic, aristocratic and monarchical political forms.
3. Schmitt observed that the blending of political forms, particularly the democratic and monarchical forms, would not be possible without aristocratic mediation. Democracy and monarchy occupied opposite poles of the political spectrum. By contrast, aristocracy 'occupies the middle point between monarchy and democracy, and because of this it embodies a mixture' (1965, p. 218). Schmitt reiterated: 'aristocracy is, in a certain sense, a *mixed* state-form' (1965, p. 218).

The aristocratic state-form was not meant to be a merely regulatory paradigm, an abstract model that balanced opposed state-forms. Schmitt's constitutional realism situated this discussion of state-forms within the context of the struggles of the bourgeoisie during the nineteenth century. When the bourgeoisie stepped into the political arena, it favoured neither democracy nor monarchy. Its political exertions were aimed at the establishment of the rule of law as prevention 'against all forms of state absolutism, democratic or monarchical' (1965, p. 216). This kind of mediation fitted naturally with the aristocratic spirit, whose principle was moderation. And moderation found institutional expression in a parliamentary style of government. 'Parliamentary rule is an instance of aristocratic rule' (1965, p. 218).

Historically, parliaments were the perfect platform to defend the demands claimed by the bourgeoisie. Schmitt observed that in 1848 the bourgeoisie was able to stake an 'intermediate position' between absolute monarchy and 'expanding proletarian democracy' (1965, p. 309). Against monarchy, it asserted the democratic rights of parliaments and professed to be the genuine representative of the people. Against democracy, the bourgeoisie advocated a strong monarchical government as the best protection for private property (1965, p. 309).

After 1848, and particularly during the Weimar Republic, parliamentary rule identified itself with democracy. Here lay the root of the crisis of contemporary parliamentarism. When deputies were taken as agents or commissars of the people, parliaments lost their representative capacity. According to 'old liberalism', representatives were selected because of their abilities 'to attend to the needs of the political whole as such' (1965, p. 217). But the rise of democracy brought with it a decline in the representative nature of parliaments and the transformation of deputies into 'dependent agents of interest and electoral groups' (1965, p. 217). These observations defined the core of Schmitt's critique of Weimar parliamentarism. It was a critique directed against the one-sided actualisation of the democratic principle. Schmitt believed that the emphasis on democracy at the expense of the monarchical element was incongruous with the design of the Weimar constitution. A strong state stood out as an enduring principle in Schmitt's political theory. The constitutional *status mixtus* fostered by the aristocratic form ensured that strong monarchical characteristics would be able to tame democratic indiscipline.

Schmitt's politicisation of liberalism was not an untried idea. Schmitt attempted to retrieve the agenda of classical liberals like Constant, Hegel and Tocqueville who were not averse to deriving conservative conclusions from liberal premises. Hayek, a liberal who closely observed the authoritarian liberal compromise struck by Schmitt in Weimar, would not find it objectionable.

the concept of the political

In his *Verfassungslehre*, Schmitt deviated from standard conceptions of liberalism in order to incorporate the political aspects he saw hidden in constitutionalism. To delve explicitly into the nature of the political he published an article in 1927 entitled 'The Concept of the Political', which he later expanded into what would become his most famous book (1976).

Much earlier he had noticed how Lenin and Trotsky politicised Marxism by abandoning scientific rationalism and developing a theory of a state that relied on the direct use of force. 'The bourgeois is not to be educated, but eliminated. The struggle, a real and bloody struggle that arises here, requires a different chain of thought and a different intellectual constitution from the Hegelian construction, whose core always remains contemplative' (1985b,

p. 64). In *The Concept of the Political*, Schmitt enhanced the role of the state in Leninist fashion and excoriated humanitarian liberalism for its abdication of the political. The political has specificity and autonomy, and it intersects with the realms of morality, economy, law, aesthetics, and so on. 'The specific political distinction to which political action and motives can be reduced is that between friend and enemy' (1976, p. 26). The struggle between enemies does not mean 'competition, ... purely intellectual controversy [or] symbolic wrestling'. The notions of friend, enemy and struggle 'receive their real meaning precisely because they refer to the real possibility of physical killing' (1976, p. 33). As Schmitt saw it, Lenin's 'concrete-enemy concept' derived from Hegel, whom he now interpreted not as a contemplative, but as a political thinker in all respects (1976, pp. 62–3). Like Lenin, he rejected the liberal contraction of politics to legal and constitutional affairs. By anchoring legitimacy within established constituted powers, liberalism sought to ensure the protection required by the bourgeoisie. But legality tied the hands of the bourgeoisie in the face of emergencies. To untie them, Schmitt brought to light the affinity of sovereignty with prerogative. During periods of exception, breaking through the limits of legality did not necessarily cancel legitimacy. This earned him the epithet 'Lenin of the bourgeoisie'.

Schmitt's repudiation of liberalism was tempered by his acknowledgement that classical liberalism did not share anarchist tendencies. He recognised that liberal neutralisation and negation of the state, hence the inability to develop a political theory, had a determinate 'political meaning' (1976, p. 61). This incipient 'political' understanding of liberalism was reflected in the distinction he drew between classical liberalism and the 'pure and consequential notion of individualist liberalism' (1976, p. 70). From the latter one could not derive a specific political idea, but the former was capable of adopting a political stance. Earlier, Schmitt had detected the political significance of Locke's notions of prerogative and federative powers (1928, pp. 41–2).

This book was intended to refute the views advanced by syndicalists (Duguit, Leroy) and pluralists (Barker, Cole, Laski) who robbed the state of its sovereignty and presented it on a par with other institutions like churches, business corporations, labour unions and sports clubs. Radical liberals went even further. Franz Oppenheimer attempted the wholesale 'destruction of the state' (1976, p. 76). His radical liberalism even denied the state the role of armed protector of civil society. The political methods employed by the state implied robbery, economic onslaught and criminal behaviour. Instead, civil society meant exchange, reciprocity, equality and peace. Oppenheimer thus reversed Hegel's conception that placed the state above selfish civil society. Like Hegel, Schmitt distrusted democracy. And like Hegel, who thought that only a state that was strong could adopt a more liberal attitude, Schmitt espoused the view that a strong state was a condition for the possibility of a free economy.

strong state, free economy

On 28 March 1930, Hindenburg appointed Brüning as Chancellor without previously consulting the political parties. The new government would function as a non-parliamentary regime resting on Hindenburg's authority. This event marked the beginning of a presidential regime. In his *Der Hüter der Verfassung* (1st edn 1931), Schmitt sought to justify this regime as Weimar's only politically viable option. Much of Schmitt's work as a jurist had been devoted to demonstrating the need for an enhanced political role for the *Reichspräsident*. A consistent application of Article 48 was the procedure he had suggested. This would break the hegemony of a parliamentary system gone astray and restore the balance between legislative and executive functions. By becoming involved in what were the exclusive concerns of civil society, the state had lost its autonomy and independence. Hindenburg's presidential regime was intended to save the state by reinforcing its executive functions.

Schmitt charted the evolution of the modern state and distinguished four distinct configurations: the judicial, executive, legislative and 'total' forms of the state. A judicial state (*Juridiktionsstaat*) was discernible when a regime came to rest on jurisdictional functions. Feudalism and the American 'judicial review' exemplified this kind of state (1969, p. 75). Schmitt dismissed it as a tradition alien to Germany and Continental Europe generally. The next two configurations – the executive and the legislative state – arose as typically modern phenomena. They rested on the dualist structure that distinguished between civil society and the state. The executive state (*Regierungsstaat*) resulted from the rise of the absolutist state and found its proper expression 'in the sovereign personal will and authoritarian mandate of an executive head of state' (1932, p. 9), and was the appropriate outlet for decisionist attitudes. This was Schmitt's preferred state configuration. Parliamentarism, marked by the hegemony of the legislative functions, determined the ascent of the legislative state (*Gesetzgebungsstaat*). Schmitt defined it as the state 'ruled by impersonal, general and predetermined norms, by lasting norms of determinable and measurable content' (1976, p. 8). Typical of this state was the distinction between laws and decrees, between law and its execution. The legislative state, and its parliamentary embodiment, realised the ideal of the *Rechtsstaat*. The old Aristotelian dictum that laws and not men ought to rule implied that personal sovereignty was extinguished. Whoever claimed exercise of sovereignty, could do so only 'according to the law or in the name of the law' (1932, p. 8).

Finally, marking the disappearance of the separation between civil society and the state, civil society organised itself as a state. Schmitt employed a number of descriptions to refer to the resulting entity: economic state, cultural state, welfare state. But his most striking formula was one inspired by Ernst Jünger: total state (1969, p. 79). Schmitt maintained that the total state was most visible in the economic sphere. Abandoning the postulates of liberal state neutrality, the total state demanded extensive economic intervention and regulation. Schmitt acknowledged the factual existence of this state, but strongly opposed its constitutional entrenchment. This led to the following option: either abandon the idea of an interventionist state, or fully accept its regulatory function (1969, p. 98). At first sight, an interventionist corporatist state, either fascist or soviet, had the advantage of corresponding to the current situation. When Schmitt wrote that 'the demand for non-intervention is utopian', this was meant to apply only to the circumstances generated by the total state in Weimar. Only 'in such a situation' would intervention be advisable (1932, p. 81). But in principle, Schmitt thought that intervention was 'dangerous and erroneous', for it would weaken the unity of the state and its capacity to distinguish between friends and enemies (1969, p. 99). The form of state activity he advocated did not constitute an alternative brand of interventionism. On the contrary, it matched the non-interventionism advocated by neo-liberals like Alexander Rüstow, who explicitly agreed with his views on the strong state.

In *Legalität und Legitimität* (1932), he again postulated that the happy balance attained in the nineteenth century between executive and legislative functions could no longer be duplicated. Confronted with the weakness demonstrated by the legislative state in its ability to withstand the democratic avalanche that led to the total state, he saw that the only alternative was to turn back to a strong executive state (1932, p. 98). This coincided with his support for the authoritarian disposition of Papen's regime inaugurated on 1 June 1932, and his mounting frustration with the aims of democratic party politics. In his estimation, the state's very existence was compromised by the rise of democratic party politics and the administrative or total state. Democracy, furthermore, was responsible for weakening the unitary and decisive will of parliament. Parliament had become the 'scenario of a pluralist system' (1932, p. 90) and party-politics meant that the will of the majority shifted according to unstable compromises between heterogeneous organisations. This situation compromised the legislative state's capacity to govern. The total state obliterated the separation between civil society and the state and thus imperilled state autonomy. Schmitt proposed the retrieval of an executive state as a solution to the crisis which resulted from the extinction of an authoritarian ethos and decisionist temper that could sustain a strong state. The task of reinforcing executive state functions did not mean cancelling the autonomy of civil society and the substantive liberal values it embodied – individual liberty and private property. Schmitt condemned democracy as the matrix of the total state and espoused a strong authority necessary 'for the restoration of the free spheres and domains of life' (1932, p. 93).

A few months later, Schmitt would substantially reiterate this view in his address to a conference convened by big business in a show of support for Chancellor Papen's policies of minimum state intervention. Schmitt was invited to address this forum because he shared its liberal views on the economy. His views on a strong state and a free economy coincided with the 'new liberalism' of German economists like Rüstow, Eucken and Röpke. According to these authoritarian liberals, only a strong state could guarantee the self-regulation of the market.

In his address, Schmitt recognised that depoliticisation involved political decisions. The quantitative total state could only be confronted by a similarly total state capable of making the political decisions required to depoliticise civil society:

> In this respect the total state is at the same time an especially strong state. It is total in the sense of quality and energy. The fascist state calls itself *stato totalitario* ... A state does not allow that forces inimical to it, or those that limit or divide it may develop within in its interior ... It does not contemplate surrendering new powers of coercion to its own enemies and destroyers, thus burying its power under such formulae as liberalism, rule of law, etc. It can discern between friends and enemies. In this sense, as has been said, every true state is, and always has been, a total state. (1998, p. 217)

Schmitt did not hesitate to identify the strong state he proposed with the *stato totalitario* of Italian fascism. But his expressed sympathy for the fascist state did not necessarily translate into a support for the Nazis. He thought Schleicher represented the best chance for the realisation of his authoritarian ideas. Ultimately, not a piecemeal reform of the constitution but its overhaul would be the aim of a strong state. 'We need, in the first place, a strong state that is capable of acting and ready for its great tasks. Were we to have it, we would then create new arrangements, new institutions, new constitutions' (1998, p. 230). The foundations of the bridge that allowed him to cross the Rubicon on 24 March 1933 had been laid here.

the nazi adventure

On 24 March 1933, the Reichstag enacted an enabling law that abrogated the constitutional separation of powers. Hitler could formally inaugurate his sovereign dictatorship. On 1 April, Schmitt published a commentary defining the scope and meaning of the enabling act. He noted that the executive had gained the 'faculty to promulgate new laws to replace existing ones' (1933a, p. 456). This meant that a 'portion of power to enact constitutional laws' had been conferred on the executive. This was Schmitt's first step towards determining the revolutionary implications of the enabling act. A few weeks later, he would formally declare that the enabling act of 24 March was the provisional constitution, and a few months later he would not hesitate to acknowledge that the Weimar constitution had been abrogated. Finally, in 1936, Schmitt acknowledged that the enabling act had formally abrogated the

Weimar constitution (cf. 1988, p. 227). By bringing to the fore the notion of constituent power and the distinction between commissarial and sovereign dictatorship he was able to pave the way for the Nazi takeover and provide the legal foundations for the Nazi regime.

In his *Staat, Bewegung und Volk* (1st edn 1933), Schmitt countersigned the death certificate of the Weimar constitution. The book opened with his acknowledgement that 'the entire body of public law of the present German state rests today on its own foundation ... The Weimar constitution is no longer valid' (1933b, p. 5). Since the enabling act of 24 March complied at least formally with the provisions stipulated for constitutional reform, it could be argued that the Nazi regime remained under its aegis. Schmitt wrote this book to lay this view to rest. He interpreted the enabling act as having brought forth a new constitution. The Weimar regime had not just succumbed politically. On 24 March 1933, its philosophical underpinnings had been also demolished. 'All the principles and rules which were essential to this constitution, both ideologically and organically, have been eliminated together with all its presuppositions' (1933b, p. 5). Under his guidance the revolution was now complete.

Staat, Bewegung und Volk was the declaration of principles of this self-appointed *Kronjurist*. In it Schmitt discussed the principles that should guide the new regime. He defined the principles of the new constitution to be enacted and contrasted them with the *Grundkonzeption* of the former 'liberal-democratic' one. Its basic structure was a dyadic arrangement constituted by civil society and the state. Democratic liberalism demanded the shackling of the state, the pacification of the leviathan (1933b, p. 24). This was the aim of the political forces that had swept through the late nineteenth and early twentieth centuries and had taken away from parliaments their sovereign representative nature. As the commissioned agent of the diverse interests pullulating in civil society, parliament could not retain the autonomy required by a genuine representative function. With the leviathan securely tied and bound, civil society, fragmented by multiple parties embodying opposed interests, faced a neutralised state incapable of making political decisions which demanded drawing adversarial lines of separation from its internal enemies. 'But all these liberal-democratic fabrications and fictions ended [on 30 January 1933, when] the German Reich regained its political leadership and the German state found strength to annihilate state-inimical Marxism' (1933b, p. 31).

This description of the Weimar constitution as a dyadic system corresponded to the basic distinction Schmitt drew in his *Verfassungslehre* between the liberal and the political elements of the constitution. But now there was no explicit mention of a constitutional *status mixtus* or the aristocratic state-form conceived as the mediation between the democratic and the monarchical state-forms. From the vantage-point of the Nazi Party in power, the Weimar regime did not rest on a constitutional *status mixtus*. Schmitt saw it now as a liberal-democratic document from which monarchical possibilities were excluded. Left behind was the certainty he had felt of having his own authoritarian expectations fulfilled by the Weimar constitution.

In contrast to Weimar's bipartite scheme, the Nazi regime had developed into a basic structure made up of three elements: state, movement and the people. Distinguishable, but not separable, all three aspects of the newly created Nazi order formed an integrated totality. Those aspects could be compared to 'strands', overlapping and 'running side by side each other in orderly fashion, meeting at certain decisive points, particularly at the apex, maintaining defined and articulated reciprocal contacts and cross-connections' (1933b, p. 12). But there was no balance to be struck between state, movement and people, no veritable *status mixtus*. According to Schmitt, the elements of this triad did not have an equal standing. Both the state and the people were subordinate to and borne by the movement. The movement owed its organisation to the Nazi Party. Schmitt assigned to the movement a mediating role. It stood between the state and the people and bore them both. The movement, and not the state, was responsible for leadership. The movement had thus become a repository for the aristocratic and monarchical forms distinguished in the *Verfassungslehre*. There they were profiled as counterweights to democracy. With democracy out of the picture Schmitt could now reaccommodate his conservative principles and place them at the service of a counter-revolutionary cause.

In 1936, envious colleagues, resentful of the prestige and influence Schmitt had acquired within the Nazi party, denounced him as a Catholic opportunist who maintained Jewish connections and made jokes about the Gestapo. In spite of Goering's protection, he lost many of his privileges, but was not expelled from the party, nor did he lose his university post. After his fall from grace with the SS, he wrote a book on Hobbes (1st edn 1938). This would be his last major contribution to political theory. The focus of his attention was again the state. Whereas France and Prussia became classical embodiments of the Hobbesian state, Hobbes had failed to persuade England of the virtues of state absolutism. 'The decisionism of absolutist thinking is foreign to the English spirit' (1996, p. 80). Whereas absolutism avoided 'mixing and balancing', the English constitution was the paradigm of mixed government. In the end, the Hobbesian state also failed to flourish in Continental Europe. In Schmitt's opinion, this was due to Hobbes' choice of a biblical monster, the leviathan, as political symbol. In search of emancipation, the Jews led the way in the struggle against the state. This marked the ascendancy of individualist liberalism and the beginning of the dissolution of sovereign unity of the state. '[I]n the great historical continuum that leads from Spinoza by way of Moses Mendelsohn into the century of "constitutionalism", Stahl-Jolson did his work as a Jewish thinker – that is, he did his part in castrating a leviathan that had been full of vitality' (1996, p. 70). Friedrich von Stahl, whom he had earlier extolled, together with Hobbes, as a defender of the monarchical principle, decisionism and concrete sovereignty (cf. 1985a, p. 33), he now denounced as a Jewish precursor of the liberal *Rechtsstaat*.

During Weimar, Schmitt had criticised individualist liberalism for weakening the unity of the state. Now he attempted to trace the rise of anti-étatist liberalism back to the Jewish spirit. More than that, in this book he manifested an unreserved allegiance to Nazi anti-Semitism. On 4 October 1936, he delivered a heinous address at a Nazi high school teachers' conference, laced with racist remarks and quotations from *Mein Kampf*. To 'cleanse' German legal literature and avoid 'Jewish contamination' he proposed that scholarly citations explicitly identify Jewish authors and ideas. 'Nowadays, whoever writes "Stahl-Jolson" accomplishes more in a genuine scientific manner than by making extensive comments about the Jews, abstract and general formulas by which no particular Jew may feel singled out *in concreto*' (1936, p. 1195). In his book on Hobbes, Schmitt affixed a yellow star on German intellectuals of Jewish descent and thereby cast a long shadow over his political theory as a whole.

schmitt and modern political theory

Is Schmitt the twentieth-century Hobbes, or is he the systematic theorist of fascism? If the latter were the case, there would be no philosophically valid reason to recommend the study of his work. Only historians of ideas would benefit from the clarity and articulation of his thought when trying to make sense of the fascist hotchpotch. But if the notion of a Hobbesian Schmitt were to be seriously entertained, his work would demand philosophical attention, for it would signify a sweeping re-evaluation of liberalism.

Schmitt rejected liberalism for its negation of the political, but he acknowledged that not all liberals were anarchists and that, as a matter of fact, there were liberals who did not wish to negate the state. Nineteenth-century liberalism was sensible to the political and succeeded in reaching a formula of cohabitation with monarchy, which resulted in the simultaneous affirmation of free liberal economies and an authoritarian state. In fact, confronted with emergencies, liberals will invariably set aside the rule of law and commit arbitrary authority to some magistrate. And even in the ordinary run of things, the deeply divided nature of civil society requires the unity and stability of a strong state to allow it to withstand its own injurious, and yet inevitable, fluctuations. Private property and freedom of contract are substantive values that demand protection. Only a strong state can ensure that a free economy is left to carve out its own destiny.

Like Hobbes, Schmitt believed that the survival of a bourgeois lifestyle depended on posting constant reminders of the horrible insecurity of the state of nature. But it is a mistake to think that he was Hobbes' ally in every respect. Though Hobbes acknowledged the political, his only desire was to negate it, escape the state of nature, the *status belli*, and embrace the security and peace enforced by the state. Schmitt, in contrast, thought that the dangers facing liberal society were so acute that reincarnating a leviathan would be insufficient to save it. Schmitt conjured up a darker vision than Hobbes. He grounded his conception of the political in an anthropology steeped in theological dogma that was foreign to Hobbes. He rejected cosmopolitan ideals and the intrinsic goodness of humankind. The corruption of human nature has forced us to identify the agents of evil, brand them as enemies and secure the good will and cooperation of friends. Only war and political violence could purge us from original sin. Schmitt thus warned us against engaging in any false optimism about the natural tendencies of liberal society. But it was one thing to expose the insincere political blindness and impartiality of humanitarian liberalism; and quite another to betray without remorse its most noble ideals.

further reading

Current full-length studies on Schmitt include John P. McCormick, *Carl Schmitt's Critique of Liberalism* (New York: Cambridge University Press, 1997), William E. Scheuerman, *Carl Schmitt* (Lanham, MD: Rowman & Littlefield, 1999), Gopal Balakrishnan, *The Enemy: an intellectual portrait of Carl Schmitt* (London: Verso, 2000) and Eckard Bolsinger, *The Autonomy of the Political* (Westport, CT: Greenwood, 2001). The following are recent monographs that confront Schmitt's work from the left: Jean Cohen and Andrew Arato, *Civil Society and Political Theory* (Cambridge, MA: MIT Press, 1992), Chantal Mouffe, *The Return of the Political* (London: Verso, 1993) and David Dyzenhaus, *Legality and Legitimacy* (New York: Oxford University Press, 1997). In 2000, a special issue of the *Cardozo Law Review* was devoted to Schmitt. A comprehensive bibliography of primary and secondary sources is found in Andreas Koenen, *Der Fall Carl Schmitt* (Darmstadt: Wissenschaftliche Buchgesellschaft, 1995).

references

Schmitt, C. (1924) 'Die Diktatur des Reichspräsidenten nach Artikel 48 der Weimarer Verfassung', appended to Schmitt, 1928, pp. 23–59.

Schmitt, C. (1925) *Römischer Katholizismus und politische Form* [1st edn 1923]. Munich: Theatiner Verlag.

Schmitt, C. (1926) *Unabhängigkeit der Richter, Gleichheit vor dem Gesetz und Gewährleistung des Privateigentums nach der Weimarer Verfassung. Ein Rechtsgutachten zu den Gesetzenentwürfen über die Vermögensauseinandersetzung mit den früher regierenden Fürstenhäusern*. Berlin and Leipzig: Walter de Gruyter.

Schmitt, C. (1927) 'Die Begriff des Politischen', *Archiv für Sozialwissenschaft und Sozialpoliti* 58: 1–33.

Schmitt, C. (1928) *Die Diktatur: Von den Anfängen des modernen Souveränitätsgedankens bis zum proletarischen Klassenkampf* [1st edn 1921]. Munich and Leipzig: Duncker & Humblot.

Schmitt, C. (1932) *Legalität und Legitimität*. Munich and Leipzig: Duncker & Humblot.

Schmitt, C. (1933a) 'Das Gesetz zur Behebung der Not von Volk und Reich', *Deutsche Juristen-Zeitung* 38 (1 April): 455–8.

Schmitt, C. (1933b) *Staat, Bewegung und Volk.* Hamburg: Hanseatische Verlag.

Schmitt, C. (1936) 'Die deutsche Rechtswissenschaft im Kampf gegen den jüdischen Geist. Schlußwort auf der Tagung der Reichsgruppe Hochschullehrer des NSRB vom 3. und 4. Oktober 1936', *Deutsche Juristen-Zeitung* 41: 1194–9.

Schmitt, C. (1965) *Verfassungslehre* [1st edn 1928]. Berlin: Duncker & Humblot.

Schmitt, C. (1969) *Der Hüter der Verfassung* [1st edn 1931]. Berlin: Duncker & Humblot.

Schmitt, C. (1976) *The Concept of the Political* [1st edn 1932], trans. G. Schwab. New Brunswick, NJ: Rutgers University Press.

Schmitt, C. (1985a) *Political Theology: Four chapters on the concept of sovereignty* [1st edn 1922]. Cambridge, MA: MIT Press.

Schmitt, C. (1985b) *The Crisis of Parliamentary Democracy* [1st edn 1923], trans. Ellen Kennedy. Cambridge, MA: MIT Press.

Schmitt, C. (1986) *Political Romanticism*, trans. Guy Oakes [1st edn 1919]. Cambridge, MA: MIT Press.

Schmitt, C. (1988) *Positionen und Begriffe im Kampf mit Weimar, Genf, Versailles: 1923–1939* [1st edn 1940]. Berlin: Duncker & Humblot.

Schmitt, C. (1996) *The Leviathan in the State Theory of Thomas Hobbes: meaning and failure of a political symbol* [1st edn 1938], trans. G. Schwab and E. Hilfstein. Westport, CT: Greenwood.

Schmitt, C. (1998) 'Strong State and Sound Economy' [1st edn 1932], in *Carl Schmitt and Authoritarian Liberalism: strong state, free economy*, ed. Renato Cristi, Cardiff: University of Wales Press.

9

antonio gramsci

james martin

Antonio Gramsci (1891–1937) holds a curious place in the tradition of Continental Political Thought. He was neither a professional academic (in political philosophy or otherwise) nor did he ever write a systematic treatise or study for public consumption. Whilst most political thinkers write at some remove from day-to-day events, Gramsci's thought closely corresponded to his practical engagement with revolutionary politics. Indeed, his most extensive, abstract or 'philosophical' writings were in fact the product of his enforced removal from political activity when incarcerated in one of Mussolini's prisons.

Nevertheless, since his death, Gramsci's thought has had an enormous impact, especially on the political left in Europe and America. His ideas – particularly those concerning the state and the significance of 'hegemony', or ideological leadership, in advanced capitalism – have come to us, notoriously, in an unfinished condition. This has made them amenable to a range of different enquiries and has prevented commentators from placing any final closure on the meaning and application of his thought. Thus whilst Gramsci identified with and worked through the Marxist tradition, his ideas have been uniquely inspirational to Marxists and 'post-Marxists' alike. Today his influence is felt throughout a range of academic disciplines, including cultural and media studies, sociology, anthropology and international relations.

If there is a dominant motif in Gramsci's thought, however, it is not any specific academic theme but the compulsion to maintain a connection between theory and practice, ensuring that political philosophy and all abstract knowledge remain grounded in but also critically receptive to everyday life and popular experience. This demand, as we shall see, grew out of Gramsci's response to Italy's faltering entrance into modernity at the start of the twentieth century. Today his preferred solution of socialist revolution led by a revolutionary party may not be widely shared, but his unique ability to see the fractures in cultural and political modernity continues to mark him out as an inspirational thinker, one who took politics to be a way of transcending these divisions.

gramsci and italian modernity

Gramsci was born on the island of Sardinia, off the coast of the Italian peninsula. Like other zones on the periphery of Italian society, especially in the south, Sardinia was economically underdeveloped and culturally marginalised from the mainland. Italy's formal unification as a nation-state at the end of the nineteenth century is generally thought to have failed to develop an integral national culture or a stable institutional order. This left tensions of various kinds: between the narrow governing class and the wider populace (most of whom could not vote or indeed speak Italian), between the economically developed north and the underdeveloped south, between modernising elites and the anti-modern impulses of landowning classes and the Catholic Church. By the end of the first decade of the twentieth century, these overlapping tensions were spiralling into a widespread cultural and political crisis. Gramsci's originality as an intellectual and political leader stems from both his position as a critical 'outsider' to northern Italy's modernity and his timely intervention into its gathering storm.

Though Gramsci's early years were not comfortable, in 1911 he managed to escape these initial vicissitudes via a scholarship to study languages at the University of Turin. Nevertheless, the difficulties of life in the Italian south remained with him throughout his life and left their imprint on his intellectual and political preoccupations. Gramsci's displacement from the culture and experiences of the developed, capitalist north ensured that he arrived in Turin bearing a strong identification with the experiences of southerners who could not know the ideas of freedom and progress associated with modern society. However, Turin was then developing into the industrial powerhouse of Italian capitalism, and its sheer scale and dynamism inspired Gramsci to embrace the revolutionary socialism of the Italian Socialist Party.

Gramsci's early socialist inclinations diverged significantly from the predominant tradition of crude, positivist-inspired Marxism. That tradition encouraged other parties in the 'Second International' socialist movement, particularly the highly influential German Social Democratic Party, to view revolution as the inevitable result of ineluctable societal 'laws', an event for which revolutionary parties could only prepare but not substantially instigate. This outlook left parties in a peculiar situation of promoting revolution in principle but organising rather pragmatically around piecemeal reforms. Gramsci, however, was inspired by radical cultural critics, particularly the idealist philosopher Benedetto Croce, who repudiated the notion that society was subject to transhistorical laws. Instead, his idealism understood social change to be the creative intervention of subjective agents acting to shape the material world and to impose on it their own aesthetic and moral judgements. Against the popular Marxism and reformist practice of the Italian Socialist Party, Gramsci aligned his socialism with those looking for cultural renewal in Italian society.

Gramsci viewed the northern industrial proletariat as the agency of this renewal, a revolutionary political subject whose growing self-awareness would serve as the basis for a total transformation of Italian cultural life and the formation of a new national consciousness, taking up the project of social and political integration where the Italian bourgeoisie had manifestly failed. He undertook to cultivate an 'intense labour of criticism', encouraging a class consciousness to grow authentically from within the workers' movement and not be imposed from outside by an external force such as a political party (Gramsci, 1977, p. 11). Abandoning his studies in 1915, Gramsci took up a post as a full time left-wing journalist and committed himself to the workers' cultural education. To the decadent and self-interested bourgeoisie he counterposed, sometimes in haughty, moralising overtones, the disciplined and culturally cohesive force of the workers (see Gramsci, 1977, pp. 10–13, 17–18). In the context of deep divisions in Italy caused by its unpopular entry into the war, Gramsci presented socialism as the modernising and unifying agency of Italy's backward capitalism (Gramsci, 1993, pp. 27–30; 1977, pp. 38–47).

However, the Russian Revolution of 1917 focused Gramsci's attention on issues of concrete organisation. For him the Bolsheviks' success was evidence that revolutions are made by a unified moral force imposing its will. The Russian Revolution, he argued in contrast to the vulgar Marxism of the day, had been 'a revolution against Karl Marx's *Capital*' (Gramsci, 1977, p. 34). Moreover, the Russians had set about creating a new state (Gramsci, 1977, pp. 28–30). He soon began to direct his attention to the question of a workers' state as the concrete expression of its own collective will. In 1919 and 1920, this direction found expression in the celebrated 'factory council struggles' that briefly turned Turin into the 'Italian Petrograd'.

The factory council struggles resulted from accumulated tensions in the postwar period. Following a strike in April 1920, workers occupied the factories in September and began to manage the production process themselves (Clark, 1977). For Gramsci, the occupations anticipated a wholly new form of workers' state, one that was autonomous from liberal ideas of parliamentary government, initiated by the workers themselves. He and a small group of his fellow socialists rapidly transformed their new cultural journal *L'Ordine Nuovo* ('The New Order') into the theoretical mouthpiece of the movement. There they published articles about workers' self-management of industry, projecting an idea of the factory as a variation on the Russian 'Soviet' system.

Gramsci argued that the factories could become 'organs of proletarian power' (Gramsci, 1977, p. 66), serving as the basis for a unification of state and civil society. Where parliamentary systems divide up citizens within civil society and unify them 'abstractly' through their affiliation to the constitutional state, a genuine workers' state unifies citizens within the organisation of the production process (Gramsci, 1977, pp. 142–6). In the factory, citizens were united as 'producers' who would participate democratically in the functioning of industry through membership of 'factory councils'. That way, workers' particular labour tasks would be 'organically' linked to those of the collective (see Schecter, 1991).

Gramsci's 'council communism' was a direct challenge to the Socialist Party's *faux* revolutionism. Emphasising workers' self-emancipation through the creation of new state structures, he and his group rejected the logic of bureaucratic and elite-led party politics that left ordinary workers passive in the workplace (Gramsci, 1977, pp. 98–102, 142–6). The factory council system opposed any waiting for the revolution; instead, it proposed setting up the organs of the new state as the old one declined. Although the socialist party leadership had passed into the hands of its revolutionary wing, its executive remained sceptical of the council's ability to function as the organ of revolution. It refused fully to support the transformation of the councils into revolutionary bodies, and the movement eventually collapsed in October 1920.

Gramsci had little time to reflect on the significance of the council movement. Already, anti-communist reaction was setting in, as he himself had predicted (Gramsci, 1977, p. 191). At the Socialist Party Congress in 1921, he joined with the communist faction led by the militant Amadeo Bordiga in splitting off from the party to create the Communist Party of Italy. Committed to Lenin's 'twenty-one conditions' for being a genuinely revolutionary party (including expelling all reformists), the communists effectively substituted theoretical purism for popular organisation, and, as a consequence the party remained small and ineffectual. Gramsci's switch from being a proponent of council communism to being a Leninist party executive member may seem improbably rapid. How could he change from being a supporter of workers' revolution 'from below', to being a supporter of leadership 'from above'? The contrast is certainly striking, but Gramsci had already become aware of the limitations of the council movement, even as the occupations were underway. As early as January 1920 he had called for a party that would actively shape the 'forces eroding bourgeois democracy' (Gramsci, 1977, p. 35). After the defeat of the factory occupations, Gramsci aligned himself with the communist faction because only they offered genuinely revolutionary leadership. There is little doubt, however, that his ambition for revolution from below was seriously compromised by Bordiga's leadership of the party. Bordiga had little care for the council movement and saw his task as one of leading a tightly disciplined vanguard at a distance from workers' immediate struggles.

In the next few years, Mussolini's National Fascist Party succeeded in mobilising popular fears of revolution and discontent with the liberal government. Coming to power in 1922, the fascists set about obstructing and then dismantling the democratic system, and after 1925, building a dictatorship. The socialist and workers' movements were thrown onto the defensive. The fascists harassed, attacked and murdered workers and arrested their political leaders. Gramsci, however, was posted to Russia as the party's representative on the Executive Committee of the Communist International (or 'Comintern'). There he came into close contact with debates over the nature of Communist Party strategy as well as the intensifying conflicts amongst the Soviet leadership that eventually led to the expulsion of Trotsky.

Gramsci proved to be a reliable, if not wholly uncritical, supporter of the Soviet leadership, but he became increasingly concerned at Bordiga's view of party tactics. From 1923 he made clear his view that the party needed to be more engaged with the proletariat and peasantry in resisting fascism. He regarded Bordiga's intransigent vanguardism and economically reductive outlook as dangerously mistaken. The Soviet leadership also distrusted Bordiga and took the opportunity in 1924, whilst Bordiga was under arrest in Italy, to install Gramsci as the party leader.

In a series of analyses, Gramsci argued (against Bordiga's remaining supporters) that it was necessary actively to prepare a class alliance between workers and peasants and not to wait for an economic crisis to produce a new revolutionary uprising. Fascism, he believed, was more than just a capitalist class reaction. It had successfully mobilised the rural bourgeoisie and large landowners in order 'to become an integral movement' (Gramsci, 1978, p. 160). Without attending to the wider 'national' conditions of the Italian state, the Communist Party could not hope to revive prospects for revolution. That meant developing a strategy attentive to the unevenness of Italian capitalism – in particular, the economic and cultural underdevelopment of the south – and the 'political and organizational reserves' that, unlike in Russia, prevented relatively developed states from collapsing after economic crisis (Gramsci, 1978, pp. 400–11). In January 1926 that view was accepted at the party's Lyon Congress (Gramsci, 1978, pp. 340–75). Later that year, Gramsci penned some notes on 'Some aspects of the Southern Question' that sketched an analysis of the key role of intellectuals, such as the philosopher Croce, in functioning as ideological leaders amongst the southern middle class (Gramsci, 1978, pp. 441–62). It was necessary, he suggested there, that the communists seek out their own intellectuals to develop a strategy of ideological and political alliances amongst Italy's various classes.

Not long after making these observations, Gramsci was arrested and sentenced to 20 years in prison. His relatively short political career was now over. However, his concern with the peculiarities of Italy's history, and the need to understand these in order to develop a revolutionary strategy, continued in prison. There he was able to develop further his sense, already expanding before his arrest, that Marxist thought required a new vocabulary of political analysis if it were to grasp the uneven, yet stubbornly enduring character of modern capitalist states.

the prison notebooks and the theory of hegemony

Enforced removal from day-to-day politics afforded Gramsci the opportunity to return to deeper historical and philosophical themes and to blend these with the practical concerns that occupied him immediately prior to his arrest. The material product of this retracing and fusing of ideas was a body of writing in 3,000 pages, collected in 33 separate notebooks or *quaderni*. Written between 1929 – when the prison authorities first permitted him to write – and 1935 – after which he was too ill to continue – the *Quaderni del carcere* (or *Prison Notebooks*, see Gramsci, 1971, 1975, 1995) consisted of notes and essays of theoretical, cultural and historical analysis. With no obvious structure, no narrative start or end, some parts rewritten, and with concepts and themes weaving in and out of different sections, modifying their meaning as they went, the *Notebooks* defy any 'straight' or literal reading. In addition, Gramsci seemed to have been forced to modify his language in order to avoid attracting the attention of the prison censor.

However, what we know of Gramsci's earlier concerns can help us to establish the broad thrust of his prison writings. Central here is the concept 'hegemony' (*egemonía*) that Gramsci used in a number of related senses to tie together his ideas. For most commentators, it is this concept and the various analyses attached to it that mark the fundamental source of Gramsci's theoretical innovations.

Hegemony refers to the leadership function of one group, class or state over others. Gramsci would certainly have come across this term in debates amongst the communist parties and the Soviet Union, for it was used widely there to refer to the leading role of the working class over others in Russia. However, it was also used by Italian commentators to describe the bourgeoisie's need to unify the country culturally in the nineteenth century (see Bellamy and Schecter, 1993). Gramsci combined these political and cultural uses to underline the theoretical point that it was necessary to abandon economic reductionism in Marxist theory and to reassert the significance of ideology and politics in revolutionary struggle. Hegemony, in his usage, referred both to a theory of bourgeois class domination and to the simultaneous political and cultural strategy necessary to build up a revolutionary alliance amongst 'subaltern' or oppressed classes. The implications of these reflections were profound and marked a significant effort to advance Marxism towards a theory of politics. We shall consider his remarks on hegemony, starting with his analysis of state and civil society in class domination, and then, in later sections, turn to his efforts to reconstruct Marxism and his proposals for a revolutionary strategy.

Gramsci employed hegemony to shift the traditional Marxist emphasis away from the idea of narrow class 'interests' as the underlying force in social change. With that obsession came an interpretation of class power as primarily coercive, that is, a situation in which one set of already-formed interests is imposed upon another. Gramsci already felt that this perspective failed to grasp the ideological and political factors in play under fascism. Whilst class interests clearly were at work there, these could not in themselves explain its success. Instead, Gramsci drew attention to cultural, ideological and political – or 'superstructural' – factors as preconditions for class rule. Economic domination by a class – that is, its wealth and its control over the means of production – was not in itself sufficient for it to exercise power over society. On the contrary, he argued, it was necessary also to wield ideological and political power over other classes, groups and organisations throughout 'civil society'. The ruling class did not rule by coercion alone, but, typically in advanced capitalist societies in the 'West', by consent, too. This consensual form of rule distinguished conditions for revolution in developed capitalist societies from those of Russia. There 'the State was everything, civil society was primordial and gelatinous; in the West, there was a proper relation between state and civil society, and when the state trembled a sturdy structure of civil society was at once revealed' (Gramsci, 1971, p. 238).

Whilst furthering particular economic interests was central to a class's political objectives, it had also to persuade others to accept its domination, otherwise they would be permanently at war in a struggle of narrow self-interest. Whilst for Marx and Engels capitalist society comprised a 'more or less veiled civil war' between classes, for Gramsci, to 'fix one's mind on the military model' of strategy 'was the sign of a fool: politics ... must have priority over its military aspect' (Gramsci, 1971, p. 232). Picking up a theme that had originated in Machiavelli's writings, he claimed that a properly political analysis must involve consideration of the prevailing balance of force *and* also a consideration of the role played by consent.

The implications of these notes is important, because they reverse some of the dominant principles of classical Marxist analysis. At one point Gramsci suggested that a class must attain consent throughout civil society *prior* to achieving state power, a claim that dramatically alters the idea that revolution consists of an initial seizure of power. More often, however, he discussed consent and coercion as combined elements of class rule without implying that one necessarily preceded the other. Nevertheless, this view involved a modification of the idea of the state as a mere instrument of class rule, another of Marxism's favoured themes. Instead, Gramsci claimed the state must be viewed in two senses, one narrow and the other broad: as an apparatus of power designed to impose order ('political society') *and* as a combination of coercive force and consent in civil society. In a way not dissimilar to Hegel, this is what he called the general or 'integral' sense of the state: 'The general notion of the state includes elements which need to be referred back to the notion of civil society (in the sense that one might say that state = political society + civil society, in other words hegemony protected by the armour of coercion)' (Gramsci, 1971, p. 263).

How is hegemony exercised? Gramsci did not offer much evidence to substantiate his emphasis on consent; but he did make some crucial suggestions. First, he referred to the interventions of political society (the state in the narrow sense) in undertaking an 'ethical' function through the education system – 'to raise the great mass of the population to a particular cultural and moral level' – and also, in a negative way, through the legal system. Second, he pointed out that in civil society there exists 'a multitude of other so-called private initiatives ... which form the apparatus of the political and cultural hegemony of the ruling classes' (Gramsci, 1971, p. 258). These 'private initiatives' might include newspapers, churches, charities and other organisations that are formally independent of the state apparatus but which disseminate ideas and values supportive of the ruling class.

It is clear, then, that by 'consent' Gramsci did not mean a rationally agreed 'contract' in the classical liberal sense, or even a parliamentary democratic method of reconciling different interests. Rather, he understood consent as a form of 'intellectual and moral leadership', a kind of ideological power exercised over subjects' consciousnesses. Thus Gramsci also returned to the role of 'intellectuals' as agents of class hegemony. By intellectuals he understood not professional academics but all those who work with ideas and knowledge: 'all men are intellectuals, one could therefore say: but not all men have the function of intellectuals' (Gramsci, 1971, p. 9). Intellectuals were defined by their social function as disseminators of truths, whether they were scientists, engineers, journalists, philosophers or teachers. It was they who brought ideas to ordinary people and justified these as universal and practically useful truths. 'Organic' intellectuals, as Gramsci called them, helped organise their class by conferring on it a sense of purpose and identity beyond its narrow 'economic-corporate' interests. Other types of intellectual included the 'traditional' variety that comprised members of classes no longer in the ascendant, such as ecclesiastics or, indeed, philosophers.

marxism and ideology

The philosophical target of Gramsci's analyses in the *Notebooks* lay principally in the 'scientific' Marxism of the time, particularly orthodox accounts of historical materialism then circulating amongst the Soviet leadership. As with his early writings in Turin, Gramsci was excoriating in his opposition to positivist Marxism, accusing it of 'primitive infantilism'. Now, however, he endeavoured to reconstruct Marxism by taking full account of the insights that he believed could be culled from Italy's own philosopher of history, Croce. Properly readjusted to incorporate Croce's emphasis on values and ideas and their basis in practical experience, Marxism could become what Gramsci called a 'philosophy of praxis'. That is, Marxism could be both a theory of, and a practical guide to, revolutionary action.

In his critique of vulgar Marxism, Gramsci had a precise text in mind: Nicolai Bukharin's *The Theory of Historical Materialism* of 1921. A deliberate attempt to popularise Marxism as a science of history based on the primary determination of society by economic relations of production, Bukharin's book exemplified for Gramsci all that was wrong in positivism. By reducing Marx's thought to the discovery of self-sufficient laws, Bukharin had assimilated it to a mechanical sociology, replacing the 'historical dialectic ... by the law of causality and the search for regularity, normality and uniformity' (Gramsci, 1971, p. 437). Thus Bukharin effectively ruled out Marxism's critical, political engagement with human experience and practice. 'Scientific' laws presuppose a passive humanity whilst 'political action tends precisely to rouse the masses from passivity' (Gramsci, 1971, p. 429). Vulgar economism simply misinterpreted the role of subjects in constituting their own world. Ideology was dismissed as 'pure appearance', and the role of subjective motivations in stimulating or hindering revolutionary practice was ruled out of analysis (see Gramsci, 1971, pp. 376–7).

Gramsci argued that the antidote to economic reductionism and positivist scientism was a return to the insights of idealism, that is, to its positive evaluation of ideas and beliefs. Thus the philosopher Croce figures centrally in the *Notebooks* as a critical interlocutor, a source from whom Gramsci struggled to separate wheat from chaff. Croce's so-called 'historicist' philosophy had set out a non-teleological view of history as the constant working-out of human creativity: ideals and values were inseparable from the contingent problems individuals face in their daily lives. All thought and meaning, therefore, was bound up with immediate historical circumstances, and no outlook – however 'scientific' – could claim to be 'outside' history.

For Gramsci, when pared of its excessively liberal trappings, this philosophy could be assimilated into historical materialism in order to rebalance the scales, opening up Marxism to the contingency of history and the importance of ideals and beliefs in motivating, as well as obstructing, historical change (Gramsci, 1971, pp. 442–3). Historical materialism, he argued, should lay more stress on the *historical* and less on the *materialism* of its terms (Gramsci, 1971, p. 465). In so doing, emphasis would be placed on actual human practice, on the ideas that motivate social classes and give them a conscious sense of their surroundings, rather than on abstract notions of interests. Of course, for Gramsci, Croce's philosophy was itself excessively idealistic, focusing too much on creative subjects and not enough on the material circumstances within which they become conscious. This had the effect of eliding any sense of material conflict and overstating the self-sufficiency of human creativity. Gramsci's proposed philosophy of praxis, therefore, was designed to conjoin Marxism and idealism by detaching their insights from an overemphasis on either economic conditions or subjective creativity. Praxis implied the dialectical interplay of consciousness and materiality, and it was only by grasping this mutual interdependence that Marxism could succeed. Marxism, too, was a philosophy that grew from genuine historical experience and social contradictions (Gramsci, 1971, p. 421). The important task was not to make it a 'speculative' theory, but to make it a philosophy that engaged with real experience and laid the foundation for a new form of civilisation.

towards a proletarian hegemony

The *Prison Notebooks* are not replete with direct recommendations for revolutionary strategy. This would have been impossible given the conditions under which they were written. Nevertheless, Gramsci made a number of important remarks that set out a view of revolution suited to conditions in which the bourgeoisie had succeeded, to some extent, in establishing a hegemony over civil society. In that context, revolution was conceived, not purely as a moment of violent rupture from the old order – what Gramsci termed a 'war of manoeuvre' – but as a *process* of cultural and political resistance that gradually generated an alternative 'bloc' of class support around the interests of the proletariat. Gramsci called this a 'war of position', that is, a situation comparable to the military strategy of gradually taking key positions in the defences of the enemy so as to ensure that the final assault (the classic moment of revolutionary violence) would not be defeated (Gramsci, 1971, pp. 235–9). Having conceived bourgeois domination in terms of that class's capacity to shore up ideological and political support throughout key sectors of civil society, Gramsci's view of revolution was of a process disassembling the hegemonic bloc and rebuilding consent around a new class leadership.

The key agency in this hegemony-building project was the political party, conceived as a 'Modern Prince'. Whereas Machiavelli invested the successful prince with all the virtues and skills necessary for strong political leadership, Gramsci transposed this function to the collective agency of the party. Here he was drawing on a common Italian understanding of Machiavelli's *Prince* as an agency of national unification. The Modern Prince, therefore, was no isolated vanguard preparing only to storm the palace at the key moment. More than that, it was an agency of cultural and moral reform. Drawing on Sorel's idea of 'myth', Gramsci argued that the party had to conceive its task, in part, as a symbolic one, that is, the 'creation of a concrete phantasy which acts on a dispersed and shattered people to arouse and organise its collective will' (Gramsci, 1971, p. 126).

Gramsci's comments on the party as a cultural as well as a political force seem to position him outside what is commonly understood as Leninism, the idea of the party as an elite vanguard preparing a revolution external to the working class. The Modern Prince appears much more inclusive an organisation than that in the Bolshevik theory of the party expounded by, for example, Bordiga. However, it is clear from other comments that Gramsci was trying to reconcile two opposing views of party organisation. In his conception, the party remained the leading agency of revolution, but it would lead by engaging with the experience of working people and the peasantry: 'a matching of thrusts from below with orders from above' (Gramsci, 1971, p. 188). Thus the party had to be a disciplined organisation based on a commitment by all its members to the central party line, yet it had to work amongst subaltern classes and win their support. The party had to be the source of commands, yet develop its own intellectuals amongst the highly skilled workers of industrial capitalism. It had to display a commitment to Marxism as a worldview, but also understand the commonsense attitudes of the peasant classes and draw them in to the party. Gramsci expressed this dual logic at one point as a combination of 'feeling' and 'knowing', producing amongst the 'simple' masses a 'critical self-consciousness' that would transform their commonsense worldview (see Gramsci, 1971, pp. 418, 330–1, 334).

It is in Gramsci's notes on party strategy that many of the latent tensions in his theory of hegemony come to the fore. Distinctions such as force/consent, intellectuals/masses, feeling/knowing, and war of manoeuvre/position here involve issues of judgement and are not just abstract principles. It is necessary in political action to decide when one term might have priority over the other; when, for example, classes must be regarded as enemies rather than potential allies, when intellectual leadership must be asserted over the views of mass membership, when revolutionary assault must substitute wars of position, and so forth. More than any other Marxist, Gramsci's idea of revolutionary strategy was sophisticated enough to incorporate these distinctions. But he did not offer a satisfactory way of reconciling them. Despite his insistence on 'democratic centralism' and an 'organic' relation between leaders and led (Gramsci, 1971, pp. 188–90), Gramsci provided no reasoning that could ensure that the party would not become an instrument of repression or authoritarian violence against dissenters.

Nor did Gramsci say much about future communist society. Again, that might be too much to expect given his circumstances. However, what suggestions there were did give an indication of his reasoning. For Gramsci, proletarian hegemony was rooted in the experience of the industrial working class, even if that class required leadership from the party. Gramsci devoted a whole notebook to what he called 'Americanism and Fordism' (see Gramsci, 1971, pp. 279–318). This referred to the forms of industrial organisation based on routinised production-line techniques developed by the car manufacturer Henry Ford, which were then spreading across Europe. As an early observer of the expansion of these techniques, Gramsci was aware that Fordism was emerging as the basis of a whole new form of social (and not just economic) organisation based on the deep incorporation of the working class into industrial society and the extension of state functions. In short, Fordism was the economic basis to a new form of capitalist society. Although Gramsci could not foresee the development of Fordist mass consumer societies in the postwar period, he was attuned nevertheless to the basis of class hegemony in the restructuring of capitalism then under way.

For Gramsci, the organic intellectuals of the working class had to come from this material basis in economic production. The engineers and mechanics, production managers and designers, would supply the intellectual foundations for a new hegemonic commonsense and a new civility. Gramsci looked forward to what he described as the formation of a 'regulated society', as workers' self-management rendered a separate state unnecessary. In this utopian view, not uncommon to Marxists as they projected their ideas into the future, civil society would effectively 'absorb' the state, and the apparatus of coercion would give way to a society based entirely upon consent (see Gramsci, 1971, p. 253).

gramsci's legacy

In the 1960s and 1970s, Gramsci's ideas were at the forefront of an intellectual revival of Marxism, especially in Italy and France. His emphases on subjective agency in revolutionary politics, on the role of ideology and consent in understanding the survival of capitalism, his analyses of the historic weaknesses of the Italian bourgeoisie in developing its own state, and his views on the party and its capacity to lead a 'national-popular' rather than class-sectarian politics, all became crucial areas of discussion as postwar Western economies began to falter. In Italy, Gramsci's thought was the point of reference for a variety of debates concerning the strategy of the Communist Party and its ability to advance a pluralistic and democratic politics distinct from Soviet authoritarianism (see Bobbio, 1979; Femia, 1981; Salvadori, 1979).

Outside of Italy, Gramsci emerged as the Marxist 'theoretician of the superstructures', of developed or 'Western' capitalism, and hence a vital source for radicals who wanted to avoid the stale, reductive and deterministic Marxism of the Stalin era. Unlike other Marxist thinkers of his age, Gramsci's notes offered sketches for political analysis, posed problems about state power rather than dogmatic solutions, and provided a range of terminology concerning class political domination that could be extended into a variety of contexts. With the arrival of new translations, the theory of hegemony provided a means of focusing on the peculiarities of western capitalism, in particular its complex ideological formations, its form of state and the symptoms of its decline.

In the early 1960s Gramscian analyses were published in journals such as *New Left Review* by the Marxist historians Perry Anderson (1964, 1992) and Tom Nairn (1964, 1981), who used this method to examine the peculiarities of the British state. A decidedly more theoretical approach to Gramsci's work was taken by Nicos Poulantzas (1973, 1978), who assimilated hegemony into the 'structuralist Marxist' framework of Louis Althusser. Though critical of Gramsci's Hegelian background (that is, the influence of Croce), Poulantzas attempted to wrest the theory of hegemony from what he viewed as a simplistic ('humanist') account of politics and ideology. For him hegemony was not simply one class's ability to propagate 'its own' worldview, as British Marxists had implied. Rather, it depended more on the state's capacity to build a 'power bloc' of support than on a class's ideological predominance. So long as capitalist relations of production cohered over time, it did not matter exactly *which* ideology dominated, that of the bourgeoisie, the aristocracy or some mixture of both. This state-centred approach to hegemony was later refined to considerable effect in the work of Bob Jessop (1990).

As postwar capitalist democracies stumbled through economic and political crises in the 1970s, Gramsci's work was also used to theorise the unsteady and shifting balance of forces. In the work of Stuart Hall and others in the Birmingham Centre for Contemporary Cultural Studies (BCCCS), Gramsci's analyses helped illuminate this volatile conjuncture from the perspective of popular culture. Gramsci's writings on ideology and common sense and their role in supporting and contesting structures of power provided a vital source for theorising the way that wider structural forces are translated into 'lived' experience. The BCCCS used Gramsci's ideas to make connections between the symbolic worlds constructed through the media and popular culture and the structural crises of capitalism (Hall et al., 1978). Here the emphasis was on how 'subcultures' or media campaigns helped construct popular narratives that translated unsettling social change into a meaningful story.

In the early 1980s Hall's use of Gramsci's ideas culminated in his seminal account of 'Thatcherism', the new ideology of the British Conservative Party under the leadership of Margaret Thatcher. Hall defined Thatcherism as a hegemonic project aimed at rebuilding popular consent to the British state through a novel fusion of neo-liberal and traditional conservative values (Hall, 1988). By working at the level of common sense and not just party ideology or class interests, Thatcherism redefined the terms by which public policy and the roles of the state and citizen were understood. Others, however – in what was a common concern amongst Marxists eager to emphasise 'material' as opposed to 'ideal' factors – maintained that Hall's focus was too much on ideology and not enough on the state and capitalism (Jessop et al., 1988).

Perhaps the most controversial deployment of Gramscian themes to date comes in Ernesto Laclau and Chantal Mouffe's theoretical re-elaboration of hegemony (Laclau and Mouffe, 1985). Setting aside the 'sociological' uses of Gramsci's thought to examine specific ideologies or state forms, Laclau and Mouffe read hegemony as a theory of the 'articulation' or linking-together of social orders. For them Gramsci's great insight was to conceive society not as something governed by an economic essence but as constructed in a radically contingent way. Hegemony was not merely a political addition to Marxist theory of economic determination, but rather exposed that theory's fundamental incoherence. Its 'logic', they argue – in underscoring the need for political intervention to make capitalist society cohere and survive – is to reveal how society is not governed by *any* necessary determination, economic or otherwise.

Taking this logic further than did Gramsci – and by inflecting it with insights from 'poststructuralist' theories of language such as those of Derrida, Foucault and Lacan – Laclau and Mouffe reject the idea that society is an 'objective' order, one knowable through a properly scientific theory, in which economic classes and class interests have ultimate priority. They argued instead that the working class has no 'necessary' or objective interest in overcoming capitalism; thus left-wing politics need not be conceived as a strictly anti-capitalist struggle led by the working class. This view permits contemporary radicals to view class as merely one historical source of progressive hegemonic politics and also enables them to legitimate the democratic struggles of non-class social movements.

Laclau and Mouffe's work takes Gramsci's insights far beyond his explicit theoretical and political agenda. For many critics, particularly Marxists, they have too willingly embraced a postmodern framework emphasising language and 'discourse' as opposed to 'social and economic structures' (for a useful discussion, see Ives, 2004). This, it is claimed, loses touch with the social basis for politics and actually disarms radical politics of its foundational critique, a desire that inspires much of the recent uses of Gramsci in the study of international politics (see Gill, 1993). Whilst many of these criticisms are wildly overstated and often elaborated in the very terms that Laclau and Mouffe themselves reject, it is certain that in making the transition to a 'post-Marxist' outlook they have ensured that Gramsci's insistence on the link between theory and practice remains as problematic than ever.

conclusion

For all its lack of systematic unity and scholarly precision, Gramsci's work nevertheless places him firmly in a Continental tradition of thought. His rejection of positivism and scientific Marxism, his concern with subjectivity, ideology and lived experience, and his focus on the state and the active building of civil orders, all underscore a sense of politics and 'the political' that is more subtle and more inclusive than that of other Marxists either before or after him. Combining both a modern, 'republican' sense of politics as the formation of a unified public alongside an older, Machiavellian awareness of the intrinsic unevenness and uncertainty of political action, Gramsci succeeded in theorising politics in two different registers. For this reason, despite the evident incompleteness of his work, Gramsci's insights continue to speak to a variety of contemporary concerns at some distance from his own socialist project.

further reading

Gramsci's work is best accessed directly in the available selections of translations of his writings both before prison (Gramsci, 1977; 1978; 1993) and during incarceration (1971; 1995), as well as his prison letters (1994). Columbia University Press has begun to publish a full translation of the Prison Notebooks by Joe Buttigieg, a number of which are now available. Forgács (1988), however, offers the best short collection of his writings as a whole. Biographical details can be found in Fiori (1990) and Davidson (1977). Theoretical assessments of Gramsci's Marxism vary in their focus. For an emphasis on his intellectual and political context, see Bellamy and Schecter (1993); on interpretations amongst later Italian communists, see Femia (1981). Laclau and Mouffe's (1985) approach is complex, and helpfully presented in Torfing (1999). A comprehensive collection of the last 30 years of scholarly studies can be found in Martin (2002).

references

Anderson, P. (1964) 'Origins of the Present Crisis', *New Left Review* 23: 26–53.

Anderson, P. (1992) *English Questions*. London: Verso.

Bellamy, R. and Schecter, D. (1993) *Gramsci and the Italian State*. Manchester: Manchester University Press.

Bobbio, N. (1979) 'Gramsci and the Conception of Civil Society', in *Gramsci and Marxist Theory*, ed. C. Mouffe, pp. 21–47. London: Routledge and Kegan Paul.

Clark, M.N. (1977) *Antonio Gramsci and the Revolution that Failed*. New Haven, CT, and London: Yale University Press.

Davidson, A. (1977) *Antonio Gramsci: Towards an intellectual biography*. London: Merlin Press.

Femia, J.V. (1981) *Gramsci's Political Thought: Hegemony, consciousness, and the revolutionary process*. Oxford: Clarendon.

Fiori, G. (1990) *Antonio Gramsci: Life of a revolutionary*. London: Verso.

Forgács, D. (ed.) (1988) *A Gramsci Reader: Selected writings, 1916–1935*. London: Lawrence & Wishart.

Gill, S. (ed.) (1993) *Gramsci, Historical Materialism and International Relations*. Cambridge: Cambridge University Press.

Gramsci, A. (1971) *Selections from the Prison Notebooks of Antonio Gramsci*, eds Q. Hoare and G. Nowell-Smith. London: Lawrence & Wishart.

Gramsci, A. (1975) *Quaderni del carcere*, ed. V. Gerratana. Turin: Einaudi.

Gramsci, A. (1977) *Selections from Political Writings (1910–1920)*, ed. Q. Hoare. London: Lawrence & Wishart.

Gramsci, A. (1978) *Selections from Political Writings (1921–1926)*, ed. Q. Hoare. London: Lawrence & Wishart.

Gramsci, A. (1993) *Pre-Prison Writings*, ed. R. Bellamy. Cambridge: Cambridge University Press.

Gramsci, A. (1994) *Letters from Prison*, 2 vols, ed. F. Rosengarten. New York: Columbia University Press.

Gramsci, A. (1995) *Further Selections from the Prison Notebooks*, ed. D. Boothman. London: Lawrence & Wishart.

Hall, S. (1988) *The Hard Road to Renewal: Thatcherism and the crisis of the left*. London: Verso.

Hall, S. et al. (1978) *Policing the Crisis: Mugging, the state, and law and order*. London: Macmillan.

Ives, P. (2004) *Language and Hegemony in Gramsci*. London: Pluto Press.
Jessop, B. (1990) *State Theory: Putting the capitalist state in its place*. Cambridge: Polity Press.
Jessop, B. et al. (1988) *Thatcherism: A tale of two nations*. Cambridge: Polity Press.
Laclau, E. and Mouffe, C. (1985) *Hegemony and Socialist Strategy: Towards a radical democratic politics*. London: Verso.
Martin, J. (ed.) (2002) *Antonio Gramsci: Critical assessments of political philosophers*. London: Routledge.
Nairn, T. (1964) 'The British Political Elite', *New Left Review* 23: 19–25.
Nairn, T. (1981) *The Break Up of Britain*. London: Verso.
Poulantzas, N. (1973) *Political Power and Social Classes*. London: New Left Books.
Poulantzas, N. (1978) *State, Power, Socialism*. London: New Left Books.
Salvadori, M. (1979) 'Gramsci and the PCI: Two conceptions of hegemony', in *Gramsci and Marxist Theory*, ed. C. Mouffe, pp. 237–58. London: Routledge and Kegan Paul.
Schecter, D. (1991) *Gramsci and the Theory of Industrial Democracy*. Aldershot: Avebury.
Torfing, J. (1999) *New Theories of Discourse: Laclau, Mouffe and Žižek*. Oxford: Blackwell.

10

georg lukács

timothy hall

Georg Lukács (1885–1971), the Hungarian Marxist philosopher and aesthetician, is one of those ambivalent figures of twentieth-century social and political thought whose influence is widely acknowledged yet whose writings languish for the most part in a state of critical neglect. The son of a wealthy Hungarian banker, he was to become one of the most influential figures in Marxist thought in the twentieth century. His literary career spanned many generations and included writings on philosophical aesthetics, literary theory, social philosophy and politics. His political career, on the other hand, involved a brief spell as People's Commissar for Culture in the ill-starred Hungarian Workers Republic in 1919, and also a key role in the 1956 Hungarian uprising against Soviet forces. He was a principal figure in the left opposition to the emerging Soviet orthodoxy of the 1920s. The mere mention of his name today, however, suffices to summon up a host of stock debates: these range from arguments against the authoritarian tendencies of his thought as expressed in concepts like 'imputed' class consciousness to claims of its sheer obsolescence in adhering to 'macro' historical agencies and a teleological conception of history (see Kolakowski, 1972). At a time, however, in which there has been a marked movement towards the centre ground in critical social theory, it will perhaps be illuminating to look again at Lukács' original project and to assess where we stand in relation to it. Needless to say, such a second glance cannot proceed by prejudging the outcome by placing Lukács' thought in a received history. Rather 'our' standpoint must be allowed to emerge immanently from the experience of the limits of Lukács' project. Such a strategy would enable us to arrive at a more accurate picture of his place in the modern tradition and also perhaps enrich a debate in contemporary critical social theory that has tended to polarise between Habermas' neo-liberalism and Adorno's aesthetic modernism.

By Lukács' original project I refer to his 1923 *History and Class Consciousness* and the writings leading up to it (see Lukács, 1990). This work, written in exile in Vienna in the immediate aftermath of the fall of the Hungarian Soviet Republic, sets out Lukács' critique of modern social institutions as 'reified'. It argues that the possibility of social critique is tied to the emergence of the proletariat as a social class and that a critical social theory is an extended elaboration of the experience of this class in modern society. As such it departs from the view that the value of a social theory lies in its strict adherence to scientific method, whether this is thought of as the 'value-neutrality' of positivist conceptions of social science or as the suspension of normative assumptions in Weber's conception of social scientific methodology. For Lukács, all social theories proceed from definite standpoints, and truth is to be thought, not in representational terms, but in the success it meets with in elucidating a contradictory social experience. This leads us to the last key claim in the work, namely that a critical social theory is to be understood as a *praxis*. That is to say, as an attempt by the proletariat at self-understanding, in the face of their inability to make sense of themselves and their relation to the world in terms of existing categories of thought and action – an attempt which is at one and the same time a form of activity and a transformation of the social world.

My concern will be to set out and elaborate these claims, drawing out their implications and anticipating received readings along the way. Lukács' claim, for example, that a critical social theory is to be understood as a *praxis* seems to set him at odds with the dominant concern in contemporary social theory, namely to uncover a normative basis for social theory – at least if this is taken to mean the discovery of some founding normative principle that can be action-guiding. The chapter will then proceed to an evaluation of Lukács' position. To what extent, for example, is his social theory based on a classical Marxian conception of history as the product of a struggle between social classes? Such an analysis and evaluation will, I suggest, reveal the perhaps surprising conclusion that Lukács' conception is not as redundant as is often portrayed.

theory, truth and history

Lukács' social and political thought is frequently characterised as Marxist even though it makes some substantial departures from orthodox theory. The problem is that these departures are often difficult to see because of the heavily Marxist terminology used in *History and Class Consciousness*. His preferred strategy seems to be to retain, wherever possible, the classical terminology and to transform its meaning from within. This of course means today that his work is widely open to misinterpretation as the extent of his departure from classical Marxist theory is constantly underestimated.

Lukács, for example, defines 'historical materialism' as the 'self-knowledge of capitalist society' (Lukács, 1990, p. 229). At first glance this sounds a very unpromising claim if we understand by historical materialism the fundamental 'laws of motion' of historical development. Thus, for example, new productive forces, such as machinery or an industrial labour force, come to exert a critical pressure on existing productive relations and – insofar as these relations determine all others in society – social relations in general. The result of this pressure is a breaking of the 'fetters' of existing relations and a reorganisation of society on this basis. The creation of a concentrated, urban, industrial labour force is as decisive a factor in the transformation of capitalist society as the application of technology to industry was to feudal society (see Marx, 1971). If historical materialism is understood in this way – that is, as an abstract philosophy of history comprehending the transition from feudal to capitalist society as much as the transition from capitalist to socialist – then Lukács' claim appears to mean the following: at a certain point in historical development – that is, in the transition from capitalism to socialism – the laws of historical development themselves become comprehensible. This means that the historical process itself is rendered transparent and history effectively comes to an end in coming to be comprehended under laws. This 'scientific' knowledge also presents an infallible basis for action, as everything undertaken by the proletariat is to be seen in the light of liberating the new society from the repressive fetters of the old.

If indeed this were what Lukács meant, his social and political thought would hold little interest for us. However it is more than clear that this is *not* what he means. To begin with, Lukács is careful to stipulate that 'historical materialism' – however we are to understand this – is the self-knowledge of *capitalist* society – not society as such. It therefore affords us an insight into the *capitalist* historical process and not the historical process as such. On this restriction of the scope of historical materialism Lukács' is adamant:

> The substantive truths of historical materialism are of the same type as were the truths of classical economics in Marx's view: they are truths within a particular social order and system of production. As such, but only as such, their validity is absolute. (Lukács, 1990, p. 228)

Whatever is understood by 'historical materialism', one thing that it cannot be is an ahistorical theory of historical development. In fact this conclusion would be plainly absurd with the nomological form of the theory giving the lie to the historical content. Indeed given the basic premise of Marx's critique of classical political economy – that it extrapolates the basic characteristics of capitalist societies and mistakes them for universal characteristics of any society whatsoever – it would be a palpable absurdity to repeat this error with history itself.

Marxian social theory is the self-knowledge of capitalist society. As such its insights are restricted to the modern social world. It offers no insight into precapitalist societies with different social structures and perhaps more importantly it has nothing to say about postcapitalist societies. Again, on this last point, Lukács is explicit. Whilst the truths of historical materialism have an absolute validity in respect of capitalist society:

> [t]his does not preclude the emergence of societies in which by virtue of their different social structures other categories and other systems of truth prevail. (Lukács, 1990, p. 228)

Lukács understands the truth of Marxian social theory not in representational terms – that is, not in terms of the accuracy with which it represents or models the social world in thought – but in praxical terms. Crudely stated, a social theory is true to the extent that it succeeds in realising itself, and, in so doing, transforming the social world (Lukács, 1990, pp. 198–9). In postcapitalist societies it is quite possible for social theories to be true in radically different ways. Praxis has no monopoly on the concept of truth.

These preliminary considerations should cast considerable doubt on the summary dismissal of Lukács as an orthodox Marxist. For Lukács, Marxian social theory is the self-knowledge of *capitalist* society. As such it cannot represent the 'basic laws of motion' of history. Nor can it form the dogmatic and infallible basis of a theory of class action. Nor, for that matter, is it a theory that contemplates the end of history and the entrance into a realm of universal freedom. Insofar as its application is restricted to modern capitalist societies and the forms of social domination specific to these, its 'prescriptions' do not imply that social relations can be rendered transparent: nothing precludes the possibility of the emergence of new societies with different social structures along with different and unanticipated forms of social domination.

the economic structure of modern societies

However, even if we concede that Lukács' conception of social theory is free of dogmatic commitments to a materialist philosophy of history it surely remains 'classical' in one important sense, namely in its reductivism. Lukács does after all assert that modern societies have an 'economic structure' (Lukács, 1990, p. 229). What can this mean if not that the key to understanding society lies in understanding its specific mode of production – a possibility unique to modern capitalist society with its purely economic articulation of social classes? If Marxian social theory is the self-knowledge of capitalist society, and if the key to understanding the latter lies in its mode of production, then his account is surely reductive because it supposes that society and culture can only be understood through their material-economic relations. Thus if we suppose that an understanding of society follows from an analysis of its mode of production then we are attributing a primacy and determinacy to the economic aspect of social existence in respect of all others. This is historically wrong and methodologically reductive, as Weber demonstrated in *The Protestant Ethic and the Spirit of Capitalism* (see Weber, 1976). In this study he showed how certain religious and cultural factors – ascetic ways of life in the early Protestant sects – were the precondition for the emergence of capitalism and not the reverse. These cultural and religious factors gradually disappear or, like the dignified aspects of a constitution, sink into empty ritual, leaving the economic practice without the religious worldview. The crucial point for Weber, however, was that these factors were central to the emergence of capitalism and to the economic practices that characterise it.

To understand why Lukács' conception of social theory is not reductive will, to a large extent, involve understanding Weber's influence on it. Weber, his friend and mentor in Heidelberg in the interwar years, exercised a profound and decisive influence on his thought, especially in respect of the shortcomings of classical Marxist social theory. This influence is discernible, centrally, in his pivotal claim that modern social relations are reified. In this concept Lukács first read Weber *against* Marx and then a distinctly Hegelian Marx back *against* Weber.

Modern societies have, in Lukács' view, an 'economic structure', but this does not mean that society as a whole can only be understood through its economic relations – that is, through its relations of production, distribution, exchange and consumption (Lukács, 1990, p. 29). Lukács argues that in modernity the social structure fragments into separate and distinct sectors of social activity. These sectors – the economy, the legal sphere, the state and the cultural sphere – become autonomous. As self-regulating spheres of social activity they become autonomous from one another and also from human intervention and control. Laws and regularities governing the economic sphere are, for instance, distinct from the sociological laws governing the familial sphere or the behavioural laws investigated by political science. Lukács' conception of the structure of modern societies is closer to Weber's than it is to Marx's. Whereas Marx viewed the modern bureaucratic state as an essentially bourgeois institution guaranteeing through its judicial system and police force the laws of contract and property (see Marx and Engels, 1984), Weber tended to view the development of the modern state as a prerequisite for capitalism. A rational system of law and a highly centralised bureaucratic state were essential for the emergence of a modern capitalist economy because, as rational developments, they reduced the uncertainty and unpredictability of the social world. On Weber's integrated account of the structure of modern societies, far greater emphasis was given to the social, legal-political and cultural contexts of capitalist economies – on the reciprocal conditionings and interdependencies, without which a capitalist economy cannot develop.

The implications of this are far-reaching. On the classical Marxist reading the state and the legal system are viewed as 'superstructural' formations whose existence can only really be explained with reference to the mode of production that gave rise to them. This suggests a one-way determinacy of economic factors on legal and political factors that is simply not borne out in historical experience. Whilst many orthodox Marxists concede the capacity of the legal-political and the cultural spheres to react back upon the economic, the fact that an independent reality is withheld from these spheres indicates that its capacity for doing so is at best secondary. In traditional Marxist idiom the legal-political sphere *reinforces* the economy whilst the cultural sphere serves to *mystify* productive and social relations. Moreover, underpinning this reductive account of the social structure is a reductive account of human existence in which the necessity of the economic reproduction of life – the fact that no life is possible without it – is mistaken for its essence. But the fact that 'spiritual' relations are supported by the material reproduction of human existence should not lead us into the error of supposing that the former are wholly reducible to the latter. Lukács does not make this reductive error and so he follows Weber in attributing a reciprocal determinacy to the separate aspects of the social structure.

The same point about the integrated and reciprocally determining character of the social structure can also be put into Hegelian language in terms of the primacy of the whole over the parts. Whilst the immediate appearance of the social world is that of a composite made up of separate and distinct parts, each impacting on the other externally, the reality is an underlying *interdependence* in which the production and reproduction of economic and productive relations is conditioned by the existence of other spheres of social activity. Rather than speak of the reproduction of capital, Lukács refers to the 'total social process' – the process, that is, through which society reproduces itself in its fragmentation (Lukács, 1990, pp. 10, 15).

Lukács, therefore, follows Weber in adopting an integrated account of the social structure, as opposed to the sedimented or layered account that it is given in classical Marxism. This means that he is not committed to the view that societies are comprehensible through their basal relations or for that matter that the fundamental human activity is labour. Both 'materialist' commitments have been comprehensively criticised from a variety of different theoretical perspectives, and the reductivism of classical Marxist theory is widely accepted today (see Arendt, 1998; Habermas, 1994). However, whilst these acknowledged shortcomings in classical theory should if anything increase interest in a non-reductive materialism such as Lukács', the fact that an orthodox approach is often attributed to him prevents this from happening.

Nonetheless, Lukács still insists that the key to understanding the social process lies in the commodity-form, as if relations of consumption, exchange, distribution and production are somehow generalisable in modern societies (Lukács, 1990, p. 83). How does he maintain this without backsliding into a reductive materialism?

Lukács agrees with Weber that there are tendencies evidenced in modern societies like fragmentation, specialisation and rationalisation that are sociologically general. The division of labour, for example, evidenced in the modern productive process can equally be found in the modern administrative process. Similarly, the general tendency of the rationalisation of the productive process, the legal process and the administrative process is an increased capacity for calculating and predicting social events. Where his analysis moves beyond Weber's is in the manner through which he relates these tendencies back to the commodity form.

Marx's analysis of the commodity form in the opening chapters of *Capital* is concerned to show how, through abstraction from the quantitative, material use-value of a good, it becomes possible to express its value in terms of another good (see Marx, 1990, ch. 1). Since value originates in productive labour this 'equating of the unequal' has an analogous source in production. If the value of one commodity is expressible in terms of another, then the labour that went into its production must be homogeneous and undifferentiated. Exchange is therefore possible by an analogous suppression of qualitative material labour in and by homogeneous labour power. On this basis a thorough-going rationalisation of the productive process – that is, a dividing up into specialised tasks – becomes possible.

For Lukács, the significance and import of Marx's analysis could not be overstated because it provides an account of how human activity comes to be objectified in mechanically functioning social systems (the modern, rationalised, productive system). Clearly this 'alienation' of human activity in mechanically functioning social systems presupposes the ubiquity of the commodity form, because unless modern labourers relate to themselves as objects, the thoroughgoing rationalisation of the labour process would not be possible.

Marx's analysis of the commodity form is thus the source of Lukács' concept of reification, that is, the theory that in modern societies social relations between people appear as the objective properties of things, and that in this process their origin – social relations between people – comes to be concealed (Lukács, 1990, p. 83). It is the source of this theory but with the following crucial difference: whereas Marx thought that this process, along with the illusion that it generates, was restricted to the economy and the economic aspect of social existence, Lukács believes it to be sociologically general. Thus, for example, he maintains that the same objectification of human activity underlies the development of a rational system of law and the modern administrative process in the centralised bureaucratic state. This objectification or reification takes the form of an abstraction from all content in order to make possible the imposition of a closed system of formal concepts, procedures and cases that anticipate any eventuality in advance. Moreover, as previously stated, the emergence of the centralised state and a rational system of law is the precondition of the emergence of a developed capitalist economy. The domain of the calculable must extend way *beyond* the projected forecasts of profit and loss if large-scale capitalist enterprises are to be possible. Minimally it must also extend to the outcome of administrative processes and legal procedures as well.

However, it is at this juncture that the advance of Lukács' social theory beyond Weber becomes perceptible. For if Weberian social theory is the corrective to the inherent reductivism of Marxian social theory, it is a Hegel-fortified Marx that acts as the corrective to the fatalism of Weber's social theory. By relating Weberian concepts back to the commodity form and to the illusion arising from it, Lukács charts a course beyond the impasses of the former. For Weber, rationalisation and specialisation were viewed as fateful and inexorable for the modern individual. For Lukács, however, the fact that these tendencies are predicated upon the objectification of human activity in rationalised social systems leaves open the possibility that the dormant subjectivity alienated in these systems could awaken and, in doing so, dispel the illusion of the commodity-form. This is a possibility that is never countenanced by Weber, but it is precisely this possibility that is thought through by Lukács with respect to the position of the proletariat in modern society.

the subject and social theory

Marxian social theory, for Lukács, is the elucidation of the contradictory present. As such it has no application beyond modern societies. It does not afford us an insight into premodern societies with different (non-economic) structures. Neither does it point to a society 'to come' in which social relations are wholly transparent. It is simply the inner most contradictory tendencies of the modern age taken to their logical extreme (Lukács, 1990, p. 121). Neither can the truth or validity of Marxian social theory be thought in representational terms, since the 'reality' that would 'confirm' it does not yet exist. This confers a curious logical status on the categories of Marxian social theory that, although they present a compelling narrative account of an otherwise opaque and contradictory experience, they have only a *retrospective* validity. In praxical terms then the categories of Marxian social theory have no *a priori* validity and are at best *tropes* in terms of which a contradictory life is comprehended (see Bernstein, 1988).

Unlike the post-Kantian German idealists, Lukács does *not* think that transcending the contradictory present requires only a broader more encompassing concept of reason – Hegelian *Geist* rather than Kantian *Vernuft* – nor indeed does he construe this task in purely philosophical terms. The point for Lukács is less that the contradictions of the present are real rather than imagined but that the possibilities of overcoming them are tied to concrete potentialities existing in the present; in other words, the historical emergence of the proletariat as a class in itself. Of course the question that immediately arises is whether or not this is still *our* present, a question that any reappraisal of Lukács inevitably runs up against. What should not be lost sight of, however, is the historical contingency of any attempt to transcend the contradictory present. Idealists, in viewing this task in *purely* philosophical terms – as the need for a broader concept of reason – are in danger of construing it as a more or less *permanent* possibility unrelated to any concrete potentiality in the present.

Like the idealists, Lukács maintains the need for a broader conception of reason, one in which it becomes possible to reconcile or advance beyond the oppositions of subject and object, theory and practice, understanding and reason. Unlike the idealists, however, he views this concept of reason as at bottom the *elucidation* of contradictory experience. As such it has no application or justification outside this experience. There is no – and can be no – 'dialectical logic' outside of and independent of the opaque, contradictory experience of which it constitutes an essential elucidation. For Lukács this represents the cardinal difference between an idealist and a materialist theory.

The ramifications of this are that Lukács' praxical conception of social theory is neither a philosophical theory nor is it an empirical social theory, at least as these have been understood hitherto. If it were, then it would be inscribed in an intellectual division of labour that simply represents the fragmentary form of the modern social world rather than any attempt to go beyond it. There can, for instance, be no suspension of the empirical existence of the real in order to account for its transcendental conditions of possibility. Rather the reverse for Lukács. The proper *theoretical* mode of comportment is one of passivity in which the emergent object – the *in itself* existence of the proletariat as a class – is allowed to self-form. This *cognitive passivity* has, of course, a Hegelian provenance (see Hegel, 1977, p. 54, para. 84). The central difference, however, is that whereas Hegel views these self-articulating contents as already overcome in the self-genesis of reason – the recapitulation of the genesis of absolute spirit in absolute knowledge – Lukács sees the historical process as precisely that which defies any definitive systematic presentation (Lukács, 1990, p. 147). As a consequence there is a genuine open-endedness and lack of closure in Lukács' concept of praxis, born of the unceasing dialectic of reason and history that forecloses the possibility of a transcendental accounting through a general concept of reason.

However, herein surely lies its unbreakable ties with orthodox Marxism and the principal reason why the contradictory present to which Lukács refers is no longer *our* present. For in his insistence that the subject of overcoming is the proletariat – the identical subject-object of the historical process – lies his fundamental Marxist commitment to the theory of social classes and to the view that history is the outcome of the struggle between classes. Whilst it is then possible to exonerate Lukács from the charge of dogmatism and reductivism, it appears impossible to rid his theory of its commitments to collective social subjects that somehow *make* history and to the related view that modern social domination is essentially class domination. Both positions have been severely criticised: the first for effectively mystifying subjectivity and viewing history as the product of demiurges; the second for an oversimplistic analysis of class structure and the ignoring of other (non-class based) forms of social domination. However, before we prejudge Lukács social theory, it would do as well to explore his central claim about the proletariat and examine what precisely it commits him to.

For Lukács the contradictions of the present are real and not imagined, and they represent the necessary and ineluctable point of departure for the proletariat and their attempt to make sense of their existence. Lukács maintains that the categories of modernity are contradictory and thus alike for both classes (Lukács, 1990, p. 197). However, what is specific about the experience of the proletariat is the extent to which these contradictions are lived and suffered. There is a gap between its self-definition and its actual experience. Whilst ordinarily it understands itself as the *subject* of events (fabricating use-values, freely entering into mutually advantageous contracts, and so on), day-to-day experience everywhere confirms it to be the pure *object* of these events (that is, a homogeneous 'input' into mechanically functioning social systems) (Lukács, 1990, p. 165). What sets the proletariat apart and gives it its potential insight into the social process is the fact that it *suffers* this contradiction between concept and reality, self-definition and social experience. In the face of the negation of its subjectivity, the proletariat is driven to reinterpret its identity and relation to world and is thereby propelled beyond the contradictory categories of the present.

The clue for this self-interpretation is the commodity form, and also the peculiar status of the proletariat as a commodity capable of becoming aware of itself as such (Lukács, 1990, p. 168). Commodities *qua* commodities do not have the capacity for self-consciousness, of course, so the consequence of proletarian self-reflection is the rupturing of social appearances structured by the commodity form. A self-conscious commodity implies an awakening of the alienated subjectivity that has lain dormant in things. Through this recovery of its subjectivity new ways of organising the labour process suggest themselves: forms of organisation based directly on the social relations between people rather than the manipulation of reified social relations. This provides a tentative basis for the reorganisation of productive relations and social relations generally.

From the point of view of existing categories of thought and action this activity (praxis) *defies* categorisation. It proposes a reorganisation of society but one that implies a new self-understanding and relation to world. As such it can neither be understood as subjective (that is, moral) action nor can it be subsumed under the categories of means and end. Both forms of action (moral and prudential) pertain to the rigid opposition of subjective and objective realms implied in societal reification. For Lukács, however, the inner-worldly domain of subjective reason is an alienated standpoint. It represents a subjective point of view from which to judge events, yet without being able to influence or affect them (Lukács, 1990, p. 124). On the other hand the objective sphere, governed by the principle of causality, is an equally illusory standpoint resulting from the misrecognition of social relations as the objective characteristic of things. The modern subject is effectively cleaved in two: between the alienated subjectivity 'in' things and the residual subjectivity that contemplates the objective sphere (Lukács, 1990, p. 87). The former represents the ineliminable premise of prudential rationality and the adjusting of means to ends that this involves.

By contrast the outcome of praxical action is a new self-understanding, along with new categories of thought and action, and a new relation to world. Through praxis the proletariat reinvents or reimagines itself and its relation to world (see Merleau-Ponty, 1973, p. 4). In terms of existing categories of action, it is *action from the middle*, neither subjective nor objective. Of course this is not to deny that class action cannot be given a moral or strategic interpretation. What is being suggested, however, is that the *meaning* of this action is lost if its ontologically creative dimension in respect of self and world is overlooked.

With this, an overall picture emerges: social theory has its origins in the self-consciousness of the proletariat and the praxical transformation of the world that this involves. The development of self-consciousness, however, evolves along essentially Hegelian lines: that is, a staking of self without a guarantee of a recovery of self (see Hegel, 1977, ch. IV). The proletariat, in risking its identity in praxical activity, cannot assuage itself by appeal to 'dialectical logic' – for example, the positive 'result' of a negation – for this logic has no validity apart from the *experience* it is to elaborate. In the face of the ontologically new, the validity of the categories governing reality can only ever be retrospectively conferred.

It is for this reason that Lukács' praxical conception of social theory differs from other conceptions in not having a normative basis. Unlike other conceptions, such as Habermas' communicative theory (see Habermas, 1987), there is no practical, evaluative principle underpinning Lukács' social theory. This is because of the character of praxical action, which is inherently risk-laden, transgressive and improvised. The praxical subject cannot avail itself of any normative principle that would *guarantee* the outcome and rightness of its action. For this reason the model of *judgement* involved in praxis more closely approximates to Kant's account of aesthetic judgement than it does his account of practical judgement. Whilst the latter is subsumptive, the former is 'ascending' in character, and better described as in search of a universal. This is not, of course, to say that rules play no part in praxical action. It is just that in searching for a rule that comprehends the action there is an implicit admission that its meaning cannot be 'read off' from existing categories, that is, means–end, rational and moral. Lukács claims that existing categories do not exhaust the significance of human action and that there is an ineliminable element of self-discovery and novelty in all genuinely significant human action.

broadening the concept of praxis

In the light of this presentation, the problem of the contemporary relevance of Lukács' social theory emerges very clearly: what is the role of class in Lukács' argument? To what extent is modern social domination, at bottom, a form of class domination, and how far is his theory of praxis predicated upon class-analysis of society? Does Lukács' exclusive focus on the proletariat entail a denial of other forms of social domination, such as those linked to gender, ethnicity or sexuality?

There is no question that Lukács focuses exclusively on class politics in *History and Class Consciousness* and that he has almost nothing to say about other social struggles in modernity, such as the women's movement, the struggle for recognition of ethnic minorities or the struggle of the colonised against the coloniser. The fact that Lukács has nothing to say about these, however, invalidates neither his account of modern domination nor his concept of praxis. To begin with, societal reification is not identical with class domination for Lukács. The latter involves the domination and expropriation of one social class by another, through the wage-labour form and the extraction of surplus labour value. Societal reification on the other hand, involves the wholesale domination of institutions over individuals. The proletariat is the subject of overcoming for Lukács, because their position in society enables them to 'see through' the commodity form and to rupture the reified appearance of the social world, not primarily because the prospect of their seizing power represents the promise of social justice. For Lukács we lack freedom, principally through the loss of subjectivity and not because the greater part of our lives is taken up with reproducing the material conditions of our existence. The recovery of subjectivity is the precondition of the realisation of social justice and the reinstituting of the social world that this involves. Without the recovery of a praxical standpoint that follows from the rupturing of social appearances, the realisation of any claim to social justice can only be partial. It will amount to enfranchisement and participation in an increasingly fragmented and devalued social whole.

The experience is a familiar one: equality and social justice for workers, women and ethnic minorities, to the extent that it has been realised, has somehow coincided with the wholesale devaluation of participation in civil society and the polity (literally, the rights and equalities secured are worth less). From a Lukácsian perspective, the reason for this is plain to see. The pursuit of social justice in its various forms has done nothing to arrest the increased penetration – extensive and intensive – of societal reification. The unchecked development of reification means that we relate to ourselves first and foremost as objects in every aspect of social existence, not simply in our working and economic lives. For Lukács, the question is what makes human behaviour increasingly predictable and calculable, thereby facilitating its take-up and assimilation in rationally functioning social systems. His answer is societal reification. If, for example, in our political lives we did not first and foremost relate to ourselves as objects by reifying our own activity, the sampling of 'dead opinion' in opinion polls would not be possible. Neither would the manipulation of this knowledge in what passes for politics today.

If societal reification is not identical with class domination, then it is equally clear that Lukács' concept of praxis is broader than proletarian praxis. Since praxis involves a staking of identity in the face of the contradictory present, there is no reason in principle why the concept cannot be extended to other social struggles in modernity. If it is possible, for example, to talk about the nominally free wage-labourer staking his identity in collective struggle, then why not also the nominally free black European or American or the formally emancipated woman? In each experience the possibility of social transformation is tied to the question of identity ('Who am I?'), which cannot be adequately answered under existing categories and can only emerge through praxical struggle.

Clearly it lies beyond the scope of this chapter to give a praxical interpretation of these histories. I simply want to point out that Lukács' concept of praxis need not be restricted to proletarian praxis. Vis-à-vis other forms of social domination and social struggle, Lukács' only proviso would be the following: if these social struggles are to result in a transformation and reinstitution of the social world – if in other words they are to be truly revolutionary – then there must be a rupturing of social appearances out of which a new self-relation and relation-to-world can emerge. Nothing prevents or precludes this for Lukács, because the commodity form and the illusion to which it gives rise is a general social phenomenon, and not an illusion restricted to the economic aspect of life. That said, however, it is undoubtedly the case that here we run up against the limits of Lukács' social theory: his constant return to the proletariat and to the factory experience as the putative site of overcoming. Despite the fact that this is only a contingent and therefore transient site of overcoming, his case would have been considerably aided by identifying other standpoints from which the fractured present might have been overcome.

conclusion

Lukács' lasting contribution to social and political thought was to have recognised and set out the impersonal form of modern social domination – namely the wholesale domination of institutions over individuals – and to have made its overcoming the condition of the realisation of any claim for social justice. This is a form of domination that 'levels-down' human spontaneity and individuality and progressively robs the social world of value and meaning. As Lukács states, from the point of view of mechanically functioning social systems, these human traits appear, increasingly, as mere sources of error that reduce the likelihood of functioning smoothly and predictably (Lukács, 1990, p. 89). It may come as a surprise that the thinker of collective subjectivity *par excellence* should view human spontaneity and individuality as the precondition of any collective action, but there is little doubt that that is what Lukács had in mind. The more rationalised and reified society becomes, the more individuals come to fulfil organisationally and functionally defined roles, and the more their personalities come to figure as potential sources of error. If collective political action is to be possible, however, it must be possible for people to relate to one another directly and not in a mediated way through things. In this sense, a recovery of subjectivity involves a reversal of the depersonalising character of modern society and a recovery of those spontaneous and human traits that have been suppressed.

Finally it should be noted that Lukács' analysis and critique of modern society provides a basis for thinking about the seeming disappearance of 'macrological' social struggles in late modernity. The increased penetration of societal reification leaves fewer aspects of social existence and less of the total personality free from the corrosive effects of reification and thus provides less of a basis for the type of self-interpretive practices involved in praxical struggle. In this respect it is only a short walk from Lukács' social theory to the breakdown of socialisation at the social and psychical level that Adorno and Horkheimer argued was decisive in the transition to late capitalism.

further reading

For introductory accounts of Lukács see Arato and Breines (1979) and Jay (1984). The former contains much useful biographical detail on the development of his thought. For more advanced analysis, see Feenberg (1981) and Bernstein (1984; 1988). For Feenberg, Lukács theory of praxis needs supplementing with a Marxian dialectic of nature. Bernstein (1988), on the other hand, offers a brilliant reading of Lukács through Heidegger and Derrida. On the reception of *History and Class Consciousness*, see the recently discovered *A Defence of History and Class Consciousness* (Lukács, 2000). This also contains a useful introductory essay by John Rees and a Postface by Slavoj Žižek. See also the review by Fredric Jameson in *Radical Philosophy* 110 (November/ December 2001).

references

Arato, A. and Breines, P. (1979) *The Young Lukács and the Origins of Western Marxism.* London: Pluto Press.
Arendt, H. (1998) *The Human Condition.* Chicago: University of Chicago Press.
Bernstein, J.B. (1984) *The Philosophy of the Novel: Lukács, Marxism and the Dialectics of Form.* Brighton: Harvester Press.

Bernstein, J. (1988) 'Lukács' Wake: Praxis Presence and Metaphysics', collected in *Lukács Today: Essays in Marxist Philosophy*, ed. Tom Rockmore. Dordrecht: Riedal.

Feenberg, A. (1981) *Lukács, Marx and the Sources of Critical Theory*. Totowa, NJ: Rowman & Littlefield.

Habermas, J. (1987) *The Theory of Communicative Action*, 2 vols, trans. T. McCarthy. Cambridge: Polity Press.

Habermas, J. (1994) *Knowledge and Human Interests*, trans. J. Shapiro. Cambridge: Polity Press.

Hegel, G.W.F. (1977) *The Phenomenology of Spirit*, trans. A.V. Miller. Oxford: Oxford University Press.

Jay, M. (1984) *Marxism and Totality: The Adventure of a Concept from Lukács to Habermas*. Berkeley, CA: University of California Press.

Kolakowski, L. (1972) 'Lukács' Other Marx', *Cambridge Review* 28 January: 85–90.

Lukács, G. (1990) *History and Class Consciousness: Studies in Marxist Dialectics*, trans. R. Livingstone. London: Merlin.

Lukács, G. (2000) *A Defence of History and Class Consciousness: Tailism and the Dialectic*, trans. E. Leslie. London: Verso.

Marx, K. (1971) *Preface to A Contribution to the Critique of Political Economy*, trans. S.W. Ryazanskaya. London: Lawrence & Wishart.

Marx, K. (1990) *Capital*, Vol. 1, trans. B. Fowkes. Harmondsworth: Penguin.

Marx, K. and Engels, F. (1984) *The Communist Manifesto*, with an introduction by A.J.P. Taylor. Harmondsworth: Penguin.

Merleau-Ponty, M. (1973) *Adventures of the Dialectic*, trans. J. Bien. Evanston, IL: Northwestern University Press.

Weber, M. (1976) *The Protestant Ethic and the Spirit of Capitalism*. London: Allen & Unwin.

11
hannah arendt

roy t. tsao

Hannah Arendt was born in 1906 to a secular Jewish family in Hannover, Germany. At an early age she moved with her family to the Baltic city of Königsberg in East Prussia (then part of Germany), where she spent her childhood and youth. A precocious student, she left home at age 16 to study classics and Christian theology as a special student at the University of Berlin. Two years later, she began studies in philosophy at the University of Marburg. There she became a student of Martin Heidegger, who was then on his way to becoming one of the most important and influential Continental philosophers of the twentieth century. Arendt's philosophical apprenticeship with Heidegger in the mid-1920s marked an epoch in her intellectual life (and his); it was accompanied by an intense but short-lived romantic affair between them. (Heidegger was 17 years her senior, and married; he had not yet begun his now-notorious involvement with the Nazi party.) In 1926 she broke off their affair and left Marburg to study at Heidelberg with Heidegger's friend Karl Jaspers, who was then the leading exponent of 'existentialism' in Germany.

In Jaspers Arendt found a lifelong intellectual mentor; under his supervision she completed her doctoral dissertation, a phenomenological analysis of Augustine's concept of love, published as *Love and Saint Augustine* in 1996 (Arendt, 1996). She published her dissertation in 1929 (when she was only 23). In the same year she married her first husband, Günther Stern (who later became known as a writer under the pen-name Günther Anders). By that time, with National Socialism on the rise, she had taken an interest in questions of Jewish politics, and had befriended the Zionist leader Kurt Blumenfeld. In 1930 she and her husband moved to Berlin where she began work on her second book, a biography of an early nineteenth-century Jewish diarist Rahel Varnhagen. Arendt took Varnhagen's struggles for social acceptance to be paradigmatic for the insoluble dilemmas of Jewish assimilation into Christian society. After the Nazi takeover in 1933, Arendt was recruited by Blumenfeld to collect instances of the Nazis' anti-Semitic propaganda for publication abroad. While doing so, she was arrested and briefly detained. She and her mother succeeded in escaping and fleeing to France.

As a refugee in Paris, Arendt became active in Zionist resettlement organisations, and worked for a time as the secretary for a Rothschild baroness. During those years in Paris she befriended Walter Benjamin and other exiled writers. (It was to Arendt that Benjamin later entrusted his last manuscripts, just prior to the ill-fated escape from German-occupied France that ended in his desperate suicide.) With Benjamin's encouragement, she completed her study *Rahel Varnhagen*, though it remained unpublished until 1958 (Arendt, 1997). She also attended some of the famously influential seminars on Hegel conducted by the Russian émigré philosopher Alexandre Kojève, and became acquainted with many of the writers who were later the leading lights of postwar French intellectual life – from Raymond Aron (whom she befriended) and Albert Camus (whom she admired) to Jean-Paul Sartre and Simone de Beauvoir (both of whom she loathed). During this period, too, she became estranged from her first husband and met her second one, a German leftist and fellow refugee Heinrich Blücher; they were married in 1940. Shortly afterward, with France at war with Germany, she and her mother (like other refugee Jews in the country) were interned by the French in a camp for 'enemy aliens'. They were able to escape only on account of the general confusion following the German invasion. (The Jewish inmates of that camp who missed that brief chance to escape all ended up in Auschwitz.) Together with Blücher, she and her mother managed to get first to Lisbon and then to the United States. They arrived in New York in 1941.

Once in the US, Arendt began writing for *Aufbau*, a German-language Jewish newspaper based in New York; her intellectual attention remained fixed on the situation in Hitler's Europe and the politics of the Zionist settlers in Palestine. (Her columns for *Aufbau* have two recurring themes: a call for the formation of a Jewish army to fight Hitler alongside the Allies, and an increasingly vocal dissatisfaction with the Zionists' failure to come to terms with the Palestinian Arabs.) Within a few years she was publishing in English as well, writing articles for various publications on aspects of Jewish and European history. Her writing began to coalesce by 1946 into a project for a book-length study on European imperialism, whose culmination she then saw in the openly racist, implacably expansionist politics of Nazi Germany. Her thinking on these matters would soon after take a dramatic turn, however; by the time she completed her manuscript, she had decided that Hitler's politics had more to do with Stalin's than with any imperialist antecedents. The somewhat hybrid book that resulted from this mid-stream correction is *The Origins of Totalitarianism* (1973). First published in 1951, this work incorporates both her earlier analyses of anti-Semitism and imperialism with a powerful and insightful new theory of totalitarianism, which stressed the totalitarian movements' unyielding antagonism toward factual reality as such. Its publication established her reputation as an intellectual in the United States. The book raises many of the theoretical issues that occupied her attention in later years, though it generally does so only in passing, over the course of an amazingly wide-ranging chronicle of events in the prior two centuries of European history.

Arendt adopted a more explicitly theoretical framework in her next book, *The Human Condition* (1958). This book is Arendt's true *magnum opus*, a consummate expression of her mature political philosophy. Its theoretical scope and ambition is as great as its title would indicate; the very nature of its endeavour is such that it implicitly lays claim to a place beside such classics as Hobbes's *Leviathan* or Hegel's *Phenomenology of Spirit*. It contains the fruit of her sustained intellectual engagements with the prior thinkers she takes to be her philosophical predecessors: not just her former teacher Heidegger but figures such as Aristotle, Augustine, Kant, Hegel and Marx. Most of the essays contained in her collection *Between Past and Future* (1961) were written around this time, and represent either preliminary statements or further elaborations of arguments in *The Human Condition*. (She later published two other volumes of essays in her lifetime as well: a collection dealing mainly with contemporary political events, *Crises of the Republic* [1972], and a collection of biographical portraits, *Men in Dark Times* [1968].)

Arendt's next project after *The Human Condition* was a comparative study of modern revolutions, focusing primarily on the eighteenth-century political revolutions in America and France. The book that came out of this project, *On Revolution* (1965b), does not show the same impressive level of original historical insight as does *The Origins of Totalitarianism*; its primary importance lies rather in the application and extension of the abstract arguments from *The Human Condition* to more concrete problems in political theory. These problems include the nature of a constitutional founding and the prospects of participatory democracy in the conditions of modern society.

The writing of *On Revolution* was interrupted by an event whose consequences for Arendt's career would do more than anything else to make her name known to a wider public, and would shape the intellectual trajectory of her later years. That event was the trial in Israel of the former Nazi official Adolf Eichmann, the SS officer who had been responsible for administering the Nazis' arrest and transport of Jews from all over Europe to their eventual deaths at Auschwitz and other extermination camps. Eichmann had been captured in Argentina in 1960 by Israeli agents, and brought to Jerusalem to stand trial the following year for crimes against humanity and against the Jewish people. After a protracted and highly publicised trial, Eichmann was found guilty on nearly every count, and soon after hanged. Arendt had obtained an assignment to report on the trial for *The New Yorker* magazine; her caustic reportage was assembled into a hugely controversial book, *Eichmann in Jerusalem: A report on the banality of evil* (1965a). The remarkable phrase in the subtitle, 'the banality of evil', became indelibly associated with Arendt's name; unfortunately, its intended meaning is to this day very often misunderstood. Contrary to common opinion, Arendt never meant to suggest that Eichmann's crimes were merely banal, or that he was somehow less than culpable for them; she fully endorsed the death sentence that he received. Nor did she mean to suggest that Eichmann's circumstances were such that anyone in his position would have done what he did. Her point was rather that Eichmann *himself* regarded his crimes in that light; she argued that his self-oblivion – what she called his 'inability to think' – represented a syndrome of evil that the moral and philosophical traditions of the West were ill-prepared to recognise. *Eichmann in Jerusalem* itself engages in no sustained theoretical discussion of this problem. But the question of the relationship between mental 'activities' and moral conduct remained a central concern for Arendt in her remaining years, even though she published fairly little on the topic during her lifetime.

Arendt's reflections on these matters eventually led her to her last, unfinished work, *The Life of the Mind*, a tremendously ambitious investigation of the mental faculties of thinking, willing and judging. At the time of her death, in 1975, this last project remained incomplete, but two posthumously edited volumes, *Thinking* and *Willing*, were eventually published in 1978.

the origins of totalitarianism

The greatest obstacle to understanding *The Origins of Totalitarianism* is the book's title. Contrary to what that title seems to suggest, it does not offer a comprehensive narrative of the rise of totalitarianism from its historical origins. Instead, it presents a loosely linked sequence of discrete historical episodes, with totalitarianism only the last and most malignant in the series. Each of these episodes is in effect a different variation on a single political theme: the failure of the modern states of Continental Europe to integrate their populations into the active life of the body politic. The subjects of the book's three parts – 'Anti-Semitism', 'Imperialism' and 'Totalitarianism' – each represent for her what we might call a form of 'anti-politics', an assault on the state and on the legal order it was supposed to uphold. Her analyses of each challenge the conventional wisdom of her own time, and also that of today.

In the case of anti-Semitism, Arendt's aim is not to trace the historical genealogy of religiously inspired hostility toward the Jews on the part of Germans or other Europeans, but something more specific: to explain the rise of the use of anti-Semitism in the late nineteenth and early twentieth centuries as an efficacious *political* argument that could be brought to bear on a host of seemingly unrelated issues, and capable of rallying the anger of politically aggrieved groups against the institutions of the constitutional state (1973, pp. 25, 39).

In the case of imperialism, Arendt's topic is the transformation (or, in a sense, creation) of world politics that began with the European powers' 'scramble for Africa' in the last decades of the nineteenth century. That process led with astonishing swiftness to those powers' carving up nearly the entire globe into competing spheres of military control – and whose ultimate upshot was World War I. (Arendt is oddly silent about US imperialism in Latin America and the Pacific during that same period, but it fits into the general pattern of her analysis.) Arendt's analysis coincides with the Marxist view that the impetus for imperialist expansion was the class interests of a politically dominant bourgeoisie, yet she fundamentally breaks with the Marxist reduction of that process to the workings of economic laws. Instead, she regards that expansionism as the belated expression of a perverse ethos that she claims the bourgeoisie had always harboured; their true aspiration had always been to accumulate an extortionate monopoly of power in whatever form that was available (1973, pp. 138, 145). (Her argument thus has the curious implication that the bourgeoisie's classic function of accumulating capital was merely a manifestation of this more fundamental ethos, which for contingent reasons had until then not received its full political expression.) Moreover, she argues that the ultimate basis of this perverse ethos lay in the bourgeois mentality of estrangement from genuine political community; the imperialist abuse of state power for the bourgeoisie's expansionist aims was thus a boomerang effect of that same class's alienation from the body politic (1973, p. 141).

In the case of totalitarianism, finally, Arendt sees an even more profound form of alienation at its basis. As noted above, she had originally regarded Nazism as an outgrowth of imperialism; over the course of writing her book she came to see it as an even more virulent phenomenon, more closely related to the Bolshevism of Stalin. (She consistently avoids referring to the latter as 'Stalinism', a label that she believed attached too great importance to Stalin's own personality, and not enough to the system he created and led.) The object of her account is not the totalitarian state, but rather what she calls the totalitarian 'movement'; this is a reflection of her view that the 'so-called totalitarian state' – Hitler's Reich and Stalin's Soviet Union – is not really a state at all, but rather the subordination of government functions to the momentary aims of the movement's all-embracing ideology (1973, pp. 392–7).

Arendt's central thesis is that the sinister success of these movements resulted from their ability to attract and sustain a following of adherents whose loyalty was completely detached from self-interest of any kind. She argues that this following was drawn primarily from the segment of population that she calls 'the masses', and the attraction of the movements lay in those masses' longing to escape from human reality into the sheer fiction of ideology. As Arendt uses the term, the 'masses' do not represent the members of any particular class, but are simply agglomerations of otherwise isolated individuals who are estranged from any settled class or social interest group, and who are cut off from traditional forms of political organisation (1973, pp. 311–15). According to her, the masses' condition of social atomisation deprives them of any shared perspective of common solace or solidarity with which to make sense of their disappointments (1973, pp. 352–3). As a result, she argues, they come to find the contingency that pervades all human affairs unbearably frustrating, and are drawn to totalitarian movements primarily in order to escape it (1973, p. 358).

It is in this way that Arendt explains how such people could be so hypnotically drawn to Hitler's and Stalin's outrageous claims to trace all the recalcitrant features of reality to the workings of some all-encompassing, hidden conspiracy; the purported ubiquity of those enemy conspiracies provided the totalitarian movements with a rationale for their movements' own conspiratorial organisation. Arendt notes that the principle of that organisation is precisely to *heighten* the sense of atomisation experienced by the movement's adherents, so as to make them all the more hostile and contemptuous toward the reality of the world outside the movement (1973, p. 385). Because the totalitarian movement is so deeply invested in the reality of its ideological fictions, the very existence of the outside world is bound to appear as a threat. Arendt argues that it is this that accounts for such movements' incomparable belligerence. She argues further that the inevitable tendency of such a movement in power is a project of 'total domination', whose true aim is to destroy the feature of reality that is most fundamentally responsible for the contingency of human affairs – which is nothing other than the existence of other human beings capable of free, spontaneous action at their own independent initiative (1973, pp. 458, 466).

labour, work and action

The Human Condition could be regarded in part as an extended meditation on the very facts about the human condition that Arendt says the totalitarian mentality finds so unbearable. A central strand of its argument concerns that same human faculty for spontaneous action, and its bearing on the fact we find ourselves in a world with other people equally capable of it. Yet Arendt's reflections on this matter are bound up in a much more complex and comprehensive philosophical undertaking, and its immediate political concerns are quite different from those that had inspired her prior study of totalitarianism. The complexity of *The Human Condition* derives primarily from the fact that Arendt carries out several distinct theoretical projects more or less simultaneously, often without clearly indicating which one is her primary concern at any given point in the text. The most fundamental of these projects is literally an analysis of the human condition: or, more precisely, an analysis of the ineluctable conditions common to all human life as we know it, and a specification of certain basic human activities whose essence is to respond to, and have their character determined by, these same conditions. The aim of this project is to set forth the 'elementary articulations' of the activities that fall within what she calls the *'vita activa'*.

The book's second major project is a critique of modernity in the light of these basic activities. That critique is framed by an immediate concern that modern technology in its various guises constitutes a 'rebellion' against the basic facts of the human condition, and has had the effect of undermining our ability to find satisfaction in, or even to recognise our full capacity for, those basic human activities – especially insofar as they pertain to political life. The aim of this second project is therefore to explain the basis of a cluster of syndromes that Arendt describes as 'world alienation', which she believes to be the 'hallmark of the modern age' (1958, sec. 35, p. 254). (Interwoven with these two projects is at least one other, a polemical history of Western philosophy and political theory since Plato.)

The starting point of the first project is a set of 'basic conditions under which life on earth has been given to man' (1958, sec. 1, p. 7). Those conditions are: the fact that we are living creatures with natural, bodily needs like those of all other organic life (the condition of 'life'); that we inhabit a world composed of non-natural objects of our own making (the condition of 'worldliness'); and that we find ourselves in this world with other human beings, each of whom is a distinct individual (the condition of 'plurality'). Corresponding to those three conditions are three basic human activities: 'labour', whereby we provide for our bodily needs; 'work', whereby we create and sustain the world of artifacts; and 'action', whereby we carry out projects in relation to those of our fellow human beings. 'Labour' consists in the expenditure of bodily energy to provide the means for continued life; together with consumption and reproduction, it belongs to the living organism's metabolic cycle of exhaustion and renewal. Arendt sharply distinguishes labour from the separate activity that she (somewhat idiosyncratically) designates as 'work' (which she also calls 'fabrication'). While labour conforms to the cycles of nature, and yields no product apart from the regeneration of life, the activity of work is responsible for making the durable implements and objects – tools, shelter and the countless manmade things that surround us – that shield us from natural forces and afford us a measure of mastery over it. It is thanks to the 'human artifice' erected through work that we experience anything like an 'objective' world that subsists apart from our immediate needs, and which potentially outlasts the life of any one person. Action, finally, refers to the field of activity that 'goes on directly between men without the intermediary of things or matter'; its medium is rather the intangible 'web' of interpersonal relationships that bestow meaning on human affairs (1958, sec. 1, p. 7; sec. 25, p. 183). Action consists in fulfilling, disappointing, surprising, or otherwise altering the expectations that inhere in those relationships; it is the stuff of the stories of each of our lives. Every instance of action constitutes what

Arendt calls a new 'insertion' into this 'web' of relationships; for this reason, she associates the activity with the human condition of 'natality' – the fact that each human birth marks the beginning of a unique person's life story (1958, sec. 1, p. 8; sec. 24, p. 176).

The aim of Arendt's threefold classification of human activities is not to provide a definitive taxonomy of possible activities, as if to shunt every instance of human endeavour into one and only one of three rubrics. Instead, it is to provide a set of discrete abstractions from the welter of worldly activity, each with its own logic of explanation, and each corresponding to a different dynamic of change and persistence in time. Her claim is that *insofar* as whatever we do belongs to one of those activities, it will necessarily conform to that activity's particular explanatory logic and temporal dynamic. Consider the case (made in the gendered language that Arendt used) of a wage-earning artisan, whose craft is also his living. Insofar as he *works*, his craft will yield a final result, a lasting product that will persist in the world apart from its maker; the activity ends when its intended design is fulfilled. Insofar as he *labours*, though, that singular sequence is subsumed within the ongoing rhythm of effort and rest, our artisan's daily grind. The bodily needs he serves in earning his wages will never be sated as long as he lives, and so the activity never will cease – though he may contrive to get others to bear the brunt of its toil for him. And insofar as he *acts* – if he shares tools, say, or carries out a contract – his doings will make sense only as the story of singular deeds (however modest) of a unique individual interacting with others.

Arendt's whole theory of politics amounts to an elaboration on her thesis that all political activities and institutions are essentially a matter of action, and that all involvement with them is therefore subject to the same possibilities and predicaments that action invariably is. It is the human condition of plurality that makes action possible, but it is this same condition that makes for the contingency pervading all human affairs. Because action is meaningful by virtue of the 'web of relationships' in which it transpires, the meaning of any given person's deed is always dependent on its intersection with the overlapping or conflicting projects of other people; its outcome is always unpredictable, and its consequences always at least potentially boundless (1958, sec. 26, pp. 190–2). By the same token, the lasting significance of any political act depends entirely on whether and how it is carried forward by others. Stated in this general form, such truths sound obvious, as they are meant to be. Arendt's most fundamental contribution to political theory consists in her unyielding insistence on those truths in opposition to seductive habits of thought that are unconsciously or even wilfully forgetful of them. One example is the escapist, ideological mindset she had already exposed in her analysis of totalitarianism. Another is the wish to avoid the uncertainties of action through a kind of politics modelled on the activity of fabrication instead, with the latter activity's characteristic mastery over its materials and control of its product. Arendt argues that this wish, conscious or not, is endemic to much of the Western tradition of political theory. As she puts it, 'This attempt to replace acting with making is manifest in the whole body of argument against "democracy", which, the more consistently and better reasoned it is, will turn into an argument against the essentials of politics' (1958, sec. 31, p. 220). In her view, putting that wish into practice invariably tends toward impotence or violence (and if violence, then impotence too): toward impotence, because the essence of human power is nothing but the capacity of agents to act in concert; or toward violence, because to manipulate human beings as if they were things is precisely what violence is (1958, sec. 28, pp. 200–2; 1972, pp. 142–6).

Now, to claim, as Arendt does, that violence breeds impotence is not to deny that it can be an effective instrument of domination (there is none better). But it is to claim that to rule by brute force negates the freedom to act of the person who wields it, at least in relation to the people that person rules over. That is simply because the capacity to act itself depends on the readiness of others to recognise one's projects and to respond with initiatives of their own; the generative potential of action inheres in the fact of that mutual recognition. That means that freedom, as Arendt understands it, is incompatible with control: 'If men wish to be free, it is precisely sovereignty they must renounce' (1968, p. 165).

the public realm and modern society

The bridge between Arendt's theory of human activities and her critique of modernity is her distinctive conception of the public realm. What she understands as the public realm has two distinct dimensions. (Note that neither of these involves any specific identification of 'the public' with the domain of the modern state.) First, it refers to the linguistically mediated 'space of appearance' in which the agents are recognised by one another as such – 'where I appear to others as others appear to me, where men exist not merely like other living or inanimate things but make their appearance explicitly' (1958, sec. 27, pp. 198–9). More generally, the public realm in that sense encompasses the whole of human experience that has been rendered intersubjectively communicable through the medium of language (1958, sec. 7, p. 50).

The other major dimension of the public realm for Arendt is the 'common world' of manmade things that situate and stabilise our interactions. Created through the activity of work, the artifacts that compose this common world range from written documents and artworks to the buildings and streets of cities and towns. This other dimension of the public realm is closely related to the first; in Arendt's words, it 'gathers us together yet prevents us from falling over one another' (1958, sec. 7, p. 52). It does so in part by erecting boundaries between public and private, so as to protect those aspects of human life and human experience (like those related to physical intimacy, and bodily functions) that require shelter from the 'glare' of publicity.

Arendt's critique of modernity revolves around her views on the relationship between the public realm in both of the two senses just described and the activity of labour. Unlike action and work, labour is alien to both of these senses of the public realm just described. Although we all have the same bodily needs, our satisfaction of them is private (in the sense that one person's hunger is never satisfied by another's eating, nor fatigue by another's sleeping). The cycle of labour and consumption leave no lasting product that might contribute to a common world. Yet despite this, Arendt argues, the emergence and inexorable growth of the modern market economy has allowed labour to dominate what passes for the public realm in our time. (Confusingly, she typically refers to this historical change as the 'rise of the social', with only oblique indications that what she has in mind is the rise of *market* society.) Her understanding of that great transformation (and indeed her understanding of labour generally), is profoundly indebted to Marx's analysis of the same phenomenon in *Capital*. Like Marx, she regards the decisive event in the making of modern capitalism to have been the expulsion of peasants from their small holdings and common pasturage starting around the sixteenth century; as Marx had said, this created an 'emancipated' labour force that was 'free' to be exploited in the market for wage labour.

Marx had argued that the illusion of freedom in this new market for labour masked a reality in which the labourer was compelled by bodily needs to submit to a system of production that involved even more exploitation than the outwardly coercive systems like slavery or serfdom had done. At the same time, capitalist production allows for an unprecedented increase in the division of labour in society; in Marx's view, the production process is well on the way to being fully 'socialized' even under the regime of capitalist ownership. Arendt has something like this in mind when she speaks of the 'unnatural growth of the natural' that she says followed the emancipation of labour from the former constraints on its productivity; she characterises the new 'social' realm of the market as one in which the human capacity for action is put in the service of bodily necessity (1958, sec. 6, p. 47).

Arendt differs with Marx on the eventual destiny of this development, though. Marx famously believed that the spiralling growth of productive capacity in such a system would ultimately come to grief over its ever more polarised class divisions, leading in turn to a proletarian revolution. With a century's hindsight, Arendt argues instead that the long-range tendency of modern society (with the help of trade unions and the welfare state) is to become ever more inclusive in the distribution of consumer goods and material security (1958, sec. 6, p. 45; sec. 30, p. 219). In her view, the modern 'consumers' society' is one in which the activities of labour and consumption have (almost) completely overrun the public realm; both the 'space of appearances' for action and the 'common world' produced through fabrication have been stunted and deformed. Action and work are still performed in such a society, but increasingly both are done solely in what Arendt calls 'the mode' of labour. On the one hand, the human institutions that occupy our time and attention are overwhelmingly those through which we make our living, so that our interactions and self-understandings are governed by the imperatives of economics (1958, sec. 45, p. 322). On the other hand, the manmade things that make up our human artifice are degraded to the status of disposable goods for consumption, and the built structures that compose the human habitat become no more than fungible instruments for the production of wealth (1958, sec. 35, p. 256).

Writing nearly a century after Marx, in the 1950s, Arendt was able to see that his prediction for an inevitably worsening cleavage between the interests of an idle bourgeoisie and a propertyless proletariat mistook circumstances that were peculiar to his historical moment for universal tendencies. Today, another half century later, it is easy to see that in one respect Arendt, too, mistook the contingent circumstances of her time for an irreversible trend. The long prosperity of the postwar years, coupled with the historical advances of the trade unions in the United States and Western Europe, unduly coloured her confidence that the future of industrialised nations lay assuredly with an ever more inclusive welfare state and ample consumer goods for all. That the welfare state might turn out to be a fragile achievement, or that a large share of such nations' working populations might be persistently deprived a place at the social table are possibilities that she seems never even to have considered. She offers no help whatsoever for thinking about the problems of distributive justice within the framework of a complex market economy. (But then again, neither does Marx.) That hardly detracts from the pertinence of her critique of modernity, though. The upshot of that critique is that the syndromes of social conformism and 'world alienation' that she analyses would still beset our society even if those other problems were to be surmounted. Indeed, our greater anxiety about the prospects for prosperity only makes us that much more vulnerable to them.

freedom in politics

In her writings after *The Human Condition*, Arendt further explores the fate of the human capacity to act under modern conditions. (Her equally pressing concern about the fate of the human capacity to make and sustain a durable 'common world' does not receive comparable attention in her later writings, but this should not be taken to diminish its importance in *The Human Condition* itself.) This theme receives its fullest elaboration in *On Revolution*. Among her aims in that book is to recover a conception of participatory politics that she takes to be the 'lost treasure' of the American and European revolutionary traditions (1965b, pp. 275–81). In her somewhat stylised telling, the history of those revolutions was punctuated by intermittent efforts to

establish republican political institutions that would give citizens a direct
opportunity to engage with their fellows as 'participators in government' (to
use a phrase she takes from Thomas Jefferson). She is especially interested in
the networks of locally based, democratic councils that fleetingly emerged
over the course of the failed European revolutions from the Paris Commune
of 1870 to the Hungarian Revolution of 1956 (1965b, pp. 255–65). What she
admires about these short-lived experiments in participatory democracy is that
the citizens who took part were not motivated by class interest or concern for
material welfare, but instead sought to assume responsibility as individuals
for their common political future. (In her later essay 'Civil Disobedience',
she later celebrated a similar virtue in the American civil rights and anti-war
movements of the 1960s [1972, pp. 95–102].) In her view, these thwarted
experiments in participatory democracy should be a standing reproach to the
party-dominated representative institutions of modern liberal states, which
give little opportunity for citizens to act in concert with their fellows about
matters of common concern.

At the very end of *On Revolution*, Arendt goes so far as to propose scuttling
those representative institutions entirely, to be replaced with a federated
system of democratic councils open at the grassroots level to all citizens who
cared enough to take part. Her idea, roughly, is that the participants would
choose leaders from among their own number to serve on a higher tier of
councils, whose members could then be trusted to do the same at each of
the successive stages of a pyramidal hierarchy (1965b, p. 278). It must be
said that this proposal to reconstitute democratic politics from the ground
up is presented in too sketchy a manner to bear much weight as a practical
prescription for institutional change. Its primary significance lies rather in
the vivid expression it gives to Arendt's abiding political concerns. On the
one hand, the council system she envisions would give citizens access to
a public setting in which their opinions and actions as individuals would
actually matter, providing an institutional framework for the kind of mutual
recognition without which action amounts to no more than furtive or futile
gestures. On the other hand, by restricting political voice to those citizens who
chose to take part – eliminating the election of representatives by secret-ballot
suffrage – the system would grant power only to those who were willing to
assume some measure of public responsibility for its exercise. Arendt freely
concedes that perhaps only a minority would choose to do so, and that her
vision of participatory politics is in some sense 'elitist' on that account. (Lest
that seem an invitation to oligarchic usurpation, through the permanent
disenfranchisement of the 'passive' citizens not taking part, it should be noted
that Arendt also stresses the importance of a stable, constitutionally based
legal culture with vigorous judicial review [1965b, p. 200].) Her point is that
this elite – unlike the entrenched, professional elites that inevitably rise to
the top no matter what in all party-based, representative systems – would be
entirely self-selected, and its members distinguished from other citizens on

the basis of qualities that indeed ought to matter in public life: a willingness to step forward, to speak out, and to build trust among peers with whom one may disagree for the sake of common political aims. She does not pretend that people with such genuinely political qualities are any more altruistic or intelligent than anyone else, or any more capable of managing government policy for the sake of collective welfare. What she believes, rather, is that the active manifestation of those qualities themselves – when given a space to become publicly significant – uniquely contribute toward sustaining the kind of common world in which human beings can find themselves at home with their fellows.

challenges and contributions

During her lifetime, Arendt often maintained a certain aloofness from the dominant discourses of political thought and philosophy; her work maintains a similar distance from the equivalent discourses today. For instance, she had little to say about the role of the state in the management of economic activity, and even less of immediate bearing on such contemporary issues as globalisation, multiculturalism or identity politics. The continuing importance of her work is due rather to the enduring pertinence of the questions that did concern her, no matter how alien they may seem to our usual habits of mind. The historical circumstances that she analysed in *The Origins of Totalitarianism* may have passed, but the phenomena of extremist movements and political terror are still very much with us, and her unshrinking efforts to confront the mentalities that give rise to them – in that book, and in *Eichmann in Jerusalem* as well – still merit our close attention. The theory of modern society she presents in *The Human Condition* may take the success of the welfare state far too much for granted, but that hardly detracts from the acuity of her warnings about the way a society organised chiefly for the sake of labour and consumption corrodes our capacity to sustain a viable public realm. The ideas for participatory politics she ventures in *On Revolution* may have little prospect for their realisation; nevertheless, they pose a bracing challenge to our preconceived notions of the purposes of, and possibilities for, democratic institutions under modern conditions.

Arendt's most profound contribution to political theory may well be her unyielding insistence on the paradoxical incompatibility between the freedom to act in a world with others and the aspiration to sovereign independence, whether on the part of individuals or groups. To be sure, she is hardly alone among twentieth-century thinkers to have warned against a covert will to a domineering mastery that is inscribed in the Western philosophical tradition. What sets Arendt apart from others who voiced similar warnings (among them her sometime teacher Heidegger) is that her alertness to the dangers of this syndrome does not spill over into a more generalised suspicion of the human capacity for concerted political action. From beginning to end, her political thought is grounded in the conviction that through speaking and acting men and women can indeed make themselves at home in the world they inhabit together. It is precisely for the sake of a richer appreciation of what these capacities make possible that she counsels an acceptance of the inherent uncertainties in their exercise. In her own words, 'the impossibility [for human beings] of remaining unique masters of what they do, of knowing its consequences and relying upon the future, is the price they pay for plurality and reality, for the joy of inhabiting together with others a world whose reality is guaranteed for each by the presence of all' (1958, sec. 34, p. 244).

futher reading

All of the works by Arendt mentioned in this chapter, with the exception of *Rahel Varnhagen* (1997), are readily available in paperback editions. Apart from *The Origins of Totalitarianism* (1973), which stands alone, all are best understood in light of *The Human Condition* (1958). (This applies even in the case of *Eichmann in Jerusalem* [1965a], the underlying theoretical arguments of which are otherwise hard to discern beneath its journalistic surface.) Readers seeking a more immediate entry to her political thought may wish to start with the essays 'What is Freedom?' and 'The Crisis in Culture' in *Between Past and Future* (1961), or 'On Humanity in Dark Times', in *Men in Dark Times* (1968). A large proportion of Arendt's unpublished correspondence, lectures, and manuscripts, held at the US Library of Congress, have recently been made available online via the Library's 'American Memory' website <http://memory.loc.gov/anmem/arendthtml/arendthome.html>.

The only complete biography of Arendt in English is Elisabeth Young-Bruehl, *Hannah Arendt: For love of the world* (New Haven, CT: Yale University Press, 1982). The standard scholarly overview of her thought is Margaret Canovan, *Hannah Arendt: A reinterpretation of her political thought* (Cambridge: Cambridge University Press, 1992); this study is the best general guide to Arendt's diverse writings, particularly for her many uncollected or unpublished essays, lectures and manuscripts. Other accessible, useful studies include Richard J. Bernstein, *Hannah Arendt and the Jewish Question* (Cambridge, MA: MIT Press, 1997), Jeffrey Isaac, *Arendt, Camus, and Modern Rebellion* (New Haven, CT: Yale University Press, 1992), and George Kateb, *Hannah Arendt: Politics, conscience, evil* (Totowa, NJ: Rowman & Allanheld, 1984). Readers interested in further elaboration on the interpretation of Arendt's thought offered in the present chapter may wish to consult the following articles by Roy T. Tsao: 'Arendt Against Athens: rereading *The Human Condition*', *Political Theory* 30(1) (February 2002): 97–123; and 'The Three Phases of Arendt's Theory of Totalitarianism', *Social Research* 69(2) (summer 2002): 579–619.

references

Arendt, H. (1958) *The Human Condition*. Chicago, IL: University of Chicago Press.

Arendt, H. (1961) *Between Past and Future* [enlarged edn 1968]. New York: Viking.

Arendt, H. (1965a) *Eichmann in Jerusalem: A report on the banality of evil* [1st edn 1963]. New York: Viking.

Arendt, H. (1965b) *On Revolution* [1st edn 1963]. New York: Viking.

Arendt, H. (1968) *Men in Dark Times*. New York: Harcourt.

Arendt, H. (1972) *Crises of the Republic*. New York: Harcourt.

Arendt, H. (1973) *The Origins of Totalitarianism* [1st edn 1951, rev. edn 1958]. New York: Harcourt.

Arendt, H. (1978) *The Life of the Mind* [posthumous], 2 vols, ed. Mary McCarthy. New York: Harcourt.

Arendt, H. (1996) *Love and Saint Augustine* [1st edn 1927], ed. J. Stark and J. Scott. Chicago, IL: University of Chicago Press.

Arendt, H. (1997) *Rahel Varnhagen* [1st edn 1958, 2nd edn 1974], ed. L. Weissberg. Baltimore, MD: Johns Hopkins University Press.

12
louis althusser

benjamin arditi

More than a quarter of a century after Louis Althusser's heyday, one wonders how this rather troubled French professor managed to create such a buzz with the publication of only two books – *Reading Capital* and *For Marx*. The first was written in collaboration with students, and the other was a compilation of essays. In *The Future Lasts Forever*, his posthumous memoir that claims not to be one, it is often difficult to distinguish fact from fantasy. Althusser (*alte Haüser*, 'old house' in Alsatian dialect) tells us that he knew very little of either the history of philosophy or Marx, and that he never quite managed to understand Freud ('He remains a closed book to me') despite the regular use of psychoanalytical concepts in his work. He also claims that he often learned by hearsay from what friends mentioned in conversations or from reading papers written by his students, a remark that will certainly strike a chord with many academics.

Althusser had the twin fantasies of solitude and mastery. He saw himself as being 'alone against the world' intellectually, because philosophers must lead a lonely life if they are to break with existing consensus, and also alone politically, because not even the party went along with his anti-humanism, so it seemed. His desire to be the 'master's master' was equally strong. It appears in petty details, as when he brags that compared to him the greatest chefs are unimaginative or that de Gaulle once asked him for a light in a chance encounter in the street and then invited him for dinner to talk about his work and political experience. Or when he describes himself as a regular womaniser, claiming to have cheated continually on his first love interest and lifelong partner Hélène Rytman – whom, tragically, he killed – while demanding her approval of his mistresses. It also appears in his efforts to position himself in the place of the 'subject supposed to know'. This is particularly noticeable in his 'return to Marx' through a 'symptomatic reading' of his texts – one that 'divulges the undivulged event in the text it reads, and in the same movement relates it to *a different text*, present as a necessary absence in the first' (Althusser and Balibar, 1970, p. 28). This reading, he says, enabled him to detect 'the places where Marx's discourse is merely the unsaid of his silence' (1970, p. 143), to restore to Marx 'what he required: coherence and intelligibility', and to master 'his own thought better than he had done' (1993, pp. 221–2).

Despite his reputation for being generous with students, he was somewhat unkind to those who challenged him. Rancière's contribution to *Reading Capital*, together with the contributions of Establet and Macherey, were dropped from the second edition of 1968 – the one used for the English translation – allegedly to abridge and improve the book. Only the texts by Althusser and Balibar remained. Rancière (1974) had criticised Althusser for his politically paralysing theoreticism (philosophy as the 'theory of theoretical practice'), his ambiguous position toward the student movement in 1968 and his unwillingness to break with the French Communist Party (PCF). Althusser had joined the PCF in 1948 and remained within it despite his disagreements. He voiced these without ever exceeding the limits of its tolerance and so never risked expulsion (Althusser, 1993, p. 197). Membership gave him a certain real-world aura, a semblance of practical action through a deflected link to the working class, not to mention the prestige of being the leading party intellectual at a time when the PCF was a reference point for French intellectuals.

However, there is a more convoluted explanation of his refusal to break with the party. Althusser had been a prisoner of war in a German camp. He thought of ways of escaping, but never dared to implement them, partly due to his avoidance of physical danger and because he believed that his having found the perfect means of escape was sufficient reward. Indeed, his acts of daring were committed under the protection of the camp, and for someone who vindicated the primacy of struggle, he was happy to respond to practical problems with theoretical solutions. Althusser describes his regular internments in psychiatric hospitals – where he spent almost 15 years of his adult life – and his living quarters at the École Normale Supérieure in similar terms: they provided him with a protective embrace. Connecting these experiences – in the camp, the hospital, the École, and the party – one can begin to understand his self-referential claim that 'how to escape the circle while remaining within it' was the core of all philosophical, military and political problems (1993, pp. 108–9, 319).

In between depressions, Althusser flourished as a writer, teacher and polemicist. He was part of a remarkable group of postwar thinkers – many of them marked by structuralism – that included Gaston Bachelard, Roland Barthes, Georges Canguilhem, Jacques Derrida, Michel Foucault, Jean Hyppolite, Roman Jakobson, Jacques Lacan and Claude Lévi-Strauss, to mention just a few. He also taught a host of scholars like Étienne Balibar, Roger Establet, Pierre Macherey, Jacques-Alain Miller and Jacques Rancière. The connection between them was not simply a question of timing – 'the 1950s' or 'the 1960s' – but also of shared themes and a willingness to engage in disciplinary crossings.

Althusser's work in this respect was exemplary. He believed that just as Lacan had called for a 'return to Freud' and had broken with psychologism, his own return to Marx had contributed to a renewal of historical materialism by announcing a break with the prevalent Marxist orthodoxies built on economism, historicism, and humanism. To do so, he drew on history and politics, from philosophy (above all Spinoza, but also Machiavelli, Rousseau and Bachelard) and psychoanalysis (Freud and Lacan), effectively opening up Marxism to the debates of the times.

In the eyes of his followers, who were fascinated by his conceptual wizardry, Althusser was the master theorist, and his writings enjoyed a semi-canonical status. His style played a part. It was seemingly less concerned with proving complex points than with seducing readers by presenting his arguments as if they were self-evident conclusions. Althusser takes great pains to create this impression, confiding that he owes part of his academic success to two maxims of Jean Guitton, one of his teachers at the *lycée*. These were to be as clear as possible when writing, and to present arguments on any subject coherently and convincingly in order to make them appear as *a priori* and purely deductive (Althusser, 1993, pp. 93–4).

Yet Althusser's style also had irritating traits replicated by many of his followers. With the passing of Althusserianism, there was a sense of linguistic relief among readers who had been punished mercilessly – and long enough – by its abuse of italics and inverted commas, the predilection for capitalised terms, and the obscure nomenclature made more bearable only by Ben Brewster's glossary in *Reading Capital* and *For Marx*. This notwithstanding, the combination of assertive prose, discursive crossings and communist militancy paid off. By the late 1960s, the name Althusser had become synonymous with cutting-edge philosophy among young Marxist intellectuals in France, the UK and Latin America. The early work of Nicos Poulantzas (1973) extended Althusserian categories into Marxist accounts of class, politics and the state. Marta Harnecker (1969), a former student of Althusser's, returned to Latin America to publish a manual of Althusserianism that, despite its annoying 'taxonomic excesses' – as Ralph Miliband once said of the work of Poulantzas – managed to sell well over 150,000 copies and is still in print. In the UK, Barry Hindess and Paul Hirst became his most celebrated advocates until they began to question his theoreticism in the mid-1970s. Ernesto Laclau's (1977) creative use of the notion of 'determination in the last instance' sought to undermine economism and class reductionism in Marxist discussions of politics, ideology and populism. Like Althusser, he did not escape the metaphysical trappings of 'the last instance', but his critique of essentialism fired the opening salvos for what was later to be known as post-Marxism.

Althusserianism, however, was less a system than work in progress. It emerged through the publication of a dozen or so articles – the most influential between 1960 and 1969 – that were shaped by very public controversies with Paul Lewis and E.P. Thompson. Althusser made it clear in various prefaces and in *Essays in Self-Criticism* that he had changed his position on many issues. In a letter to the English translator of *For Marx* he expressed his fears that readers will be misguided 'if they were allowed to believe that the author of texts that appeared one by one between 1960 and 1965 has *remained in the position* of these old articles whereas time has not ceased to pass' (1969, p. 258). But even if he reformulated 'his' Marx as he went along, one can identify Althusserianism in the reasoning behind the critiques of humanism, historicism, economism and ideology. In what follows, I will look in some detail at his efforts to vindicate the scientific status of Marxism, to distinguish the Marxist dialectic and totality from the Hegelian ones, and to counteract the mechanicism of the Second International through the thesis of 'determination in the last instance' by the economy.

the epistemological break and overdetermination

Althusser's reading of Marx is governed by the hypothesis of an 'epistemological break' or discontinuity in Marx's intellectual development. The motif comes from Bachelard (1947), who speaks of the epistemological obstacles faced by science, and he borrows it 'to designate the mutation in the theoretical problematic contemporary with the foundation of a scientific discipline' (Althusser, 1969, 'Today', p. 32). One could also link it to Kuhn, who characterises scientific revolutions by a shift from one paradigm to another and by the incommensurability of those paradigms. The force of an epistemological break is that it 'establishes a science by detaching it from the ideology of its past and by revealing this past as ideological' (Althusser, 1969, 'On the Materialist Dialectic', p. 168). Althusser uses it to distinguish the work of the early, pre-scientific Marx, from the mature Marx of dialectical and historical materialism.

His basic premise is that while all beginnings are necessary and contingent, they do not prefigure what is to come: 'Marx did not choose to be born to the thought German history had concentrated in its university education, nor to think its ideological world. He grew up in this world, in it he learned to live and move, with it he "settled accounts", from it he liberated himself' (Althusser, 1969, 'On the Young Marx', p. 64). This espousal of a purely contingent link between genesis and consequences reverberates in Foucault's Nietzschean invocation of genealogy to criticise the myth of origins, that is, the belief in an absolute beginning from which one might deduce the present. It also prefigures Poulantzas' claim that the class origin of an agent does not determine its class position in a political conjuncture. The 'beginning' of Marx refers to the period of his early works that culminates with the Paris Manuscripts of 1844, when his writing was still caught up in the humanist problematic of the theory of alienation. The latter is troublesome because of its concurrent anthropological assumptions of a universal essence of man, which presupposes an original uncontaminated human nature that can and should be restored. One might add that this betrays an eschatological view, for liberation conceived as the reinstatement of an alienated essence entails the telos of a fully reconciled society.

The turning point comes with the writing of *The German Ideology* in 1845, in which Marx and Engels claim to have settled their erstwhile philosophical conscience. This text triggers the break with humanist ideology that would eventually lead to the theory of exploitation whose mature form is *Capital*. New concepts appear after the break (mode of production, productive forces, relations of production, infrastructure–superstructure) as Marx gradually founds the science of history (Althusser, 1976, 'Reply to John Lewis', p. 66). The passage from alienation to exploitation induces Marx to replace the ideological postulates of subject and essence with a theoretical anti-humanism that gives rise to a materialism of *praxis* (Althusser, 1969, 'Marxism and Humanism', p. 229). This 'retreat from ideology towards reality', as Althusser calls it, led to Marxism 'at the price of a prodigious break with his origins, a heroic struggle against the illusions he had inherited from the Germany in which he was born' (Althusser, 1969, 'On the Young Marx', pp. 81, 84). This reality is nothing other than the discovery of the science of history (historical materialism) and the development of a non-ideological philosophy, dialectical materialism or 'Theory' as such. An Althusserian would thus say that while Marx was always Marx, before the break he was a non- or pre-Marxist Marx.

Althusser claims that the critique of humanism was necessary to counteract the theoretical confusions generated by the widespread use of the term after the Twentieth Congress of the Communist Party of the Soviet Union in 1956 (Althusser, 1969, 'To My English Readers', pp. 9–12). Some invoked it, thinking that recasting communism as humanism would wash the ugliness of the cult of personality and the barbarism of Stalinism away, forgetting the implications of humanist ideology. History, as he famously put it, is a 'process without a subject'. The real target, however, was Hegel, or rather the effects of Hegel, on what passes as Marxist thought. Althusser set himself the task of extricating Marxism from the economism that had reduced 'the dialectic of history to the dialectic generating the successive *modes of production*' (Althusser, 1969, 'Contradiction and Overdetermination', p. 108). He did so through an ingenious deconstruction of the Hegelian dialectic. This involves an initial reversal of a binary opposition (speculative versus materialist dialectic) in order to identify the traits held in reserve by the subordinate term (the complexity of materialism). Then comes a displacement of the opposition into a new terrain (Marxism) whereby Althusser keeps the old name (dialectic) but grafts onto it a new meaning that renders it 'overdetermined' – a term 'borrowed from another discipline'. In describing the Marxist dialectic as 'overdetermined in its principle', he is drawing on Freud and building bridges between Marxism and psychoanalysis.

Althusser's reasoning proceeds from the premise that the distinction between Marx and Hegel's dialectic has been obscured by the interpretation of the metaphor of inversion used by Marx. In the 'Afterword' to the second edition of *Capital*, Marx states: 'With [Hegel, the dialectic] is standing on its head. It must be turned right side up again, if you would discover the rational kernel within the mystical shell' (Althusser, 1969, 'Contradiction and Overdetermination', p. 89). Commentators have stressed the topos of the inversion, claiming that Marx corrected Hegel by putting the dialectic on its materialist feet. This argument, Althusser says, is correct but also misleading, as 'a philosophy inverted in this way cannot be regarded as *anything more* than the philosophy reversed' (Althusser, 1969, 'On the Young Marx', p. 73). In Althusser's reading, the 'rational kernel' has not one but two mystical wrappings. One is the external speculative system, which is removed through the celebrated inversion. The other refers to the very structure of the dialectic, for Althusser argues that the simplicity of the Hegelian contradiction leads Hegel to conceive totality as the manifestation of a single internal principle, or, to put it differently, to derive all discrete phenomena from that principle (Althusser, 1969, p. 102). Marx, he says, gains access to the rational kernel of the dialectic through the removal of this second mystical shell in 'an operation which transforms what it extracts' (Althusser, 1969, 'Contradiction and Overdetermination', p. 93). Here we must quote Althusser at length:

The simplicity of the Hegelian contradiction is made possible *only* by the simplicity of the *internal principle* that constitutes the essence of any historical period. If it is possible, *in principle, to reduce the totality*, the infinite diversity, of a historically given society (Greece, Rome, the Holy Roman Empire, England, and so on) to a *simple internal principle, this very simplicity* can be reflected in the contradiction *to which it thereby acquires a right* ... the reduction of *all* the elements that make up the concrete life of a historical epoch ... to *one* principle of internal unity, is only possible on the *absolute condition* of taking the whole concrete life of a people for the externalization-alienation ... of an *internal spiritual principle* ... I think we can now see how the 'mystical shell' affects and contaminates the 'kernel' – for *the simplicity of Hegelian contradiction is never more than a reflection of the simplicity of its internal principle of a people, that is, not its material reality but its most abstract ideology*. It is also why Hegel could represent Universal History from the Ancient Orient to the present day as 'dialectical', that is, moved by the simple play of a principle of *simple* contradiction. (Althusser, 1969, p. 103)

Economism, Althusser says, replicates the Hegelian argument by conceiving the superstructures as manifestations of the underlying economic nucleus. It reduces the dialectic to the play of a simple principle. That is why the mere abandonment of Hegel's speculative system leaves the central problem of the dialectic untouched. One can embrace materialism and still interpret historical processes as if they were the direct effect of a single contradiction – in this case, the contradiction between forces and relations of production – that operates as the founding locus of the totality and as the explanation of its transformations. In peeling off the mystical wrapping of the dialectic, he says, Marx will have to supplement the inversion of Hegel with a transformation of the very structure of the contradiction. The key to this transformation is the notion of 'overdetermination', which Althusser introduces through the metaphor of the 'weakest link', used by Lenin in his essay on imperialism.

Lenin invokes this metaphor to explain why the revolution could take place in Russia, the most backward country of Europe, instead of where the orthodox interpretations of Marx had predicted – advanced capitalist nations. A chain, says Lenin, is as strong as its weakest link. In the system of imperialist states of the time, Russia represented the weakest point because of '*the accumulation and exacerbation of all the historical contradictions then possible in a single state*' (Althusser, 1969, 'Contradiction and Overdetermination', p. 96). Althusser cites contradictions of a feudal system at the dawn of the twentieth century, of colonial exploitation and wars of aggression, of large-scale capitalist exploitation in major cities, of class struggles between exploiters and exploited but also within the ruling classes, and so on. In Russia, the imperialist chain could be broken on account of the accumulation of contradictions that provided the conditions for a socialist revolution. This, he says, indicates that, contrary to the caricature painted by economism, the capital–labour contradiction never acts on its own: an accumulation of circumstances is needed to activate it. Another extensive quote is warranted:

Marxist revolutionary experience shows that, if the general contradiction ... is sufficient to define the situation when revolution is the 'task of the day', it cannot on its own simple, direct power induce a 'revolutionary situation' ... If this contradiction is to become '*active*' in the strongest sense, to become a ruptural principle, there must be an accumulation of 'circumstances' and 'currents' so that whatever their origin and sense ..., they '*fuse*' into a *ruptural unity* ... The 'contradiction' is inseparable from the total structure of the social body in which it is found, inseparable from its formal *conditions* of existence, and even from the *instances* it governs; it is radically affected by them, determining, but also determined in one and the same movement, and determined by the various *levels* and *instances* of the social formation it animates; it might be called *overdetermined in its principle*. (Althusser, 1969, pp. 99, 101)

The Hegelian contradiction is never overdetermined. Therein lies the difference between Hegel and Marx and between economism and Althusser's reading of Marx. The contradiction between forces and relations of productions cannot explain historical change on its own. It only acquires ruptural force through its overdetermination by contradictions arising in different levels of the social formation. Instead of a direct causal link between base and superstructure, which conceives of politics and ideology as epiphenomena or by-products of the economy, the superstructures acquire their own specificity and effectiveness in the historical process, to the extent that changes in the base do not automatically modify the superstructures (Althusser, 1969, pp. 111, 115). The latter are part of the conditions of existence of the economic level, if only because labour legislation intervenes to organise the process of production (Althusser and Balibar, 1970, p. 178). The superstructures always already contaminate the base.

Althusser supplements the critique of the solitary causal determination of the economic base by invoking a letter that Engels wrote to Bloch in 1890, stating that their followers had exaggerated the role of the economy in the explanation of extra-economic phenomena. Moreover, to say that the contradiction is always overdetermined undermines the principle of necessity of orthodox Marxism and its belief in the inescapable laws of history. The Russian exception loses its exceptional character or, as Althusser put it, 'the exception thus discovers in itself the rule', for the general contradiction can be overdetermined in the direction of a historical break or of a historical inhibition (Althusser and Balibar, 1970, pp. 104, 106). This claim about the undecidability of historical events is Althusser's way of saying that contingency is lodged in the heart of the Marxian dialectic. The economy is determinant, but only in the last instance, to which he adds: 'From the first moment to the last, the lonely hour of the "last instance" never comes' (Althusser and Balibar, 1970, p. 113).

If the emphasis falls on the final part of this phrase, 'the lonely hour of the "last instance" *never comes*', we have a powerful critique of economism, but also an abandonment of the Marxist or mature Marx. This is something that Althusser was unlikely to consider as it would have compromised his position in the PCF. Yet if one underlines the beginning, 'the *lonely* hour of the "last instance" never comes', then what is lost is the mechanistic interpretation of Marxist orthodoxy and its belief in the solo work of the economy. The latter retains a place of honour while politics and ideology cease to be its epiphenomena. The thesis of 'the last instance' thus provided breathing space for those who were suspicious of economism but were not yet prepared to break with historical materialism or to contemplate the possibility of post-Marxism.

Althusser reiterates the ubiquitous reference to the last instance in his depiction of the Marxist totality as a 'structure in dominance'. Unlike the Hegelian expressive totality, that 'presupposes in principle that the whole in question be reducible to an *inner essence*, of which the elements of the whole are then no more than the phenomenal forms of expression' (Althusser and Balibar, 1970, p. 187), Marx proposes a totality that is as complex as his dialectic. It is a structured whole containing distinct, unevenly developed, relatively autonomous and dislocated instances or levels that include the economic structure – forces and relations of production – and the legal-political and ideological superstructures. Following Mao, Althusser contends that 'in real history determination in the last instance by the economy is exercised precisely in the permutations of the principal role between the economy, politics, theory, etc.' (Althusser, 1969, 'On the Materialist Dialectic', p. 213). But he also maintains that in order to escape relativism we must accept that the various levels 'coexist within this complex structural unity, articulated with one another according to specific determinations, fixed in the last instance by the level or instance of the economy' (Althusser and Balibar, 1970, pp. 99, 97). The Marxist whole is a 'structure in dominance', an articulation of instances whose play is governed by the economic level.

This notion of totality brings forth a critique of linear causality and the 'absent cause' inspired by Spinoza, for whom 'a cause is taken to be anything which *explains* the existence or qualities of the effect' (Hampshire, 1978, p. 3). Spinoza maintains that the substance is *causa sui*, a cause of itself, one whose 'essence involves existence and whose nature cannot be conceived unless existing' (Spinoza, 1963, *Ethics*, Def. I). A substance is composed of infinite attributes, 'each expressing the reality of being of the substance' (*Ethics*, Prop. IX). This infinite (unbound) and eternal (timeless) self-creating totality is logically prior to its parts (*Ethics*, Prop. I), and it exists or may be conceived through its modifications (*Ethics*, Def. V, Axiom I). Similarly, for Althusser the structure 'is not an essence outside the economic phenomena which comes and alters their aspects, forms and relations and which is effective on them as an absent cause, absent because it is outside them'. Instead, it is 'a cause immanent in its effects in the Spinozist sense of the term, that the whole existence of the structure consists of its effects, in short, that the structure ... is nothing outside its effects' (Althusser and Balibar, 1970, pp. 188–9). So Althusser uses the idea of the primacy of the whole over its parts and the determination of the latter by the former to enunciate the thesis of the structure in dominance, and he takes the existence of the substance through its modifications as the basis to account for the immanence of the structure in its effects. Both provide the ground for claiming that subjects, political or otherwise, are nothing but effects of the structure. For Althusser, 'the structure of the relations of production determines the *places* and *functions* occupied and adopted by the agents of production, who are never anything more than the occupants of these places, insofar as they are the "supports" (*Träger*) of these functions' (Althusser and Balibar, 1970, p. 180). Subjects are therefore conceived as bearers or supports produced and reproduced by the structures.

the philosophico-political underside

The accomplishments of Althusser – renewing Marxist discourse by disentangling Marx from Hegel and by combating economism – did not shield him from criticism. The analytic status of the epistemological break, for example, is debatable. For Althusser, the distance between the two 'problematics' – alienation and exploitation, ideology and science – is so radical that they become incommensurable, to the extent that the mature or Marxist Marx detaches himself altogether from the thoughts entertained by his former self. This effort to discard everything deemed pre-scientific in order to deliver a distilled Marx who is above metaphysical suspicion is tactically convenient but also simplistic. It rests on the tacit assumption of change without remainder. The Jacobins also wished to make *tabula rasa* of the past, even changing the calendar to enshrine 1789 as year zero. They failed because the very idea of revolution as a rupture without residues was flawed. The persistence of superstition or non-republican ideologies was not a sign of an imperfect revolution but of the exorbitant demand that it should have produced an absolute new beginning, a relation of pure exteriority with the past. Similarly, the presumption that the break would render an anti-humanist Marx immune to all teleo-eschatology is questionable when one recalls the thesis of a communist end of history, something Althusser only acknowledged 20 years later (Althusser, 1993, p. 224). Derrida put it very well: all ruptures are inevitably reinscribed in an old fabric that we must pull apart endlessly; this endlessness is not accidental but systematic and essential (Derrida, 1981, pp. 24, 1993, p. 195).

The opposition between science and ideology is equally problematic. For Althusser, 'ideology, as a system of representations, is distinguished from science in that in it the practico-social function is more important than the theoretical function (function as knowledge)' (Althusser, 1969, 'Marxism and Humanism', p. 231). Both are systems of representation, a claim that brings him close to discourse-theoretical approaches that have become popular in the social sciences. He also sees ideology as a superstructure, and therefore as an organic part of every social totality. 'Only an ideological world outlook could have imagined societies *without ideology* and accepted the utopian idea of a world in which ideology ... would disappear without trace, to be replaced by *science*', for 'it is in ideology (as the locus of political struggle) that men *become conscious* of their place in the world and in history'; that is, ideology 'is a matter of the *lived* relation between men and their world' (Althusser, 1969, pp. 232, 233). Ideology is not a passing phenomenon and science is not the telos of revolutionary politics. Yet Althusser chooses to stress Marx's scientific innovation, his foundation of a non-ideological philosophy or capitalised 'Theory' and to grant Marxist philosophy the status of sole scientific philosophy.

Why would Althusser advocate this scientific monotheism? One is tempted to dismiss it as an intervention in the politico-theoretical struggles of the time, as the work of a will to power in the field of knowledge. Marxism had to be dignified as a science, a task that Althusser radicalises by claiming that dialectical and historical materialism alone can guide us to attain true knowledge of the world and ground politics. 'Marxism', he says, 'is like a "guide for action". It can be one because it is a science, and only because of this … [S]ciences also need a "guide", not a false but a true guide … [a] theoretically qualified one: dialectical materialism' (Althusser, 1966, p. 122). The claim about the scientific guidance of politics is baffling, as it comes closer to the sprit of positivism than to a philosophy of praxis. It inverts the Marxist primacy of practice over consciousness through the ill-conceived definition of philosophy as the 'Theory' of theoretical practice. This in turn insinuates a naive theory of truth that combines unveiling – Marxism shows us the reality behind illusions – and correspondence – its knowledge depicts the reality of the real. Of course, Althusser's scientism might also spring from the desire for mastery mentioned earlier. Sorting out good interpretations of Marx from merely ideological ones is a way of affirming the correctness of his Marx as opposed to that of Lukács, Gramsci or Colletti. 'In an epistemological and critical reading' of Marx, he says, 'we are simply returning to him the speech that is his own' (Althusser, 1970, pp. 143–4). Althusser's symptomatic reading restores the truth to Marx. Here hermeneutics is reduced to interpretation as the unveiling of a hidden text, except that the referent – the truth of Marx's discourse – is an effect of his own reading.

Althusser's work on ideology (1971) criticises the thesis of false consciousness and tries to fill the gap left by his earlier dismissal of subjects as mere effects – 'bearers' or 'supports' – of the structure. He reiterates that ideology represents the imaginary relationship of individuals to their real conditions of existence, but also invokes a Gramscian trope by saying that it is embodied in apparatuses, notably state apparatuses, and adds that ideology is a practice that transforms individuals into subjects through the mechanism of hailing or interpellation typified in the police call, '*Hey, you there!*' Interesting as this was, the argument had a clear functionalist slant. For Althusser ideology works to secure the reproduction of capitalist class relations, which makes it difficult to think of ideologies of resistance and emancipation, or of ideological struggle as such. Class reductionism also plagued it, as the postscript added to counter the accusations of functionalism and the absence of struggle in his depiction of ideology led him to assign a class nature to all social phenomena. This prevented any possibility of conceiving either non-class ideologies or the specificity of non-class identities. The circularity of his argument was a problem, too. If ideologies transform individuals into subjects, there must be something like a pre-ideological condition, but as only subjects recognise interpellations, Althusser has to claim that we are always already subjects and therefore never outside ideology. This begs the question of how can anyone ever manage to escape its grip – or bother to do so – in order to elaborate a scientific philosophy or engage in revolution. Moreover, he simply ignores the gap between the conditions of production and the conditions of reception of interpellations. One can hail people as fascist or sexist, but this does not mean that they will recognise themselves as such. He admits that mechanisms of recognition *and* misrecognition are at work in ideology, but only recognition seems to count, as misrecognition applies to real conditions of existence, not hailing. By focusing on interpellation alone, Althusser has no way of assessing the actual efficacy of the ideological constitution of subjectivity.

Finally, while 'determination in the last instance' did provide some breathing space for Marxism, Althusser's critique of economism and the ensuing resurrection of historical materialism were done at the price of misinterpreting or counterfeiting Freud's concept of overdetermination, either intentionally or by accident (one cannot take seriously his confession that Freud 'remains a closed book to me'). Freud speaks of overdetermination to account for the asymmetry between the dream-thoughts and the manifest content or brief text that one remembers when waking up. His explanation for this is that only the overdetermined dream-thoughts – those that 'have been represented in the dream-thoughts many times over' – find their way into the manifest dream (Freud, 1976, pp. 388, 389). These operate as anchoring points that centre the dream, but – and this is a decisive 'but' – the overdetermined dream-thoughts or nodal points have no ontological consistency: they are only identified as the result of analysis, not *ex ante*. Althusser, however, has already decided that the general contradiction alone can be overdetermined to trigger or block a revolutionary rupture. In doing so, he cancels out the possibility of the overdetermination of religious, racial or national oppositions. This turns 'determination in the last instance' into the metaphysical closure of his intellectual project, an article of faith enunciated by a PCF theoretician to comply with Communist Party orthodoxy.

This was the flip-side of Althusserianism. He eventually recanted his theoreticism, saying that it was prompted by the desire to find a compromise between his own speculative-theoretical yearnings and his obsession with real practice and contact with physical reality (Althusser, 1993, p. 215). But this fascination with practical and political life coupled with scientism and theoreticism was not without consequences for Marxism. Perhaps the most significant is that one wanders through the Althusserian landscape without ever encountering an ethics or a theory of political action. His Spinozist structural causality left agency unexplained. Class struggle, invoked repeatedly, remained buried in the unswerving defence of science and the purity of theory. The critique of theoretical humanism dismissed the problems of the essence of man at the expense of leaving the theory of exploitation without resources with which to conceptualise emancipation (Rancière, 1974). In the end, like many of his followers, he contributed not so much to the renewal of socialist political practice as to the introduction of Marxism into the academic curriculum, where it prospered in post-Marxist and cultural studies.

Althusser's originality is that he subjected Marxism to what Derrida calls the law of iterability: if a repetition or effort to recover something invariably incorporates something new, then every retrieval is also a form of reinstitution as it cannot leave the 'original' unscathed. The return to Marx through a symptomatic reading of his texts modified what it sought to retrieve. Althusser aimed to deliver us a distilled Marx, one that would show critics and vulgar emulators alike that there was no trace of economism, historicism, humanism, or a transcendental subject in his writings. In weeding out the youthful mistakes of the theory of alienation from the historical materialism of the mature Marx, Althusser was not so much clarifying Marx as inventing Althusserianism. His return to Marx thus mirrored Lacan's return to Freud in the double sense that while both sought to restore the dignity of the source through a careful textual reading, both also reinstituted that source as they retrieved it.

further reading

Of Althusser's works listed below, *Reading Capital*, *For Marx* and *Lenin and Philosophy* are the most significant. The first two develop the familiar tropes of the epistemological break and the critiques of humanism and economism, whereas the latter contains the essay on ideology. Amongst the secondary literature, the essays in Kaplan and Sprinker (1993) and Elliott (1994) cover relevant aspects of his thought in a clear and elegant manner. The polemic with Thompson (1978) raises the question of his paralysing theoreticism, as does Rancière's (1974) critique of the gap between his theory and his politics.

references

Althusser, L. (1966) 'Matérialisme historique et matérialisme dialectique', *Cahiers marxistes-léninistes* (11 April): 90–122.

Althusser, L. (1969) *For Marx* [1st edn 1965], trans. B. Brewster. London: Allen Lane.

Althusser, L. (1971) *Lenin and Philosophy and Other Essays*, trans. B. Brewster. London: New Left Books.

Althusser, L. (1976) *Essays in Self-Criticism*, trans. G. Lock. London and New Jersey: New Left Books and Humanities Press.

Althusser, L. (1993) *The Future Lasts Forever*. New York: The New Press.

Althusser, L. and Balibar, É. (1970) *Reading Capital* [1st edn 1965], trans. B. Brewster. London: New Left Books.

Bachelard, G. (1947) *La formation de l'esprit scientifique. Contribution à une psychanalyse de la connaissance objective*. Paris: J. Vrin.

Derrida, J. (1981) *Positions* [1st edn 1972], trans. A. Bass. London: Athlone.

Derrida, J. (1993) 'Politics and Friendship: An Interview with Jacques Derrida' [1st edn 1989], in *The Althusserian Legacy*, ed. A. Kaplan and M. Sprinker, pp. 183–231. London: Verso.

Elliot, G. (1994) *Althusser: A critical reader*. Oxford and Cambridge: Blackwell.

Freud, S. (1976) *The Interpretation of Dreams* [1st edn 1900], The Pelican Freud Library, vol. 4, trans. and ed. J. Strachey. Harmondsworth: Penguin Books.

Hampshire, S. (1978) *Spinoza*. Dallas: Penguin.

Harnecker, M. (1969) *Conceptos elementales del materialismo histórico*. México: Siglo XXI.

Kaplan, A. and Sprinker, M. (eds) (1993) *The Althusserian Legacy*. London: Verso.

Laclau, E. (1977) *Politics and Ideology in Marxist Theory*. London: New Left Books.

Poulantzas, N. (1973) *Political Power and Social Classes* [1st edn 1968]. London: New Left Books.

Rancière, J. (1974) 'On the Theory of Ideology (The Politics of Althusser)', *Radical Philosophy* 7: 2–15.

Spinoza, B. (1963) *Ethics*, trans. A. Boyle. New York: Everyman.

Thompson, E.P. (1978) *The Poverty of Theory and Other Essays*. London: Merlin.

13
jürgen habermas

Jürgen Habermas is one of the most important political philosophers today, and one of those authors about whom everybody seems to have an opinion. He has published dozens of books on a variety of subjects and has been influential in a number of disciplines, especially in the social sciences. Indeed, his influence is such that ideas and writers associated with his work are often referred to as 'Habermasian'.

Habermas is the best-known representative of the second generation of the Critical Theory of the Frankfurt School, the first generation of which included Theodor Adorno and Max Horkheimer. Habermas has developed Critical Theory in important respects, drawing on Continental as well as analytic philosophers like John Searle and John Rawls. Thus he straddles the traditional Continental/analytic divide in philosophy.

Today, Habermas is best known for two things. The first is his defence of reason, modernity and the Enlightenment together with his critique of so-called postmodernists, such as Michel Foucault, Gilles Deleuze and Jacques Derrida. The second is his idea of deliberative democracy, which has gained increasing influence among political philosophers as well as experts and practitioners.

Habermas was born in 1929 in West Germany, and he grew up during World War II, an experience that made a lasting impact on him and his thought. In 1954 he finished his PhD thesis on the philosopher Friedrich von Schelling at Bonn University, and later in the 1950s he became Adorno's assistant at Frankfurt. After spells at other universities, he became professor of philosophy at Frankfurt in 1964, where – apart from a period at the Max Planck Institute in Starnberg and several visiting professorships in the US – he has been ever since. He is now Professor Emeritus at Frankfurt and continues to write at the pace of one book every year or two.

Habermas's work can usefully be divided into three periods. During the first period, from the early 1960s to the early 1970s, he tried to develop a quasi-Marxist Critical Theory of late capitalism, criticising scientism and positivism in particular. This work was based on a notion of human interests, which he later abandoned (Habermas, 1987b). The second period consists of his theories of communicative action and discourse ethics from the 1970s and 1980s (Habermas, 1984; 1987a; 1990; 1998b). During the third period, stretching from the late 1980s until the present, he developed his theory of deliberative democracy. Although Habermas's political philosophy is mostly of a more recent date, his work in philosophy and sociology was permeated by political concerns from the very beginning. Moreover, Habermas is a proliferate public intellectual, and his political writings have been collected in ten volumes, the latest English translation of which is *Time of Transitions* (Habermas, 2005).

Given that Habermas's work escapes summary in its entirety in a brief introduction like this, I shall focus on what will be of most interest to students of political philosophy, namely his work on communicative action, discourse ethics and deliberative democracy.

communicative action

Habermas developed the theory of communicative action in *The Theory of Communicative Action* (1984; 1987a) and in a number of articles (1998b). This theory is his attempt to save a normative content for reason and modernity, and it is the basis for his discourse ethics and deliberative democracy, to which I will turn in the succeeding sections.

The philosophical background for the theory of communicative action is Habermas's critique of what he calls 'the philosophy of the subject', which he finds in Immanuel Kant, G.W.F. Hegel and Karl Marx, among others. In Kant, for instance, a clever individual subject tries to imagine what the moral law must be. However, a problem arises when a plurality of subjects have to come to agreement on the moral law; this is particularly a problem in pluralist societies with deep moral disagreements. For Habermas, it is therefore necessary to shift the focus from the individual to the public sphere where individuals come to agreement about moral and legal norms.

Hegel partly provides a solution to this, because he thinks of individual subjects as always embedded in ethical life. Yet Hegel dissolves the intersubjectivity of ethical life into a subject writ large: the modern bureaucratic and bourgeois state is the highest point of rationality in a teleological unfolding of History. This has implications for pluralism, because if the state incarnates rationality, all dissent can be suppressed with reference to this.

Like Hegel, Marx focuses on the collective rather than the individual. For Marx, however, the essence of human beings is not some form of intersubjectivity, but instead the subject–object relation of *Homo laborans'* appropriating nature. Politically, Marxism gives a privileged position to a particular subject (the proletariat, the party or the vanguard) capable of predicting and acting upon history. This idea of a privileged subject had dire consequences, for instance, for those who dissented from the official party line.

Habermas's problem with the philosophy of the subject – as found in Kant, Hegel and Marx – is that it locates rationality and validity in a subject, whether an individual or a collective subject. This kind of philosophy takes rationality to be a means–end relationship: a subject with certain goals or principles stands opposed to the world, including the world of other subjects, which it can only treat as objects that need to be overcome in order to realise its goals and principles. This is not just a philosophical problem, but a sociological and political problem, too. The philosophy of the subject cannot explain how actions can be coordinated, especially in modern pluralist societies.

Habermas's response to the philosophy of the subject is to take the 'linguistic turn' and to argue for a shift to an intersubjectivist paradigm. The latter avoids the problems with the philosophy of the subject by locating rationality and validity in the intersubjectivity of free and open dialogue. This is the basis for the theory of *communicative* action and, later, *discourse* ethics and *deliberative* democracy.

In *Knowledge and Human Interest*, Habermas (1987b, p. 313) argues that *'work, language, and power'* are constitutive of human experience. From then onwards, he focuses on the second of these: language. He writes:

> What raises us out of nature is the only thing whose nature we can know: *language*. Through its structure, autonomy and responsibility are posited for us. Our first sentence expresses unequivocally the intention of universal and unconstrained consensus. (Habermas, 1987b, p. 314)

And he speculates that 'In this way, perhaps the Kantian notion of the fact of reason can be revitalized' (Habermas, 1987b, p. 380). What defines us as human beings, then, is the fact that we are linguistic. We always find ourselves within language, and we only have access to the world, including any human essence, through language. This is more than an empirical fact, however. Habermas wants to locate in it a normative force; that is, he finds an 'ought' in the 'is'. Only in this way can the Kantian belief in reason and Enlightenment be revived.

Habermas attempts to save reason and modernity from their critics. Among the latter are Adorno and Horkheimer, who criticise reason but, according to Habermas (1987c, ch. 5), confuse reason as such with what is only one particular kind of reason, namely instrumental reason. Habermas differentiates action and rationality, thus linking sociology and philosophy in a way that is characteristic of Critical Theory. Instrumental rationality refers to a subject–

object relationship. Strategic rationality refers to a situation where a subject treats another subject as an object; like instrumental rationality, the criterion of success is the efficiency of the means in achieving dominance, whether dominance over nature or other human beings.

These kinds of action and rationality can be distinguished from communicative action and rationality. Communicative action is oriented towards mutual understanding or agreement, not towards the assertion of power or instrumental efficiency. The rationality of communicative action is located not in a subject but in the character of the relations among subjects or, more specifically, in relations that are free from relations of power.

Habermas's method is one of rational reconstruction (Habermas, 1990, p. 31f.). He claims to reconstruct the constitutive and unavoidable assumptions of social practices, in this case of social action in general. The structures of action and language that he reconstructs are universal or 'quasi-transcendental'. They are not something one can choose, but are necessarily presupposed when one engages in social action and linguistic communication. These universal structures are not just empirical facts, however; they have a normative force as well.

Habermas argues that, without an account of communicative action, it is impossible to explain how societies can, in the long run, be integrated peacefully, that is, without violence and power. Of course one may argue – and Habermas's critics have done so – that violence and power are characteristics of all hitherto existing human societies. Habermas does not deny that violence and power are facts of life, and he is himself the first to point to these phenomena in current societies.

Nonetheless, he argues that it is necessary to distinguish communicative action and rationality from instrumental/strategic action and rationality. Only then can one criticise power and pull oneself above the fray of power relations. Only if one has established a point where there is no power (communicative action) can the critique of power itself claim to be not just another expression of power. If everything is reduced to instrumental reason, then the critique of it can itself only be an expression of instrumental reason. For instance, Adorno and Horkheimer's total critique of reason saws off the branch on which they are sitting. In Habermas's terms, they are making a performative contradiction. They cannot claim to be engaged in critique without having first secured a ground on which to stand. Habermas concludes that if Adorno and Horkheimer's critique is to have any force and not be self-defeating, it must presuppose something like communicative rationality. This is a critique he also levels at so-called postmodernists, such as Foucault (Habermas, 1987c, chs 9 and 10).

With the argument of the performative contradiction Habermas has shown that even the starkest critics of reason have to presuppose something like communicative reason in order for their critique to have any force. Hence he can argue that communicative rationality is indeed unavoidable; even when we communicate to criticise rationality, we implicitly take a form of it for granted.

A final aspect of the theory of communicative action is the 'colonisation thesis' (Habermas, 1987a, ch. 6 and pp. 332–73). Although Habermas has not addressed this thesis directly since *The Theory of Communicative Action*, it is nonetheless an important part of the theory and serves to illustrate its potential for social critique.

Habermas divides society into system and lifeworld, where the former is integrated through instrumental-strategic action and the latter through communicative action. The lifeworld is a taken-for-granted background consensus for communicative action, which can nevertheless be problematised by social agents. Although the system–lifeworld distinction is analytical, the lifeworld is typically found in institutions like the family and civil society. The two most important systems are the state and the market, which are integrated through the steering media of power and money respectively.

Both systems and lifeworld are necessary parts of complex modern societies. State and market solve important problems that could not be solved otherwise, so Habermas is not against the state or the market as such. However, a problem arises when system media colonise the lifeworld, that is, when system media are used in contexts that are best integrated through communicative action. This happens when money and power rule relationships like friendship, family and the public sphere. If that happens, then the orientation towards mutual agreement is pushed aside by concerns for money and power. For instance, in the case of the family, increasing legal regulation makes family members view one another as legal subjects rather than as persons taking part in a communicative context. And, in the case of the public sphere, a concern with truth and normative rightness is pushed aside by the desire for power and money.

The colonisation thesis gives Habermas a critical take on alienation in contemporary Western societies. Significantly, the thesis is not confined to a critique of capitalism and the market but extends to other areas, including state bureaucracy. What is more, the colonisation thesis rests neither on a nostalgic longing for a lost premodern past nor on a utopian ideal; all it states is that the lifeworld must be protected against intrusion from the systems.

discourse ethics

Discourse ethics is an answer to the question: how can we talk about something as true or right in modern, secular and divided societies? Habermas's answer is a procedural account of truth and normative rightness, which, like the theory of communicative action, locates rationality in intersubjective relations (Habermas, 1990). Validity or what is true and normatively right is the outcome of discourse, and rationality is ascribed by Habermas to the character of the discourse. When certain requirements are met, Habermas refers to the discourse as rational, something which he earlier referred to as an 'ideal speech situation', a term he later abandoned.

The argument is as follows. When engaging in communicative action we take an implicit background consensus for granted. When problematising the background consensus – for instance, some taken for granted truth or norm – we move to the level of discourse. For instance, I might put forward the validity claim that 'society ought to be more equal', which is a claim, among other things, to what is normatively right.

When raising a validity claim in this way, the claim to validity is raised in a particular context, here and now. Yet it contains the implicit claim that I could defend it with reasons under idealised circumstances of equal access, absence of power, and so on. This is what Habermas refers to as rational discourse, where only the force of the better argument counts. The result of a rational discourse is a rational consensus, where the agreement to the validity claim is universal. Thus, while particular, the validity claim also contains an implicit claim to universality.

The rationality of the consensus is attributed to the character of the discourse. Earlier, Habermas believed that rational discourse and rational consensus were in fact possible; later he held that they were impossible to realise, but that they are unavoidable assumptions of communicative action and argumentation; and most recently he has argued that the idea of a rational consensus may be self-defeating (Habermas, 1998b, p. 365f.). The end of discourse (namely, consensus) would also be the end to discourse, because there would be no point in further discussion (see also Mouffe, 2000, p. 98).

Habermas believes that his discourse ethics is a modest theory of rationality and validity. First of all, it is procedural. The procedures stipulated by discourse ethics do not determine the outcome of discourses; they only give us a way of finding out what is the best and right thing to do. In this sense, discourse ethics is deontological: it does not tell us what to strive for, only how to find out what to strive for. With regard to norms, this is stipulated in the discourse principle (D): 'Just those action norms are valid to which all possibly affected persons could agree as participants in rational discourses' (Habermas, 1996, p. 107). In addition, Habermas believes that he has reconstructed in a rational fashion the unavoidable assumptions one makes when engaging in communicative action and argumentation. As quoted above: 'Our first sentence expresses unequivocally the intention of universal and unconstrained consensus' (Habermas, 1987b, p. 314). In this sense, too, discourse ethics is modest. He sometimes refers to his project of communicative action and discourse ethics as 'formal' or 'universal pragmatics' in order to capture these points: it is merely a reconstruction of the universal structures of pragmatic use of language and only provides a formal (as opposed to a substantive) theory of morality (Habermas, 1990; 1998b, ch. 1).

With discourse ethics, Habermas is able to claim that it is possible to discuss truth and rightness in rational ways and thus not reduce validity to power. At the same time, having taken the 'linguistic turn', he rejects the correspondence theory of truth, which holds that validity depends on the (non-)correspondence of claims with a state of affairs. The problem is that the correspondence cannot be determined independently of language, because we always find ourselves within language. Habermas also rejects any claim by an individual or collective subject to have a monopoly on truth or rightness. This is particularly important in pluralist societies where subjects need to get along despite their different views of what is true and right. Finally, the idea of rational discourse and rational consensus gives Habermas a way to criticise the shortcomings of any particular discourse or consensus, for instance the exclusion of groups from discussions about norms that would apply to those groups. This also leads him to reject any reference to tradition as the basis of validity, thus distinguishing him from communitarians (for example, Charles Taylor) and hermeneuticists (for example, Hans-Georg Gadamer).

'Discourse ethics' is actually a misnomer. It is more adequately described as a discourse theory of validity, including truth, normative rightness and ethical authenticity. Habermas makes a distinction between different questions that can be asked in a discourse, and which are often raised at the same time. There are pragmatic questions of efficiency and truth. More importantly for Habermas's moral and political philosophy are moral and ethical questions. Moral questions concern what is right and just; they concern norms and what is equally good for all. Ethical questions concern what is good for me or us in the long run; they concern values, that is, what I or we value, or what Habermas, following John Rawls, sometimes calls conceptions of the good life. It means that there is a limit to dialogue about ethical questions. In the end, they are relative to a subject, an 'I' or a 'we'. Discussions about ethical questions are teleological not deontological, and this has important consequences for politics in societies where there is a plurality of ethical conceptions of the good life. In this sense, too, 'discourse ethics' is slightly misleading as it is actually more focused on morality.

So, to sum up, we have moved from the theory of communicative action and rationality to the discourse theory of validity. The latter includes answers to how to deal with pragmatic, moral and ethical questions. The discourse principle applies to norms: only those norms to which all who are possibly affected have consented in rational discourse are valid. However, the discourse principle bifurcates, because it covers both moral norms and legal norms. The former are covered by the moral (or Universalisation principle: U), which states that 'For a [moral] norm to be valid, the consequences and side effects that its *general* observance can be expected to have for the satisfaction of the particular interests of *each* person affected must be such that *all* affected can accept them freely' (Habermas, 1990, p. 120). Legal norms are covered by the democratic principle and the theory of deliberative democracy.

deliberative democracy

Habermas developed his theory of deliberative democracy and law from the late 1980s onwards and, in particular, in *Between Facts and Norms*, published in German in 1992 and in English in 1996. It would be wrong to refer to this as a 'political turn', however, because Habermas's earlier work was already very political. For instance, throughout his career, Habermas has taken part in a number of public debates about the organisation of the university, student protests, nuclear protests and civil disobedience, and German history. His interventions were all informed by his philosophy, thus combining the two roles of academic philosopher and public intellectual. Moreover, as argued above, his theories of communicative action and discourse ethics are linked to the possibility of social critique and social integration in pluralist societies.

With deliberative democracy, Habermas turns from moral to legal norms. The reason for this turn is that modern, complex societies cannot be integrated through moral norms only. Morality only carries a weak force, especially in impersonal contexts (the force of bad conscience, and so on). Law, on the other hand, is enforceable (fines, prison, and so on) and better fits the impersonal relations of modern societies. For these and other reasons, Habermas concludes that law is the only available medium for social integration in modern societies. However, it is not enough for law to be enforceable, that is, for the subjects of law to stick to the law out of fear of reprisals. In such a situation, people would relate to the law in a strictly instrumentalist fashion, weighing up the costs and benefits of breaking it on an *ad hoc* basis. In the end, it would lead to disrespect of the law and, eventually, disintegration of society. So Habermas needs to give an account of how law can be legitimate, that is, how the subjects of the law may relate to it out of respect.

Law can be seen on analogy with morality. To be legitimate, both legal and moral norms must be rooted in discourse, hence they are linked by the discourse principle (D). The foundation of legitimate law is discursive opinion and will formation – in short, *deliberative* democracy. This is expressed in the democratic principle: 'only those [legal] statutes may claim legitimacy that can meet with the assent (*Zustimmung*) of all citizens in a discursive process of legislation that in turn has been legally constituted' (Habermas, 1996, p. 110).

Habermas here draws on a notion of autonomy rooted in Kant and Jean-Jacques Rousseau. In order for the law to be legitimate, the addressees of the law must be able to see themselves simultaneously as the authors of the law. However, according to Habermas, Kant's and Rousseau's notions of autonomy are limited by the philosophy of the subject. Kant has an account of individual autonomy, but he does not have an adequate account of the relations among subjects and of how individuals come together to make the law. Rousseau, on the other hand, has an account of collective autonomy and lawmaking but risks imposing the general will on individuals, thus violating their individual autonomy.

Habermas wants to take the best from both and avoid the problems. His notion of autonomy holds that the 'citizens [are] able to understand themselves also as authors of the law to which they are subject as addressees' if democracy is organised as deliberative democracy (Habermas, 1996, p. 449). That is, if the addressees have made the laws under conditions that secure the equality and freedom of each citizen, the law is the result of collective lawmaking that respects individual freedom. The conditions Habermas refers to here are the idealised conditions behind the discourse principle: equal access for everybody, any issue can be raised, and so on. Since everybody has to consent freely, Habermas believes that public autonomy (collective lawmaking or popular sovereignty) and private autonomy (individual rights) are reconciled.

This view of autonomy is reflected in the democratic principle. The validity of legal norms can only be settled in public deliberations under idealised conditions of full information, equal access, symmetry, and so on. Constitutional democracy is the concrete realisation of these principles. The addressees of the law must simultaneously be its authors, and this condition extends to the laws of lawmaking, that is, the constitution. In large and complex societies, the immediate identity of addressees and authors is possible neither in everyday lawmaking nor in constitutional lawmaking. Yet the addressees of the law must at least be able to *understand* themselves as simultaneously the authors of the law. So the constitution must be subject to democratic will-formation. At the same time, however, the latter must be constitutionally regulated in such a way as to protect the pluralism of modern societies and the singularity of each individual. Citizens can only understand themselves as the authors of the law if they are simultaneously constituted as free and equal subjects under the law. Habermas's thesis of the co-originality of constitutionalism and democracy reflects this: there is a relation of mutual implication and support between constitutionalism (individual rights) and democracy (popular sovereignty). So only a political system that is both constitutional and democratic is legitimate (Habermas, 1996, ch. 4; 1998a, ch. 10). To sum up, at the core of Habermas's theory of deliberative democracy is a notion of autonomy, which is expressed in the democratic principle, in the identity of addressees and authors of the law, and in the co-originality thesis.

As suggested by the democratic principle, Habermas views the politics of deliberative democracy on the model of public argumentation. It is precisely *deliberative* democracy. For instance, he understands civil disobedience as the continuation of public argumentation with different means (Habermas, 1996, pp. 382–4). To Habermas, civil disobedience must be non-violent and take a symbolic form, and it must not be rooted in self-interest but should appeal to the majority and to principles of justice. It should follow public discussion in both formal and informal settings, and the civil disobedient person must take a fallibilist attitude to his or her own views. This all suggests that Habermas understands civil disobedience as a way of continuing public discussion after a formal political decision has been taken.

For Habermas, the public sphere, and more broadly civil society, is central to deliberative democracy (Arato and Cohen, 1992). The core of the discursive opinion and will formation on which law rests takes place in the public sphere, which must be as free as possible from relations of power. The public sphere was the subject of Habermas's first book, *The Structural Transformation of the Public Sphere: An Inquiry into a Category of Bourgeois Society*, first published in German in 1962 and then in English in 1989 (see also Calhoun, 1992). The book was a critique of what Habermas saw as the erosion of the public sphere and its increased manipulation by the state and capital. One need only think of the way election campaigns are fought today in order to see that this is not a phenomenon of the past. Yet although the book referred to the public sphere as a 'category of bourgeois society', Habermas found in it a normative potential, namely the promise that the force of the good argument will prevail, the promise that he also finds inherent in language as such. This normative content of the public sphere can be retrieved and turned against the ills of bourgeois society, including the way the public sphere functions. This is a good example of Habermas's method. He reconstructs the normative and rational content of Enlightenment ideals in order to turn them against real existing (bourgeois) democracies.

Modern political systems do not allow for day-to-day direct democracy, at least not on a big scale. Hence, we need a system of representative government, and the theory of deliberative democracy tries to take this into account. However, Habermas highlights two things (Habermas, 1996, ch. 8). First, the institutions of the representative system must themselves be organised like small public bodies, for instance in a parliament or in juries. In these institutions, the force of the better argument, not self-interest, must prevail.

Second, representative government must be rooted in the public sphere, that is, in the citizens' deliberations on the laws of the country. Consequently, Habermas thinks of the political system as having a core (the formal political system comprising parliament, courts and government) and a periphery (the informal institutions of civil society and the public sphere). The public deliberations in the informal parts of the system must feed into the formal system, because formal lawmaking must originate in the citizens' deliberations. In addition, during the process of making and interpreting the law, the formal system must be porous, that is, open to inputs from the public sphere.

Modern societies are pluralist, that is, they contain a plurality of ethical conceptions of the good life. This 'fact of pluralism' leads Habermas to argue that, if society were integrated at the ethical level, that is, if the laws expressed a particular ethical conception of the good, then other conceptions of the good would be disadvantaged or excluded. For instance, if schoolchildren are made to pledge allegiance to the flag and that pledge contains a reference to a (Christian) God, it will discriminate against atheists, agnostics and non-Christians. So the law must be distinguished from any particular ethical view, for instance, a religious one.

Habermas here makes a distinction between the plurality of ethical conceptions of the good and the political integration of society through society-wide laws:

> The ethical integration of groups and subcultures with their own collective identities must be uncoupled from the abstract political integration that includes all citizens equally ... The neutrality of the law vis-à-vis internal ethical differentiations stems from the fact that in complex societies the citizenry as a whole can no longer be held together by a substantive consensus on values but only by a consensus on the procedures for the legitimate enactment of laws and the legitimate exercise of power. (Habermas, 1998a, p. 225)

This distinction should not be confused with the one between ethical and moral questions. Laws will inevitably express some values, because they are the positive expression of the will of a people. But Habermas distinguishes between particular ethical values (for instance, a particular religion), which the law should not reflect, and political values (for instance, equality among religious and non-religious faiths), which the law may reflect.

Political values crystallise around a 'constitutional patriotism' (Habermas, 1996, p. 500; 1998a, p. 225f.). Constitutional patriotism must be distinguished from nationalism. Indeed, constitutional patriotism is necessary because there is often more than one nation (or other subculture) within a single country. Constitutional patriotism refers to a political culture of political and procedural values, allegiance to which ensures that different groups can see themselves as belonging to the same *political* unit despite their *ethical* differences. Of course there will be differences over the interpretation of these values, but these differences can be played out in public deliberations.

Tolerance, too, is important in contemporary multicultural societies, and it is a good example of Habermas's method of rational reconstruction. He argues that, traditionally, tolerance is a hierarchical relationship between the tolerating and the tolerated parties, where the former bestows tolerance on the latter as an act of grace. Yet this does not lead him to reject tolerance, because he argues that it is possible to appropriate a normative kernel of equal respect from it. Hence he conceives of tolerance as a relationship between equal partners in a dialogue. So Habermas reconstructs the concept of tolerance on the model of public deliberation.

In his most recent work, Habermas has looked beyond the nation-state towards what he calls a 'postnational constellation' (Habermas, 1998a; 1998b; 2001). There are two fundamental problems with the nation-state, according to Habermas. First, as already mentioned, states only rarely correspond to nations: some states contain more than one nation, and some nations are spread across different states. Second, the (nation-)state is too small to meet regional and global challenges of terrorism, migration, pollution and, especially, capitalism.

As a consequence, Habermas argues for a change of focus from the nation-state to the regional (European) and global (cosmopolitan) level. He argues for increased integration in the European Union so that it will become more like a state, including a common foreign policy. True to his theory of deliberative democracy, an EU polity must develop together with an EU-wide public sphere, because EU legislation must be rooted in EU-wide opinion and will formation.

At the global level, Habermas argues for the use of international organisations (like the United Nations) and international law (like the International Criminal Court) to regulate global capitalism and enforce human rights. This is also the context of his critique of the unilateralism of the US government under George W. Bush. Habermas's work in this area is informed by a critical appropriation of Kant's ideas of cosmopolitan government and a federation of peoples. Habermas finds signs in the present that cosmopolitanism is not impossible, for instance the emergence of a human rights regime after World War II. He argues that cosmopolitanism must move beyond (nation-)state sovereignty, a step that Kant was not prepared to take with his federation of peoples.

This leaves Habermas at odds with the Realist paradigm of international relations and with Carl Schmitt in particular. For Schmitt, it is ultimately impossible to go beyond state sovereignty, because there is always a particular 'we' opposed to a 'them', and this relation between sovereigns is the political relation *par excellence*. Habermas, on the contrary, thinks of international politics as the domestication of conflict and the constitutionalisation of international relations.

habermas and his critics

Habermas's theory of deliberative democracy is the most influential of what John Dryzek (2000, p. v) has called the 'deliberative turn' in democratic theory. Drawing on Habermas's writings, Dryzek, Simone Chambers (1996), Shane O'Neill (1997) and Andrew Arato and Jean Cohen (1992) have developed a more practical account of deliberative democracy. These attempts at concretising Habermas's theories are undoubtedly some of the most interesting discussions of his work today.

Axel Honneth occupies the chair of philosophy that Habermas held in Frankfurt, and he is considered the main representative of the third generation of the Frankfurt School. Although working within the Habermasian Critical Theory paradigm, Honneth is also critical of Habermas on central points. He is more inclined towards Hegel than Kant, focusing more on ethical life than on universal norms (Honneth, 1995).

Feminists have criticised Habermas along similar lines. Seyla Benhabib (1986), Nancy Fraser (1997) and Iris Marion Young (1990), who are sympathetic to Critical Theory and deliberative democracy, put less emphasis on rationalism and universalism and more on the concrete contexts of individuals, including power relations. This reflects a more widespread feminist critique of Habermas, arguing that he relies on a particular rationalistic conception of subjectivity and the public sphere.

Habermas is often taken as a defender of reason, modernity and Enlightenment against so-called postmodern attacks (d'Entrèves and Benhabib 1996). This is also Habermas's own view in his most systematic work on this matter, *The Philosophical Discourse of Modernity* (1987c), which engages with the alleged critics of reason from Friedrich Nietzsche through Martin Heidegger to Foucault, Deleuze and Derrida. The critics associated with the label 'postmodern' argue that Habermas's ideas of universal structures of language, rational consensus and the transparent language of rational discourse exclude constituencies who do not want to, or are not able to, cast their validity claims in a rational discursive way (Lyotard, 1984).

A related critique of Habermas is that coming from agonistic theories of democracy (Mouffe, 2000). They believe that Habermas's emphasis on rational discourse and consensus stifles democracy. Instead, they argue, it is disagreement that is and should be at the centre of a vigorous democracy.

Over the years, Habermas has developed his theories through the critical appropriation of the thoughts of others. Given his continued productivity, his thought is bound to develop further in the future, and it remains to be seen in what directions. One area of development is the recent rapprochement between him and Derrida (Thomassen, 2006). Other areas of recent interest to Habermas are genetic engineering (Habermas, 2003, pp. 1–100) and the role of religion in modern, secular societies (Habermas, 2003, pp. 1–15, 101–15).

conclusion

Habermas is undoubtedly a towering figure in contemporary political philosophy. Whether one agrees with Habermas's vision of politics or not, his most profound contribution to political philosophy is no doubt a distinct theory of law and democracy as public deliberation. His theory of deliberative democracy not only offers a clear alternative to communitarian, liberal and agonistic theories, but also includes a sophisticated philosophical foundation, linking empirical and normative concerns. While commentators have rightly put Habermas's Critical Theory credentials into question, he is nevertheless one of the most important contemporary inheritors and renewers of Kantian political philosophy.

further reading

The best introductions to Habermas's work are McCarthy (1978), for his earlier work, Rasmussen (1990), for communicative action and discourse ethics, and Eriksen and Weigård (2003) for his political philosophy. Habermas's own work is vast and complex and is perhaps best approached through his political writings, (2001) and (2005) being the most recent. His theory of deliberative democracy is found in (1996) and the more accessible companion volume (1998a). White (1995) contains a good collection of critical essays on Habermas's work, and Rosenfeld and Arato (1998) contains critical essays on Habermas's deliberative democracy.

references

Arato, A. and Cohen, J. (1992) *Civil Society and Political Theory*. Cambridge, MA: MIT Press.

Benhabib, S. (1986) *Critique, Norm, and Utopia: A study of the foundations of critical theory*. New York: Columbia University Press.

Calhoun, C. (ed.) (1992) *Habermas and the Public Sphere*. Cambridge, MA: MIT Press.

Chambers, S. (1996) *Reasonable Democracy: Jürgen Habermas and the politics of discourse*. Ithaca, NY: Cornell University Press.

Dryzek, J. (2000) *Deliberative Democracy and Beyond: Liberals, Critics, Contestations*. Oxford: Oxford University Press.

d'Entrèves, M.P. and Benhabib, S. (eds) (1996) *Habermas and the Unfinished Project of Modernity: Critical essays on 'The Philosophical Discourse of Modernity'*. Cambridge: Polity Press.

Eriksen, E.O. and Weigård, J. (2003) *Understanding Habermas: Communicative action and deliberative democracy*. London: Continuum.

Fraser, N. (1997) *Justice Interruptus: Critical reflections on the 'postsocialist' situation*. New York: Routledge.

Habermas, J. (1984) *The Theory of Communicative Action. Volume 1: Reason and the rationalization of Society*, trans. T. McCarthy. Cambridge: Polity Press.

Habermas, J. (1987a) *The Theory of Communicative Action. Volume 2: The critique of functionalist reason*, trans. T. McCarthy. Cambridge: Polity Press.

Habermas, J. (1987b) *Knowledge and Human Interest*, trans. J.J. Shapiro. Cambridge: Polity Press.

Habermas, J. (1987c) *The Philosophical Discourse of Modernity: Twelve lectures*, trans. F.G. Lawrence. Cambridge: Polity Press.

Habermas, J. (1989) *The Structural Transformation of the Public Sphere: An inquiry into a category of bourgeois society*, trans. T. Burger. Cambridge, MA: MIT Press.

Habermas, J. (1990) *Moral Consciousness and Communicative Action*, trans. C. Lenhardt and S. Weber Nicholson. Cambridge: Polity Press.

Habermas, J. (1996) *Between Facts and Norms: Contributions to a discourse theory of law and democracy*, trans. W. Rehg. Cambridge, MA: MIT Press.

Habermas, J. (1998a) *The Inclusion of the Other: Studies in political theory*, trans. C. Cronin. Cambridge: Polity Press.

Habermas, J. (1998b) *On the Pragmatics of Communication*. Cambridge, MA: MIT Press.

Habermas, J. (2001) *The Postnational Constellation: Political essays*, trans. M. Pensky. Cambridge: Polity Press.

Habermas, J. (2003) *The Future of Human Nature*, trans. W. Rehg, M. Pensky and H. Beister. Cambridge: Polity Press.

Habermas, J. (2005) *Time of Transitions*. Cambridge: Polity Press.

Honneth, A. (1995) *The Struggle for Recognition: The moral grammar of social conflicts*, trans. J. Anderson. Cambridge, MA: MIT Press.

Lyotard, J.-F. (1984) *The Postmodern Condition: A report on knowledge*, trans. G. Bennington and B. Massumi. Manchester: Manchester University Press.

McCarthy, T. (1978) *The Critical Theory of Jürgen Habermas*. London: Hutchinson.

Mouffe, C. (2000) *The Democratic Paradox*. London: Verso.

O'Neill, S. (1997) *Impartiality in Context: Grounding justice in a pluralist world*. Albany, NY: SUNY Press.

Rasmussen, D. (1990) *Reading Habermas*. Oxford: Blackwell.

Rosenfeld, M. and Arato, A. (eds) (1998) *Habermas on Law and Democracy: Critical exchanges*. Berkeley, CA: University of California Press.

Thomassen, L. (ed.) (forthcoming 2006) *The Derrida–Habermas Reader*. Edinburgh: Edinburgh University Press.

White, S.K. (ed.) (1995) *The Cambridge Companion to Habermas*. Cambridge: Cambridge University Press.

Young, I.M. (1990) *Justice and the Politics of Difference*. Princeton, NJ: Princeton University Press, 1990.

part iii
'postmoderns'

14
jacques lacan
kirsten campbell

Is political action conscious and rational? How are political identities formed? What are the politics of sex? How does language shape political life? Contemporary theorists as diverse as Luce Irigaray, Judith Butler and Homi Bhabha have all used the work of the French psychoanalyst Jacques Lacan to answer these important and difficult questions. One of Lacan's most notable political interpreters, Louis Althusser, ascribes the influence of Lacanian theory to its account of the passage of the infant from 'biological existence to human existence' (1996, p. 25). For Lacan, language is the foundation of culture. The infant's entry into language marks its passage from biological being to human subject. Drawing extensively upon philosophy and linguistics, as well as political and anthropological theory, Lacan developed Freudian psychoanalysis in terms of his theory of language as a symbolic structure. In Lacan's theory, language constitutes the human subject. It is this account of the link between culture and subject that has made Lacan's work of such interest for political theory. In particular, political theory has appropriated Lacan's model of the tie between the collective and the individual to explain the relationship between political and subjective structures.

Born in 1901 into a bourgeois Parisian family, Lacan trained as a psychiatrist at L'Hôpital Sainte-Anne, the major psychiatric hospital serving central Paris. In 1933, Lacan became a member of the leading French psychoanalytic society, the Société Psychanalytique de Paris (SPP), and in 1936 he established his private psychoanalytic practice in Paris. While the Nazis occupied France during World War II, Lacan worked as a doctor in a military hospital in Paris. After the war, the SPP resumed its activities and elected Lacan as its President in 1953. Lacan resigned shortly thereafter to join the newly established Société Française de Psychanalyse. However, the international body governing psychoanalysis, the International Psychoanalytic Association, refused to allow Lacan to train other analysts because of his practice of using clinical sessions of variable rather than standard length. Lacan subsequently founded his own psychoanalytic school in 1964, the École Freudienne de Paris, which he dissolved in 1980. He practiced as a psychoanalyst in Paris until his death in 1981.

From his first psychoanalytic paper presented in 1936, 'The Mirror Stage', Lacan's work was central to the development of French psychoanalysis. However, the influence of Lacanian theory extended beyond practising psychoanalysts. In the 1930s, Lacan's early studies of paranoia were taken up by Surrealists such as Salvador Dali, and were published in the Surrealist journal, *Minotaur*. From the 1950s onwards, Lacan's psychoanalytic work shaped a generation of French intellectuals, including Jean Baudrillard, Jacques Derrida, Gilles Deleuze, Luce Irigaray and Julia Kristeva. In 1966 Michel Foucault commented:

> Lacan, in the case of the unconscious, showed us that 'meaning' was probably no more than a superficial impression, a shimmer, a foam, and that what was really affecting us deep down inside, what existed before us, and what was supporting us in time and space, was system. (Roudinesco, 1997, p. 296)

The publication of *Écrits* in 1966 established Lacan as a major figure in French thought, and it remains his most influential work. *Écrits* consists of a collection of papers from 1936 to 1966 that Lacan selected as representative of his psychoanalytic theory. Slavoj Žižek characterises *Écrits* as the 'classical Lacan' because it explores his central concepts of the unconscious, language and subjectivity (1992, p. 130). Lacan's other influential works include his year-long seminars given from 1953 to 1981. A significant proportion of the seminars remain unpublished (for an account of the complex history of the publication of the seminars, see Roudinesco, 1997). Each of these seminars explored different themes such as the ego, the object, the unconscious and psychoanalytic ethics.

Anglophone commentators frequently characterise Lacan's work as theoretically and rhetorically complex. While Lacan's theory and rhetoric are not more difficult to read and understand than the works of many classical political theorists, readers often find the associative and literary quality of his texts disconcerting. Lacan intends his writing to have this effect, so that it evokes an experience of the resistance of the unconscious to conscious representation. Therefore it is unsurprising that there is considerable debate about how best to understand Lacanian texts and theory, given their deliberate enactment of the unconscious *glissement*, or sliding of meaning. However, these texts are neither incomprehensible nor incoherent despite their uncanny effects. Rather, they offer a subtle and sophisticated theory of psychoanalysis that has clear implications for many areas of political thought.

During the political disturbances in France in 1968, Lacan engaged in a now famous exchange on politics with radical students attending his seminar at Vincennes University. In this exchange, Lacan described his own political position as 'liberal, like everyone else, only insofar as I am anti-progressive. With the single modification that I am caught in a movement which deserves to be called progressive' (1969, p. 128). For Lacan, psychoanalysis is a radical movement because it reveals the relationship between the unconscious and the political. For this reason, Lacan told the rebellious students that psychoanalysis could 'allow you to situate what precisely is at stake, what it is that you are rebelling against' (1969, p. 128). However, he insisted that psychoanalysis does not offer political liberation (1969–70), a *Weltanschauung* (worldview) or a universal philosophy (1964). Moreover, his work does not provide a conventional account of political institutions, actions or systems. Rather, Lacan's work aims to provide a theory of psychoanalysis, 'which is historically defined by the elaboration of the notion of the subject' (1964, p. 77).

For political theory, this notion of the subject has proved to be both productive and contentious. Since political theory's appropriation of Lacan centres upon his account of the subject, focusing on this model of subjectivity is a useful means of exploring his theory. We begin this exploration by considering the 'classical' notion of the subject that Lacan presents in *Écrits*, and examining its three conceptual foundations: the imaginary, the symbolic and the real. We will then briefly consider Lacan's later reworking of the notion of subjectivity and his account of the 'sexuation' of the subject. We then turn to three key areas of political thought that exemplify contemporary debates concerning the use of Lacan's work: feminist theory and the subject of 'sexual difference'; queer theory and the subject of 'sexuality'; and postcolonial theory and the subject of 'race'. While there is a long history of psychoanalytic work at the intersection of these three fields – such as anti-racist feminist appropriations of Lacanian psychoanalysis stretching from the journal *m/f* (see Adams and Cowie, 1990) to the more recent work of Seshadri-Crooks (2000) and Khanna (2003) – each of these fields emerges from particular political debates and concerns that shape their specific relationship to Lacanian psychoanalysis. Finally, we briefly consider contemporary challenges for Lacanian theories of the political.

subjectivity and the unconscious

From his earliest psychoanalytic papers of the 1930s, Lacan argued that the subject should not be confused with our conscious sense of self. The subject has a divided structure because it is split between the conscious and unconscious. The unconscious is radically other to our conscious experience.

For this reason, we are 'excentric' to our 'self' (Lacan, 1966, p. 189). In his papers of the 1940s, Lacan focused upon the ego that forms the self, its development in the 'mirror stage', and its distinction from the unconscious. By 1955 Lacan clearly insisted upon the 'fundamental distinction between the true subject of the unconscious and the ego' (1966, p. 141), which he sustains in subsequent reformulations of his theory of subjectivity. His work of the 1960s developed his 'classical' account of the subject as an effect of language. For Lacan, language produces the true subject of the unconscious.

Lacan rejects the notion of the unconscious as a repository of repressed instincts. For Lacan, '[t]he unconscious is neither primordial nor instinctual' (1966, p. 187). Rather, Lacan argues that 'the unconscious is structured in the most radical way like a language' (1966, p. 259). The Lacanian unconscious consists of chains of signifying elements, in which each signifying element is linked to another. The particular ordering of these signifying elements produces the specific clinical structure of the subject, such as neurosis or psychosis. The subject is an effect of the relationship between the symbolic elements (or signifiers) that comprise language. It has no positive content in itself, because symbolic elements of language produce it. Unlike much conventional political philosophy, Lacan does not characterise the subject as a substance or an essence, because '[t]here is nothing substantial about this subject; it has no *being*, no substratum or permanence in time' (Fink, 1995, p. 42). Rather, the Lacanian subject is the *parlêtre* – the speaking being – that language produces by knotting together different registers of psychic functioning. Lacan describes these registers as the imaginary, the symbolic and the real.

the imaginary

For Lacan, the imaginary order emerges during the formation of the ego in the mirror stage. Lacan first develops this theory in his early papers, such as 'Aggressivity in Psychoanalysis' (1948) and 'The Mirror Stage as Formative of the Function of the I' (1949) that are collected in *Écrits*. In these papers, Lacan argued that the self forms in the mirror stage through a process of identification with an image of the body. Drawing on the work of the French psychologist Henri Wallon, Lacan developed a theory of the formation of the ego, the psychic agency which functions as the core of our sense of 'self', through a process of imaginary recognition of 'self' and 'other'. The mirror stage can be understood as an identification, in the psychoanalytic sense of a psychic process in which 'the subject assimilates an aspect, property or attribute of the other and is transformed, wholly or partially, after the model the other provides' (Laplanche and Pontalis, 1973, p. 205). The mirror stage involves a process of narcissistic identification, in which the infant establishes a relationship to their 'self' through a libidinal tie to an image of its body. The infant identifies with the specular image of its own body and incorporates that image to form the nucleus of the ego (Lacan, 1966, p. 2). This process of identification establishes a relation between the infant's inner and outer worlds, and between its sense of self and its others. The image of the body enables the infant to perceive its experience of a fragmented body as a totality. However, that process also forms 'an alienating identity' for the infant (1966, p. 5). This identity is alienating because the infant's identification with its body image constitutes its imagined other as a rival. In this process, the infant directs the aggression formerly directed at its own image to the ego's other. The infant uses this aggression to construct the relation of its ego and its other. This process marks the ego with an aggressive and objectifying relation to its imagined others. For Lacan, this process of the construction of ego and other represents the transition from an imaginary relation to self to an imaginary relation to others.

The imaginary, then, is part of the genesis of the ego in a series of alienating and objectifying identifications that are misrecognitions. Lacan argues that imaginary misrecognition is not a 'false' understanding of reality, but 'a certain organization of affirmations and negations, to which the subject is attached' (1953–54, p. 167). The imaginary order captures the ego in the illusion that the 'self' and its others possess permanent and substantial identity. The ego narcissistically and aggressively perceives itself as having mastery of its self and its others, which it sees as reflections of its self. Dylan Evans notes that, '[t]he principal illusions of the imaginary order are those of wholeness, synthesis, autonomy, duality, and, above all, similarity' (1996, p. 82).

the symbolic

For Lacan, the Symbolic order structures the imaginary. He first elaborates his theory of the Symbolic in his papers of the 1950s, such as 'The Function and Field of Speech and Language in Psychoanalysis' (1953), 'The Freudian Thing' (1955), and 'The Agency of the Letter in the Unconscious or Reason since Freud' (1957), all of which are collected in *Écrits*. Lacan's account of the Symbolic draws on the work of the structuralist linguist, Ferdinand de Saussure. Saussure (1916) defined language as a synchronic structure of signs, the arbitrary association of sound-image (the signifier) and concept (the signified). The differential relation of each sign to other signs produces meaning. However, Lacan argued that language is not a relationship between signs, but rather it consists of a chain of signifiers, the signifying element of the sign. Signifiers combine 'according to a closed order', which is the Symbolic (1966, p. 169). In this model, the Symbolic order is a structure of signifiers in which the differential relationship between signifiers produces meaning. Language is not a neutral or conscious act of representation that allows us to say what we want to say, but rather it is an overdetermined combination of signifying elements in which we always say more than we intend (the Freudian slip, the symptom).

Drawing on the anthropological theory of Claude Lévi-Strauss (1958, 1967), Lacan developed his model of language as a differential system of signifiers in terms of a structuralist notion of culture. Lacan's theory adapted Lévi-Strauss' notion of culture as a symbolic system that is structured by a foundational prohibition against intrafamilial marriage. For Lacan, this prohibition upon incestuous desire for the mother is Law-of-the-Father, which structures culture as a system of symbolic exchange. The Law-of-the-Father symbolises the father as the bearer of cultural law. This symbolic father functions as the figure of the prohibition upon the infant's desire for the mother (1966, pp. 72–4). This symbolic function represents the separation of child and mother, and should not be confused with the real or imaginary father who acts as an agent of the paternal Law that bars the child's desire for the mother. It is this Law that structures the chains of signifiers of the Symbolic order. However, that symbolic structure is contingent and incomplete. In his later work, Lacan emphasises the contingency and incompleteness of the Symbolic, with its fundamental lack that is the Real.

the real

Žižek claims that the notion of the Real represents 'the most radical dimension of Lacanian theory' because it recognises that 'the big Other, the symbolic order itself, is also *barré*, crossed-out, by a fundamental impossibility, structured around an impossible/traumatic kernel, around a central lack' (1989, p. 122). In Lacan's earlier work, the Real is the register of psychical reality, that is, the order of unconscious desires and fantasies. Lacan's later work emphasises the impossibility of the Real, which is not possible to represent within the Symbolic (1969–70, p. 143). At the level of the subject, the Real marks the unconscious desire that the subject cannot symbolise within its existing symbolic structures. At the level of the Symbolic, the Real marks a foundational and excluded element for which there is no signifier, and hence that is impossible to symbolise (see Lacan, 1964). Because it is not possible to symbolise this 'missing' element, it appears as a 'lack' or 'gap' in the Symbolic order. The Real is a lack in the Symbolic order, not in the sense of a referent 'outside' a structure of representation but rather as a traumatic antagonism 'inside' every symbolic network. According to Lacan, there is always a lack *in* the Other of the Symbolic order.

the subject of *jouissance*

The subject defends itself against the lack in the Symbolic order through phantasy. For Lacan, 'phantasy is never anything more than the screen that conceals something quite primary', namely, the lack in the Symbolic order (1964, p. 60). Phantasy consists of an imaginary scene, a frozen image that 'fills' the gap in the structure of symbolic elements that produce the subject. Phantasy veils this lack, and hence functions as a defence against it. Lacan argues that there is a fundamental phantasy from which all other phantasies derive. This fundamental phantasy structures the subject's *jouissance*, the French word for 'enjoyment' (which also has the connotation of sexual enjoyment). The Lacanian concept does not imply pleasure as such, for the subject can find enjoyment in pain. In his later work of the 1970s, Lacan put forward a model of the subject that focuses upon how a particular symbolic element organises our subjective *jouissance*, our mode of enjoyment. For Lacan, this privileged signifier 'names' the subject, knotting together the real, symbolic and imaginary orders. In his seminar of 1975 on James Joyce, Lacan called this structure the *sinthome*, a French pun on the symptom. Žižek describes the *sinthome* as 'a signifier as a bearer of *jouis-sense*, enjoyment-in-sense ... the binding of our enjoyment to a certain signifying, symbolic formation which assures a minimum of consistency to our being-in-the-world' (1989, p. 75).

the sexed subject

Žižek points out that '[o]ne of the crucial differences between psychoanalysis and philosophy concerns the status of sexual difference: for philosophy, the subject is not inherently sexualised ... whereas psychoanalysis promulgates sexualisation into a kind of formal, a priori, condition of the very emergence of the subject' (1998, p. 81). In Lacan's account of the formation of the sexed subject in the papers of *Écrits*, such as the 'The Signification of the Phallus' (1958) and 'Guiding Remarks for a Congress on Feminine Sexuality' (1960), the child becomes a subject after the intervention of the paternal interdict of the Law-of-the-Father in the Oedipus complex. In the Oedipus complex, the infant desires its mother and perceives its father as a rival to its mother's love. The child 'resolves' the Oedipus complex through identification with the symbolic father, and thereby enters the Symbolic order. In the Symbolic order, subjects are sexually differentiated according to their relation to the phallus, a symbolic element (1966, pp. 320–1). The phallus represents the lack of the signifier in the Symbolic order. In this account, the masculine subject has the phallus while the feminine subject lacks it. In Lacan's later work (most notably in his seminar of 1972–73, *Encore*), he describes the feminine subject as ~~The~~ Woman – a fantasy in which Woman desires the phallus, confirming that the masculine subject has it. For this reason, Lacan argues that ~~The~~ Woman does not exist other than as fantasy (which he represents by a strikethrough '~~The~~'). In *Encore*, Lacan makes it clear that with that formulation, he does not mean that women do not exist, but rather that the masculine fantasy of ~~The~~ Woman is an impossibility (1972–73).

feminism and the subject of 'sexual difference'

Contemporary feminist theory has predominantly read this theory of the formation of sexed subjectivity as (and for) an account of the constitution of 'sexual difference' and 'identity'. Feminists such as the literary theorist, Jacqueline Rose, argue that Lacan's work is useful because it understands sexual identity as problematic, and sexual difference as contingent. For these feminist theorists, Lacan's work is useful because it offers a social, rather than biological, account of sexual difference. For example, the feminist philosopher Robyn Ferrell argues that 'Lacan transfers the debate on sexuality from the biological, the natural and even the cultural to the order of the symbolic, the realm of law and logic' (1996, p. 91). This model explains sexual difference as a symbolisation of the body that constitutes subjects as masculine or feminine. In contrast to models of gender identity that understand masculinity and femininity in terms of social gender and biological sex (see Nicholson, 1999), this account contends that the Symbolic order constructs the very notion of 'biological' sexual difference through its signification of bodies. Sexual difference is therefore integral to the formation and experience of embodied subjectivity. However, the Lacanian account also reveals the 'problematic, if not impossible, nature of sexual identity' (Rose, 1982, p. 28). According to this psychoanalytic model, there is only a contingent relation between sexual bodies and identities. Since the unconscious reveals the failure of identity, this model understands sexual identity as unstable, incomplete, and lacking (Rose, 1986, p. 90). In particular, it understands 'femininity' as a problematic identity. Lacanian feminists argue that because there is no symbolisation of 'femininity' other than in terms of the masculine, feminist politics needs to consider both the difficulties for women of a femininity which masculinity defines, and the challenge of how to understand 'femininity' in other terms. Lacan's theory of the symbolic constitution of sexual difference offers feminist politics the possibility of deconstructing sexual difference in order to change it.

However, the pivotal role of the phallus in Lacan's account of masculinity and femininity has also given rise to contentious debates concerning feminist appropriations of his work. The difficulty of 'phallocentrism' (a term taken from Jacques Derrida's (1980) philosophical analysis of Lacan) centres on two main objections. The first objection is that Lacan ties his concept of the phallus to the biological organ of the penis, and second is that by doing so Lacan privileges masculinity and the male body as his model of sexual difference and its formation. For this reason, the political philosopher Nancy Fraser contends that Lacan's account is irrevocably phallocentric and that feminism should not 'use or adapt the theory of Jacques Lacan' because its structuralist determinism naturalises women's oppression (1992, p. 182). Similarly, the cultural theorist Teresa de Lauretis rejects Lacan's theory of the subject, arguing that it proposes 'a subject constructed in language alone, an "I" continuously prefigured and preempted by in an unchangeable symbolic order' (1988, p. 9).

Another strand of feminist work undertakes a post-Lacanian project of challenging the existing Symbolic order in order to change the symbolic structures that produce sexed subjects. An important example of this can be found in the work of the French feminist philosopher, Luce Irigaray. Irigaray argues that the Symbolic order represents a horizontal relation between men, and forms a society and culture 'between-men' to the exclusion of women. Against this exclusion of women, Irigaray aims to construct 'a female sociality (*les femmes entre elles*), a female symbolic and female social contract, a horizontal relation *between* women' (Whitford, 1991, p. 79). Irigaray proposes two key strategies for this rewriting of the Symbolic order. The first strategy, which is set out in Irigaray's classic work, *Speculum of the Other Woman* (1974), undertakes a deconstruction of philosophical discourse. Irigaray argues that philosophy is the master discourse of modern Western culture, and founds itself upon a masculine subject. The second is a reconstructive project that calls for the creation of a female imaginary and symbolic. An important example of this project in Irigaray's work is her creation of different symbolisations of the female body, such as the 'two-lips' vaginal metaphor of *This Sex Which Is Not One* (1977). More recently, Irigaray has attempted to produce a new civic identity for women by drawing up a civil code of 'positive rights of citizenship in the female mode' (1994, p. 38). Irigaray rejects a conservative reading of Lacan's work that holds that the Symbolic order is the only possible symbolic structure. Instead, she insists upon the possibility of a different symbolic order in her argument that women should create a new language and social contract that are appropriate for them.

queer theory and the subject of 'sexuality'

By contrast, queer theorists such as the influential American philosopher Judith Butler argue that feminism should not found itself upon the politics of sexual identity. Using psychoanalysis, theorists such as Butler and Tim Dean (2000) argue that the politics of sexual identity assumes a heterosexual norm. For example, Butler argues that it is necessary to displace 'the hegemonic symbolic of (heterosexist) sexual difference' (1993, p. 91). Butler is the leading queer theorist to engage with Lacanian psychoanalysis, which she uses for its account of the formation of the sexed subject by the symbolic order. However, Butler also uses the work of the French philosopher Michel Foucault to provide a re-reading of the Lacanian Symbolic. She understands the symbolic order as 'a register of regulatory ideality', which produces the 'regulatory norms' that demarcate and delimit forms of family, identity and love (1997, p. 66). According to Butler, the symbolic represents 'reigning epistemes of cultural intelligibility' by functioning as a set of cultural rules that constitute social norms (1997, p. 24). Butler argues that these normative and regulating discourses produce the subject and structure desire.

Butler's account ties the Lacanian concept of foreclosure to 'the Foucauldian notion of a regulatory ideal' (1997, p. 25). Butler reconceives foreclosure 'as an ideal according to which certain forms of love become possible, and others, impossible' (1997, p. 25). For Butler, the regulatory ideal is that of heterosexuality. Identification with this social norm forecloses attachment to 'homosexual' same-sex objects. Butler argues that the foundational prohibition that forms the subject is not the bar against incestuous oedipal desire that underpins Lacanian psychoanalysis, since that desire is already heterosexual and so based upon the preclusion of a homosexual desire. Rather, the foundational prohibition bars homosexual attachments to same-sex objects. According to Butler, every heterosexual identity founds itself upon a primary and foundational prohibition upon homosexual attachments.

While Lacan has been central to Butler's rethinking of a feminist queer theory, she insists that it is necessary to understand the symbolic order as a social order rather than as a foundational myth which functions as the condition of subjectivity and culture. Butler argues that the notion of a transcendental Symbolic 'presupposes a sociality based in fictive and idealised kinship positions that presume the heterosexual family as constituting the defining social bond for all humans' (2000, p. 142). Butler's objection to the Lacanian Symbolic is both philosophical and political. In philosophical terms, she argues that the notion of a transcendental Symbolic is itself historical, since it emerges in a particular historical and political moment. In political terms, she argues that a refusal to recognise this historical and political specificity of the Symbolic acts to prevent a more 'radically democratic formulation of sex and sexual difference' (2000, p. 147). Butler suggests that reading of the Symbolic order as a particular register of regulatory norms of identity requires displacing sexual difference as *the* ontological condition of the subject. While Butler does not develop in detail her reconception of the Symbolic as a 'racialising set of norms', such a re-reading can be found in postcolonial theory.

postcolonial theory and the subject of 'race'

For important strands of contemporary postcolonial theory, 'the convergence of the problematic of colonialism with that of subject-formation' has led to an engagement with Lacanian psychoanalysis (Gates, 1991, p. 485). This engagement with Lacan has emerged from the recent interest in the work of Frantz Fanon and his reading of Lacan, taken up by postcolonial theorists such as the influential cultural theorist, Homi Bhabha (see Khanna, 2003). Theorists such as Bhabha have found Lacanian psychoanalysis useful for the development of accounts of the formation of colonial and postcolonial identities and their relationship to the cultures of empire. These accounts often centre on the issue of how '[r]acial identity and racist practice alike are forged through the bonds of identification' (Fuss, 1995, p. 14).

In these readings of Lacan, 'racial' identity is neither completely 'successful' nor successfully 'complete'. Kobena Mercer's postcolonial adaption of Jacqueline Rose's Lacanian feminism exemplifies this understanding of identity:

[w]hat distinguishes psychoanalysis from sociological accounts of black masculinity ... is that whereas for the latter, the internalisation of norms

is roughly assumed to work, the basic premise and indeed starting point for psychoanalysis is that it does not. The unconscious constantly reveals the 'failure' of identity ... Black people's affinity with psychoanalysis rests above all ... with this recognition that there is a resistance to identity at the very heart of psychic life. (1994, p. 170)

This account conceives ethnic identity as neither originary nor as essential. Rather, it emphasises how complex psychic processes of identification and dis-identification operate to form postcolonial ethnicities.

For Bhabha, Lacanian psychoanalysis permits us to link 'the traumatic ambivalences of a personal, psychic history to the wider disjunctions of political existence' (1994, p. 45). His influential account of postcolonial identity develops Lacan's notion of the mirror stage to explain how the processes of colonial identification produce an ambivalent psychic relation between the subject and its colonial other. Bhabha contends that the postcolonial subject's assumption of the image of identity does not involve a simple reflection of the self in the mirror of the other, 'for the question of identification is never the affirmation of a pre-given identity ... it is always the production of an image of identity and the transformation of the subject in assuming that image' (1994, p. 45). Rather, there is a psychic process of constitution of an image of 'racial' identity, which misrecognises white identity as presence and black identity as its imaginary other. However, that process also produces the ambivalence of colonial discourse, because the relational constitution of these identities calls into question their prior and essential 'nature' (1994, p. 86).

Bhabha argues that these identifications occur in the context of the colonial representation of subjectivity. Bhabha insists that colonialisation involves a symbolic process, in which the symbolic field of colonial culture structures fantasies of identity. However, the cultural signification of identity is not fixed, but instead is contingent, incomplete and contested. For this reason, Bhabha argues that there is a 'third space' of postcolonial culture, a new space of the translation of cultures and the negotiation of subjectivities. For Bhabha, the 'third space' which enables other positions to emerge ... displaces the histories that constitute it, and sets up new structures of authority, new political initiatives' (1990, p. 211). It produces the hybrid identities of postcolonialism and hence new possibilities of understanding identities and cultures.

The usefulness of Lacanian psychoanalysis for theorising 'the postcolonial' has also been challenged. This debate primarily concerns Lacanian theory's 'often intractable claims of universality [and] its desire to privilege sexual difference over other forms of difference' (Seshadri-Crooks, 1998, p. 354). This critique contends that Lacanian psychoanalysis is a universalising and ahistorical theory that fails to acknowledge its own historical and political specificity as a modern European philosophy. Moreover, it argues that Lacan's theory of the formation of subjectivity posits 'sexual' rather than 'racial' difference as the condition of the emergence of the subject, and so does not provide a theory of the racialised subject (see McClintock, 1995).

One strand of postcolonial work argues that in order to deploy Lacanian theory in the postcolonial field, psychoanalysis itself must first be 'decolonised' (McClintock, 1995, p. 74). This strategy involves understanding how 'colonial history shapes the very terms in which psychoanalysis comes to understand the process of identification' (Fuss, 1995, p. 14). It argues that placing psychoanalysis within the historical context of colonialism permits a reconfiguring of psychoanalytic explanations of psychic process. Other strands of postcolonial theory suggest a strategy of evolving 'a procedure that does not require an analogy between sex and race ... to discover the intricate structural relations between race and sex, to see how race articulates itself with sex to gain access to desire or lack – the paradoxical guarantee of the subject's sovereignty beyond symbolic determination' (Seshadri-Crooks, 2000, p. 3). For example, Seshadri-Crooks uses Lacanian theory to engage in a careful reading of cultural texts of 'race' to work through those fantasies that guarantee the sovereignty of the racial subject, so as 'to resist the specious enjoyment promised by Whiteness' (2000, p. 160).

A third strand of postcolonial theory, exemplified by the work of cultural theorist Rey Chow, argues that postcolonial studies have focused upon 'the elaboration of the psychic mutabilities of the postcolonial subject alone', while neglecting the issue of the formation of communities and collectivities (1999, pp. 34–5). Chow argues that to address the issue of community 'it would be necessary to reintroduce the structural problems of community formation that are always implied in the articulation of the subject [and to address] issues of structural control – of law, sovereignty, and prohibition – that underlie the subject's relation with the collective' (1999, p. 35). This engagement with the relation between subject and collective requires a reconsideration of the symbolic order as a political order. Like Irigaray, Chow proposes a post-Lacanian project which analyses and challenges the existing symbolic order that produces racialised identities.

the political

The influence of Lacan's account of the subject upon feminist, queer and postcolonial theories of the formation of political identities and the unconscious drives of political action show that Butler is right to argue that 'psychoanalysis has a crucial role to play in any theory of the subject' (2000, p. 140). However, the challenge for contemporary Lacanian political theories is theorising the subject of the unconscious with the subject of politics. If sexual difference has been regarded as a foundational difference of Lacanian psychoanalytic theory, contemporary Lacanian political theory has fully to develop an 'intersectional' account of the subject which addresses the differences of race and sexuality.

To develop this theory of the subject requires constructing a theory of the political that is informed by Lacanian psychoanalysis. The Lacanian theory of the subject entails a particular understanding of politics. This conception of politics emphasises how the symbolic, imaginary and real orders of language shape the political field. It understands the political field as necessarily incomplete, since the symbolic order that structures it contains a fundamental lack. The incompleteness of the political field entails that its formation is contingent, so that it becomes possible to contest its formation and to create political change. An influential example of the development of Lacanian psychoanalysis as a political theory can be seen in the post-Marxist work of Ernesto Laclau, Chantal Mouffe and Slavoj Žižek. However, the recent exchange between Butler, Laclau and Žižek (2000) concerning how to understand 'the political' itself reveals both the difficulty and productivity of the development of a Lacanian model of politics. A key moment of that contestation concerns the relationship between political and subjective structures. In particular, this issue concerns whether Lacanian psychoanalysis functions as a theory of the subject which supplements a theory of politics, such as feminism or Marxism, or whether it is possible to develop a theory of politics from the theoretical framework which Lacanian psychoanalysis offers. This fundamental challenge for contemporary Lacanian political theory once again places the relationship between the subject of the unconscious and the subject of politics at the centre of political theory.

further reading

Lacan's major work is *Écrits* (1966). A useful introduction to this text is Muller and Richardson's *Lacan and Language: A Reader's Guide to Écrits* (1994). Other major works by Lacan include the translated seminars (see Lacan, 1953–54, 1954–55, 1955–56; 1959–60, 1964, and 1972–73). Roudinesco's fascinating biography, *Jacques Lacan* (1997), places Lacan's life and work in its context of French cultural and political history.

An excellent introduction to Lacan's work is Malcolm Bowie's *Lacan* (1991). *An Introductory Dictionary of Lacanian Psychoanalysis* (Evans, 1996) is invaluable for understanding Lacan's key terms and concepts. A sophisticated account of Lacan's work in relationship to clinical practice can be found in *Jacques Lacan and the Freudian Practice of Psychoanalysis* (Nobus, 2000). For an analysis of the relationship between Lacanian psychoanalysis and the contemporary politics of subjectivity, see *Jacques Lacan and Feminist Epistemology* (Campbell, 2004). An excellent overview of Lacanian political theory can be found in *Lacan and the Political* (Stavrakakis, 1999). Slavoj Žižek is perhaps the most interesting Lacanian political theorist writing today. *The Ticklish Subject* (Žižek, 1999) is an exhilarating discussion of the relationship between Lacanian and political theory.

references

Adams, P. and Cowie, E. (eds) (1990) *The Woman in Question*. Cambridge, MA: MIT Press and October Books.

Althusser, L. (1996) *Writings on Psychoanalysis: Freud and Lacan*, trans. Jeffrey Mehlman. New York: Columbia University Press.

Bhabha, H. (1990) 'The Third Space', in *Identity: Community, culture, difference*, ed. J. Rutherford, pp. 207–21. London: Lawrence and Wishart.

Bhabha, H. (1994) *The Location of Culture*. London and New York: Routledge.

Bowie, M. (1991) *Lacan*. Cambridge, MA: Harvard University Press.

Butler, J. (1993) *Bodies That Matter: On the discursive limits of 'sex'*. London and New York: Routledge.

Butler, J. (1997) *The Psychic Life of Power: Theories in subjection*. Stanford, CA: Stanford University Press.

Butler, J. (2000) 'Competing Universalities', in *Contingency, Hegemony, Universality: Contemporary dialogues on the left*, ed. J. Butler, E. Laclau and S. Žižek. London and New York: Verso.

Campbell, K. (2004) *Jacques Lacan and Feminist Epistemology*. London and New York: Routledge.

Chow, R. (1999) 'The Politics of Admittance: Female Sexual Agency, Miscegenation and the Formation of Community in Frantz Fanon', in *Frantz Fanon: Critical perspectives*, ed. A. Alessandri. London and New York: Routledge.

Dean, T. (2000) *Beyond Sexuality*. Chicago, IL: University of Chicago Press.

Derrida, J. (1980) *The Post Card: From Socrates to Freud and beyond*, trans. Alan Bass, Chicago, IL: University of Chicago Press, 1987.

Evans, D. (1996) *An Introductory Dictionary of Lacanian Psychoanalysis*. New York and London: Routledge.

Ferrell, R. (1996) *Passion in Theory: Conceptions of Freud and Lacan*. London: Routledge.

Fink, B. (1995) *The Lacanian Subject: Between language and jouissance*. Princeton, NJ: Princeton University Press.

Fraser, N. (1992) 'The Uses and Abuses of French Discourse Theories for Feminist Politics', in *Revaluing French Feminism: Critical essays on difference, agency and culture*, ed. Nancy Fraser and Sandra Lee Bartky, pp. 177–94. Bloomington and Indianapolis, IN: Indiana University Press.

Fuss, D. (1995) *Identification Papers*. New York and London: Routledge.

Gates Louis Jr., H. (1991) 'Critical Fanonism', *Critical Inquiry* 17: 457–70.

Irigaray, L. (1974) *Speculum of the Other Woman*, trans. G. Gill (1985). Ithaca, NY: Cornell University Press.

Irigaray, L. (1977) *This Sex Which Is Not One*, trans. C. Porter (1985). Ithaca, NY: Cornell University Press.

Irigaray, L. (1994) *Democracy Begins Between Two*, trans. K. Anderson (2000). London: Athlone.

Khanna, R. (2003) *Dark Continents: Psychoanalysis and colonialism*. Durham, NC, and London: Duke University Press.

Lacan, J. (1948) 'Aggressivity in Psychoanalysis', in *Écrits: A selection*, trans. A. Sheridan (2001). London: Routledge.

Lacan, J. (1949) 'The Mirror Stage as Formative of the Function of the I', in *Écrits: A selection*, trans. A. Sheridan (2001). London: Routledge.

Lacan, J. (1953) 'The Function and Field of Speech and Language in Psychoanalysis', in *Écrits: A selection*, trans. A. Sheridan (2001). London: Routledge.

Lacan, J. (1953–54) *The Seminar of Jacques Lacan. Book I. Freud's papers on technique, 1953–1954*, trans. J. Forrester, ed. J.-A. Miller (1991). New York and London: Norton.

Lacan, J. (1954–55) *The Seminar of Jacques Lacan. Book II. The Ego in Freud's theory and in the technique of psychoanalysis, 1954–1955*, trans. S. Tomaselli, ed. J.-A. Miller (1991). New York and London: Norton.

Lacan, J. (1955) 'The Freudian Thing', in *Écrits: A selection*, trans. A. Sheridan (2001). London: Routledge.

Lacan, J. (1955–56) *The Seminar of Jacques Lacan. Book III. The psychoses, 1955–1956*, trans. R. Grigg, ed. J.-A. Miller (1993). London: Routledge.

Lacan, J. (1957) 'The Agency of the Letter in the Unconscious or Reason since Freud', in *Écrits: A selection*, trans. A. Sheridan (2001). London: Routledge.

Lacan, J. (1958) 'The Signification of the Phallus', in *Écrits: A selection*, trans. A. Sheridan (2001). London: Routledge.

Lacan, J. (1959–60) *The Seminar of Jacques Lacan. Book VII. The ethics of psychoanalysis, 1959–1960*, trans. D. Porter, ed. J.-A. Miller (1992). London: Routledge.

Lacan, J. (1960) 'Guiding Remarks for a Congress on Feminine Sexuality', in *Feminine Sexuality: Jacques Lacan and the école freudienne*, ed. J. Mitchell and J. Rose. London and New York: Norton.

Lacan, J. (1964) *The Four Fundamental Concepts of Psycho-Analysis*, trans. A. Sheridan (1986). London: Peregrine.

Lacan, J. (1966) *Écrits: A selection*, trans. A. Sheridan (2001). London: Routledge.

Lacan, J. (1969) 'Impromptu at Vincennes', in *Television: A challenge to the psychoanalytic establishment*, ed. Joan Copjec (1990). London and New York: Norton.

Lacan, J. (1969–70) *Le Séminaire. Livre XVII. L'envers de la psychanalyse, 1969–1970*, ed. J.-A. Miller (1991). Paris: Seuil.

Lacan, J. (1972–73) *The Seminar of Jacques Lacan. Book XX. Encore: On feminine sexuality, the limits of love and knowledge, 1972–1973*, trans. B. Fink, ed. J.-A. Miller (1998). New York and London: Norton.

Laplanche, J., and Pontalis, J.-B. (1973) *The Language of Psychoanalysis*, trans. D. Nicholson-Smith. New York and London: Norton.

Lauretis, T. de (1988) 'Feminist Studies/Critical Studies: Issues, terms, and contexts', in *Feminist Studies/Critical Studies*, ed. T. de Lauretis, pp. 1–19. London: Macmillan.

Lévi-Strauss, C. (1958) *Structural Anthropology*, trans. C. Jacobson and B. Grundfest Schoepf (1963). New York: Basic Books.

Lévi-Strauss, C. (1967) *The Elementary Structures of Kinship*, trans. J. Harle Bell and J. von Sturmer, ed. R. Needham (1969). London: Eyre and Spottiswoode.

McClintock, A. (1995) *Imperial Leather: Race, gender and sexuality in the colonial contest*. London and New York: Routledge.

Mercer, K. (1994) *Welcome to the Jungle: Positions in black cultural studies*. London and New York: Routledge.

Muller, J. and W. Richardson (1994) *Lacan and Language: A reader's guide to Écrits*. Madison, CT: International Universities Press.

Nicholson, L. (1999) 'Interpreting "Gender"', in *The Play of Reason: From the modern to the postmodern*. Buckingham: Open University Press.

Nobus, D. (2000) *Jacques Lacan and the Freudian Practice of Psychoanalysis*. New York and London: Routledge.

Rose, J. (1982) 'Introduction – II', in *Feminine Sexuality: Jacques Lacan and the école freudienne*, ed. J. Mitchell and J. Rose. London and New York: Norton.

Rose, J. (1986) *Sexuality in the Field of Vision*. London: Verso.

Roudinesco, É. (1997) *Jacques Lacan*, trans. B. Bray. Cambridge: Polity Press.

Saussure, F. de (1916) *Cours de linguistique générale*, trans. R. Harris (1992). LaSalle, IL: Open Court.

Seshadri-Crooks, K. (1998) 'Psychoanalysis and the Conceit of Whiteness', in *The Psychoanalysis of Race*, ed. C. Lane. New York: Columbia University Press.

Seshadri-Crooks, K. (2000) *Desiring Whiteness: A Lacanian analysis of race*. London: Routledge.

Stavrakakis, Y. (1999) *Lacan and the Political*. London and New York: Routledge.

Whitford, M. (1991) *Luce Irigaray: Philosophy in the feminine*. London and New York: Routledge.

Žižek, S. (1989) *The Sublime Object of Ideology*. London and New York: Verso.

Žižek, S. (1992) *Looking Awry: An introduction to Jacques Lacan through popular culture*. Cambridge, MA, and London: MIT Press.

Žižek, S. (1998) 'Four Discourses, Four Subjects', in *Cogito and the Unconscious*, ed. S. Žižek. Durham, NC, and London: Duke University Press.

Žižek, S. (1999) *The Ticklish Subject*. London and New York: Verso.

15
paul ricoeur
dimitrios e. akrivoulis

Undoubtedly one of the most distinguished Continental philosophers and leading hermeneutic thinkers of the twentieth century, Jean Paul Gustave Ricoeur (1913–2005) was born in Valence, France. Having lost his already widowed father in the Great War, the young Ricoeur was raised as a *pupille de la nation*. Nourished by the Protestant education he received, his participation in the socialist youth movement and the existential and phenomenological currents of thought reigning in French intellectual life in the 1930s, his intellectual and political conscience soon developed as a singular amalgam of pacifism and socialism. Captured early in World War II, Ricoeur was allowed access as a prisoner of war to German philosophy, which he also taught to his fellow prisoners. His thorough explorations of the writings of Husserl, Heidegger and Jaspers during his five-year captivity were soon reflected in his work published in the immediate postwar years: *Karl Jaspers et la philosophie de l'existence* (1947), *Gabriel Marcel et Karl Jaspers: philosophie du mystère et philosophie du paradoxe* (1948), and his translation and authoritative commentary on Husserl's *Ideen* (1950).

In 1948 Ricoeur was called to succeed Jean Hyppolite as *Maitre de conférences* in the history of philosophy at the University of Strasbourg. The Strasbourg years marked Ricoeur's critical transition from existential phenomenology to an investigation of the philosophy of the will, an attempt to develop a more reflexive philosophy in which human freedom becomes meaningful in its dialectical relating to necessity. This exertion was soon evident in his 1950 *Le volontaire et l'involontaire* and underpinned the essays included in *Histoire et vérité* (1955). His following two-volume *Finitude et Culpabilité* (1960) (*L'homme faillible* and *La symbolique du mal*) reflected his further explorations towards the development of a philosophical anthropology and a more detailed deliberation on the problems of language and interpretation.

In 1956 Ricoeur was named to the chair of general philosophy at the Sorbonne, where he remained until 1967. Then he moved to the newly established University of Nanterre and was soon elected as doyen of the Faculty of Letters, a position from which he resigned in 1970, discouraged by his unfortunate efforts to deal with the aftermath of the 1968 student revolt that had erupted there. During a three-year leave due to his failing health, Ricoeur was also invited to teach at the Catholic University of Louvain in Belgium. In 1967 he was named to succeed Paul Tillich as the John Nuveen professor of philosophical theology at the University of Chicago, with a joint appointment in the Divinity School, the Philosophy Department and the Committee on Social Thought. He held this position until 1992. During the 1960s and 1970s Ricoeur's philosophical anthropology reached its more mature stage with the development of his hermeneutics of action, agency and human identity. Enunciated in *De l'interprétation: essai sur Freud* (1965), a response to the challenges posed by the popular subject-centred disciplines of structuralism and psychology, Ricoeur's hermeneutic theory was further developed in the 1969 collection of essays *Le conflit des interprétations*, in *Interpretation Theory: Discourse and the surplus of meaning* (1976), as well as in his 1975 study on the creative capacity of metaphoricity, *La métaphore vive*, which marked his critical encounter with the late Heidegger (Bourgeois and Schalow, 1990) and his unresolved polemic with Derrida on the relation between philosophy and metaphor (Lawlor, 1992).

Ricoeur continued teaching at the University of Chicago as Professor Emeritus. The main themes of his hermeneutics were now reworked in a substantial number of articles and books on practical reason, the social imaginary, ethics, narrative and the fundamental temporality of human existence. During the 1980s, Ricoeur published amongst others five major works, which soon became widely known and highly regarded both in France and in the United States: the three volumes of *Temps et récit* (1975, 1983, 1984), *Du texte à l'action* (1986) and his first systematic exploration of Marx in his *Lectures on Ideology and Utopia* (1986). His most prominent recent publications in the 1990s include his authoritative *Soi-meme comme un autre* (1990), a work mostly drawn from his 1986 Gifford Lectures, as well as his *Le Just* and *La Critique et la Conviction*, both published in 1995.

Covering a vast range of topics such as aesthetics, ethics, religion, linguistics, humanistic sciences, Marxism, action theory, biblical narrative and interpretation theory, Ricoeur's writings had a considerable impact on such disparate fields as theology, psychoanalysis, historiography, literary theory, political economy and political philosophy. Built on a congenial appropriating and reconciling of seemingly incommensurable philosophical heritages (Kant *and* Hegel, Descartes *and* Nietzsche, Gadamer *and* Habermas, Anglo-American analytic philosophy *and* hermeneutic phenomenology), Ricoeur's admittedly interdisciplinary work is an exemplary exercise in collaborative mediation and academic modesty. So abstemious, disciplined and studious, his rhetorical practice seems at first almost un-Parisian, an impression further amplified by his relative reticence towards figures often associated with French 'postmodernism'. And yet, more often than not, this sobriety or silence entails quiet but difficult responses that soon reveal their combative character. Once one considers Ricoeur's painstaking objections to Saussurean linguistics, as well as his uncompromising and often acrimonious contentions with many of his contemporaries like Sartre, Lévi-Strauss, Althusser, Lacan, Derrida or Habermas, his humble rapprochement divulges anything but an elision of disputation, an academic sheathing of the sword.

ricoeur's philosophical anthropology and the 'political'

Despite their polycentricity, Ricoeur's many writings form parts of a 'philosophical anthropology' and reflect his undaunted engagement with politics and the *polis* (Dosse, 1997, p. 7). Ricoeur's political thought both springs from his philosophical anthropology and supplements it. The political resides not only or merely in those of his writings that explicitly address political matters. Instead it could and, perhaps, should be traced in his overall contribution to the hermeneutics of imagination, action and time. Thus read, most of the themes explored in Ricoeur's philosophical anthropology become parts of his constant yet unfinished exploration of our material involvements with other people. Politics, for Ricoeur, is the principal domain where the recurrent themes of his philosophical anthropology find expression, such as his investigations into the embodied, situated character of freedom and the centrality of the element of hope in our responsible engaging with politics; the obligation to seek a non-totalitarian version of socialism as a viable alternative to both Marxist communism and capitalism; the *poetic* power of metaphorical language and imagination in the symbolic mediation of sociopolitical life; and the historical and paradoxical character of power and the ineliminable character of human fallibility and political fragility.

Ricoeur's overall work, his engagement with the political included, is mostly built on a series of pairings between two antithetical poles (*Verstehen/auslegung*, rationality/evil, ideology/utopia, justice/violence, selfhood/otherness, teleological ethics/nomological morality). In order to investigate the subtle relationship between these pairs, Ricoeur attempts what he calls a 'difficult *detour*' into their initial disproportionality, showing that their phenomenal opposition is also a form of dialectic. Typical of the way Ricoeur appropriates a series of philosophers and philosophical heritages in his work, this 'obsession for reconciliation' betrays nothing of a mere methodological compromise. His dialectic results neither in a merely eclectic combination of elements from both poles, nor in a Hegelian third term that would surpass their antithesis and render them useless. Situated *in* the heart of the dialectic and completely implying *both* of its poles, Ricoeur's 'third term' can only be understood as a practical mediation between them, a reading through from one pole to the other disclosing their constant interplay (Ricoeur, 1998a, pp. 61, 76). This third position leads neither to the evasion of politics, nor to the levelling of differences, nor even to the elimination of political risk. To the contrary, it demonstrates that the preservation of this subtle way of relating is intrinsically pertinent to the very perseverance of politics, namely that the political is 'always already' conditioned by this riskiness.

For Ricoeur, everything political is historical, paradoxical and inescapably fragile. Politics is historical because it is always already embedded in concrete material practices and contextual contingencies, which are nonetheless conditioned by past experiences and become socially meaningful in their dialectical relationship with them and with the future anticipations of a historically and culturally specific community. The paradox of politics is but an expression of the paradoxical character of the power exercised in the community. It is born out of the 'internal contradiction' between sovereignty and the sovereign, between *form* and *force*, in the establishment of political power. Although the constitution of a state gives *form* to the will of a group of people to participate in a good common life, to 'live with and for others in just institutions' (Ricoeur, 1992, p. 172), it also demands their acceptance of an authority that legitimises the domination of some by others. As this domination has never been free from the exercise of excessive legalised *force* by the rulers, a certain gap is created between power and domination, giving rise to conflict. This in turn threatens to undercut the people's will to live together and hence endangers the durability of politics (Ricoeur, 1993, pp. 14–15). Hence politics, for Ricoeur, fosters both a specific rationality *and* specific evils, evils of political power. It is always open, an always unfinished project, but it is also unavoidably risky. It is always already shot through with an ineliminable fragility which has its roots in the very human condition:

> Henceforth, man cannot evade politics under penalty of evading his humanity. Throughout history, and by means of politics, man is faced with *his* grandeur and *his* culpability. One could not infer a political 'defeatism' on the basis of this lucidity. Such a reflection leads rather to a political *vigilance*. It is here that reflection, ending its long detour, comes back to actuality and moves from critique to praxis. (Ricoeur, 1998b, p. 261)

The political paradox conforms to shapes of the paradox of authority in society. It is the task of the always already fragile political discourse to manage all shapes of this paradox. Political discourse is fragile because it always already contains, for Ricoeur, both ideological and utopian elements. In order to investigate the rationale of this fragility, a core theme in Ricoeur's engagement with politics, let us follow more closely his investigation of the constant, paradoxical interplay between the ideological and utopian elements inherent in political discourse. Thus instead of resorting to his earlier writings that are directly related to social and political issues (see, for example, Ricoeur, 1974), the following discussion will render Ricoeur's understanding of political fragility more intelligible by following a less direct way, passing through Ricoeur's hermeneutics of imagination and his discussion of the relationship between tradition and innovation in the symbolic mediation of sociopolitical life. This analytical choice flows from the conviction that Ricoeur's contribution in the investigation of the Janus face of social imagination is of political significance and contemporary relevance.

the janus face of social imagination: ideology/utopia

Ricoeur discusses ideology and utopia as concepts rather than as phenomena. They are approached as two limit-ideas, two conflicting yet complementary functions of the social imaginary and thus constitutive expressions for any durable society. Through a 'regressive analysis of meaning' he attempts to 'dig under the surface of the apparent meaning to more fundamental meanings' of these two concepts, so that their range of possibilities will be disclosed. Both ideology and utopia, according to Ricoeur, pertain to certain representational qualities and social functions. More crucially they should not be treated as forms of noncongruence. Ideology critique is possible neither from the point of reality (Marx and Engels of *The German Ideology*) nor from that of science (orthodox Marxism). Instead, as he notes,

> what we must assume is that the judgement on ideology is always the judgement from a utopia. This is my conviction: the only way to get out of the circularity in which ideology engulf us is to assume a utopia, declare it, and judge an ideology on this basis. Because the absolute onlooker is impossible, then it is someone within the process itself who takes the responsibility for judgement ... It is to the extent finally that the correlation ideology – utopia replaces the impossible correlation ideology – science that a certain solution to the problem of judgement may be found, a solution ... itself congruent with the claim that no point of view exists outside the game. Therefore, if there can be no transcendent onlooker, then a *practical* concept is what must be assumed. (Ricoeur, 1986, pp. 311, 172–3)

For Ricoeur, Marx's understanding of ideology as *distortion* is a definition of the concept at the surface level. In order to explore ideology genetically Ricoeur relates it to the planes of both representation and praxis. Although ideology claims to provide the true representation of material reality, it never ceases to function as such, that is, in representational terms. In that sense, distortion becomes a mere phase and not *the* model of ideology. As he remarks (1986, p. 136), 'to give an account of ideology we must speak the language of ideology; we must speak of individuals constructing dreams instead of living their real life'. It is by virtue of its representational function that ideology relates to the realm of praxis. Representation and praxis should not be treated as opposed; rather, representation should be regarded as a constitutive dimension of praxis.

It should be emphasised here that by referring to the distorting function of ideology Ricoeur does not imply the pre-existence of a real, *correct* social and political structure that then becomes dissimulated ideologically. Ricoeur's treatment of the 'reality' of sociopolitical life is based on his reading of Marx and Engels' *The German Ideology*, where the real (the way people are, *wirklich*) is equated with the *actual* and the *material*, as individuals are put together with their material conditions, the way they operate (*wirken*) (Marx and Engels, 1970, pp. 46–7). Instead, Ricoeur discusses distortion as the process through which the established sociopolitical order is uncritically vindicated and the community's symbols become fixed and fetishised. This process is the meeting point of representation and praxis:

> The process of distortion is grafted onto a symbolic function. *Only because the structure of human social life is already symbolic can it be distorted.* If it were not symbolic from the start, it could not be distorted. The possibility of distortion is a possibility opened up only by this function. (Ricoeur, 1986, p. 10; emphasis added)

Moving to the next, deeper level of meaning, Ricoeur proceeds from the distorting to the *legitimating* function of ideology. He notes that it is the task of ideology to legitimate existing reality by filling in the gap between a sociopolitical ordering that provides society with a specific ideological pattern or *Gestalt* (*Ordnung*) and the individual intellectual representations of this order (*Vorstellung*). Put in Weberian terminology, this is the gap between the *claim* made for a specific ordering and the *belief* in such a correspondence. In other words, the belief in the legitimacy of the given order is always in need of a supplement, a surplus value, and it is the role of ideology to provide it through its legitimating function.

At this second level of meaning ideology meets power. By filling in the gap between claim and belief, the ideological imaginary becomes intrinsically related to the discourses of political ontology. Everything novel becomes assimilated and accommodated only insofar as it fits into the typologies of the original schema. Whatever is assimilable is legitimate and whatever legitimate, in turn, exists. The ideological imaginary comes to function as a form of blindness and closure because only those forms of (inter-)action that have been already symbolically represented as legitimate are the ones ascribed with political existence. Its goal becomes less the mobilisation of society than the justification of what society has become. It ceases 'to be mobilising in order to become justificatory; or rather, it continues to be mobilising only insofar as it is justificatory' (Ricoeur, 1997, p. 307). Hence its singular capacity of dynamism is revealed. It animates society only insofar as motivation serves the affirmation of the righteousness, justness and necessity of the current forms of social existence. According to Ricoeur (1986, p. 266), this occurs 'when the integrative function becomes frozen ... when schematization and rationalization prevail'. This moment is marked by the perpetual duplication of certain sociopolitical stereotypes that, due to their conformity with the ideological symbolic system, appear as legitimate and true, finally leading to a 'stagnation of politics' (Ricoeur, 1981, p. 229). The danger here is immanent:

> this reaffirmation can be perverted, usually by monopolistic elites, into a mystificatory discourse which serves to uncritically vindicate or glorify the established political powers. In such instances, the symbols of a community become fixed and fetishized; they serve as lies. (Ricoeur, 1995a, p. 230)

The third level of meaning that Ricoeur discusses in his 'unmasking' of the concept of ideology is that of *integration*. In this final, deepest level ideology integrates society by providing a shared symbolic system that mediates social action. Through the codifying function of the modes of its representation, the ideological imaginary is maintained by the transmission of the ideas it enhances about society and politics into commonly shared opinions. It is through its symbolic schematisation that ideology renders possible the idealisation of the existing forms of sociopolitical organisation and interaction, as well as the perpetuation of this idealised image in the future. With thought mutated into *doxa*, the ideological imaginary functions at the level of rationalisation, as its political representations are gradually added into political rhetoric as maxims or slogans. It comes to function as a non-reflective image of reality, and, by virtue of its being so, it facilitates the social efficacy of its implicit ideas along with the integration of society. Hence, Ricoeur maintains, it is because ideology already functions symbolically in an integrating manner that it can function as both distortion and legitimation.

As we have noted above, ideology becomes *constitutive* of social existence by virtue of its symbolic function. In that sense, a critique of ideology would be incomplete if it failed to acknowledge the strong linkage between the functions of ideology and the symbolic articulation of sociopolitical interaction through the ideological imaginary. Otherwise the critique of ideology would be limited to unmasking its intellectual malfeasance and thus incomplete, for what would be missing is the very ideological relating of 'the mask to the face' (Ricoeur, 1982, p. 116). This relating would be impossible and the 'unmasking' would be meaningless if we failed to acknowledge the ways in which the ideological imaginary is related to the symbolic systems that constitute and integrate a specific community.

A similar regressive analysis of meaning is followed in order to investigate the functions of utopia. His aim here is not only to explore the deeper levels of meaning of the concept of utopia, but also to bring the two opposing imaginaries (ideological and utopian) closer together so that their subtle relationship would be disclosed. For Ricoeur, this involves making a double analytical move towards what Raymond Ruyer has called the mode and the spirit of utopia. On the one hand, the mode of utopia relates to the existence of society in a way similar to the one invention relates to scientific knowledge:

> The utopian mode may be defined as the imaginary project of another kind of society, of another reality of another world. Imagination is here constitutive in an inventive rather than an integrative manner, to use an expression of Henri Desroche.

On the other hand, the spirit of utopia encompasses:

> the fundamental ambiguities which have been assigned to utopia and which affect its social function. We discover at this level a range of functional variations which may be paralleled with those of ideology and which sometimes intersect those functions which earlier we described as ranging from the integrative to the distorting. (Ricoeur, 1982, pp. 118–19)

Whereas with the utopian mode we come closer to the realisation of the more general inventive function of the utopian imaginary, once we take this second step towards the spirit of utopia we can ascribe a more meaningful content to this inventiveness.

Ricoeur starts his genetic phenomenology of utopia by discussing its first level of function, that is, utopia as *possibility*. Contrary to the usual critique of utopia as either unreal or unscientific, he approaches the concept by way of its symbolic element. Similarly to ideology, Ricoeur maintains that it is because of its symbolic function that utopia plays 'a *constitutive* role in helping us *rethink* the nature of our social life'. This dynamic is inherent in the mode of utopia. But whereas ideology's positive trait is integration, utopia's positive function lies in its disclosing a series of future political possibilities by providing us with an alternative imaginary variation on the real. It paves the way towards what is not yet, as well as what could be. In any utopia there is an inherent anticipation of and an intrinsic claim for a future that although not existent at present still wants to be realised. This is what Ricoeur (1986, p. 310) calls utopia's 'function of the nowhere', inasmuch as this nowhere is not merely the un-real but the not-yet. It is the unreal that makes a claim to reality. This is a function that dialectically relates to *Dasein*: 'To be here, *Da-sein*, I must also be able to be nowhere. There is a dialectic of *Dasein* and nowhere.'

Moving from the surface level of function (utopia as *possibility*) to the second, intermediate level, Ricoeur discusses the utopian function of *challenge*. This function is the counterpart of the legitimating function of ideology, for what is questioned in challenging the given order or the present authority is exactly the legitimating process that sustains it. Whereas ideology provides the necessary supplement needed for belief in an authority, utopia aims at divulging the undeclared surplus value. Utopia is not only 'the fantasy of an alternative society'. It is a political 'nowhere' that functions 'as one of the most formidable contestations of what is' (Ricoeur, 1986, p. 16). By situating our viewpoint in the no-place of utopia we are able radically to rethink the given, for

> the shadow of the forces capable of shattering a given order are already the shadow of an alternative order that could be opposed to the given order. It is the function of utopia to give the force of discourse to this possibility. (Ricoeur, 1982, pp. 117–18)

This view from the *u-topos* of utopia, the society that is not yet, functions as an *epoché*, calling for a suspension of our assumptions about reality. But this glance from nowhere is metacritical in the sense, not of some form of detachment from the historical and cultural specificities of the ideological schematisation at work, but of its self-awareness as a utopian gaze. In other words, whereas utopia understands itself as such, ideology has no knowledge of itself whatsoever. At this second level, utopia encounters the problem of authority as a manifestation of power. It becomes an imaginary variation of power itself.

At the third deepest level, Ricoeur discusses utopia as a *form of escapism*. Through a complete denial of the real, utopia may lead to a full embrace of the unrealisable and a total indifference to its realisation. This pathology leads to 'the eclipse of praxis, the denial of the logic of action which inevitably ties undesirable evils to preferred means and which forces us to choose between equally desirable but incompatible goals' (Ricoeur, 1991a, p. 322). Furthermore, utopia bears the inherent danger of constituting a new orthodoxy itself, sharing the dogmatism of the ideological imaginary it seeks to destabilise. Unless it provides the practical conditions for this realisation, all a utopian imaginary could do is 'project a static future', thus coming to function itself as ideology (Ricoeur, 1995a, p. 230). This pathology is rooted in the eccentric function of utopia, offering a parody of an ambiguous phenomenon that fluctuates between fantasy and creativity. As the negative function of ideology, distortion is possible because it already functions in a legitimating and integrating manner. Similarly the pathology of utopia emerges out of its most positive trait, its leaping beyond the point where the reimagination of society and politics is possible.

As the deeper levels of the functions of utopia are disclosed, our steps towards the 'spirit' of utopia become more meaningful, for it is here that the ambiguities and variations of the utopian imaginary are brought together with those of the ideological one. At first glance, it seems that their traits are placed as *opposed* to each other: integration *contra* challenge, legitimation *contra* possibility, distortion *contra* escapism. But this subtle relationship is one not only of conflict but also of *complementarity*, which involves a dialectical relating or, better, a dialectical implicating of each other. For example, although the utopian imaginary would seem but erratic in its subversive and challenging exertion, its eccentricity is but a manifestation of utopia's double move: to question the given we have to be elsewhere; but what gets us elsewhere also leads us back to the here and now. Moreover, this eccentricity is the potential result of the gap introduced by the ideological symbolic mediation of sociopolitical reality. Conversely, it is this eccentricity that the ideological imaginary aims at taming by filling in this gap through its imaginary schematisations.

Thus both the existence and the functions of these imaginaries are caught into a constant, unsurpassable interplay. They are complementary expressions of social imagination reflecting the paradoxical effects of the political phenomenon itself. The relating between the dysfunctions of the ideological and utopian imaginaries reflects, for Ricoeur, the Janus face of imagination at the level of pathology. It reflects the subtle relationship between their dysfunctions and the fundamental directions of the social imagination. On the one hand, the pathology of the ideological imaginary (distortion) becomes meaningful within the symbolic constitution of the political order reflecting one of the fundamental directions of the social imagination, that is, the integrating function. On the other hand, the dysfunctioning of the utopian imaginary should be appreciated as a reflection of the other fundamental direction of the social imagination, that is, its tendency to step outside and question the given.

Yet if utopian imagination does not manage fully to escape its own pathology, why should one insist on imagining alternative forms of social and political life? To what extent are we to count on and value such an imaginary? Our reimagining might be the aptest medium for destabilising the given symbolic forms that mediate sociopolitical organisation and interaction. But it would have to 'fly away' *and* 'return to' the specificities and necessities of our current imaginary schematisations. It is in the very pathological traits of such an erratic imaginary that perhaps one should trace its most positive function as well. For as Ricoeur has asked:

> who knows whether such and such an erratic mode of existence may not prophesy the man to come? Who even knows if a certain degree of individual pathology is not the condition of social change, at least to the extent that such pathology brings to light the sclerosis of dead institutions? To put it more paradoxically, who knows whether the illness is not at the same time a part of the required therapy? (1982, p. 124)

As we have seen, ideology and utopia are bound together, interacting in the form of a practical circle that transcends their oppositional structuring, as opposed to either science or reality. According to Ricoeur, we always already find ourselves entangled yet not helplessly entrapped within this circle, for the circle is not closed, rigid and immutable. It is our task, Ricoeur concludes (1986, p. 312), to turn it into a spiral: '[W]e must try to cure the illnesses of utopias by what is wholesome in ideology – by its element of identity – and try to cure the rigidity, the petrification, of ideologies by the utopian element.' Hence the complementarity between ideology and utopia does not imply their mere coexistence in terms of polarity. It should be read in terms of pathology, to the extent that their positive sides stand in complementary relation to the negative and pathological ones of the other. This is especially evident in the case of the utopian imaginary, which as we saw bears an unfulfilled promise that wants to be realised. The not-yet-realised horizon of its promise may function not only as an ongoing sociopolitical critique but also as the integrating imaginary ground of human emancipation (Koselleck, 2002, pp. 261–4). It is only when we make sure that our reimagining brings together this horizon of expectation with the actual field of lived experience that it could function positively: 'It is not that we are without utopia, but that we are without *paths* to utopia. And without a path towards it, without concrete and practical mediation in our field of experience, utopia becomes a sickness' (Ricoeur, 1995a, p. 231).

What is involved in such a path-finding pertains, we think, less to the destabilising function of utopian reimagining, than to the *relationship* sustained between the horizon disclosed by imagining the not-yet and the symbolically mediated field of current political experience. If we accept that 'the most challenging political problems of our time ... arise primarily from a need to re-imagine what we mean by politics' (Walker, 2000, p. 23), then perhaps it is not hard to assess the contemporary relevance and political significance of Ricoeur's path-calling. How does the horizon of the future political possibilities opened up by our reimagining politics relate to our present? In Reinhart Koselleck's terms (1985), how does our 'horizon of expectations' relate to our 'space of experience' when reimagining politics? These are the questions that we will attempt to tackle in our concluding remarks, so that both the relevance and the significance of Ricoeur's contribution to the investigation of the political will become conspicuous.

conclusion: radically reimagining democratic politics

Contemporary dialogues on the left have often noted the necessity of *radically* reimagining democratic politics. Ranging from (post-)Marxism to feminism and poststructuralism, the theoretical variants of such a radical democratic imaginary demonstrate a certain affinity at the level of function. Despite their diversity in terms of content, they all pertain to functions that could be addressed as 'utopian', meaning the challenges they pose to the given political order that is symbolically mediated by the neo-liberal imaginary, the possibilities they disclose by imagining not-yet-existent forms of sociopolitical life, and the possible dangers they bear when not providing the means for their realisation. Once we place our analytical focus upon the functions of these imaginary variants, we soon realise that there is something more involved here than a mere theoretical exchange within the boundaries of the left. This something more concerns the very relationship sustained between a radical democratic imaginary and the neo-liberal imaginary that mediates our present political experience. As soon as these two conflicting imaginaries are examined in parallel, the very extent and limits of the radicalness involved in our reimagining are implicitly interrogated. What is problematised here, that is, is the modern meaning of radicalness, according to which the future is registered but only after and through its total rift with the present.

Indeed, when referring to the horizon opened up by our radical democratic imaginary as one of possibilities, we already presuppose that it is always already a horizon of expectations aimed at the future of politics. But these anticipations are also always already inscribed *in* the present. Put in Ricoeur's Heideggerian terms (1998c, p. 208), it is 'the future-become-present (*vergegenwärtigte Zukunft*), turned toward the not-yet'. This implies that our reimagining is not only a self-aware glance from the *u-topos* of an aspired political future *towards* our historical present, but also a projection towards our political future *from* this present. It is a projection that by being always already inscribed in the present should respond to the necessities, callings and commitments of present political experience, radicalising the present liberal political institutions (see also Bobbio, 1987, p. 59; Mouffe, 1996, p. 20). In that sense, there has to be sustained a certain relevance between our present political experiences and future expectations within our radical democratic imaginary, in order to avoid our gaze ending up as a form of escapism. We have to make sure that this relevance preserves its tensional character and does not end up creating a schism; 'we have to keep our horizon of expectation from running away from us' (Ricoeur, 1998c, p. 215). When radically reimagining democratic politics, we are still the heirs of the discourses and practices that have been mediated by the neo-liberal imaginary. No matter how distant our future anticipations might seem, we would never be in the position of being 'absolute innovators', but rather we would be 'always first of all in the situation of being heirs' (Ricoeur, 1998c, p. 221).

Hence the paradox: We cannot reimagine politics and anticipate an alternative political future without breaking with the neo-liberal symbolic forms mediating our present political experience. But equally we cannot suppose that our hopes about this political future become more meaningful in deficit of any historical household. In that sense, we could say that what we have been so keen on overcoming, rejecting and substituting – the neo-liberal imaginary schematisation of politics – is finally what has constituted and continues to underpin what we allow ourselves to hope for through our reimagining. By finding unconditional refuge in an alternative imaginary of a totally different kind of society and politics, we simply reaffirm that our historical present is in Ricoeur's words wholly a 'crisis', to the extent that 'expectation takes refuge in utopia and ... tradition becomes only a dead deposit of the past' (1998c, p. 235).

Perhaps then it is far more useful to acknowledge the significance of placing our radical democratic imaginary in parallel with the neo-liberal imaginary it longs to overcome. This in-parallel-situating could then demonstrate better that the opposing imaginaries are caught in a tensional relationship characterised by both conflict and complementarity. Investigating what imaginary variations or hybrids such a dialectics might bear in our reimagining the future of politics appears to be a task both timely and demanding. But even our mere posing the question is always already pregnant less of answers than of new difficulties. It presupposes a certain act of instantiation that leads us to a state of *aporia*. As time becomes thematised into historical past, present and future, there comes forth the issue of legitimacy of both our lived experiences and our aspired futures. And with the question of legitimacy there emerges the need for an ahistorical transcendental, a new ethical standard; we need a new criterion for the critique of critique. What is going to validate our future aspirations? How could we avert the danger of returning to a principle of radically monological truth, as in the Kantian transcendental deduction?

This is a political moment, a moment of risk and fragility. Our criteria of truth and legitimacy need a dialogical dimension rooted in history. We have to ensure that our horizon of future expectations opened up by our political reimagining and its validation are articulated on the basis of thinking about history as the future-being-affected-by-the-past (see Ricoeur, 2000; Akrivoulis, forthcoming 2006). In that sense, our anticipations would be conditioned by a 'fusion of horizons' rather than by a multitude of distinct, incommensurable ones (Ricoeur, 1998c, p. 220). In this fusion of horizons the historical past, present and future are bound together in a form of dialectics. It is our task to keep this dialectics alive. Perhaps then we could come closer to the realisation that the utmost significance of our reimagining is one of an intrinsically political essence. Perhaps then we could speak of politics as always open and unfinished; we could speak of politics with Ricoeur (1986, p. 179) as 'not a descriptive concept but a polemical concept provided by the dialectics between utopia and ideology'.

further reading

Of Ricoeur's works listed below the most significant is his three-volume *magnum opus Time and Narrative*. His *Lectures on Ideology and Utopia* and the essays collected in *History and Truth* and *From Text to Action* are significant sources with regard to Ricoeur's understanding of political fragility. His more recent works *Oneself As Another* (1992), *The Just* (1995b) and his still untranslated *Lectures I: autour du politique* (1991b) are equally important and of strong political relevance. Both Reagan (1996) and Dosse (1997) provide accessible and philosophically informed biographies of Ricoeur. Dauenhauer (1998) represents a valuable account of the political significance and relevance of Ricoeur's overall work, whereas Clark's (1990) critical introduction to Ricoeur's hermeneutics still remains unsurpassed. Some informative extensions and critical interrogations of Ricoeur's thought are hosted in numerous edited volumes dedicated to his overall work, such as Cohen and Marsh (2002), Hahn (1995), Kearney (1996), Kemp and Rasmussen (1989), Klemm and Schweiker (1993), Wall et al. (2002) and Wood (1991).

references

Akrivoulis, D.E. (forthcoming 2006) 'The Efficacity of History and the Limits of Emancipation: Ricoeur's hermeneutics of historical consciousness', in *Interpretation, Values, Action: A collection of essays on Paul Ricoeur*, ed. Y.B. Raynova. Vienna: Vienna Institute for Axiological Research and Peter Lang Publishing Group.

Bobbio, N. (1987) *The Future of Democracy*. Oxford: Oxford University Press.

Bourgeois, P.L. and Schalow, Fr. (1990) *Traces of Understanding: A profile of Heidegger's and Ricoeur's hermeneutics*. Würzburg/Amsterdam/Atlanta: Königshausen/Neumann/ Rodopi.

Clark, S.H. (1990) *Paul Ricoeur*. London/New York: Routledge.

Cohen, R.A. and Marsh, J.I. (eds) (2002) *Ricoeur as Another: The ethics of subjectivity*. Albany, NY: SUNY Press.

Dauenhauer, B.P. (1998) *Paul Ricoeur: The promise and risk of politics*. Lanham, MD: Rowman & Littlefield.

Dosse, F. (1997) *Paul Ricoeur: les sens d'une vie*. Paris: La Découverte.

Hahn, L.E. (ed.) (1995) *The philosophy of Paul Ricoeur*. Chicago/La Salle, IL: Open Court.

Kearney, R. (ed.) (1996) *Paul Ricoeur: The hermeneutics of action*. London/Thousand Oaks, CA/New Delhi: Sage.

Kemp, T.P. and Rasmussen, D. (eds) (1989) *The Narrative Path: The later works of Paul Ricoeur*. Cambridge, MA/London: MIT Press.

Klemm, D.E. and Schweiker, W. (eds) (1993) *Meanings in Texts and Actions: Questioning Paul Ricoeur*. Charlottesville, VA/London: University Press of Virginia.

Koselleck, R. (1985) *Futures Past: The semantics of historical time*, trans. K. Tribe. Cambridge, MA: MIT Press.

Koselleck, R. (2002) 'The Limits of Emancipation: A conceptual-historical sketch', in *The Practice of Conceptual History: Timing history, spacing concepts*, trans. T.S. Presner, pp. 248–64. Stanford, CA: Stanford University Press.

Lawlor, L. (1992) *Imagination and Chance: The difference between the thought of Ricoeur and Derrida*. Albany, NY: SUNY Press.

Marx, K. and Engels, F. (1970) *The German Ideology*, Part I. New York: International Publishers.

Mouffe, C. (1996) 'Radical Democracy or Liberal Democracy?', in *Radical Democracy: Identity, citizenship, and the state*, ed. D. Trend, pp. 19–26. London: Routledge.

Reagan, Ch.E. (1996) *Paul Ricoeur: His life and work*. London/Chicago, IL: University of Chicago Press.

Ricoeur, P. (1974) *Political and Social Essays*, trans. D. Stewart and J. Bien. Athens, OH: Ohio University Press.

Ricoeur, P. (1981) 'Science and Ideology', in *Hermeneutics and the Human Sciences*, ed. and trans. J.B. Thompson, pp. 222–46. Cambridge: Cambridge University Press.

Ricoeur, P. (1982) 'Ideology and Utopia as Cultural Imagination', in *Being Human in a Technological Age*, ed. D.M. Bochert and D. Stewart, pp. 107–25. Athens, OH: Ohio University Press.

Ricoeur, P. (1984, 1985, 1998c) *Time and Narrative*, Vols 1–3, trans. K. McLaughlin and D. Pellauer. Chicago, IL: University of Chicago Press.

Ricoeur, P. (1986) *Lectures on Ideology and Utopia*, ed. G.H. Taylor. New York: Columbia University Press.

Ricoeur, P. (1991a) 'Ideology and Utopia', in *From Text to Action: Essays in hermeneutics II*, trans. K. Blamey and J.B. Thompson, pp. 308–24. Evanston, IL: Northwestern University Press.

Ricoeur, P. (1991b) *Lectures I: autour du politique*. Paris: Seuil.

Ricoeur, P. (1992) *Oneself As Another*, trans. K. Blamey. Chicago, IL: University of Chicago Press.

Ricoeur, P. (1993) 'Morale, éthique, et politique', *Pouvoirs: revue française d'études constitutionelles et politiques* 65: 5–17.

Ricoeur, P. (1995a) 'The Creativity of Language', in *States of Mind: Dialogues with contemporary thinkers*, ed. R. Kearney, pp. 216–45. New York: New York University Press.

Ricoeur, P. (1995b) *The Just*, trans. D. Pellauer. Chicago, IL: University of Chicago Press.

Ricoeur, P. (1997) *The Rule of Metaphor: Multi-disciplinary studies in the creation of meaning of language*, trans. R. Czerny with K. McLaughlin and J. Costello. Toronto: University of Toronto Press.

Ricoeur, P. (1998a) *Critique and Conviction: Conversations with François Azouvi and Marc de Launay*, trans. K. Blamey. New York: Columbia University Press.

Ricoeur, P. (1998b) 'The Political Paradox', in *History and Truth*, trans. K. Blamey, pp. 247–70. New York: Columbia University Press.

Ricoeur, P. (2000) *La mémoire, l'histoire, l'oubli*. Paris: Seuil.

Walker, R.B.J. (2000) 'Both Globalization and Sovereignty: Re-imagining the political', in *Principled World Politics: The challenge of normative international relations*, ed. P. Wapner and L.E.J. Ruiz, pp. 23–34. Lanham, MD: Rowman & Littlefield.

Wall, J., Schweiker, W., and Hall, W.D. (eds) (2002) *Paul Ricoeur and Contemporary Moral Thought*. New York/London: Routledge.

Wood, D. (ed.) (1991) *On Paul Ricoeur: Narrative and interpretation*. London/New York: Routledge.

16
michel foucault

andrew barry

Michel Foucault was born in Poitiers in France in 1926 and died in Paris in 1984. He was trained in philosophy and psychology, and one of his first posts was as an assistant in psychology. His work was influenced strongly by the work of the historian of medicine, Georges Canguilhem. He also wrote widely on contemporary literature (Macey, 1993). An appreciation of this intellectual background is significant to an understanding of Foucault as a political thinker. For Foucault did not come to the study of politics from any training in political theory. He wrote rather as someone with a background in philosophy and the history of science, whose approach to the study of politics was indirect. Part of the importance of Foucault's work is the way that he demonstrated the critical significance of the life sciences and social sciences to contemporary political life. At the same time, part of his originality derives from the way he was able to bring many of the analytical tools that he had developed in his studies of science to the study of politics and government.

In the 1960s Foucault wrote a series of books on madness, the history of medicine and the analysis of discourse (Foucault, 1970; 1972; 1973). His most explicitly political thought, as well his involvement in political activities, dates from the end of the decade, after the events of May 1968. In December 1968 he was appointed to the Chair of Philosophy at the University of Vincennes, and subsequently became Professor at the Collège de France (Eribon, 1991). During the 1970s he became increasingly well known as a public intellectual, taking part in demonstrations, contributing to petitions and contributing articles on contemporary political events in newspapers and journals. His public lectures, which he was required to give as a Professor at the Collège de France, also dealt with explicitly political themes in the 1970s. In the early

1980s, his research turned towards the study of ethics and what he termed practices of the self (Foucault, 1986a; 1986b; 1997a; 1997b). Both Foucault's earlier work from the 1960s and his later work on ethics and technologies of the self have important implications for the study of politics. However, in this chapter I introduce Foucault's political thought through a discussion of his explicitly political writings from the 1970s. A central theme of this chapter is that if we are to understand Foucault as a political thinker, it is important to read not just his published books, but also his less well known lectures and journalism (Foucault, 1994). In recent years these have become increasingly widely available in translation (Foucault, 1997a; 1997b; 2000; 2003a; 2003b).

Foucault's writing became partially translated and extensively discussed in the Anglo-American academy in the period from the 1970s onwards. However, some of the most intense debates regarding the implications of his work for the study of politics in the US and UK occurred in the late 1970s and 1980s (Gordon, 1996). The time lag between the original date of publication in France and the period of greatest interest in Foucault's work in the US and UK is significant. At the beginning of the 1970s, Marxism had a strong presence in French universities. Foucault's biographer, Didier Eribon, writes of the intensity of political debate and unrest at the time when Foucault took up his position at Vincennes (Eribon, 1991, pp. 201–11). By contrast, Foucault's work was read and discussed in the US and UK during a period when neo-liberal political thought, associated particularly with the governments of Margaret Thatcher and Ronald Reagan, became dominant. At the same time, his work became caught up in an Anglo-American academic debate concerning the differences between Critical Theory and poststructuralism, and between modernism and postmodernism (Ashenden and Owen, 1999; Bauman, 1991; Dews, 1987; Foucault, 1984a; Habermas, 1990). Part of the interest in reading Foucault is certainly the way in which his work establishes multiple connections between the modernism and political radicalism of France in the 1960s and 1970s and the neo-liberalism and postmodernism of Britain and the US in the 1980s. However, part of the difficulty of re-reading Foucault today may result from the need to rescue his thought from these specific, recent, and possibly overwhelming contexts of writing and reception. In this chapter I do not address the relation between Foucault's work and the largely theoretical debates surrounding the notion of postmodernism. Instead I argue that part of the contribution of Foucault to political thought today derives from the particular form through which he communicated his attention to historical and empirical detail.

theory

In the Anglo-American context it is commonplace to draw a clear line between social and political theory and the more empirical concerns of political science and social research. Although there are significant exceptions, for many Anglo-American theorists, social and political 'theory' is quite distinct from empirical or historical research. Of course, empirical materials may be used to illustrate more general theoretical arguments, but, with exceptions, it is not normal to do theoretical work by empirical means.

Viewed in the context of Anglo-American social and political thought, reading Foucault presents three clear difficulties. One difficulty is that Foucault's work is full of empirical and historical detail. *Discipline and Punish*, a book clearly relevant to any assessment of Foucault as a political thinker, begins with a lengthy and graphic description of the public execution of the regicide Damiens in 1757, contrasting this with an account of Léon Faucher's disciplinary rules for the 'House of young prisoners in Paris' (Foucault, 1977, pp. 3–7). Later Foucault approvingly quotes Marshal de Saxe's instruction that it is not enough to know architecture, one must also know 'stone-cutting' (Foucault, 1977, p. 139). The clear implication is that it is not enough to know political theory if one is to understand politics; one must also attend to the details of what Foucault terms 'political technologies', such as Faucher's rules. Continental Political Thought is broadly hostile to Anglo-American empiricism, but Foucault's work complicates the terms of this opposition. His work is full of empirical detail, and, I shall suggest, could point towards a rethinking of empiricism in political thought.

A second difficulty in reading Foucault as a political thinker is that he did not write any text about the kinds of things that you would expect a political thinker to write about. His most explicitly 'political' books (*Discipline and Punish* and the *History of Sexuality*, Vol. 1) concern such matters as prisons, schooling, architecture, the body and sexuality. He never wrote a book on democracy, the state, or social justice, nor on the work of any other political thinker. His brief comments on the work of Machiavelli, Marx and the Frankfurt School are largely to be found in interviews and lectures (Foucault, 1984a; 1991a; 1991b). His analysis of the work of Bentham focuses not on his utilitarianism, but on his proposal for the design of a prison, the Panopticon. Moreover, instead of framing his discussions of discipline and sexuality in terms of a more general social and political theory, Foucault stubbornly affirms the necessity of analysing them as elements of 'concrete systems' which have to be situated in their own 'field of operation' (Foucault, 1977, p. 24). In doing so, Foucault wrote not as a social and political theorist at all, but, to use his description, as an 'historian of systems of thought'. He was simply not interested in providing a general account of society or of politics. Indeed, from the point of view of mainstream social theory he seems simply to be a bad sociologist (Osborne, 1998).

A third difficulty relates to the first two. A central theme in Foucault's later work on politics is his concern with the materiality of bodies, as well as the materiality of non-human objects such as prison buildings. Foucault is as much concerned with 'stone-cutting' as a technique and as a problem, as with the theory of architecture. In his later work he is concerned with the study of bodies, muscles and bones, as much as with language and ideas. Yet twentieth-century social and political thought has tended to split off the study of material objects, such as human bodies and the natural environment, from the study of social and political entities such as states, social movements and political ideologies (Barry, 2001; Latour, 2004). Political science, for example, analyses democratic institutions and parties in great detail, but has little to say about such topics as the architecture of parliaments, the technology of ballot papers or the political significance of new genetic technologies. These objects are bracketed outside, or to the margins, of the frame of political thought. Within Marxism, as Foucault recognised, politics has tended to be regarded as a superstructural phenomenon, related to, but distinct from, material productive forces and the social relations of production. Although Foucault's account of materiality remains underdeveloped, as we shall see, it nonetheless disturbs the distinction of political from material phenomena that is still so often taken for granted in political thought.

If Foucault does not write as a social or political theorist, then how are we to read him as a political thinker? One starting point is suggested by Gilles Deleuze (1992), who divides Foucault's writings on politics into two parts. One part begins with *Discipline and Punish* (1977) and the *History of Sexuality*, Vol. 1 (1979). These books can be read as studies in what Foucault terms political technologies (1977, p. 30). Foucault's central concern is not to try to develop something like a general account of politics and government. Rather he focuses on the role of various mundane techniques (such as examination procedures and disciplinary methods) in the formation of individual and collective subjects. *Discipline and Punish* and the *History of Sexuality* are often read as general accounts of a society of surveillance (for example, Giddens, 1985). This is a limited way of reading Foucault as a political thinker. A potentially more fruitful approach is to see how his work points us more generally towards the importance of examining the technical character of politics and the performativity of political discourse. Rather than understand politics and government in terms of the conventional categories of political science and political sociology (the state, ideology, society), Foucault radically shifts our focus. His key terms (apparatus, problematisation, technology, biopower, micro-physics of power, governmentality, the subject) indicate the possibility of a different approach to the analysis of contemporary political life. His topics (the body, sexuality, punishment, population, madness) shift our attention away from the conventional preoccupation with political systems, parties, elections and ideologies onto a very different terrain. In a 1975 interview, Foucault remarked that when he 'began to be interested in subjects that were the lowest depths of social reality a few people ... focused on it with interest. But I must say that neither the philosophical community nor the political community was interested' (quoted in Eribon, 1991, p. 116).

The second side to Foucault's work on politics, which is not contained in his academic books, but largely in his interviews and journalism, provides what Gilles Deleuze calls a 'diagnostics' of contemporary political actions and events. While it is commonplace in social and political theory to denounce the media as superficial or ideological, Foucault reckoned that there was a close relation between his work and the work of journalists: 'intellectuals work with journalists at the intersection of ideas and events' (Foucault, 1978, p. 707). In this respect Foucault's trajectory can be contrasted with that of Habermas. As Thomas Osborne argues: 'whereas Habermas started out as a journalist and ended as a philosopher, Foucault, as a consequence of his philosophy, ended up – amongst other things – as something like a journalist' (Osborne, 1999, pp. 56–7). Although Foucault wrote much less about contemporary political events than the history of systems of thought, his discussions of political events both complement and highlight the limitations of some of the more extended analyses of discipline and governmentality. In this chapter I shall follow Deleuze's scheme, introducing Foucault's books and lectures on what I have termed political technologies, followed by a discussion of the significance of his political journalism.

political technologies

A characteristic feature of Foucault's style is to begin an argument with a negative statement. In this manner, the opening chapter of *Discipline and Punish* contains the following suggestion:

> Instead of treating the history of penal law and the history of the human sciences as two separate series whose overlapping appears ... to have a disturbing or useful effect, according to one's point of view, see whether there is not some common matrix ... in short, to make the technology of power the very principle both of the humanization of the penal system and of the knowledge of man. (Foucault, 1977, p. 23)

This statement is significant. Foucault's approach to the history of the human sciences in *Discipline and Punish* was distinctive. He does not seek to show whether such knowledges are more or less true. He does not treat them as sciences or as ideologies (Barrett, 1992; Foucault, 1972; 1979; 1980). Nor does he seek to contextualise the history of the human sciences in terms of a more general analysis of a capitalist society. Rather he treats them as elements of political technologies. The history of the human sciences demands, according to Foucault, attention to their quite specific entanglement into disciplinary apparatuses of power.

Two points follow from this observation. One concerns Foucault's relation to the academic disciplines of sociology and politics. In one reading, *Discipline and Punish* does look something like a social and political history of punishment. Although Foucault's work may have something to contribute to such a history, such a reading would be misleading. For rather than make a contribution to historical sociology or political history, Foucault points to the need to locate sociology and politics themselves within the framework of an analysis of political technologies (Foucault, 2000, p. 5). And rather than accept the conventional terms of social and political analysis (the individual, society, the state), his work points to the ways in which the 'individual' and 'society' are themselves the product of political technologies, of which the disciplines of sociology and politics are themselves parts.

Second, according to some commentators, Foucault's lack of interest in the question of the truth or falsity of specific knowledge claims leads him towards postmodernism. In this view all Foucault can do is simply describe different systems of power-knowledge as simply different, without offering any grounds for critical evaluation (Ashenden and Owen, 1999). But such a view would also be to misinterpret Foucault's argument. His intention is not to denounce the claims of the human sciences to knowledge as untrue, but neither is it simply to make the banal observation that the categories of the human sciences are constructed. Rather his argument indicates that if we are to understand how the human sciences have worked as elements of apparatuses it is fruitless to restrict ourselves to the forms of analysis inherited from the human sciences themselves. We need, Foucault argues, to think from a different conceptual space. In this respect, his work may owe less to postmodernism than to an earlier tradition of literary modernism. His constructivism should not be equated with social constructivism. Rather, it derives a sense of the need for continual conceptual invention in the face of the limitations of contemporary forms of social and political thought (Foucault, 1986a).

Thus the effect of *Discipline and Punish* is not to explain or to contextualise, but to shock. The book raises a question: are our contemporary forms of political thought still rooted in a model which should have been abandoned in the nineteenth century? Foucault's book shocks us in four ways. One is to question the adequacy of the model of sovereignty, and its continual hold on our political imagination. Power, he argues, should not be thought of as possessed by a sovereign power, but instead should be understood as a mode of action on the action of others. Power is not possessed, but exercised. Second, Foucault is rigorously constructivist. Power does not exist simply to repress, for there is no essence to the human person to be repressed. Rather, persons are formed and moulded through the exercise of power. Third, power is not just exercised through the medium of ideas or language or through ownership of the means of production, but also directly on the body. In this way, Foucault replaced the Marxist interest in the production of ideology with a different and much more specific emphasis on the political technology of the body: an analysis of the 'micro-physics' of power. Fourth, disciplinary power is exercised through the existence of disciplinary apparatuses. Such apparatuses contain both discursive and non-discursive and human and non-human elements.

They are made through the conjunction of bodies, scientific knowledges, architectural forms, techniques and practices. Jeremy Bentham's design for a prison, the Panopticon, illustrates the form of the disciplinary apparatus:

> This enclosed, segmented space, observed at every point, in which the individuals are inserted in a fixed place, in which the slightest movements are supervised, in which all events are recorded, in which an uninterrupted work of writing links the centre and the periphery, in which power is exercised without division, according to a continuous hierarchical figure, in which each individual is constantly located, examined and distributed among living beings, the sick and the dead – all this constitutes a compact model of the disciplinary mechanism. (Foucault, 1977, p. 197)

Nearly 30 years after its first publication the shock effect of the publication of *Discipline and Punish* has arguably been both too little and too great. Too great, because it was all too easy to translate Foucault's analysis of disciplinary power into the form of a more general analysis of a disciplinary society. For some, Foucault's work provides the starting point for an analysis of new forms of a digital panopticon (Poster, 1996). But also too little, because despite Foucault's provocation, political theory and political science remain largely oblivious to its force. Politics still tends to be seen as the study, above all else, of the state. Foucault's unfashionable preoccupation with mundane and material political technologies, such as examination methods and the architectural design of prisons, has been taken up enthusiastically by some, but remains marginal to the mainstream of political thought (Power, 1997; Rabinow, 1984; Rose, 1999).

sexuality

In the *History of Sexuality*, Vol. 1, Foucault developed the argument of *Discipline and Punish* further and in a new direction. One of the striking themes of *Discipline and Punish* was its focus on the materiality of the body. The book begins with the physical dismemberment of the regicide Damiens and continues with a meticulous description of disciplinary regimes. In the *History of Sexuality* Foucault extended this concern with the materiality of the body to the terrain of sexuality. Sexuality itself was produced through the exercise of power. Sexuality was not the last point of resistance of the human body to power – 'a stubborn drive' – but itself the product of a particular historical form of power. Again, Foucault stresses not the repressive effects of political technologies, but their inventiveness:

> It is clear that the genealogy of all these techniques, with their mutations, their shifts, their continuities and ruptures, does not coincide with the hypothesis of a great repressive phase that was inaugurated in the course

of the classical age and began to slowly decline in the twentieth. There was rather a perpetual inventiveness, a steady growth of methods and procedures, with two especially productive moments in this proliferating history: around the middle of the sixteenth century, the development of procedures of direction and examination of conscience; and at the beginning of the nineteenth century, the advent of medical technologies of sex. (Foucault, 1979, p. 119)

Foucault's account of the historical invention of sex brought his concerns close to Anglo-American feminist theory. Judith Butler's work, in particular, extended Foucault's account in order to rethink the distinction between sex and gender in feminist theory. For Butler, as for Foucault, sex could no longer be understood as the firm ground on which the discursive construction of gender was subsequently established (Butler, 1993). Sex itself needed to be analysed in terms of its historical and political formation.

But if Butler followed Foucault in his account of the politics of sex, feminist theory also raised a more general difficulty with Foucault's analysis of the materiality of the body. In Foucault's work the body appears to be almost a blank slate onto which the effects of power can be imprinted. In *Discipline and Punish*, the body is rendered 'docile' through the exercise of disciplinary power, and in the *History of Sexuality* sex is viewed as the product of power and knowledge. Although Foucault acknowledges that the exercise of power is never fully effective (1979, p. 143), he does not address the question of the body's 'resistance' to the exercise of power. In his account, power has effects, but matter remains simply resistant, and is otherwise inert.

Foucault's own analyses of the importance of the biological body in politics are suggestive, but remain, as he recognised, underdeveloped. In *Discipline and Punish*, he had already interrogated the notion of sovereignty through the analysis of disciplinary power, and towards the end of the *History of Sexuality* he developed a further theme – biopolitics. For Foucault, a biopolitics of population complemented what he termed the anatomo-politics of the body:

One of these poles – the first to be formed, it seems – centred on the body as a machine: its disciplining, the optimization of its capabilities, the extortion of its forces, the parallel increase of its usefulness and its docility, its integration into systems of efficient and economic controls, all this was ensured by the procedures of power that characterized the *disciplines*: an anatomo-politics of the human body. The second, formed somewhat later, focused on the species body, the body imbued with the mechanics of life and serving as the basis of the biological processes: propagation, births and mortality, the level of health, life expectancy and longevity, with all the conditions that can cause these to vary. Their supervision was effected through an entire series of interventions and *regulatory controls: a biopolitics of population*. (1979, p. 139)

The notion of biopolitics has been further developed within sociology and anthropology, particularly by writers concerned with the study of the new bio and genetic technologies. Paul Rabinow, in particular, coined the notion of 'biosociality' to highlight the ways in which natural biological processes 'will be known and remade through technique and will finally become artificial' (1996, p. 99). Foucault's work is often read as anti-scientific. Yet Rabinow argues for a different reading of Foucault's work that opens up the possibility of a constructive form of engagement between the natural and the social sciences. Rather than provide a critique of science, Foucault points Rabinow towards a recognition of the inventiveness and political significance of the new biosciences (Rabinow, 1999). After Foucault, it is difficult to ignore the importance of biology and medicine in political life.

governmentality

Foucault never wrote a major study of political thought. However, in a series of lectures towards the end of the 1970s he developed the outlines of an account of what he termed governmentality, or the rationality of government. For Foucault, the notion of government did not refer to *the* government. Rather, what we know as government is but one of a number of actors engaged in the practice of governing. As Graham Burchell argues, Foucault applies the notion of government to a range of different forms of the 'conduct of conduct' (Burchell, 1996, p. 19). Government in this sense could refer to the government of the economy, but also to the government of the family or of children, or of oneself. Government does not operate through the suppression of freedom, or through meticulous discipline, but rather entails both the production and utilisation of freedom. One of the great strengths of liberal and neo-liberal governmentality, Foucault noted, was that liberalism recognised the value of freedom in the activity of government.

Since the 1980s there have been a substantial number of studies of governmentality, in relation to a variety of topics, ranging from sexual abuse to alcoholism, and from sanitation to schooling (for example, Barry et al., 1996; Cruikshank, 1999; Dean and Hindess, 1998; Hunter, 1988; Rose, 1999). For some commentators, the development of studies of governmentality represents nothing less than the development of a new subdiscipline of the social sciences and humanities (Dean, 1999). This is surely to exaggerate its significance. Nonetheless, the Foucaultian notion of government has considerable value. First, it points to the *technical* character of liberal government. Rather than regard freedom as a product of the absence of control, or as an ideological fiction, it highlights the technical devices involved in the practice of freedom. Second, it draws attention to the inventiveness of government, without necessarily endorsing it. Critical political thought has been very good at tracing the links between the state and forms of economic and political domination. It has been less good at analysing government as a constructive and inventive practice. Third, Foucault's work on government points to the historical formation of 'society' and the 'economy'. In this account, 'economy' and 'society' do not have a natural existence but are themselves formed through the development and dispersion of the social sciences. The social sciences assist in the formation of 'society' and the 'economy' as objects of knowledge and regulation (Barry et al., 1996; Callon, 1998; Mitchell, 2002; Rabinow, 1999).

One of the strengths of *Discipline and Punish, History of Sexuality* and the analysis of governmentality is that they expand our sense of politics. In this way, their historical analyses resonate with the expanded sense of the space of politics associated with contemporary social movements. Yet if this is part of the strength of Foucault's writing, it is also a weakness. For many readers of Foucault everything seems to become political. There are two difficulties with this. First, it reduces any sense of the specificity of politics as a practice. Second, in telling us that everything is political, Foucault's analyses may themselves short-circuit the work that must be done in making things political. Curiously, given his concern with technology and practice, Foucault seems to have little to say in these books on political practice itself.

A second strength of Foucault's method in these works is their attention to common forms. Foucault is both concerned with the details of particular disciplinary practices, but also with their formal similarities. He is alert to the different ways in which sexuality becomes the object of knowledge and regulation, but he is primarily concerned with their formal similarities. In this respect at least, Foucault is a structuralist (cf. Dreyfus and Rabinow, 1982). Yet this attention to common form is a weakness as well as a strength of his analysis. Foucault's apparatuses of power seem too static and too rigid. There is no sense of dynamism, irregularity and instability. Foucault cautions us that power 'always fails', but the forms of its failure remain mysterious. Both the human and non-human elements of Foucault's apparatuses remain extraordinarily inert.

Both weaknesses point in a similar direction. Although Foucault is a political thinker, his published books contain little sense of the dynamics of contestation, negotiation and disagreement that is a characteristic feature of political life. His historical methodology certainly produces shocking and disruptive effects. It asks us to interrogate the role of social and medical sciences in the creation of social and medical phenomena (Hacking, 1999; Osborne and Rose, 1999). And it forces us to examine the historical conditions of existence of our most basic analytical categories: economy, society, the individual, agency and sexuality (Gordon, 1980). Yet it is difficult to know how Foucault's thought might give insight into the complexity of political events and the mechanics of political conflict. In order to gain a sense of Foucault's approach to the study of political events it is necessary to turn from his major published books to his journalism.

political events

In his methodological writings Foucault emphasised the importance of contingent events in the history of systems of thought. One of the tasks of genealogy, he noted, 'is to identify the accidents, the minute deviations ... the errors, the false appraisals, and the faulty calculations that gave birth to those things that continue to exist ...' (Foucault, 1984b, p. 81). Yet as I have noted, many commentators ignore Foucault's explicit concern with the singularity of events. On the one hand, his work has tended to be read as a source for purely 'theoretical' arguments which then can be judged against other purely theoretical alternatives. On the other hand, more historically minded writers have focused on very broad historical forms (discipline, liberal governmentality, biopolitics, and so on) at the expense of an attention to the study of the 'accidents and minute deviations' of history.

Foucault's most explicit accounts of his approach to the study of political events are to be found, not in his published books, but in his journalism. During the 1970s, in particular, Foucault contributed articles on a whole series of subjects ranging from the Polish solidarity movement to human rights, dissidents in Eastern Europe and the Soviet Union, and the Vietnamese boat people (Foucault, 1994; Osborne, 1999, p. 49). In relation to such events, Foucault argued that the task of the intellectual was not to act as a leader or a strategist but rather to engage in what he termed a form of 'anti-strategic' practice that would respect the singularity of the event (Foucault, 1979, p. 794). In this context, it was necessary to be attentive to the emergence of new possibilities and forces, rather than to account for the occurrence of events in terms of some more general analysis. There was a need, he argued, to be 'witness to the birth of ideas and to the explosion of their force, in the struggles into which one is led for the sake of ideas, whether for or against' (Foucault, 1978, p. 707, quoted in Osborne, 1999, p. 51). Foucault argued that intellectuals should not distance themselves from the media, but rather should work with journalists.

Foucault's emphasis on the singularity of events is made explicit, for example, in his writings and commentary on the Iranian revolution. For Foucault, the Iranian revolution could not be understood simply as the expression of existing political forces or social classes. Nor could it be understood as the product of the rational calculations of political activists (Foucault, 1988, p. 211). Rather it had to be understood as a singular event, which created effects, but would then pass. It was important, he suggested, not to view the Islamic religion as false consciousness, but rather to recognise the positive revolutionary force of the Islamic religion which had helped to forge what he thought to be a single collective will: 'let's say, then, that Islam, in that year of 1978, was not the opium of the people precisely because it was the spirit of the world without spirit' (Foucault, 1988, p. 218).

Foucault's contrast between the 'absolutely collective will' of the Iranian revolution and the more mediated forms of European revolutions can certainly be faulted for its Orientalism (Said, 1981; Young, 1995, p. 57). This reflects a much wider lack of reflection by Foucault on the importance of empire in the history of Western social and political thought (Mitchell, 2000). But despite its limitations, Foucault's writing on Iran is suggestive of the importance of an attention to the singularity of events. In this respect, Foucault can be placed in a tradition of political thought that includes radical writers such as Hannah Arendt, as well as conservative thinkers such as Michael Oakeshott. For Arendt, there was a tendency of political thinkers to objectify politics in general, and to objectify revolutionary political action in particular (Arendt, 1964). In this way, the historical importance of political action was constantly explained away in terms of something else. Likewise, for Oakeshott, it was critical to be attentive to the specificity of politics. For Oakeshott, 'neither "principle" … nor any general theory about the character and direction of social change seems to supply an adequate reference for explanation or for practical conduct' (Oakeshott, 1962, p. 69).

Of course, Foucault's analyses of discourse and technology are often used to provide a critique of a certain form of empiricism. Certainly, for Foucault, empirical truths are not simply gathered through observation. The production of truth depends on the existence of specific historical systems of thought and practice that, in his later work, become associated with the exercise of power. The critical task for Foucault was not to investigate the truth or falsity of particular statements, but to analyse the conditions within which certain statements could be taken as true or false. In brief, Foucault was concerned with the question of the historical existence of specific regimes of truth:

> It is a question of what governs statements, and the way in which they govern each other so as to constitute a set of propositions that are scientifically acceptable and hence, capable of being verified or falsified by scientific procedures. In short, there is a problem of the regime, or the politics of the scientific statement. (Foucault, 2000, p. 114)

But viewed from a different perspective, Foucault's work also points to a different form of empiricism. As Deleuze suggests, empiricism can be understood not so much as a naive belief in the objectivity of observational reports, but as a form of thought which points to the existence of singularities. In this view, the occurrence of events cannot be understood as simply an expression of broader social or economic forces. Rather empiricism points to the need to be alert to the possibility that something new might be produced in the course of events (Deleuze, 1987, p. vii). The significance of Foucault's journalism lies less in the claims he makes about specific events than the fact that it points towards the importance of the analysis of their singularity.

conclusions

It is always tempting, when reading a political thinker, to try to fit the work of that thinker into a given category. In the case of Foucault there is an irony to this. For, above all else, his work alerts us to the normalising effects of categorisation. Not surprisingly, he resisted attempts to categorise him, at different times, as a structuralist, a Marxist, a postmodernist or a nihilist.

But to view Foucault simply as a theorist of the politics of classification and categorisation and normalisation misses three important points. First, Foucault's work makes us acutely aware of the materiality of politics. *Discipline and Punish*, in particular, opens up the question of how one might account for the materiality of buildings, technologies and the physicality of the human body in the study of politics. In this way his work connects directly to the concerns of contemporary feminist research and science and technology studies with the politics of physical and biological matter (Butler, 1993; Fraser, 2002; Grosz, 1995; Haraway, 1991; Latour, 2004). Nearly 30 years since the publication of *Discipline and Punish* such concerns still remain marginal to contemporary political thought. Second, Foucault's historical analyses are directed, amongst other things, at the categories of contemporary political thought itself. Rather than take categories such as 'economy', 'society' and the 'state' as tools for analysis, he alerts us to their historical formation. Foucault did not write as a political scientist or as a sociologist, nor indeed as a social or political theorist. He wrote rather as a philosopher and an historian who sought to interrogate our contemporary forms of political thought. Third, and most surprisingly, Foucault's work indicates the need for a return to empiricism in political thought. Rather than ignore the study of political events, or view political events simply as the manifestation of larger social and political forces, Foucault's work directs us towards them, in all their multiple forms.

further reading

There are numerous general accounts of Foucault's writing. Among the most useful are Cousins and Hussain (1984), Dreyfus and Rabinow (1982), McNay (1994) and Mills (2003). Foucault's biographies include studies by Eribon (1991) and Macey (1993). Gordon (1980) provides an excellent introduction to Foucault's analysis of power. For Foucault's work on governmentality, see Barry et al. (1996), Burchell et al. (1991), Dean (1999) and Rose (1999). On Foucault and political theory, see Hindess (1996). On Foucault and social theory, see Ashenden and Owen (1999) and Osborne (1998). On Foucault and feminist theory, see Bell (1993), Butler (1993), Grosz (1995) and McNay (1992).

references

Arendt, H. (1964) *On Revolution*. London: Faber and Faber.
Ashenden, S. and Owen, D. (1999) *Foucault contra Habermas*. London: Sage.

Barrett, M. (1992) *The Politics of Truth: From Marx to Foucault*. Cambridge: Polity Press.

Barry, A. (2001) *Political Machines: Governing a technological society*. London: Athlone.

Barry, A., Osborne, T. and Rose, N. (eds) (1996) *Foucault and Political Reason: Liberalism, neo-liberalism and rationalities of government*. London: UCL Press.

Bauman, Z. (1991) *Postmodernity and its Discontents*. Cambridge: Polity Press.

Bell, V. (1993) *Interrogating Incest: Foucault, feminism and the law*. London: Routledge.

Burchell, G. (1996) 'Liberal Government and the Techniques of the Self', in *Foucault and Political Reason: Liberalism, neo-liberalism and rationalities of government*, ed. A. Barry, T. Osborne and N. Rose, pp. 19–36, London: UCL Press.

Burchell, G., Gordon, C., and Miller, P. (eds) (1991) *The Foucault Effect*. Hemel Hempstead: Harvester Wheatsheaf.

Butler, J. (1993) *Bodies that Matter: On the discursive limits of 'sex'*. London: Routledge.

Callon, M. (ed.) (1998) *The Laws of the Market*, Oxford: Blackwell.

Cousins, M. and Hussain, A. (1984) *Michel Foucault*. Basingstoke: Macmillan.

Cruikshank, B. (1999) *The Will to Empower: Democratic citizens and other subjects*. Ithaca, NY: Cornell University Press.

Dean, M. (1999) *Governmentality*. London: Sage.

Dean, M. and Hindess, B. (eds) (1998) *Governing Australia: Studies in contemporary nationalities of government*. Cambridge: Cambridge University Press.

Deleuze, G. (1992) 'What is a Dispositif?', in *Michel Foucault: Philosopher*, ed. T. Armstrong, pp. 159–68. Hemel Hempstead: Harvester Wheatsheaf.

Deleuze, G. with Parnet, C. (1987) *Dialogues*. London: Athlone.

Dews, P. (1987) *Logics of Disintegration*. London: Verso.

Dreyfus, H. and Rabinow, P. (1982) *Michel Foucault: Beyond structuralism and hermeneutics*. Brighton: Harvester Wheatsheaf.

Eribon, D. (1991) *Michel Foucault*. Cambridge, MA: Harvard University Press.

Foucault, M. (1970) *The Order of Things*. London: Tavistock.

Foucault, M. (1972) *The Archaeology of Knowledge*. London: Tavistock.

Foucault, M. (1973) *The Birth of the Clinic*. London: Tavistock.

Foucault, M. (1977) *Discipline and Punish: The birth of the prison*. London: Penguin.

Foucault, M. (1978) 'Les "reportage" d'idées', in *Dits et Écrits*, by M. Foucault (1994), pp. 706–7. Paris: Gallimard.

Foucault, M. (1979) *The History of Sexuality*, Vol. 1. London: Penguin.

Foucault, M. (1980) *Power/Knowledge: Selected interviews and other writings 1972–1977*. New York: Pantheon.

Foucault, M. (1984a) 'What is Enlightenment?', in *The Foucault Reader*, ed. P. Rabinow, pp. 32–50. New York: Viking.

Foucault, M. (1984b) 'Nietzsche, Genealogy, History', in *The Foucault Reader*, ed. P. Rabinow, pp. 76–100. New York: Viking.

Foucault, M. (1986a) *The Use of Pleasure: The history of sexuality*, Vol. 2. Harmondsworth: Penguin.

Foucault, M. (1986b) *The Care of the Self: The history of sexuality*, Vol. 3. Harmondsworth: Penguin.

Foucault, M. (1988) 'Iran, the Spirit of the World without Spirit', in *Michel Foucault: Politics, philosophy, culture*, ed. L. Kritzman, pp. 211–26. London: Routledge.

Foucault, M. (1991a) 'Governmentality', in *The Foucault Effect*, ed. G. Burchell et al., pp. 87–104. Hemel Hempstead: Harvester Wheatsheaf.

Foucault, M. (1991b) *Remarks on Marx*. New York: Semiotext(e).

Foucault, M. (1994) *Dits et Écrits*. Paris: Gallimard.

Foucault, M. (1997a) *Ethics: Essential Works 1954–1984*, Vol. 1. Harmondsworth: Penguin.

Foucault, M. (1997b) *Aesthetics, Method and Epistemology: Essential Works 1954–1984*, Vol. 2. Harmondsworth: Penguin.

Foucault, M. (2000) *Power: Essential Works 1954–1984*, Vol. 3. Harmondsworth: Penguin.

Foucault, M. (2003a) *Society Must be Defended*. Harmondsworth: Penguin.

Foucault, M. (2003b) *Abnormal: Lectures at the Collège de France 1974–75*. London: Verso.

Fraser, M. (2002) 'What is the Matter with Feminist Criticism?', *Economy and Society* 31: 606–25.

Giddens, A. (1985) *The Nation State and Violence*. Cambridge: Polity Press.

Gordon, C. (1980) 'Afterword', in *Power/Knowledge: Selected interviews and other writings 1972–1977*, by M. Foucault (1980), pp. 229–59. New York: Pantheon.

Gordon, C. (1996) 'Foucault in Britain', in *Foucault and Political Reason: Liberalism, Neo-liberalism and Rationalities of Government*, ed. A. Barry et al., pp. 253–70. London: UCL Press.

Grosz, E. (1995) *Space, Time and Perversion: Essays on the politics of bodies*. London: Routledge.

Habermas, J. (1990) *The Philosophical Discourse of Modernity*. Cambridge: Polity Press.

Hacking, I. (1999) *The Social Construction of What?* Cambridge, MA: Harvard University Press.

Haraway, D. (1991) *Simians, Cyborgs and Women: The reinvention of nature*. London: Free Association Books.

Hindess, B. (1996) *Discourses of Power: From Hobbes to Foucault*. Oxford: Blackwell.

Hunter, I. (1988) *Culture and Government: The emergence of literary education*. Basingstoke: Macmillan.

Latour, B. (2004) *The Politics of Nature: How to bring the sciences into democracy*. Cambridge, MA: Harvard University Press.

Macey, D. (1993) *The Lives of Michel Foucault*. London: Hutchinson.

McNay, L. (1992) *Foucault and Feminism*. Cambridge: Polity Press.

McNay, L. (1994) *Foucault*. Cambridge: Polity Press.

Mills, S. (2003) *Foucault*. London: Routledge.

Mitchell, T. (2000) 'The Stage of Modernity', in *Questions of Modernity*, ed. T. Mitchell, pp. 1–34. Minneapolis, MN: University of Minnesota Press.

Mitchell, T. (2002) *Rule of Experts: Egypt, techno-politics and modernity*. Berkeley, CA: University of California Press.

Oakeshott, M. (1962) 'Political Education', in *Rationalism in Politics and other Essays*, pp. 43–69. London: Methuen.

Osborne, T. (1998) *Aspects of Enlightenment: Social theory and the ethics of truth*. London: UCL Press.

Osborne, T. (1999) 'Critical Spirtuality: On ethics and politics in the later Foucault', in *Foucault contra Habermas*, ed. D. Owen and S. Ashenden, pp. 45–59. London: Sage.

Osborne, T. and Rose, N. (1999) 'Do the Social Sciences Create Phenomena?: The example of public opinion research', *British Journal of Sociology* 50: 367–96.

Poster, M. (1996) 'Databases as Discourse, or Electronic Interpellation', in *Detradition-alization*, ed. P. Heelas, S. Lash and P. Morris, pp. 277–93. Oxford: Blackwell.

Power, M. (1997) *The Audit Society: Rituals of verification*. Oxford: Clarendon Press.

Rabinow, P. (1984) *The Foucault Reader*. New York: Viking.

Rabinow, P. (1996) 'Artificiality and Enlightenment: From sociobiology to biosociality', in *Essays on the Anthropology of Freedom*, pp. 91–111. Princeton, NJ: Princeton University Press.

Rabinow, P. (1999) *French DNA: Trouble in purgatory*. Chicago, IL: University of Chicago Press.

Rose, N. (1999) *Powers of Freedom: Reframing political thought*. Cambridge: Cambridge University Press.

Said, E. (1981) *Orientalism: Western conceptions of the Orient*. Harmondsworth: Penguin.

Young, R. (1995) 'Foucault on Race and Colonialism', *New Formations* 25: 57–65.

17
jacques derrida

michael dillon

Jacques Derrida was born in Algeria in 1930 and died in France in 2004, aged 74. At school in Algiers during the collaborationist government of the early 1940s, Derrida experienced the anti-Semitism of the Pétain regime. Subsequently expelled from the Lycée de Ben Aknoun, he was sent to another institution staffed by Jewish teachers themselves expelled from the public education system. Derrida skipped school, failed exams and read. He also played football. Envying the novelist Camus, who played in goal for Algeria, he said that he would rather have been known as an international footballer than a philosopher. He was never quite sure about philosophy anyway and it is difficult to know how to label him. But that is the point. He didn't label and he wasn't interested in being labelled. A thinker distinguished above all by the way he read, he was also a prolific and inspirational writer with over 60 books translated into English, and a wealth of material yet to be translated.

Having made it through school and into the mainland French system Derrida worked with the Marxist Louis Althusser at the École Normale Supérieure. Thereafter he taught at the Sorbonne, where he met Michel Foucault, later returning to the École where he taught for 20 more years. In 1979, with other colleagues, he founded the Estates General of Philosophy at the Sorbonne. He was also involved in the founding of the Collège International de Philosophie in Paris in 1983, and he became its first Director. He was then elected as directeur d'études at the École des Hautes Études en Sciences Sociales in Paris where he remained until his retirement at the age of 67. This represents quite a lot of philosophical institution building for one so productively ambivalent about philosophy and reputed to care little about the world of practice.

Derrida was also an itinerant scholar travelling widely and holding visiting appointments in the United States, notably at Yale, Johns Hopkins and the University of California, Irvine. He made his 'debut' at a conference held at Johns Hopkins in 1966. There he presented a remarkable paper 'Structure, Sign and Play in the Discourse of the Human Sciences' (Derrida, 1981). The following year he published three key texts: *Writing and Difference* (Derrida, 1981), *Of Grammatology* (Derrida, 1974) and *Speech and Phenomena* (Derrida, 1973). These initiated a change in the way we think about the way we think. Derrida revives political thinking, then, because of the way in which his thought haunts everything, hitherto, that we have thought was political: freedom, democracy, law, sovereignty, decision and ethics. What follows is how I think that haunting works in relation to politics. It is not an account of a Derridaean (political) programme. It is instead an attempt to show how Derrida's thinking makes you rethink almost everything there is to think about politics.

reading

All of Derrida's work has implications for the understanding and teaching of politics, but there is no single point of entry into his work. Derrida stops us in our tracks and makes us pay attention to things that, in a sense, we already know. For example, we think we know how to read. Once having read Derrida, especially to read Derrida reading, you discover the possibility that reading can radicalise politics because, in the first instance, it challenges the claims to the transparency of meaning and full readability of texts to which politics always lays claim. There is also more to this than critique. Positive constitutive political possibilities – rupture and surprise – are installed in the very possibility of reading. How they are realised depends upon the skill with which you read. Derrida was an astonishingly skilled reader and so his work is full of disturbing new political insight and potential.

For me, reading Derrida was an epiphany. Something opened up. I was able to think differently, and I think to greater effect, about something that I thought I already understood. It happened this way. At one time I was stuck in my work because I had no analytical or conceptual vocabulary with which to interrogate an intuition or emerging sense that I had concerning my preoccupation with the politics of 'security'. The world I already 'understood' was the world of defence and foreign policy-making. I had been researching my world for decades. In particular I was fascinated by 'decision'.

I did my PhD in defence decision-making. I can even remember being interviewed for admission to a PhD programme, and being asked what I wanted to research. I said I wanted to research defence decision-making by analysing modern defence policy. But I realise now that this was merely an entry point for understanding not just politics of security but politics as such.

In an affectionate thanks to Derrida, Simon Critchley reminds us that 'Derrida was a supreme reader of texts, particularly but by no means exclusively philosophical texts' (Critchley, 2005, p. 26). He also reminds us that reading deconstructively does two things, which is why it is sometimes called a double reading. On the one hand Derrida teaches that you have to know your text – how it was produced, the corpus of the author/authority responsible for it, its relation to allied texts, the context of its circulation and reception as well as the details of its content and what it is trying to achieve. On the other hand, the text may also be levered open through locating what Derrida sometimes called its 'blind spots'. Here the singular excesses within the text, that the text itself cannot control but upon which it necessarily relies, break through.

This recalls what Foucault said about critique, that, 'it is not a matter of saying that things are not right as they are. It is a matter of pointing out on what kind of assumptions, what kinds of familiar, unchallenged, unconsidered modes of thought the practices that we accept rest' (Foucault, 1988, p. 154). However, Derrida's deconstructive reading does more and means more than this – as we will see. The reference to Foucault helps for now because it highlights how locating these blind spots in a text both discloses how the text operates, and provides us with critical purchase upon it. To do that, especially when the texts are politically salient texts, becomes a deeply subversive move in relation to the authority invoked by texts, the meanings they seek to establish, the textual and interpretative matrix they situate themselves within, the action that the text excites, and so on.

Take my interest in security, for example; the many different ways in which texts problematise danger by specifying friends, enemies, threats and fears. In so doing they mobilise a world of power, law and economy, but also of meaning, desire and imagination. If worlds are to be mobilised differently, then, their very textual constitution has to be disrupted in its intimate details. This is no 'one-shot operation'. Textuality has to be deconstructively re-read if it is to be imaginatively reworked. And remember, too, textuality is a materiality.

Remember, also, that texts do things. They do not simply seek to tell us about the world (constative utterances). They seek to enact things (performative utterances). It is tempting to say that texts cannot do anything unless they are, in fact, read. But that is not quite so. Texts cannot 'state' or 'enact' without the very possibility of reading. Even if it is not read, but merely paraded and sanctified, for example, the existence of a text will impact. Why? Because of the very possibility of reading to which its mere existence testifies. That is why authorities (authors and institutions, the very institution of the author) go to such great lengths in writing texts also to determine the reading of texts – from holy books to manifestos – as well as their dissemination. Ultimately, Derrida's double reading enables us to interrogate how politics refuses to see itself as the writing that it is.

That said, there are other notable politically salient things to observe about the reading of texts. While you are engaged in detecting blind spots in a text, the text is busily detecting blind spots in you. How you read texts, and how they read you, opens up new worlds. By that I mean that worlds are not only disclosed or mobilised in this way. Texts continuously give themselves away. Perhaps the most important point of all, then, is that textuality – reading/writing – is subversive even of itself. Blind-spotting is the art of highlighting how texts betray themselves. But if they did not give themselves away we would remain forever trapped in the same (political) text.

Although they may appear to be so, blind spots are not incidental to a text. They are fundamental to what it is trying to state, to mean and to effect. So the operational power of a text depends upon the nature of the blind spots, where they are located and how they work. They are often located in ambiguous concepts or key terms that contain such a multiplicity of meanings, and cross such a variety of registers, that the force of their signification cannot be contained by the intended meaning of the text. Famously Derrida first did this in relation to the term 'pharmakon' in Plato. He amplified the double meaning of pharmakon – both medicine and poison – to show how this ambiguity disrupts (deconstructs) the argument of Plato's text. While it therefore empowers critical engagement there is nonetheless more to deconstruction than critique. In effect the text, as a condition of its very production is always already also deconstructing itself. This auto-deconstruction points towards some much more powerful and extensive insight at work in Derrida's thinking.

deciding, naming, haunting

Deconstruction, according to Derrida, is an uncanny fact of life: 'Deconstruction is not a method or some tool that you apply to something from the outside. Deconstruction is something that happens and which happens inside' (1997, p. 9; Derrida et al., 1997b). When Derrida first talked deconstruction he was doing the kind of close reading that allowed classical texts, not only Plato but also Husserl and Rousseau, to show us how they deconstruct themselves. In our tradition of Western thinking we think the political in the way that we do because of the way that we think. By reading the way that he did, Derrida changed the way that we think. That is why, after Derrida, we have to think politics otherwise.

From Derrida I came to understand that the moment of decision, for example, which I was so concerned to interrogate, was also the moment of 'undecidability' when the legible, the sayable and the calculable emerge as being infused through and through with the illegible, the unsayable and the incalculable (Derrida, 1992, p. 26, 1995, p. 65). I began to appreciate that the key point was this. The tradition of Western thinking called metaphysics always privileges presence, or that which *is*. For the traditional metaphysical thinking of the West, that which *is*, is, in principle, also undivided and knowable. In metaphysics that which *is* adds up. It does so by insisting that everything ultimately relies on secure foundations.

However, Derrida continually shows that it does not add up. He persistently shows, instead, how that which *is* depends upon a peculiar structure of presence and absence that makes it strategically dependent upon that which is 'not', or what he calls 'the Other' (Derrida, 1999). Derrida demonstrates the instability of that which *is* and its reliance upon conditions of possibility and operation that cannot be commanded by what we might call the sciences and practices of the present. As he does so the axis of thought and politics shifts decisively from foundation to future.

The structure of that which is, is continuously open to the advent not simply of an uncertain future but of the radical surprise induced by the advent of what he also called 'radical alterity'. What is really going on in things is this 'to-come'. Caught in the middle of things we are always open to something else that is yet to arrive and that, however much we plan, never arrives in the way that we calculated for. It, literally, takes us unawares.

Oddly enough, perhaps, defence decision-makers appreciate this as much as deconstructionists. If, as Derrida suggests in *Politics of Friendship* (Derrida, 1997), the decision must 'surprise the very subjectivity of the subject', I found them continuously surprised as well (Derrida, 1997, p. 68). This doesn't make the defence decision-maker and the deconstructionist the same thing. It's the difference that intrigues me. The one, compelled to plan and to insist on planning, even though they know that the plan never works and have to find ways of continually working around it and reworking their own policy subjectivity as the unbidden future keeps arriving. For if something is truly in the future then it cannot lie within our current system of calculable knowledge. The other, challenged to compose themselves towards discharging this obligation to the unbidden future that is nonetheless the condition of possibility and operability even for all calculative planning.

Derrida was not a political thinker in the sense of the great political thinkers of the canon of political thought: 'I think political theory is necessary, but I try to articulate this necessity of a political theory with something in politics or in friendship, in hospitality, which cannot, for structural reasons, become the object of knowledge, of a theory, of a *theoreme*' (Derrida et al., 1997a). Despite his relation to Philosophy he was always more of a philosopher in relation to politics. And yet not quite in the same way that philosophers have always had an ambiguous relation to politics. Philosophy has always had an ambivalent relationship with politics because philosophy claims to be the master discourse that teaches us about Being as such. The problem with Derrida, here, is that he departed from the view that Philosophy was a master discourse. It was a certain form of writing about the most important but contestable things. And it certainly didn't deliver the security of certainties. In changing the ways that we think about Being (Philosophy), he began to change the ways in which we think about life. From there it is but a step – the step, however, of quite a labour of thought – to think politics otherwise.

Here, also, Derrida was deeply concerned about the animal/human distinction and the privileging of the 'human'. The whole relationship – and the complex dividing practices by means of which animal and human are differentiated – concerned him especially in his reading of Aristotle and Heidegger. He wasn't simply concerned to note that in calling ourselves an animal equipped with a special quality – say the power of reason or speech – we thereby equip ourselves with a powerful device for labelling other creatures as not human or less human, including other human beings (Derrida, 2002b). Neither was he simply concerned with how we organise our politics around this cardinal distinction, and thereby also our moral and material economies deciding who gets what, where, when and how, who shall live and who shall die. He was concerned to question further, asking what kind of existence is the kind of existence that exists, first, as something that is open to the ethical call of the Other. What kind of commission is it that falls to such an ethically charged existence, and how might it be discharged?

The ethical call with which Derrida ultimately became so concerned extended for him beyond the domain of the anthropological. It is 'outwith' the domain of the anthropological. For that reason we might say that Derrida was also a kind of transcendental thinker. Transcendental means to stand above, beyond or outside the changing historical contours of the here and now of the world, untainted by the world; as it is said that God or universal principles do. He admitting to being a 'quasi-transcendental thinker' because although he was concerned with that which serves as the condition of possibility of existence he thinks that this condition remains at the same time inseparable from existence and tainted by it. For that reason he thinks that we are engaged in a responsibility which is also a response-ability that, 'assigns [us] even in [our] liberty' (Derrida, 1989, p. 130). For Derrida the condition of possibility of our existence is the wholly Other or radical alterity. It not only governs our capacity to take up our existence – response-ability – it issues an insatiable ethico-political call to us that is our individual and collective responsibility to answer. Indeed whenever we assume our response-ability we simultaneously discharge – one way or another – this responsibility.

The Other for Derrida was simply that which was not knowable, not calculable, not something one can have a relation with. And yet we are always already in relation somehow to it. Its radically disruptive absent presence is a condition of possibility for everything we write, say and do. This Otherness does not however operate as a foundation, a principle or a ground. It is not something that comes first, and it doesn't pose to us the challenge of how to access it securely. Neither is it a stable referent in relation to which we could ultimately measure everything with certainty, or move the world.

Yet it takes place in everything that takes place, and for Derrida it has a very definite structural logic or operational effect. It overturns the grounding claims of thought and politics alike, exposing them as limits that are always in the process of being overcome. He explores that structural logic in many contexts, notably in writing but also in 'giving' as well as in terms of 'deciding', whether in law or in politics. He also explores it under many names: as supplementarity, as trace, as *différance*, as promise and, towards the end of his life, as messianicity.

But how do you have a relation with the non-relationable? How do you speak about something that is essential but incalculable and not knowable? Most especially, how do you speak about something that is absent but present, present but absent? Something other than a paradox is operating here. A paradox is two opposed things coexisting. Derrida thinks the Other radically problematises these opposed and apparently unproblematic terms of presence and absence. He thinks a different structure of existence is therefore operating instead, and he searches for ways to speak about it that take our understanding of it beyond the confines of our tradition. One of the ways he does so is by calling it 'haunting'. The ghost or spectre is here but not here, present in its very absence. The Other has that spectral quality for Derrida. He finds it and celebrates it in his reading of Marx as well (Derrida, 1994). It is an absent presence that not only conditions the possibility of existence, but, like a ghost, continuously haunts it. Haunting by the spectre of the Other does not simply make existence possible for Derrida, it continuously characterises the nature of its taking place. It is the rupture that continuously disturbs the world opening it up to our response-ability and our responsibility. Ultimately, to our 'decision'.

Decision for Derrida, I learnt, is thus not the occasion simply for a choice between two or more alternatives. Decision is the moment when we assume responsibility towards ourselves and others in this Otherness that makes way for the assumption of responsibility precisely because its very peculiar structure is to ensure that we are always in the condition of having to assume responsibility without ever being able ultimately to consign that responsibility to the operation of some rule, metric, law or plan. Since the character of our existence is marked by response-ability there is no escaping responsibility with Derrida because this haunting alterity does not tell us what to do.

That omission in our make-up is our difficult freedom. The omission also issues a commission. Here it is a responsibility that devolves on us precisely because we are not told what to do. For Derrida we seem to be distinguished through and through by such a commissioning omission. There is no way out of it. Living is not something that can be definitively comprehended by calculation which is not to say that we are excused calculation. Neither is living a problem to be solved. For Derrida it is an event: and it takes place as something to be taken up and lived according to the responsibility, hospitality and the call of justice that not being told what to do continuously springs upon us. Here, accordingly, in this account of the unconditioned event of existence, lies the possibility of another kind of politics whose prospect preoccupied

Derrida. Specifically it introduces the thought of another kind of belonging – of being related together – that transcends traditional accounts of politics. This belonging together revolves around the insatiable call of the ethical to which Derrida claims that we are continuously exposed by virtue of the wholly Other: 'I am responsible to anyone (that is to say, to any other) only by failing in my responsibility to all the others, to the ethical or political generality. And I can never justify this sacrifice; I must always hold my peace about it … What binds me to this one or that one, remains finally unjustifiable' (Derrida, 1995, p. 70). One final word about this responsibility is necessary. It arises from the quotation just used. A disturbing economy of sacrifice characterises responsibility because as we respond to the singular demand of one other we cannot escape the fact that we are failing in our responsibility to other others. This insatiable responsibility is for Derrida therefore aporetic. There is no solution to this problem. It is something that we bear.

There is then no simple politics of deconstruction. There is nonetheless the challenge of thinking politics otherwise in the light of deconstruction. Whatever this politics or politicising might be there is no 'proper' place for it. In being ethically responsive to the Other, for Derrida, we are not merely being ethically responsive to another thing. We are acting in accordance with the peculiarly haunted structure of the nature of existence itself which issues that call to us – effectively calls us into being even as and when we refuse and refute it.

It has also to be admitted that reading Derrida is hard. But what is hard is this relearning and rethinking that reading Derrida forces you to do. Interrogating politics from a Derridaean perspective responsibilises you in ways you did not, could not, have anticipated. He did this first, and most insistently, in relation to the response-ability furnished by language, and specifically in relation to the very structural possibilities that underwrite the way language signifies.

language, speaking, writing

Language has been the centre of political reflection in our tradition since the Greeks, but Derrida exposes the profound importance of the uncanny nature of language. He first explored this in terms of the 'iterability' of the sign. 'In order for my "written communication" to retain its function as writing, i.e. its readability', he wrote in *Limited Inc.* (Derrida, 1988), 'it must remain readable despite the absolute disappearance of any receiver, determined in general. My communication must be repeatable – iterable – in the absolute absence of the receiver or of any empirically determinable collectivity of receivers. Such iterability (… the working out of the logic that ties repetition to alterity) structures the mark of writing itself, no matter what particular type of writing is involved' (Derrida, 1988, p. 7).

In other words, the condition of possibility of writing – which he takes as the condition of all signification, written and oral – is the possibility of repetition in the absence of another receiver. The readability of the sign on any one actual occasion, he says, is possible only if another repetition is always possible without the presence of a receiver: 'For a writing to be a writing it must continue to "act" and to be readable even when what is called the author of the writing no longer answers for what he has written ... The situation of the writer is, concerning the text, basically the same as that of the reader' (1988, p. 8).

Quite disturbing things follow from this. As Paul Patton observed: 'The permanent possibility of citation or iteration is also a possibility of transformation' (Patton, 2004, p. 28). One of the things that follows directly from it politically is the point that signification is never a wholly private act. By virtue of Derrida's account of the structural possibility of signification, signification is always already a 'public' thing. Reading and writing – signification – in no matter what kind of sense, for Derrida, must therefore structurally be for every possible language user in general. Even when talking to ourselves we are up to our necks in an uncanny form of life that we share in common. Once again, this absence that is present he calls the Other. That is what he means when he says that the structural possibility of signification is the tie to alterity.

Deconstruction is therefore not merely an analytical device. It is something that takes place in every act of signification because every act of signification depends structurally for Derrida upon this absent presence. For Derrida, then, it is not simply that something goes on in language that defeats our ambition to make everything intelligible and readable, or to make everything add up. Nor is it that something goes on which defeats our attempts to be purely 'I', or purely 'We' – the pure authors of ourselves. Without that something we would not be anything at all. Some people react violently against this because it appears to deny us all power of judgement both ethical and political.

Language, like politics then, is thus also haunted by the Other. This haunting is also a spectral presence, the presence of something absent that is nonetheless somehow uncannily also present – an odd and disturbing kind of 'presence'. Derrida's reflection on the very structural possibility of signification reinstalls language at the heart of political reflection. It does so in a way, however, that radically subverts all technical and private notions of language. Because of the structural dependence of signification on the Other, the Other is thereby also installed as the key principle of formation in any Derridaean articulation of political being.

haunted being-in-common

Politics has long been defined also in terms of the thing that we share in common. Indeed, classically, it is argued that the thing that we share in common is the very ground of politics. If we think that we share a universal subjectivity comprised of universal rights, a subjectivity that exists prior to its constitution by historically determined social and political means, one that is free to engage in contracts and exchanges in pursuit of interests, as well as insistent that its rights be represented in and by government, then what we have is representative and accountable government. Representative and accountable government has become the hegemonic understanding of politics at the beginning of the twenty-first century, the form of politics against which all others are now unflatteringly measured. An astonishing amount of violence nonetheless accompanies this politics, even as it claims to be more peaceable than any others. The voice in which it increasingly finds expression is the martial voice of (in)security. No wonder that, starting out by asking about defence decision-making under such a regime, I now find myself deeply enmeshed in the very problematic of politics as such; nationally as well as internationally, globally as well as locally as we say today. For I discovered that when Derrida writes in a most overtly political way, as he did, for example, in one of the first books to be translated into English after he died – *Rogues: Two essays on reason* (2005) – Derrida is most concerned with the deconstruction of security and its allied concepts. These define, and now also radically threaten, the political tradition of the West: sovereignty, mastery, certainty, the safe (*sauf*), sound, the immune, salvation, redemption. Here, too, he recognises the continuing intimate link between 'the safe' and 'the holy' (security and salvation, the political and the religious) and its fundamental significance even for a civilisation that claims to be secular: 'so much is at play or at stake here …', he says (2005, p. 112).

Derrida spent a great deal of time interrogating the idea that in some way seems to lie behind all these different expressions of the principle of formation that grants us the common bond that politics expresses and orders. In doing so he radicalised the very ground of politics. That in virtue of which we belong together politically, the Greeks, especially, thought is friendship. Friendship is that bond of solidarity indebted to something that we share beyond the immediacy of family, identity, race, and so on. It is something that offers a different form of social organisation, one indeed that promises to be able to function by relating different friends to the thing they have in common, friendship. As ever with Derrida, the interrogation of fraternity began to disclose more about the very nature or consistency of the political bond thought in this way. First, it was clearly gendered. It connoted the male, the phallus or phallo of fraternity. Second, it also connoted having the capacity to speak, the logos of discourse among friends who share a common capacity to speak, as opposed to barbarians who were said (by Greeks) merely to babble. It was, in short, phallo-logo-centric.

Derrida did not, however, dismiss friendship because of its phallo-logo-centrism. As Spivak observed, his style is one of critical intimacy not critical distance. He radicalised it, instead, through exploring the idea that we are linked through the logic of an originary 'amity'. As it turns out, a bit like language and a bit like life, amity, too, is an uncanny thing. For Derrida amity turns on the life we have within us that does not have our name on it, and over which we exercise no proprietorial right because it escapes all propriety.

Derrida uses the word 'amity' here, because he pursues these reflections in a most sustained way through, and against, the controversial German Jurist Carl Schmitt. Schmitt was known for his definition of politics in terms of the friend/enemy distinction. Amity and enmity are closely linked in the belonging together that forms the law of political formation, and Schmitt recognised this. He taught that we know ourselves in virtue of knowing what threatens us in our very existence. Derrida taught, instead, that we know ourselves, to the extent that we ever know ourselves, in virtue of our response-ability to the wholly Other that conditions the very possibility of our existence, inflecting how we exist in every aspect of the diverse ways in which we do exist: writing, speaking, thinking, calculating, deciding, legislating, and so on.

How odd, then, especially how disturbing politically, to discover that that thing or quality in virtue of which we belong together is that over which we have no powers of discretion, compulsion or decision. Said Derrida: 'I don't think that there is such a thing as a deconstructive politics, if by the name "politics" we mean a programme, an agenda, or even the name of a regime. We will see even the word democracy, which I try to locate, is not simply the name of a political regime or nation-state organisation' (Derrida et al., 1997a). Here, he says, 'I'm not proposing a new political content within the old frame, but trying to re-define, or to think differently, what is involved in the political as such, and for the very same reason I don't propose a political theory because what I'm saying, specifically on friendship and hospitality, on what friendship is and what hospitality is, exceeds, precisely, knowledge' (Derrida et al., 1997a). The deconstruction here lies in interrogating something that structures our possibility of existence, and structures how that existence takes place. It is a way of characterising the very operation of a form of life indebted to a radical inner difference that animates it through and through, continually opening it out and exposing it, rather than closing it down and finalising it. What that does is begin to change your thinking, your disposition and your comportment towards living; the response-abilities and responsibilities it entails.

Thus you might say that, for Derrida, we are irretrievably damaged goods, dis-placed persons inhabiting a world that is equally 'out of joint'. Being thus dis-placed is the bond of belonging that we share. Of course, he knows all about the ways in which we place ourselves, and he knows how important it is for us to belong to a place. But that is not the essential point. The point, for all thinkers like Derrida, is the very possibility of us being placed 'here' at all.

From the perspective of Derrida's thinking we are indelibly marked by an incapacity to command the terms of our existence. This thought displaces politics from its usual places and initiates the task of thinking politics otherwise. Precisely because it is something that is not amenable to being known or calculated – it is simply not knowable – having politics revolve around it transforms our very understanding of politics. Hence the radical danger, rather than mere futility, of a politics of security; whatever pole security is said to revolve around.

Since politics in Derrida revolves around this excess, then Derridaean politics is excessive too. In these his own unusual terms Derrida was thus a radical, an emancipationist and a kind of revolutionary. The continuously disruptive absent presence of the Other continually invites emancipation from our current circumstances by exercising decision and responsibility, giving the singularity of the circumstances in which we find ourselves their due: 'to reinvent in a singular situation a new just relationship' (Derrida et al., 1997b, p. 17).

democracy-to-come, force of law and the messianic

The sheer ethical radicality of Derrida's impact on thinking politically is perhaps most evident in his deconstruction of law – how his careful reflection on law allows us to appreciate the ways in which law deconstructs itself, and must deconstruct itself, if there is to be a thing called law (Derrida, 1992). Most radical of all is how he differentiates justice from law, refusing to allow justice to be conflated with law. Judges must judge and decision-makers must decide. There is no avoiding this. It gets done. Derrida, however, asks what comes before the law? What precedes the rush to judgement? What responsibility is left over when the judgement and the decision are made? How are judgements and decisions then to be read, re-read and remade?

Think about his account of the very possibility of signification. It does not depend upon another one. It depends upon the possibility of being able to communicate in the absence of any one. The same goes with justice. The claim of justice cannot be exhausted by my satisfaction of your claim on me or my claim on you in law. The structural possibility of justice is the same as the structural possibility of the sign. It depends upon the absent presence of the Other. It is by virtue of this radical alterity of an absent presence without which we could neither signify nor exist; there is always meaning to come and justice to come.

Derrida reworks the notion of democratic politics in the same way. Rather than just another political regime of government and governance, democracy, for him, is the politics of a meaning and justice to come. Always to come, never being satisfied, always making its claim on us, measuring any and every regime of rule against a measure without measure. This is the challenge to be just again and again by changing the rule according to what is now needed to be just in the very implementation of the rule. Democracy is the freedom to be that responsible; and response-able.

Derrida also calls this promise of a future to come, one that is affirmative and that calls for justice, 'messianicity'. That is another reason why he takes religion very seriously, as indeed does every classic account of politics (Derrida,

1995; 2002a). He acknowledges the debt to the Judaeo-Christian idea of the Messiah, but distinguishes it from that tradition's idea of the coming of an individual Messiah and the final realisation of some divinely ordained providential plan.

Derrida's account of the operational effect of the Other is to say that, consistent with everything else he says, it has the structure of a messianic or affirmatory promise, not that there is a divine plan, much less a Messiah prophesied to fulfil it. It's curious how critics could call someone nihilistic whose whole work explores the affirmatory structure of existence up to and embracing it as messianic in its very structural conditions of possibility and operability.

Here, then, politics revolves around something that no regime of politics can grasp, but before which every regime of politics is called to account; which is why he says that democracy is less a regime than this inexhaustible promise of justice to come, to which it is our commission to remain open. Here is an amity towards existence in virtue of the excess of life within us, knowing no name that calls for a hospitality independent of how any of our regimes of rule calibrate belonging together: as subject, citizen, migrant, stranger, refugee, asylum-seeker and even enemy. It is a call to be hospitable towards the Other. Indeed without that hospitality we cannot in fact be hospitable towards ourselves since we ourselves are also constitutively riven with this Otherness. The point is not simply how hospitable we are, or how much we should be hospitable, even towards ourselves. It is less passport and citizenship laws that therefore govern hospitality politically, for him, or the cultures and traditions of welcoming the stranger. (He is not indifferent towards them either.) Once again it is the structural necessity of being hospitable to that within and between us in virtue of which we do belong together (Derrida, 2000).

Since the Other is without measure there is no way of specifying when the ethical obligation of welcoming the Other is done. Indeed, from Derrida's perspective, this is a very odd thing to think. How could one be done with the welcome one is called upon to give to that nameless animation within us without which there would be no living to be done? Unless, of course, one hates and negates life. Nothing could be further from Derrida's thought. 'What is really going on in things, what is really happening', he says, 'is always "to come". Every time you try to stabilise the meaning of a thing, try to fix it in its missionary position, the thing itself, if there is anything at all to it, slips away' (Derrida et al., 1997b, p. 31). It is that future towards which he thinks we have to be endlessly hospitable. There could be no more fragile, urgent or comprehensive political responsibility.

further reading

For the background in Continental philosophy, see Silverman (1989). For a good collection of essential texts by Derrida, see Wood (1992). Major studies on Derrida and political theory include Beardsworth (1996), Bennington (1994) and Patton (2004). For detailed philosophical analysis and critique, see Critchley (1992), Gashé (1994), Royle (1995) and Wood (2005).

references

Beardsworth, R. (1996) *Derrida and the Political*. London: Routledge.

Bennington, G. (1994) *Legislations: The politics of deconstruction*. London: Verso.

Critchley, S. (1992) *The Ethics of Deconstruction. Derrida and Levinas*. Oxford: Blackwell.

Critchley, S. (2005) 'Derrida's Influence on Philosophy ... And on my work', *German Law Journal, Special issue: A dedication to Jacques Derrida*, 6: 26–9.

Derrida, J. (1973) *Speech and Phenomena*. Evanston, IL: Northwestern University Press.

Derrida, J. (1974) *Of Grammatology*. Baltimore, MD: Johns Hopkins University Press.

Derrida, J. (1981) *Writing and Difference*. London: Routledge.

Derrida, J. (1988) *Limited Inc*. Evanston, IL: Northwestern University Press.

Derrida, J. (1989) *Of Spirit*. Chicago, IL: Chicago University Press.

Derrida, J. (1992) *Deconstruction and the Possibility of Justice* (including 'Force of the Law'), ed. D. Cornell, M. Rosenfeld and D.G. Carlson. New York: Routledge.

Derrida, J. (1994) *Specters of Marx*. New York: Routledge.

Derrida, J. (1995) *The Gift of Death*, trans. D. Wills. Chicago, IL: University of Chicago Press.

Derrida, J. (1997) *Politics of Friendship*. New York: Routledge.

Derrida, J. (1999) *Adieu to Emmanuel Levinas*. Stanford, CA: Stanford University Press.

Derrida, J. (2000) *Of Hospitality*. Stanford, CA: Stanford University Press.

Derrida, J. (2002a) *Acts of Religion*, ed. G. Anidjar. New York: Routledge.

Derrida, J. (2002b) 'The Animal That Therefore I Am (More to Follow)', *Critical Inquiry*, 28: 369–418.

Derrida, J. (2005) *Rogues: Two Essays on Reason*. Stanford, CA: Stanford University Press.

Derrida, J. et al. (1997a) *Politics and Friendship: A discussion with Jacques Derrida*. University of Sussex, 1 December, <www.sussex.ac.uk/Units/frenchthought/derrida.htm>.

Derrida, J. et al. (1997b) 'Villanova Roundtable', in *Deconstruction in a Nutshell*, ed. J. Caputo, pp. 3–28. New York: Fordham University Press.

Foucault, Michel (1988) 'Practicing Criticism', in *Politics, Philosophy, Culture: Interviews and Other Writings 1977–1984*, ed. L.D. Kritzman, trans. A. Sheridan et al. New York: Routledge.

Gashé, R. (1994) *Inventions of Difference: On Jacques Derrida*. Cambridge, MA: Harvard University Press.

Patton, P. (2004) 'Politics', in *Understanding Derrida*, ed. J. Reynolds and J. Roffe, pp. 26–36. London: Continuum Books.

Royle, N. (1995) *After Derrida*. Manchester: Manchester University Press.

Silverman, H. (ed.) (1989) *Continental Philosophy II: Derrida and deconstruction*. New York: Routledge.

Wood, D. (ed.) (1992) *Derrida: A critical reader*. Oxford: Blackwell.

Wood, D. (2005) *The Step Back: Ethics and politics after deconstruction*. Albany, NY: SUNY Press.

18

gilles deleuze

nathan widder

Gilles Deleuze (1925–1995) studied philosophy at the Sorbonne and later taught there and at the University of Lyon before being appointed Professor of Philosophy at the University of Vincennes, where Michel Foucault had been charged with establishing the philosophy department. In 1972, having already written several monographs of figures in the history of philosophy and several works of original philosophy, Deleuze collaborated with Félix Guattari (1930–1992), a political activist and trained Lacanian psychoanalyst, to publish *Anti-Oedipus: Capitalism and Schizophrenia*, which became a bestseller in France. Deleuze continued to publish solo works and collaborative works with Guattari and others into the 1990s. Although Deleuze rarely travelled outside France, he became one of the most internationally prominent figures in contemporary Continental philosophy. He has become increasingly influential in English-speaking academia since at least the late 1980s.

Like Foucault, Derrida and other contemporary French philosophers, Deleuze has become important in attempts to think through issues of identity and politics. The problems and dangers of identity-based politics have become noticeable to even casual observers of the New Left, as diverse movements – feminist, gay and lesbian, post-Marxist, and so on – have faced fracturing and disintegration in their very attempts to establish a sense of collective identity and purpose. As this chapter will show, Deleuze presents a sophisticated analysis and critique of the centrality of identity in political thought and practice, and, through this, proposes more experimental ways of thinking and acting that move them beyond the simplifications and reductions of mainstream politics. His complex ontology of political and social life and his contribution to novel theories of power ensure that Deleuze will remain a central figure in political philosophy in the future.

identity, opposition and otherness

The displacement of identity has been a central task in contemporary Continental Political Thought. It has involved demonstrating how no identity is pregiven or natural but instead refers beyond itself to relations and differences that constitute it. However, it has also been crucial to go beyond the disarticulation of identity performed by Hegelian dialectics. Hegel maintains that once identity is no longer treated as a thing-in-itself, it must be understood to determine itself in relation to what it is not or to what negates or opposes it. For Hegel, the greatest difference from any identity is its contradictory or polar opposite, the not-X opposing any X. In showing that it is not its opposite, the place of this X is defined. This process of determination, however, also consolidates the place of the opposite and identifies it – the not-X is itself an identity, defined by its own opposition to X – and this reciprocal determination means that each opposite is also implicated in the identity of the other. This allows Hegel to declare that even the greatest differences can be mediated and brought together in an Identity of identity and opposition. In this dialectical synthesis, the difference between opposites persists, but within a more encompassing unity: opposing identities are opposed *because* they are also identical, and vice versa. Hegel's displacement of identity is therefore only partial, since the way he refers identity beyond itself and his concept of difference as opposition remain compatible with the logic of identity itself (see Deleuze, 1994, p. 49).

A complete deconstruction of identity must therefore refer to a difference that differs from identity and opposition. Many Continental thinkers therefore criticise the adequacy of Hegelian opposition while articulating a different form of difference. This Otherness must be enigmatic and paradoxical: rather than being located on a spatial or temporal continuum between some X and its opposite, it is *neither* X *nor* not-X. It is the non-identical as such, and insofar as an identity refers beyond itself to this Other, it depends on an excess that, being unlocalisable, cannot anchor its place.

But here a split occurs in contemporary Continental thought concerning the relations between identity, opposition, Otherness and meaning or sense. For those who consider meaning to be impossible outside of a structure of oppositions – that is, for those who hold that for something to have meaning or sense it requires a determinate identity, which is, however precariously, separated from its opposite – the Other that deconstructs identity is usually considered an interruption of meaning or a nonsense that is effaced when a meaningful structure establishes itself. In this kind of theory, then, a relation to opposition establishes identity and meaning, while another relation to Otherness dissolves them. This Otherness is not strictly outside the structure of sense, since this structure is necessarily related to it. Nonetheless, it serves as an internal limit to structured sense and cannot be approached further.

Lacan's understanding of subjectivity exemplifies this position. To have a sense of itself, Lacan argues, a subject must identify with an image conveyed through another, making its identity relationally constituted. But, more profoundly, the subject becomes truly a subject only through the trauma of a Law of castration that demands repression. Trauma implies a lost unity, but as no subject exists prior to this trauma, this unity cannot be recovered, because it never really existed. Subjectivity thus rests upon a desire for an impossible lost object. Lacan's subject continually seeks a sense of itself through others who provide it with an image of itself, but these others are always inadequate to the desire for this mysterious Other. The subject struggles to identify with another, but will always fail, because true unity depends on the recovery of something impossible.

Lacan applies this same logic to language and sexual difference. Words are open to slippage because their meanings refer them to other words in an oppositional structure, but they suffer from another displacement in substituting for referents that, being outside language, are meaningless. The status of the feminine for Lacan is ambiguous, because whatever meaning it has comes from being an opposite or complement to the masculine, yet the feminine also designates the Other that falls outside the symbolic realm (see Lacan, 1982). Lacan refers to this Otherness sometimes as a Lack, sometimes as excessive *jouissance* and sometimes as the sublime Real, but in all cases language cannot grasp it, and no meaning or sense can be ascribed to it. From a Lacanian perspective, assigning meaning or sense to this excess illicitly gives it a content, when such content can be structured only oppositionally.

For Deleuze, this arrangement relies on an old paradigm of identity and backs away from the implications of its own thinking of excess. It understands sense in a dialectical fashion and thus holds identity, as a bounded unity separating individuals or groups from what they are not, to be a precondition for thought. Following Nietzsche, who opens both *Beyond Good and Evil* and *Human, All too Human* by declaring oppositions to be simply metaphysical exaggerations (Nietzsche, 1966a, p. 10; 1986, p. 12), Deleuze holds opposition to be an abstract and reductive conception of the relationships that constitute sense. For Deleuze, identity and opposition presuppose a territorial conceptualisation of difference, a flattened surface upon which different identities are demarcated, but one that is, for this very reason, incomplete. If I take a piece of paper and mark two opposite corners, the difference between the marks can be conceived as the distance between them – about 36 cm with a standard A4 sheet. However, if I fold the paper so the corners approach one another, the distance along its surface remains the same, but the two marks are closer along a different dimension. Assuming more than three spatial dimensions, we can imagine further folds. Opposition is an abstract simplification, because things, Deleuze argues, relate through divergent and discontinuous axes. Even what is most opposed along one axis can be more intimately related along another, but the full and concrete sense of something refers to all these axes of difference taken together. Treating difference as opposition irons out these other axes by strictly segregating things, and even if these separations are dialectically mediated, more subtle relations within and between things are missed: 'Dialectic thrives on oppositions because it is unaware of far more subtle and subterranean differential mechanisms: topological displacements, typological variations' (Deleuze, 1983, p. 157). Here, for Deleuze, Otherness becomes implicated in the constitution of sense: the sense of something comes from its relations to others, but these relations pass through an Otherness that introduces heterogeneity, discontinuity and divergence. Otherness is a conduit that ties things together such that they never simply correspond to or oppose one another (Deleuze, 1990, p. 305). There is no oppositional structure of sense, except as a simplification of this more complex passage through Otherness.

A thing therefore refers beyond itself to a network of relations of discontinuity and disjunction. Deleuze calls this a virtual network – referring to the Latin *virtus*, meaning 'power' –underpinning actual relations of difference (see especially Deleuze, 1994, pp. 208–21). He also calls it a rhizome and a multiplicity that differs from both the One and the Many (Deleuze and Guattari, 1987, pp. 3–25). Two other relevant concepts, developed most prominently in Deleuze's collaborative works with Guattari, are 'desiring-machines' and the 'body without organs'. Desire is 'machinic' insofar as it is a working assemblage of heterogeneous components: desire is 'an *agencement* of heterogeneous elements that function' (Deleuze, 1997, p. 189). The body without organs – or BwO – refers to the Otherness that links together components of one or several desiring machines. It is produced 'in the connective synthesis' (Deleuze and Guattari, 1983, p. 8), but it also repels the components, making friction and strife always part of these machines. As a result, 'Desiring-machines work only when they break down, and by continually breaking down' (Deleuze and Guattari, 1983, p. 8). At this 'molecular' level of constitutive relations, a thing is a complex convergence of differences that are never fully in sync with one another; at the 'molar' level, where constituted things relate to one another, these relations are likewise never entirely harmonious. At both molecular and molar levels, then, any formulation in terms of identity and opposition is flawed.

The articulation of this multiplicity effects a reversal of Platonism, the task, Deleuze notes, that Nietzsche sets for a philosophy of the future (Deleuze, 1990, p. 253; 1994, p. 59). In Plato's philosophy, the central oppositions of metaphysical thought are organised into hierarchies of purity and lack. One term is treated as a pure and ideal Form while the other is considered merely an absence: Beauty, for example, is a Form that is nothing but the beautiful, while ugliness is a lack of Beauty and an absence of form. Physical objects are understood as copies of Forms, attaining their meaning or sense by virtue of conforming to the Form that is their model, the weakest copies falling furthest from the Form into its opposite. But this entire structure falters when Plato examines simulacra such as the artwork, shadows and illusions that simulate physical objects, the actors who simulate various citizens and professions, and the sophists who simulate the philosopher. Plato tries to reduce simulacra to poor copies or copies of copies (the artwork copies the physical object, which copies the Form), the opposite of true Forms. Yet while physical objects are never confused with their transcendent Forms – we never mistake a physical tree for the ideal Form of a tree – a good simulation appears to be as real and true as what it copies. Simulations, in short, contain a deceptiveness that is not accounted for by their being merely faint images of higher truths, so that they defy the status Plato gives them. As Deleuze says, simulacra are not copies of copies, but are what put the order of original and copy into question (Deleuze, 1990, p. 256). They are neither original nor copy, but exceed the terms of this dualism.

Reversing Platonism therefore means affirming the rights of simulacra (Deleuze, 1990, p. 262), which follow not a model of identity but at best 'a model of the Other' (Deleuze, 1990, p. 258). This is not a sociological claim about reality melting into a postmodern hyperreality of simulation (see Baudrillard, 1993, ch. 2), but rather an ontological claim about an underlying multiplicity that appears when the dominance of models and originals fades. What, then, of identity and opposition? They now have the status traditionally assigned to simulacra. They are simulated substantialities or surface effects appearing to have depth. They are transcendental illusions in the Kantian sense (Deleuze, 1990, p. 262; 1994, p. 126). They are blunt divisions that appear when the complexity of Otherness is lost: 'What happens when Others are missing from the structure of the world? In that case, there reigns the brutal opposition of the sun and earth, of an unbearable light and an obscure abyss: the "summary law of all or nothing"' (Deleuze, 1990, p. 306). Our dominant political, ethical and philosophical traditions treat these illusory, crude, abstract, oppositional categories as necessities, while the major critiques of our traditions (Kantian critical philosophy, Hegelian and Marxist dialectics, psychoanalysis, and so on) ultimately conform to this supposed necessity, reinforcing 'the rights of the criticized' (Deleuze, 1983, p. 89). Genuine critique, Deleuze says, is inseparable from a creation that invokes the newness of excessive Otherness. The orientations of theory and practice are henceforth modified. Both are now involved in, first, locating the conditions under which the complexity of the world is forgotten, and, second, determining how it can be reintroduced into thinking and living. Moreover, theory and practice are themselves linked together discontinuously: each necessarily refers to the other, but no smooth transition exists between them. Theory does not simply set the standards that determine practice, nor does practice inspire theory in a straightforward way. Rather, each becomes a conduit across the obstacles blocking the other: 'The relationship which holds in the application of a theory is never one of resemblance ... Practice is a set of relays from one theoretical point to another, and theory is a relay from one practice to another' (Deleuze and Foucault, 1977, pp. 205–6). The standard of success for any critical theory or practice is therefore the degree it overcomes the simplifications of identity and opposition.

force, will to power and eternal return

To account for the error of reducing complex relations to opposition, Deleuze forges a link between Lucretius, Spinoza and Nietzsche (see Deleuze, 1990, p. 279; 1995, p. 6). These thinkers all trace this error to the human demand for natural purposes that give life meaning. All three also link ethics to an overcoming of this weakness. In *Nietzsche and Philosophy* (Deleuze, 1983), the error of opposition and the ethics of overcoming are presented through the distinctions Deleuze finds in Nietzsche between active and reactive forces and affirmative and negative wills to power. Deleuze's analysis of Nietzsche presents a human ontology that explains how complex conditions give rise to a will to forget them. *Nietzsche and Philosophy* is also a particularly important contribution to political theory, with Deleuze's theory of force relations often being cited alongside Foucault's theories of power relations as developing a conception of power that moves it beyond the confines of traditional political theory. Power is usually treated as a possession of a subject who can choose to use it against another subject, who, in turn, may possess less power and can therefore be compelled to obey. Deleuze challenges this with a conception of power as a relation of discontinuity that constitutes the different subjects who may be said to hold and wield power.

Force refers to the virtual network of relations underpinning a thing's meaning or sense: 'We will never find the sense of something (of a human, a biological or even a physical phenomenon) if we do not know the force which appropriates the thing, which exploits it, which takes possession of it or is expressed in it' (Deleuze, 1983, p. 3). Force relations thereby pass through a knot of Otherness, making them relations of heterogeneity, discontinuity and strife. Deleuze here speaks of Otherness as a difference that can be either affirmed or reduced to opposition (Deleuze, 1983, p. 9). The heterogeneity of difference means that related forces can never be equal or equal and opposing: 'The dream of two equal forces, even if they are said to be of opposite senses is a coarse and approximate dream, a statistical dream' (Deleuze, 1983, p. 43). Any forceful relationship is therefore one of inequality and hierarchy, of a stronger force enforcing itself upon a weaker one: 'the relation of force to force, understood conceptually, is one of domination: when two forces are related one is dominant and the other is dominated' (Deleuze, 1983, p. 51). It is thus always a relation of command and obedience, but, crucially, there is also resistance, reversal and inversion, as the weaker can overcome the stronger (Deleuze, 1983, pp. 56–9). Strife means that force relations are relations of neither simple hierarchy (this would parallel Plato's hierarchy of superior and inferior – an oppositional schema that, as we have already seen, is inadequate) nor equality. Rather, they are relations of disequilibrium, of inequality in flux. Force relations are filled with knots, disjunctions and discontinuities – in short, differences – that keep them in motion. They can therefore be considered power relations, although Deleuze generally prefers to speak of desiring machines rather than power relations (see Deleuze and Guattari, 1987, pp. 530–1; also Deleuze, 1997): they are constitutive relations in which power is not the possession of a dominator who wields it over the dominated, but rather what prevents any relation of domination from being unambiguously fixed.

The initial difference between struggling forces is a quantitative difference of relative strength and weakness. There is also, however, a qualitative difference corresponding to this quantitative difference: dominant forces are active, meaning they command, create, transform and overcome; dominated forces are reactive, meaning they must work by adaptation, compromise and utility (Deleuze, 1983, pp. 40–4). The active or reactive quality of force therefore indicates the tactics or means by which force exercises its power (Deleuze, 1983, p. 54). Finally, in any configuration of forces, there is a will to power, which is not a will to grasp power, though this desire for power regularly appears in certain forms of the will to power. The will to power, Deleuze says, is the principle of the quality of force and the signification of the sense of related forces (Deleuze, 1983, pp. 83, 85). It is what the configuration of active and reactive relations expresses. This expression is either affirmative or negative. What emerges from relations of strife is the will either to affirm strife or to deny it: 'What a will wants, depending on its quality, is to affirm its difference or to deny what differs' (Deleuze, 1983, p. 78). Affirmative and negative wills to power are closely related but not identical to active and reactive forces. Affirmation expresses active forces becoming dominant, while negation expresses forces in their becoming reactive (Deleuze, 1983, p. 54).

Deleuze here draws on Nietzsche's genealogy of noble and slave moralities (Nietzsche, 1967) and what he calls Nietzsche's method of dramatisation (Deleuze, 1983, pp. 78–9). Slave morality expresses a denial of difference that reduces differences to a schema of identity and opposition. This appears in the slavish opposition between good and evil, whereby others are called evil in order to secure the slaves' identity and goodness through contradistinction (Deleuze, 1983, pp. 119–22). The weak, forced into passivity by the strong and driven by *ressentiment*, can affirm themselves only by denying or negating what they are not. But this affirmation through negation is generated by a profound denial of constitutive relations that go beyond opposition. Reactive forces thus 'deny, from the start, the difference which constitutes them at the start' and, as they become dominant, a negative will to power enables them 'to invert the differential element from which they derive and to give a deformed image of it' (Deleuze, 1983, p. 56). Through this deformed image, differences are compared through fixed markers and 'transcendent values' (Deleuze, 1983, p. 119). But this slavish will to power, Deleuze argues, is not peculiar to a specific group: consciousness itself is 'essentially reactive' (Deleuze, 1983, p. 41) and the negative will to power's *ressentiment* and nihilism are not psychological or historical traits, but underpin human psychology and history as such (Deleuze, 1983, p. 34): they are 'the foundation of the humanity in man. They are the principle of the human being as such' (Deleuze, 1983, p. 64).

Identity and opposition express a slavish will, but slavishness defines humanity's essence. We are constituted in complex relations of strife, but what emerges is a human, all too human will interpreting and evaluating the world with blunt abstractions. In our thinking and our acting, we treat these abstractions as necessities and even realities, when they are actually surface effects or optical illusions. And yet, this is only a perspective on the world that emerges from the flux of the world. The question is: are other perspectives available? Are there other ways of thinking, feeling and acting? In short, 'Is there another becoming?' (Deleuze, 1983, p. 64). The difficulty, Deleuze notes, is that the negative will to power, with its crude oppositions, is not only the only will we know, but the only knowable will – it is 'the *ratio cognoscenti* [reason for acknowledging the fact] *of the will to power in general*. All known and knowable values are, by nature, values which derive from this *ratio*' (Deleuze, 1983, p. 172). But reactive forces are reactive only through their relation to active forces, and the slaves' negative will to power exists only because another will to power compels them into passivity. This other will to power is that of the Overman, who transmutes values and moves 'beyond good and evil'. It is 'the *ratio essendi* [reason for the existence of the fact] *of the will to power in general*' (Deleuze, 1983, p. 173) and it is not a new knowledge, but 'another sensibility, another way of feeling' (Deleuze, 1983, p. 64).

Affirmation is not affirmation of what is (Deleuze, 1983, p. 183). It is creative, meaning that 'we make use of excess in order to invent new forms of life rather than separating life from what it can do' (Deleuze, 1983, p. 185). What is affirmed is difference, but this difference is never opposition (Deleuze, 1983, p. 188). Instead, it is the Otherness that defines things relationally through disjunction and strife. Deleuze links affirmation to Nietzsche's conception of friendship: 'the friend, says Zarathustra, is always the third person in between "I" and "me" who pushes me to overcome myself and to be overcome in order to live' (Deleuze, 1983, p. 6). The friend does not support one's identity while the enemy opposes it. Rather, the friend *is* an enemy – 'one's best enemy', as Nietzsche says (1966b, p. 56) – who enables one to go beyond the limits of one's identity. Deleuze also draws upon Nietzsche's doctrine of eternal return, holding the affirmative will to power to be inseparable from an affirmation of eternal return and an affirmative movement of returning. Standard readings treat Nietzsche's thesis as the idea that, given an infinite period of time, identical events will recur eternally. From this reading, which is consistent with Nietzsche's most straightforward statements about the doctrine, interpreters see Nietzsche's corresponding ethics as a call to perform only those acts whose eternal repetition can be affirmed. Deleuze, however, argues that the return of identical events describes only the eternal return willed by the negative will to power. More profoundly, he says, what returns is difference: 'It is not some one thing which returns but rather returning itself is the one thing which is affirmed of diversity or multiplicity. In other words, identity in the eternal return does not describe the nature of that which returns but, on the contrary, the fact of returning for that which differs' (Deleuze, 1983, p. 48). The sense of the affirmative will to power is thus the eternal return of Otherness, which dissolves identity and opposition. This generates a different ethical imperative: the eternal return effects a selection, Deleuze says, whereby only what overcomes is *fit* to return (Deleuze, 1983, pp. 68–71); but this means affirming the active destruction (Deleuze, 1983, pp. 70, 174) of the values and the being of opposition and negativity.

Given its premise of a content and sense exceeding identity and opposition, the content of this affirmation must remain somewhat nebulous. It is sufficiently clear, however, to give direction to Deleuzean politics. Affirming the dissolution of the categories of identity, this politics is pitched at the virtual level from which these fictions arise. It therefore differs from dominant political traditions – liberalism, Marxism, and so on – which either start with given social identities and aim to prevent the unjust domination of one identity over others, or treat identities as constructions, but conceive the dynamic of their construction dialectically, promising eventually to overcome current states of power and domination. The theory of forces is central, because it shows how identities are abstract fictions produced by a certain configuration of constitutive relations. This politics at the constitutive level is a micropolitics (Deleuze and Guattari, 1987, pp. 208–31) that is usually ignored by mainstream political theory. Opening up this micropolitical domain reveals possibilities and necessities for a politics that endeavours 'beyond good and evil' by endeavouring beyond identity and opposition.

a many-layered politics

Despite their fictitiousness, identity and opposition do structure a certain level of political and social life. They appear most prominently in the standards of normality and deviance that organise and seem to give sense to various practices and institutions. Deviation from the norm is considered a failure to achieve the standards and a falling away from the norm into its opposite: normality and deviance are thereby opposed. Different standards operate in different domains, yet in all cases, social forces are exercised in the name of policing and correcting deviance and compelling conformity with norms, often using both carrot and stick approaches. Ironically, however, these standards are false markers, because individuals never really encompass the model of normality (Deleuze, 1995, p. 173) and the whole oppositional structure remains abstract and reductive, unable to grasp the complex dynamic of constitutive forces underpinning it.

Given the hierarchical and exclusionary nature of these oppositional categories – being declared insane or deviant, for example, excludes individuals from various political and social freedoms and opportunities – a politics of resistance in the name of the marginalised might seem appropriate. This sort of politics is often attributed to Deleuze, but while his thought touches upon such issues, they are hardly his central concern. In this regard, Deleuze distinguishes majorities, minorities and becoming-minor or minoritarian (Deleuze and Guattari, 1987, pp. 106–7). It is not a matter, he says, of reversing the relationship between majority and minority, or between norm and marginal, but of instigating a politics that surmounts such crude divisions. This involves a creative and revolutionary becoming (Deleuze, 1995, pp. 170–1), which follows Deleuze's analysis of Otherness and of the will to power. Because oppositional categories are not pregiven but willed, and because this will is produced by virtual or micro-configurations of strife, the categories refer to other layers of political and social life, where other political possibilities and necessities reside.

There is, first, a molar level of segmentarity, comprised of diverse domains such as family, school and workplace, or classifications such as childhood, adulthood, homosexuality, and so on. At this level of sharp divisions, the various facets of one's complex identity are delineated. One assumes different roles within and across segments, but only one at a time or only within specific relations: one passes from childhood to adulthood and from school to work; one can be a father, son and husband, simultaneously, but to different people; one works from 9 to 5 and is a pensioner after 65. The segments are thereby organised by binaries, even where more than two choices are available.

> Segments depend on binary machines which can be varied if need be. Binary machines of social classes; of sexes, man–woman; of ages, child–adult; of races, black–white; of sectors, public–private; of subjectivations, ours–not ours. These binary machines are all the more complex for cutting across each other, or colliding against each other, confronting each other, and they cut us up in all sorts of directions. And they are not roughly dualistic, they are rather dichotomic: they can operate diachronically (if you are neither *a* nor *b*, then you are *c*: dualism has shifted and no longer relates to simultaneous elements to choose between, but successive choices; if you are neither black nor white, you are a half-breed; if you dress as neither man nor woman, you are a transvestite: each time the machine with binary elements will produce binary choices between elements which are not present at the first cutting-up). (Deleuze and Parnet, 1987, p. 128)

Moreover, regardless of the choices or assignments made, the segments, despite their diversity, are ominously the same – undoubtedly because they all function by policing standards of normal identity (see Deleuze, 1990, pp. 169–82).

Segments, however, refer to another micro- or molecular level, where power relations constitute the standards that 'code' each particular domain. But this same power, while constructing 'normal' identities, also produces forms of madness, delinquency and perversion that oppose the norm. On this dialectical level of constitutive power, then, resistances take the form of marginals who oppose the coding that depreciates them – yet something of these marginals is found in everyone. They persist as a pervasive and potentially revolutionary element within the segments, always threatening to overturn them.

But opposition refers to another form of difference, in relation to which it is a reduction. This second level thus refers to another molecular level of strife and flux, which is affirmative in the sense of Nietzsche's affirmative will to power – a level not of power and resistance but desiring-machines. In contrast to the segments and binaries constituted by power, this level consists of chaotic 'lines of flight' that exceed identity and opposition and 'deterritorialise' molar formations and their sharp divisions. The second level of power and resistance can only partially deterritorialise, since its resistances work in simple opposition to power (Deleuze and Parnet, 1987, p. 136). But at the third level, complete deterritorialisations are possible because lines of flight break down molar formations not by opposing but simply by exceeding them. The three levels, however, are never fully distinct. Each is immanent to the others, 'caught up in one another' (Deleuze and Parnet, 1987, p. 125), so that they form a single 'assemblage' – a multiplicity of heterogeneous but inseparable domains flowing into and through each other (Deleuze and Guattari, 1987, p. 4). Micro-levels of desire and power constitute the molar segments that seem to fix and incorporate them, reterritorialising desiring lines of flight; and lines of flight continue within molar organisations, exceeding and dissolving them.

Molecular and molar forms of power code differences within each segment, giving each domain markers of normality and deviance. Domains are independent, yet they also communicate with one another: school disciplines children in preparation for work; courts and prisons use different norms and practices, yet they resonate with one another, the first producing convicts through judgments of guilt passed on acts, and the second receiving convicts and turning them into delinquents, who often reoffend and end up back in court. Every domain similarly refers beyond itself, and the state enables these diverse domains to communicate. The state 'overcodes' the coded domains by imposing its own rigid segmentarity over the segments (Deleuze and Guattari, 1987, pp. 209–10) – or, rather, the state is the realisation of this overcoding (Deleuze and Guattari, 1987, p. 223; Deleuze and Parnet, 1987, p. 129). It regulates transfers between segments rather than reduces them to one homogeneous blob. This makes the state an important but limited site of political struggle: the problem of crime, for example, cannot be adequately dealt with at the state level only, because the state is a relay rather than an all-or-nothing power holder. Moreover, the state and its institutions of coding are always pitted against deterritorialising excesses. They maintain an uneasy alliance with the forces of capitalism, which do not code difference but instead submit them to an axiomatic of exchange value. Capitalism effects a partial deterritorialisation of the state, but is also implicated in forms of reterritorialisation. More profoundly, the state is challenged by a chaotic excess of desire that Deleuze and Guattari call a 'war machine'. The war machine lies outside the state apparatus, and is only partially integrated through military and police institutions, which give this constitutive aggressiveness a defined purpose: '*The State has no war machine of its own*; it can only appropriate one in the form of a military institution, one that will continually cause it problems' (Deleuze and Guattari, 1987, p. 355). Chaos should not be seen from the state's perspective, which considers it the simple opposite of order, like a Hobbesian state of nature. Chaos consists not of merely random or accidental events, which would suggest a domain of unrelated atoms, but rather 'nomadic' passages through Otherness. These movements are as much collective as they are personal (Deleuze and Parnet, 1987, p. 127), and though from a perspective of identity and opposition they may not even appear to move, these lines of flight can initiate 'a curious stationary journey' (Deleuze and Parnet, 1987, p. 127).

This multilayered complex of movements and codings calls for a multilayered politics and recognition of the way all things, at whatever level, are political. The personal is political, though in a special sense. It is not simply that the barrier between private and public is always drawn in the public or political realm, nor that the public and private are both organised by large scale powers such as capitalism, patriarchy, racism or heterosexism. Rather it is because any thing, in the molecular fluxes that constitute it and in which it participates, and in the creative deterritorialisations it can enact, effects a reification or overcoming of formations of identity and opposition.

The different levels of political and social life call for different politics. A politics directed towards the segments seeks to modify or reform them, perhaps even radically. Yet on the one hand, it is not a matter of simply making rigid segments more flexible, 'believing that a little suppleness is enough to make things "better"' (Deleuze and Guattari, 1987, p. 215), while, on the other hand, segmentation is undeniably necessary:

[T]he segments which run through us and through which we pass are ... marked by a rigidity which reassures us, while turning us into creatures which are the most fearful, but also the most bitter ... Even if we had the power to blow it up, could we succeed in doing so without destroying ourselves, since it is so much a part of the conditions of life, including our organism and our very reason? (Deleuze and Parnet, 1987, p. 138)

The realm of constitutive power relations suggests a politics of the marginal and the revolutionary, which seeks to overturn exclusionary standards of normality and deviance. But here lies a danger that Deleuze and Guattari call 'micro-fascism', which reinforces blunt oppositions through a spiteful friend/enemy politics common to both segmented societies and the resistance movements opposing them. In both cases, Otherness is denied from the start, just as Nietzsche's reactive forces and negative will to power reduce difference to opposition. Micro-fascisms are as common within Western democracies, across the entire left–right spectrum, as they are in totalitarian regimes. They are part of the human, all too human thinking that fails to affirm difference.

A third kind of politics is thus needed, which is about neither reform nor even revolutionary opposition, but of literally 'doing something different'. There is a kind of experimentation, Deleuze argues, which standard political theory might not consider political, but which is eminently political in its power to surmount the categories of standard politics. At this level, politics is a question of how individuals and collectivities can overcome the identities and oppositions that seem to exhaust their meaning and sense by instituting deterritorialising lines of flight. Deleuze and Guattari speak of making oneself a body without organs or BwO (Deleuze and Guattari, 1987, pp. 149–66) by disaggregating the various elements and relations that organise oneself into the segmented and stratified identity one assumes. If the concrete sense of an individual or collectivity necessarily refers to heterogeneous axes of difference, then the self itself refers to a divergent assemblage of relations, which include the material, linguistic, human, animal and more:

> For the BwO is all of that: necessarily a Place, necessarily a Plane, necessarily a Collectivity (assembling elements, things, plants, animals, tools, people, powers, and fragments of all of these; for it is not 'my' body without organs, instead the 'me' (*moi*) is on it, or what remains of me, unalterable and changing in form, crossing thresholds). (Deleuze and Guattari, 1987, p. 161)

The BwO is an experiment in the opportunities for mutation that this complex but seemingly sedimented structure provides.

> This is how it should be done: Lodge yourself on a stratum, experiment with the opportunities it offers, find an advantageous place on it, find potential movements of deterritorialization, possible lines of flight, experience them, produce flow conjunctions here and there, try out continuums of intensities segment by segment, have a small plot of new land at all times. It is through a meticulous relation with the strata that one succeeds in freeing lines of flight, causing conjugated flows to pass and escape and bringing forth continuous intensities for a BwO. (Deleuze and Guattari, 1987)

To strive beyond the crude oppositions established between the human and non-human, the male and the female, the normal and the deviant, and so on, towards more subtle and complex relations of Otherness, is to engage in a politics that seeks to overcome categories that have been treated as necessities but are in fact fictions.

The dangers at this level come largely from the constitutive nature of desiring-machines. Just as active and reactive forces can constitute a will to power that affirms or negates difference, desiring machines can affirm Otherness or reinstate opposition. Lines of flight may connect productively or they may fall into isolated and empty 'black holes'; they may fall into a trap of clarity where fascism re-emerges as a dogmatic certainty of 'the truth'; or a line of flight may become a line of self-destruction, and, if this form of desire seizes control of the state, it may become macroscopic fascism: 'in fascism the State is far less totalitarian than it is *suicidal*. There is in fascism a realized nihilism' (Deleuze and Guattari, 1987, p. 230, see pp. 227–31 generally). Similarly, Deleuze and Guattari hold that experimental BwOs can be botched (Deleuze and Guattari, 1987, p. 149). They may become empty, cancerous or fascist (Deleuze and Guattari, 1987, p. 163). The question is 'knowing whether we have it within our means to make a selection, to distinguish the BwO from its doubles: empty vitreous bodies, cancerous bodies, totalitarian and fascist' (Deleuze and Guattari, 1987, p. 165). Deleuze and Guattari ask, but arguably never adequately answer, this question. Deleuze, for example, merely says: 'There is no general prescription. We have done away with all globalizing concepts' (Deleuze and Parnet, 1987, p. 144). But this is perhaps the only possible answer, because uncertainty is what makes the body without organs both experimental and political. The BwO is a matter of both political thought and political practice, brought together neither in simple correspondence nor in relations of primacy and dependence but instead in relations of mutual imbrication and difference. Absent foundational standards, the construction of a BwO is necessarily a matter of pragmatism and strategy. Through our thought and our practice at this level, Deleuze says, we seek to negotiate the impasses imposed on us by the very identities and oppositions that seem to give us structure but are also inadequate.

further reading

Of Deleuze's works listed below, *Negotiations* and *Dialogues* (written with Claire Parnet) are considered the most accessible avenues into his political and philosophical thought. *Nietzsche and Philosophy* is a particularly important and influential text in both the bourgeoning of interest in Nietzsche that has developed since the 1960s and the incorporation of Nietzsche's thought into political theory. *Difference and Repetition* and *The Logic of Sense* represent two of Deleuze's most difficult but important contributions to poststructuralist philosophies of difference, while two of his collaborative works with Félix Guattari, *Anti-Oedipus* and *A Thousand Plateaus* are perhaps Deleuze's most important contributions to social analysis and ethics. Deleuze's entire corpus is significantly more extensive than the works used in this chapter, and it includes two works on cinema and book-length studies of Foucault, Bergson, Kant, Spinoza, Leibniz, Proust, Sacher-Masoch and Francis Bacon. There is a growing body of secondary literature on Deleuze's thought. Patton (2000) is most closely focused on Deleuze's relation to political theory. Useful chapters can be found in collections edited by Patton (1996) and Boundas and Olkowski (1994).

references

Baudrillard, J. (1993) *Symbolic Exchange and Death*, trans. I. Hamilton Grant. London, Thousand Oaks, CA, and New Delhi: Sage.

Boundas, C., and Olkowski, D. (1994) *Gilles Deleuze and the Theater of Philosophy*. London: Routledge.

Deleuze, G. (1983) *Nietzsche and Philosophy*, trans. H. Tomlinson. London: Athlone.

Deleuze, G. (1990) *The Logic of Sense*, trans. M. Lester with C. Stivale, ed. C.V. Boundas. New York: Columbia University Press.

Deleuze, G. (1994) *Difference and Repetition*, trans. P. Patton. London: Athlone.

Deleuze, G. (1995) *Negotiations*, trans. M. Joughin. New York: Columbia University Press.

Deleuze, G. (1997) 'Desire and Pleasure', in *Foucault and his Interlocutors*, ed. A.I. Davidson, pp. 183–92. Chicago, IL, and London: University of Chicago Press.

Deleuze, G., and Foucault, M. (1977) 'Intellectuals and Power', in *Language, Counter-Memory, Practice*, ed. M. Foucault, trans. D.F. Bouchard and S. Simon, pp. 205–17. Ithaca, NY: Cornell University Press.

Deleuze, G., and Guattari, F. (1983) *Anti-Oedipus: Capitalism and schizophrenia*, trans. R. Hurley, M. Seem and H.R. Lane. Minneapolis, MN: University of Minnesota Press.

Deleuze, G., and Guattari, F. (1987) *A Thousand Plateaus: Capitalism and schizophrenia*, trans. B. Massumi. Minneapolis, MN: University of Minnesota Press.

Deleuze, G., and Parnet, C. (1987) *Dialogues*, trans. H. Tomlinson and B. Habberjam. New York: Columbia University Press.

Lacan, J. (1982) *Feminine Sexuality: Jacques Lacan and the école freudienne*, trans. J. Rose, ed. J. Mitchell and J. Rose. New York: Pantheon Books; New York and London: Norton.

Nietzsche, F. (1966a) *Beyond Good and Evil: Prelude to a Philosophy of the Future*, trans. W. Kaufmann. New York: Vintage.

Nietzsche, F. (1966b) *Thus Spoke Zarathustra*, trans. W. Kaufmann. New York: Viking.

Nietzsche, F. (1967) *On the Genealogy of Morals*, trans. W. Kaufmann and R.J. Hollingdale. New York: Vintage.

Nietzsche, F. (1986) *Human, All too Human: A book for free spirits*, trans. R.J. Hollingdale. Cambridge: Cambridge University Press.

Patton, P. (ed.) (1996) *Deleuze: A critical reader*. Oxford: Blackwell.

Patton, P. (2000) *Deleuze and the Political*. London: Routledge.

19
jean baudrillard
timothy w. luke

Many who cling to Enlightenment projects, like that of deliberative democracy, individual rights, or even identity politics, dismiss Baudrillard as a minor figure on the contemporary intellectual landscape. These judgements cannot be more wrong. In the hurly-burly of globalisation during the Cold War, very few others saw as clearly as Baudrillard the radical changes that were unfolding along with 24/7 mass media coverage, world wide webs of production and consumption, and the emergence of the multitudinous mass in the circulation of transnational capitalism's goods and services. A postmodern analyst who is not always comfortable with this categorisation, Baudrillard and his project merits as much, if not more serious consideration, as the work of far more conventional thinkers like Francis Fukuyama, Jürgen Habermas, John Rawls or Jean-François Lyotard.

These very different thinkers have all addressed issues of interest to Baudrillard, ranging from History's 'end', individual liberty, collective order, or democratic processes to the nature of postmodern life, technological change, or civic disengagement. Yet their reception often has been much more favourable, because of the more conventional approaches they take toward these topics. Baudrillard arguably says more and has greater insight, but his nihilistic tone and aphoristic style offends prevailing academic tastes. Clearly, Baudrillard must be taken more seriously (Gane, 1991; Kellner, 1989; Luke, 1989). This brief overview of the twists and turns in his work can only begin this task.

As a student of German language and literature, Baudrillard's work unfolds against a background of the figures of Continental philosophy, like Kant, Hegel, Marx, Nietzsche and Heidegger. Yet his own initially semiological project departs from many of their key assumptions, even as he begins to develop a new philosophical anthropology more suited to twenty-first-century realities than those rooted in the 'classics' or 'moderns' of this Continental thought. While he is often associated intellectually with 'postmodern' contemporaries, Baudrillard's idiosyncrasies come to the fore as one reads his quite pronounced classics-doubting, moderns-questioning and postmoderns-disrupting work.

Baudrillard, then, exerts an unusual influence in cultural, political and social theory with his new philosophical anthropology project. This extraordinary undertaking explores 'the end of culture' out on global mediascape, where culture creators and consumers co-produce, through many networks and channels, the new domains of transaesthetic, transpolitical and transeconomic action. Baudrillard's innovative theories on simulation, seduction and hyperreality from the 1970s and 1980s continue to reverberate among many diverse schools of theory today, even though he has never enjoyed an enthusiastic reception among the mainstream social, political or ethical theory communities.

At one level, this can be chalked up to these communities' ties to classic canons of thought. Yet Baudrillard's notoriety, on another level, is rooted in the growing appreciation of how televisual rhetoric, cybernetic imagery and informationalised practices are thoroughly reshaping everyday life (Baudrillard, 1981; 1982; 1983b). Those who only read print texts, look back to the ideals of the bourgeois Enlightenment, or read obscure traditional journals soon go adrift in his work – so they ignore him. This response also follows from most political theorists trained in capacities to look beyond liberal conventions, which keep them from discussing Baudrillard's analysis of the end of the social as well as his views on the mutating spheres of global production and presentation. Nonetheless, no sophisticated theory can fully account for today's new global order without seeing how Baudrillard's notions of simulation and hyperreality are integral to social theory and political practice. Baudrillard has claimed, 'I have nothing to do with postmodernism' (cited in Gane, 1990, p. 331), but one need not take him at his word.

Baudrillard's biography is, in fact, closely intertwined with postmodern conditions as they unfolded during the twentieth century. He was born in Reims, France, in 1929, and his formal education concentrated on language and literature. He gained considerable notoriety in the 1960s for his French translations of German writers, thinkers and playwrights. After working as a German teacher at the *lycée* level, he began moving professionally into sociology during the 1960s by taking a teaching position in this field at Nanterre University. As a follower of debates in anthropology, philosophy and sociology, he was also involved in French solidarity groups with the Cultural Revolution in China, the Situationist movement in France, semiotic critiques of mass consumerism, and radical repudiation of classical Marxist political economy.

Baudrillard's playful enjoyment of controversial debate and provocative criticism in all of his work has continued for over four decades. Moving from a semiological methodology to a philosophical anthropology as his thinking matured, he has been one of the first, the more radical, and most accurate analysts of the information revolution's impact on economy, government and society (Luke, 1989). While other thinkers in Europe or North America, like Jürgen Habermas, Charles Taylor or John Rawls, continued to flog more conventional concepts from the Enlightenment in a struggle to explain the implosion of modernity, Baudrillard's incisive analyses of this moment in history continue to be far more prescient, powerful and productive. Consequently, his thought must be confronted by anyone intent upon knowing what is happening at the dawn of the twenty-first century.

information society, simulation and hyperreality

In many ways, Baudrillard's critiques of everyday cultural politics are both complex and confusing. Yet in a sense he essentially spins through the implications of a familiar paradox: does what is real imitate signs of reality, or do signs of reality imitate what is real? How one begins to decode these themes in Baudrillard leads, in turn, to many other insights and paradoxes.

During the late twentieth century, Baudrillard argues that advanced capitalist society experienced implosive reversals in the circulation of power between the masses and organised institutions. As he claims, 'capital only had to produce goods; consumption ran by itself. Today it is necessary to produce consumers, to produce demand, and this production is infinitely more costly than that of goods' (Baudrillard, 1983a, p. 27). As individual desires, however, are now rendered abstractly into prepackaged needs that serve as productive forces, the social lifeworld devolves into fluid aggregates of atomised individuals, whose roles are to mediate the packaged meaning of their desires in the corporate marketplace. The traditional forms of attaining both individuality and 'the social' itself both collapse under these conditions. Baudrillard concludes that individual subjects 'are only episodic conductors of meaning, for in the main, and profoundly, we *form a mass*, living most of the time in panic or haphazardly, above and beyond any meaning' (Baudrillard, 1983a, p. 11).

Today's posthistorical social mass, at the same time, is neither a subject nor an object. It bears no relation to any historical social referent – a class, a nation, a folk or the proletariat. Instead, it is often no more than a statistical entity whose main traces appear in market analyses, social surveys or opinion polls. The silent majorities of the masses are perhaps no longer representable in realist political terms or concretely identifiable in realistic social terms. The ordinarily assumed 'ontological givens' taken for granted by epistemic realism essentially evaporate, according to Baudrillard, in the black holes of this cyberspace. The complex codes of media in the global market set the outer boundaries of the social mass 'at the point of convergence of all the media waves which depict it' (Baudrillard, 1983a, p. 30). Thus the layers of contemporary existence essentially become a complex simulation of reality, designed specifically to sustain the fragile cycles of political, economic and cultural reproduction, in which signs of the real take the place of reality itself.

Modernity itself transmutates with the development of this type of advanced capitalist exchange as it becomes more entwined within the informational modes of production (Luke, 1989, pp. 2–16). A new reality logic based upon simulation rather than representation constitutes the dominant organising principle of this new era. Therefore, in Baudrillard's vision of today's new world order, 'McLuhan's formula, *the medium is the message*', appropriately is 'the key formula of the era of simulation (the medium is the message – the sender is the receiver – the circularity of all polls – the end of panoptic and perspectival space – such is the alpha and omega of *our* modernity') (Baudrillard, 1983a, p. 101). Yet if the masses no longer act as traditional historical subjects in their new posthistorical habitat, then what happens to their accustomed cultural context, namely, the modern nation-state, industrial economy, liberal democracy and Enlightenment culture?

Baudrillard thought he discovered the lever required to move toward cultural revolution by developing 'a political economy of the sign'. 'Only such a critique', he claims, 'can analyze how at the very heart of the economic mode of domination reinvents (or reproduces) the logic and the strategy of signs, of castes, of segregation, and of discrimination; how it reinstates the feudal logic of personal relations or even that of the gift exchange and of reciprocity, or of agonistic exchange – in order simultaneously to thwart and crown the "modern" socio-economic logic of class' (Baudrillard, 1981, p. 38).

In the last analysis, Baudrillard postulates that what is accepted as 'society' by agents who are regarded as individuals now runs on 'a logic of simulation which has nothing to do with a logic of facts and an order of reasons' (Baudrillard, 1988c, p. 175). This claim seconds Fredric Jameson's demand to look at the rare, the unusual, and interesting, 'for shifts and irrevocable changes in the *representation* of things and of the way they change' (Jameson, 1991, p. ix). So, Baudrillard asks, why not look at Disneyland for answers? The energy of Disneyland, as its self-defined 'imagineers' proclaim, rests in the fusion of its symbolic imaginaries with sophisticated material design and complex process engineering. As Baudrillard notes, 'simulation is characterized by a *precession of the model*, of all models around the merest fact – models come first, and the orbital (like the bomb) circulation constitutes the genuine magnetic field of events' (Baudrillard, 1983b, p. 32). The model is the medium, and it becomes the message. As Baudrillard suggests, the continuously felt effects of Disney imagineering arise from 'concealing that reality no more exists outside than inside the bounds of the artificial perimeter' (Baudrillard, 1983b, p. 26). In his account, Disneyland 'the fantasy' exists to induce belief that America, which is, in fact, 'the hyperreality', is *real*.

Disneyland is there to conceal the fact that it is the 'real' country, all of 'real' America, which *is* Disneyland (just as prisons are there to conceal the fact that it is the social in its entirety, in its banal omnipresence, which is carceral). Disneyland is presented as imaginary in order to make us believe that the rest is real, when in fact all of Lost Angeles and the America surrounding it are no longer real, but of the order of the hyperreal and of simulation. It is no longer a question of a false representation of reality (ideology), but of concealing the fact that the real is no longer real, and thus of saving the reality principle. (Baudrillard, 1983b, p. 25)

Therefore, Disneyland – the semiotic engine – essentially underpins the prevailing models of international cultural simulation where the *cultural* and the *economic* 'collapse back into each other and say the same thing' (Jameson, 1991, p. xxi). When all is said and done in contemporary culture, 'the Disneyland imaginary is neither true nor false; it is a deterrence machine set up in order to rejuvenate in reverse the fiction of the real' (Baudrillard, 1983b, p. 25).

Baudrillard also maintains that the means of information in today's global transnational economy unhinge traditional metaphorical relations, because the operative semiotic principles of this informational order are those of simulation rather than pre-industrial counterfeit or industrial mechanical reproduction. Abstractions can no longer be seen as 'the maps', 'the doubles', 'the mirrors' or 'the concepts' of any terrain metaphorically regarded as 'the real'. On the contrary, all abstract frames of the real effectively function only as simulations. For Baudrillard, 'simulation is no longer that of a territory, a referential being or a substance. It is the generation by models of a real without origin or a reality: a hyperreal. The territory no longer precedes the map, nor survives it. Henceforth, it is the map that precedes the territory – PRECESSION OF SIMULACRA – it is the map that engenders the territory ...' (Baudrillard, 1983b, p. 25). In this hyperspace, something very important has disappeared, namely, what always was the ineluctable non-identity of map and terrain. Therefore, a provisional hyperontology of sorts, which Baudrillard is more than willing to provide, must now define and describe what now 'is' beyond epistemic realism's perspectival space and neutral time.

To comprehend hyperreality, Baudrillard argues, one must rethink everything one knows:

No more mirror of being and appearances, of the real and its concept. No more imaginary coextensity: rather, genetic miniaturization is the dimension of simulation. The real is produced from miniaturized units, from matrices, memory banks and command models – and with these it can be reproduced an infinite number of times. It no longer has to be rational, since it is no longer measured against some ideal or negative instance. It is nothing more than operational. In fact, since it is no longer enveloped by an imaginary, it is no longer real at all. It is a hyperreal, the product of an irradiating synthesis of combinatory models in a hyperspace without atmosphere. (Baudrillard, 1983b, p. 3)

The order of simulation out of hyperreality rises from an elimination of representational differences between true and false, concept and object, real and representation, much like the unrelenting flow of 24-hour television headline news which creates unstable stylised narratives to report 'what is true' by merging videotaped reality and cable-feed representation. Amidst this electronic haze, for example, liberal democracy becomes a state in which viewers as voters mull over their votes by hearing other voters speculate about candidates' 'electability' on TV with voting analysts addressing voters as viewers, who only *might* vote, but will always speculate freely about how others might vote.

Simulation arises from these absences and negations. Eliminating 'the real' or 'the true' leads to emulating their appearances as ontological givens. Actually, as Baudrillard suggests:

[The] age of simulation thus begins with a liquidation of all referentials – worse: by their artificial resurrection in systems of signs, a more ductile material than meaning in that it lends itself to all systems of equivalence, all binary oppositions, and all combinatory algebra. It is no longer a question of imitation, nor of reduplication, nor even of parody. It is rather a question of substituting signs of the real for the real itself, that is, an operation to deter every real process by its operational double, a metastable, programmatic, perfect descriptive machine which provides all the signs of the real and short-circuits all its vicissitudes ... A hyperreal therefore is sheltered from the real and the imaginary, leaving room only for the orbital recurrent of models and the simulated generation of difference. (Baudrillard, 1983b, p. 4)

While systems of representation endeavour to appropriate simulation as false representation, the dynamics of simulation turn any and all representations into simulacra, reducing the sign to a free radical capable of bonding anywhere in any exchange. These shifts in the sign constitute the critical juncture in maintaining the 'hyperreal' collective order that transnational capitalism has brought to its many customers and clients today. Basically, Baudrillard claims:

When the real is no longer what is used to be, nostalgia assumes its full meaning. There is a proliferation of myths of origin and signs of reality; of second-hand truth, objectivity and authenticity. There is an escalation of the true, of the lived experience; a resurrection of the figurative when the object and substance have disappeared and there is a panic-stricken production of the real and the referential, above and parallel to the panic of material production: this is how simulation appears in the phase that concerns us – a strategy of the real, neo-real and hyperreal whose universal double is a strategy of deterrence. (Baudrillard, 1983b, p. 55)

The practical mediations of generating hyperreality, as Baudrillard appraises it, are the electronic media knitting together the posthistorical flows of informational societies.

More traditional constructions of causality, perspective and reasoning are undercut completely by electronic means of information, which often efface the difference between cause and effect, ends and means, subject and object, active and passive. Without these differences, the rationality of classical epistemic realism is left unhinged. Baudrillard observes, 'we must think of the media as if they were, in outer orbit, a sort of genetic code which controls the mutation of the real into the hyperreal, just as the other, micro-molecular code controls the passage of the signal from a representative sphere of meaning to the genetic sphere of the programmed signal' (Baudrillard, 1983b, p. 33). Simulation exceeds the distinctions of space and time, sender and receiver, medium and message, expression and content as the world's complex webs of electronic media generate unbound(ed)aries of new hyperspaces with little sense of place.

making the object testify

Although Baudrillard's work on simulation, hyperreality and the obscene rarely address it, the Internet plainly constitutes a development that is, ironically, cause and effect, map and territory, material and hyperreal. Its creation marks a peculiar moment in time, whose communicative necessities shaped an artifact with multiple potentialities. Once the changing terrain of Cold War geopolitics lessened the importance of the Internet's original purposes, those capabilities became immensely more useful in the fast-changing flows of the post-Cold War era. A device designed in the 1960s to actuate reliable communications in thermonuclear attack environments became in the 1990s a utility to enable cheap, rapid and multimedia communication environments potentially or eventually, for anyone anytime anywhere. Larger changes in the global economy, however, allowed such communicative capabilities to become so accessible to the multitudes; a materialised hyperreality opened to anyone in a new 24/7 timeframe and practically to almost all places with connectivity. The internet, like mass advertising, television or consumer goods, is merely another concrete expression of those globalising transformations, and not the ultimate cause of them in all of their complexity.

Much bigger questions need to be asked, and Baudrillard asks them. Is the apparent disconnection of political analysis from political reality a sign of the nation-state's underlying disintegration, fragmentation or underdevelopment? With little following in the halls of government, and left to themselves to play out methodological fantasies, most social scientists produce work that illustrates how brittle, compromised and defunct the state has become in an era of global neoliberalism. If 'the end of the social' has much intellectual cladding at all, then economics has been its constant conceptual covering. The misbegotten and misadministrated attempt to emulate economics in many of the social sciences only reveals the state of laggards mimicking the leading force.

Older notions of fixed, stable, enduring national publics inside stable states and cohesive societies have broken down, if they even ever prevailed outside a few privileged points of imperial power. Aggregating authority in state governments, allocating material wealth inside and between territorial regimes, articulating identities as national imaginaries are projects of the seventeenth, eighteenth and twentieth centuries, which, by and large, went awry in the twentieth century. Political analysts continue to drive forward staring into the rearview mirror, but too many of their concepts and conclusions are quaint anachronisms with no purchase outside the small conversations carried on through literatures few read or at meetings that fewer attend or in departments that few support. Here, as Baudrillard suggests:

> the social which, in its time, was a fine idea, has assumed concrete form, has substituted itself for the political and it is now itself swallowed up by the cultural. What an unhappy fate the book has met with – and sociology with it! The path Bourdieu took – that of a kind of activist regression in the name of the wretched, is perhaps the only one for sociology if it is to outlive its time ... How can you go on doing your own thing in your own little discipline as though nothing had happened. (Baudrillard, 2004, p. 56)

Baudrillard's willingness to see power flowing through signs in play everywhere and anywhere gives his critical thought both an unusual range and a frustrating limit. Like Lévi-Strauss, Debord, Barthes, Bataille, Kristeva and Lefebvre before him, Baudrillard's early work approaches the symbolic and mythic dimensions of society as a realm constructed and maintained by the play of capital and power. He approaches industrial objects or cultural products as indicators of larger social tensions, as he foreshadowed in early works on the sociology of objects and the systems of mass consumption, *The System of Objects* (1997b) and *The Consumer Society* (1998b). Baudrillard claims in *For a Critique of the Political Economy of the Sign* (1981), consumer goods with all of their objective shapes, semiotic syntax, and collective rhetoric 'refer to social objectives and to a social logic. They speak to us not so much of the user and of technical practices, as of social pretension and resignation, of social mobility and inertia, of acculturation and enculturation, of stratification and of social classification' (Baudrillard, 1981, p. 38). Thus consumer goods and services consumers, especially as they intertwine with consumers in social, political and economic exchange, provide the indicators of his claims about the political economy of the sign, the culture of consumption and the dominance of the obscene. Political theorists rarely probe such bodies of evidence, but objects as such need to be interrogated. Indeed, they are vital for Baudrillard to advance his theoretical critiques.

In these earlier works, Baudrillard maintained his stance as a revolutionary critic intent upon directing theory against society in some project of radical resistance. After his *Symbolic Exchange and Death* (1998a), however, he adopts a new persona devoted to divining the mysteries of the provocative new metaphysics that he discovers in ecstatic communication. Seeing that his previous attempts 'to grasp objects as a system already went a little way towards disrupting the traditional view of things', his most recent work looks at 'object-passions' or 'object-situations' which 'is ultimately a question of metaphysics' (Baudrillard, 1990a, p. 185). This essentialist turn, however, is extremely problematic inasmuch as he becomes bogged down in his ritually reading reality through a panoply of binary oppositions that end up favouring image over substance, seduction against production, obscene before scene.

On the one hand, Baudrillard actually sees himself appraising object-passions in terms of their 'purity', 'passions' and 'possibilities'. Hence, he denies being 'a philosopher, in the sense of being interested in arguments or terminology' (1990d, p. 20) in order to be a medium of/for the object. In this mode, Baudrillard devotes himself to 'the object, the pure object, the pure event, something no longer with an origin or end, to which the subject would like to attribute an origin and an end even though it has none, and which today perhaps begins to give account of itself. Perhaps there is now the possibility that the object will say something to us, but above all the possibility that it will avenge itself' (Baudrillard, 1990d, p. 18). By moving to this new stance, Baudrillard forsakes any prospect of revolutionary critique and embraces the mission of a metaphysician disclosing the mysteries of what he sees as truly 'what is' the substance of reality.

Regrettably, however, as Kellner notes, these readings seem to be projections of his own subjective vision over objective situations. The impasse that Baudrillard works himself into here is indeed a fatal turn for his stance as a social theorist:

Desiring to seduce and to be seduced, he projects seduction onto the being of objects. Desiring sovereignty, he projects sovereignty onto objects. Desiring revenge, he projects revenge onto objects. Supremely ironic, Baudrillard projects objective irony onto objects. Desiring to become a destiny and fatality himself – recall Nietzsche for the psychological roots of this peculiar lust – he ascribes destiny and fatality to objects, and conjures up a fatal universe. Increasingly indifferent to the fate of society and his fellow human beings, Baudrillard ascribes indifference to that supreme object of objects, the masses. Himself impatient, he ascribes impatience to the masses and to the object world. Losing critical energy and growing apathetic himself, he ascribes apathy and inertia to the universe. (Kellner, 1989, p. 180)

The seductions of the transaesthetic, transsexual, transpolitical, transeconomic (ob)scene, then, are mostly metaphysical. Unable to illustrate how such tendencies operate in reality, Baudrillard goes one better in hyperreality by ontologising them into metaphysical fatality that marks the end of culture.

Once captured within the self-replicating cycles of capital and expertise, which sustain what is still labelled liberal democratic capitalism despite its many illiberal, despotic and collectivist qualities, the mass of individuals essentially conforms to innumerable cross-cutting fields of normalisation. As Baudrillard observes:

> Individuals, such as they are, are becoming exactly what they are. With no transcendence and no image, they pursue their lives like a function that is useless in respect to another world, irrelevant even in their own eyes. And they do so all the better for the fact that there is no other possibility. No instance, no essence, no personal substance worthy of singular expression. They have sacrificed their lives to their functional existences. They coincide with the exact numerical calculation of their lives and their performances. (2004, p. 108)

Granted the truth of Baudrillard's observations, the modernist classics of both Anglo-American and Continental political thought beg some very big questions.

That is, the citizen is rarely free as an economic, political or cultural agent. Instead, he or she remains trapped within veils of expertise and ownership enshrouding the decision-making in this regime; and, once trapped, individuals cope with entrapment by merging with 'the mass' and its many polydimensional functionalities. Without any effective mechanisms for removing, or even at times, rending these veils, individuals can only submit to what are the imperatives of their functional existences. Existential functionality, however, can have registers other than those constructed by corporate or state blocs of professional-technical experts, and here is where Baudrillard finds a kind of freedom in transpolitical objects.

Most social movements, irrespective of claims made by their more vocal enthusiasts, are not much of a resistance. Moreover, in a world in which virtually everything is integrated into the circuits of capitalist reproduction, one must be, like Baudrillard, 'resistant to the idea of resistance, since it belongs to the world of critical, rebellious, subversive thought' – and especially for Baudrillard, these classic and modern constructs are 'all rather outdated' (2004, p. 71).

Ordering what is called citizenship around consumption – either in markets as 'consumers' or within bureaucracies as 'clients' – reduces its mission to another domain of imperatives which Baudrillard has envisioned as 'a generalized system of exchange and production of coded values where, in spite of themselves, all consumers are involved with all others' (1998b, p. 78). Virtually any instance of criticism or rebellion in many ways is another aspect of '*the system of needs*' that is, has been, and will be little more than '*the product of the system of production*' (Baudrillard, 1998b, p. 74). The object world of global exchange merely rearticulates beyond individual needs, enjoyment or desire newer more flexible and fungible functionalities for the consumer society's 'machine/productive force, a technical system radically different from the traditional tool' as well as 'a rational system of investment and circulation, radically different from "wealth" and from earlier modes of exchange' (Baudrillard, 1998b, p. 75).

The technified fun, pleasure or thrill of any experience only underscores how fully consumption is 'now something which is forced upon us, something institutionalized, not as a right or a pleasure, but as the *duty* of the citizen' (Baudrillard, 1998b, p. 80). Many versions of technological subjectivity can be fun-filled, pleasure-serving or thrill-based; yet it is unclear how any acts of citizenship or production in this technified register of action rises beyond the imperatives of consumerism. Here, as Baudrillard observes, the global economy's participants begin to match the profiles of what he tagged 'consumerist man' in 1970. Each of the world's buyers and sellers, builders and users or movers and shakers discover their subjectivity, even if it is only fun-filled leisure '*as an obligation*':

[H]e ['consumerist man'] sees himself as *an enjoyment and satisfaction* business. He sees it as his duty to be happy, loving, adulating/adulated, charming/ charmed, participative, euphoric and dynamic. This is the principle of maximizing existence by multiplying contacts and relationships, by intense use of signs and objects, by systematic exploitation of all the potentialities of enjoyment. (Baudrillard, 1998b, p. 80)

While the mass has many resistant qualities, it hardly is a classic emancipatory resistance with tremendous potential for transformative change.

turning to transpolitics

More recently, Baudrillard has bracketed the entire project of criticism, and purposely blended together politics, exchange, and cultural on the broadbands of what he labels the transpolitical that marks today's 'state of utter confusion' (Baudrillard, 1993, pp. 3–13). While there continue to be sign-saturated systems of production, spinning on virally, radiantly, fractally in the continually recycling of past and present styles, there are no axiomatic grounds for articulating anything like foundational theories, tied to traditional aesthetics, ethics or politics.

At this juncture, Baudrillard posits that the revolution once dreamed about by all of the movements of the 1960s has happened, but it did not turn out as expected. It morphs into the fatal strategies of the transpolitical (Baudrillard, 1988a; 1990b; 2004). Everything everywhere is being liberated 'so that it can enter a state of pure circulation, so that it can go into orbit. With the benefit of a little hindsight, we may say that the unavoidable goal of all liberation is to foster and provision circulatory networks' (Baudrillard, 1993, p. 4). With this general liberation, however, there is a wild proliferation of things and actions that overwhelms traditional logics of value, once described by Baudrillard (1981) as the natural, commodity, and structural stages, with the fractal stage. Here and now:

> there is no point of reference at all, and value radiates in all directions, occupying all interstices, without reference to anything whatsoever, by virtue of sure contiguity. At the fractal stage, there is no longer any equivalence, whether natural or general. Properly speaking there is now no law of value, merely a sort of *epidemic of value*, a sort of general metastasis of value, a haphazard proliferation and dispersion of value. (Baudrillard, 1993, p. 5)

Caught in these webs of excess signification, one also sees the eclipse of appearances in realist scenes by disappearances, obscenity, hyperrealism. When plenitude brings forth the void, for Baudrillard, 'that's the obscene' (Baudrillard, 1990d, p. 185). In the realm of the transaesthetic, the transpolitical, the transeconomic, the totality of reality washes out as a pornographic hyperreality that boils down to 'the obscenity of everything tirelessly filmed, filtered, revised and corrected under the wide angle of the social, morality, and information' (Baudrillard, 1990d, p. 189). Although Baudrillard gets carried away with his paradoxes, often claiming obscenity is more visible than the visible without exactly explaining how this might work, he also sees obscenity deriving from too much meaning, overexposure, or saturation (Baudrillard, 2000; 2001; 2002b).

For culture and politics, the obscene marks the exhausted end of anything once recognisable as culture or politics. When weighed in against his metaphysical reading of the present, very little survives intact. Baudrillard, in fact, becomes quite succinct about this side of the transpolitics or transaesthetics. First, 'when everything is political, it is the end of politics as destiny, and the beginning of politics as culture, and the immediate destitution of this political culture' (Baudrillard, 1990d, p. 188). Second, 'when everything becomes cultural, it is the end of culture as destiny, and the beginning of culture as politics, and the immediate destitution of this cultural politics' (Baudrillard, 1990d, p. 188). Finally, he contends, 'and so it goes for the social, history, the economy, and sex' (Baudrillard, 1990d, p. 188).

This alleged fractalisation of everything brings to mind a new microphysics in Baudrillard, but, in fact, it trumps ordinary existence and consciousness with a new metaphysics of disappearance (Levin, 1996). Now, as Baudrillard surveys the world:

> it is impossible to make estimations between beautiful and ugly, true and false, or good and evil, as it is simultaneously to calculate a particle's speed and position. Good is no longer the opposite of evil, nothing can now be plotted on a graph or analysed in terms of abscissas and ordinates. Just as each particle follows its own trajectory, each value or fragment of value shines for a moment in the heavens of simulation, then disappears into the void along a crooked path that only rarely happens to intersect with other such paths. This is the pattern of the fractal – and hence the current pattern of our culture. (Baudrillard, 1993, pp. 6–7)

Given this position, it is tough to take up classic or modern commitments to emancipatory moralistic discourses of interpreting good and evil, beauty and ugliness, truth or falsity, virtue and vice. Baudrillard instead sees a strange inertia enveloping everything even as everything can no longer be either understood or judged. Somehow, in this purported vacuum of calculation, he asserts that fractalisation is both stable and efficient. That is,

> when things, signs or actions are freed from their respective ideas, concepts, essences, values, points of reference, origins and aims, they embark upon an endless process of self-reproduction. Yet things continue to function long after their ideas have disappeared, and they do so in total indifference to their own content. The paradoxical fact is that they function even better under these circumstances. (Baudrillard, 1993, pp. 6–7)

At the end of the day, the metaphysical posture that Baudrillard adopts leaves one, ironically, with a hard call of either just taking or leaving his claims as so much pataphysical manoeuvring, that is, an absurdist parody of modern science (Baudrillard, 2002b; 2003b). Yet in doing so, one is also often left feeling lost in his more aphoristic later writings. Baudrillard claims that he always worked from this pataphysical point, even as a student, because it was 'a kind of very powerful cultural counter-transference' (2004, p. 4). By substituting a shocking epigram for engaging analysis, Baudrillard consciously shifts away from re-evaluating the texture of reality with a morally outraged engagement of critical negativity.

Although this was the 'pious vow' of the Enlightenment still embraced by too many contemporary intellectuals in Baudrillard's view, he sees himself going beyond this commitment, forging a new kind of theory in which the theorising evaluator essentially is, or becomes, the event. That is,

> It is not enough for theory to describe and analyse, it must itself be an event in the universe it describes. In order to do this theory must partake of and

become the acceleration of this logic. It must tear itself from all referents
and take pride only in the future. Theory must operate on time at the cost
of a deliberate distortion of present reality. (Baudrillard, 1988a, p. 99)

For Baudrillard, social theorising turns into Baudrillard's diaries, Baudrillard
driving across America, Baudrillard's interviews, or Baudrillard cruising
academic conferences to discover the right kind of theoretical event venues
(Baudrillard, 1988b; 1990c; 1996b; 2000). Here, Baudrillard is consciously
ejecting projects of 'systematic totality' as he moves from work that 'presents
things in a mode that's still theoretical' to new styles of 'aphoristic writing.
In the aphorism, the fragment, there is a desire to sum things down as much
as possible' (Baudrillard, 2004, p. 22).

With this new aphoristic style, Baudrillard presents theory with different
goals:

> the function of theory is certainly not to reconcile it, but on the contrary,
> to seduce, to wrest things from their condition, to force them into an over-
> existence which is incompatible with that of the real ... it must become
> simulation if it speaks of about simulation, and deploy the same strategy
> as its object. If it speaks about seduction, theory must become seducer, and
> deploy the same stratagems. If it no longer aspires to a discourse of truth,
> theory must assume the form of a world from which truth has withdrawn.
> (1988a, p. 99)

Baudrillard takes this stance, because he believes that theory is always 'destined
to be diverted, deviated, and manipulated' (1988a, p. 63). Since he believes
it would be better for theory to divert itself, than to be diverted from itself,
he retorts that all theory producers and consumers must heed a new calling:
'Let us be Stoics'. That is,

> If the world is fatal, let us be more fatal than it. If it is indifferent, let us be
> more indifferent. We must conquer the world and seduce it through an
> indifference that is at least equal to the world's. (Baudrillard, 1988a, p. 98)

Unfortunately, by refusing to ground his arguments in more concrete forms
of social analysis, as he once did in his early works on the anthropology of
consumption or the political economy of the sign, Baudrillard diminishes the
overall credibility of this style of social theorising in the eyes of many critics.

This attitude is captured well by Ritzer's 1998 introduction to Baudrillard's
The Consumer Society. Suggesting that Baudrillard is a pivotal theorist, Ritzer
(1998, p. 20) at the same time chides him on his scholarly practices:

> This early work bears none of the arrogant disregard for academic canons
> that characterizes his most recent work. In *The Consumer Society* Baudrillard

is clearly working hard at the academic craft. He is reading the relevant literature, adopting its useful insights, critiquing its weaknesses and using all of it, as well as a sensitive eye towards the social world, to develop his theoretical ideas. While *The Consumer Society* is not nearly as important, at least theoretically, as say *Symbolic Exchange and Death*, it is far better and far more important than works like *Cool Memories* (1980–5/1990) or *America* (1988/1989).

Nevertheless, Baudrillard does not respond to dismissals by critics like Ritzer, because he will also not reconcile himself to continuing the naive epistemic realism deployed in conventional social science analysis. Instead, he speculates that pataphysics may provide the only 'way out', because 'pataphysics is both a science of imaginary solutions and a myth of imaginary solutions. It's the imaginary solution that the current state of affairs might be said to constitute' (Baudrillard, 2004, p. 5).

Baudrillard steers away from classical or modernist genres of social theorising, because 'it is here that language and theory alter their meaning. Instead of acting as a mode of production, they act as a mode of disappearance ... This enigmatic game is no longer that of analysis; it seeks to preserve this enigma of the object through the enigma of discourse' (1988a, p. 97). For Baudrillard, his aphoristic fragments are a gamble that challenges 'reality' rather than continuing shopworn conceptual conventions with it. That is, 'the fragment is a wager, not a continuous management of things. You have to gamble, you have to up the stakes' (Baudrillard, 2004, p. 41).

Even in his apparently extreme moments, as in *The Gulf War Did Not Take Place* or *Symbolic Exchange and Death*, Baudrillard is neither denying troops were deployed, armies destroyed, or military actions faked in the Kuwait war nor asserting that cities are now sublated. Instead he wants to disclose how hyperreal war-gaming, simulation, standoff weaponry or electronic imaging have looped into actual combat as the reality of killing and the representations of death are blurred in clips of TV-guided laser bombs obliterating buildings or infrared cameras documenting infantry casualties in primetime news footage of midnight skirmishes. Likewise, in asking why people agglomerate in New York 'to live', he sees the recursive electric systematicity of technostructures straining to survive amidst 'the final fling of baroque verticality, this centrifugal excentricity' (1998a, p. 22). In what he calls 'autistic performance', hyperrealities of distinguished urbanity loop into the realities of extinguished urbanism as the scripts and packages of consumer society. The annual ritual of the New York marathon typifies this 'fetishistic performance, of the mania for an empty victory, the joy engineered by a feat is of no consequence' (1988a, p. 20).

The loss of a profound transcendent purpose or a collective social telos marks the postmodern moment spinning on endlessly past the goals of modernist progress. With hyperreal simulation suffusing the programmed performativity of life, Baudrillard sees subversion seeping into people's souls:

> When they are ordered to get the maximum efficiency and pleasure out of themselves, they remain out of sorts and live a split existence. In this strange world, where everything is potentially available (the body, sex, space, money, pleasure) to be taken or rejected *en bloc*, everything is there; nothing has disappeared physically, but everything has disappeared metaphysically ... Individuals, such as they are, are becoming exactly what they are. With no transcendence and no image, they pursue lives like a function that is useless in respect to another world, irrelevant even in their own eyes. (Baudrillard, 2004, p. 108)

Reality is preprocessed, pretested, and preprogrammed in far too many domains of being, so individuals are left to 'carrying out any kind of program that produces the same sense of futility that comes from doing anything merely to prove to yourself that you can do it' (1988a, p. 21). This stance does not answer all of Ritzer's protests, but it shows where Baudrillard stands when he argues what are less classical theoretical and more extreme postmodern positions.

If one accepts Baudrillard's assessment, there is little that can be said for or about culture, economy or politics as points for progressive intervention. Utopian moments or avenues for liberation, in Baudrillard's vision, completely dissolve away in the diverting, alluring flux of sign flows. Thus producers and consumers, decision-makers and citizens, artists and audiences are all either duped entirely by the processes of mediated production or are caught up as duplicitous co-conspirators in the end of the real – deflating forever rhetorics of *avant garde* engagement. Perhaps in the end, as Stearns and Chaloupka (1992, p. 4) maintain, 'Baudrillard can never be confirmed. This is his seduction.' While this twist adds to his attraction, it also sparks many readers' befuddled distraction. If one accepts his notions of representation in hyperreality, there is little to do but become indifferent as a fatal strategy on the obscene. If one strategises in this manner, moreover, what can be written critically, said reliably, or done effectively about 'the present'? Instead of engaging with his projects as insightful criticism, most discussions of Baudrillard only quibble over his odd terminology or ridicule out-and-out the hyperbole behind so many of his claims, which then allegedly is reason enough for completely dismissing him.

It is impossible in this brief analysis to do much more than introduce Baudrillard to those unfamiliar with his extraordinary new philosophical anthropology – no matter how strange his love for odd wisdom or unusual his sense of humanity is – as well as his unrelenting efforts to account for how new media and information technologies are reshaping everyday life. Like Debord, he advances a vision of societies rooted in spectacle, consumption and new collectives of identity, but he repudiates orthodox Marxism, state socialism and other twentieth-century resistances that Debord finds difficult to release. Like Lyotard, he lays out another vision of modernity and its aftermath, but feels much less compelled to bring modern values, practices and attitudes into the picture. And, like Guattari, he articulates an alternative critique of capitalism, which releases the assumptions of bourgeois and proletarian political economy, but does not see the capitalist order crumbling amidst new challenges from below or without. What is, still is, and its obscure transpolitical imperatives create more than enough for critics to criticise as they philosophise about how the world is changing.

As his reputation has grown, Baudrillard has in many ways become more hyperreal in his own writing and work. Beginning with *America*, his books, especially in their English translations published and marketed by Verso, appear in a unique size with mass media-anchored cover art, special text block layouts, and wide margins. Baudrillard's words and voice are made by the print artefact to seem more extraordinary, insightful and special than those of many other human beings via the commodification of his thought through print. This turn in representing his work has also made him seem more superficial, ephemeral or ignorable to some, because the image seems to swamp ideas. For others, there is an honest, if perhaps troubling, consistency in such communicative performances to the degree that he acknowledges, accepts and accelerates the displacement of what is mentally mapped by the conceptual aesthetics of the map and mappers themselves. Thus, when one contrasts his earlier critical works, like *The System of Objects* or *The Mirror of Production* to his more recent compilations of conceptualisation, like *America*, *The Perfect Crime* or *Cool Memories I*, *Cool Memories II*, *Cool Memories III*, and *Cool Memories IV*, there is a shift in authorial voice, tone and representation. As we all swirl away further into the mediascapes of hyperreality, Baudrillard's print presence plainly pushes his own basic theses with both its substance and form, hype and hypotheses, image and text.

Baudrillard's infatuation with excess often seems to many as much more than excessive, but this reaction misses the insights that a theoretical commitment to excess can reveal. If the presumption of excess allows the analysts and analysands to see how it shapes social relations, collective purposes and ordinary subjectivity, then one ought not to shrink from such difficult, but nonetheless quite concrete, realities (Baudrillard, 2001; 2002a).

These ideas are only a few of the contributions that Baudrillard brings to tables of theoretical analysis today. Plainly, Baudrillard's writings are challenging; and, at times, style can obscure what he is seeking to say. His disregard for the usual progressive pieties of secular scientific and technological reasoning force many to ignore him. And, those that do not still tend to dismiss him and his work as misdirected, misbegotten or even miscreant examples of a postmodernist critique that lacks a *gravitas* or continuity with the canon, which more conventional voices cast as a burden that everyone must to carry. Here Baudrillard's spare and singular vision of posthuman living, the postnational constellation, political liberty, the inhuman or postmodern conditions discloses much more than the sparse glimpses of change thrown forth in the more voluminous writings of Fukuyama, Habermas, Rawls or Lyotard.

further reading

The intellectual backdrop to Baudrillard's work is surveyed in Jameson (1991). For an introductory selection of Baudrillard's writings, see Baudrillard (1988c). Major studies are Kellner (1989), Gane (1991), Stearns and Chaloupka (1992) and Levin (1996).

references

Baudrillard, J. (1981) *For a Critique of the Political Economy of the Sign*. St Louis, MO: Telos Press.

Baudrillard, J. (1982) 'The Beaubourg Effect: Implosion and deterrence', *October* 20 (spring): 3–13.

Baudrillard, J. (1983a) *In the Shadow of the Silent Majorities*. New York: Semiotext(e).

Baudrillard, J. (1983b) *Simulations*. New York: Semiotext(e).

Baudrillard, J. (1988a) *The Ecstasy of Communication*. New York: Semiotext(e).

Baudrillard, J. (1988b) *America*. London: Verso.

Baudrillard, J. (1988c) *Selected Writings*, ed. M. Poster. Stanford, CA: Stanford University Press.

Baudrillard, J. (1990a) *Seduction*. New York: St Martin's Press.

Baudrillard, J. (1990b) *Fatal Strategies*. New York: Semiotext(e).

Baudrillard, J. (1990c) *Cool Memories*. London: Verso.

Baudrillard, J. (1990d) *Revenge of the Crystal: Selected writings on the modern object and its destiny, 1968–1983*. London: Pluto Press.

Baudrillard, J. (1993) *The Transparency of Evil*. London: Verso.

Baudrillard, J. (1995) *The Gulf War Did Not Take Place*. Bloomington, IN: Indiana University Press.

Baudrillard, J. (1996a) *The Perfect Crime*. New York: Verso.

Baudrillard, J. (1996b) *Cool Memories II*. Durham, NC: Duke University Press.

Baudrillard, J. (1997a) *Fragments: Cool Memories III, 1990–1995*. London: Verso.

Baudrillard, J. (1997b) *The System of Objects*. London: Verso.

Baudrillard, J. (1998a) *Symbolic Exchange and Death*. London: Sage.

Baudrillard, J. (1998b) *The Consumer Society: Myths and structures*. London: Sage.

Baudrillard, J. (2000) *The Vital Illusion*. New York: Columbia University Press.

Baudrillard, J. (2001) *The Impossible Exchange*. London: Verso.

Baudrillard, J. (2002a) *The Spirit of Terrorism*. London: Verso.

Baudrillard, J. (2002b) *Screened Out*. London: Verso.

Baudrillard, J. (2003a) *Cool Memories IV, 1995–2000*. London: Verso.

Baudrillard, J. (2003b) *Passwords*. London: Verso.

Baudrillard, J. (2004) *Fragments: Conversations with François L'Yvonnet*. London: Routledge.

Gane, M. (1990) 'Ironies of Postmodernism: Fate of Baudrillard's fatalism', *Economy and Society* 19: 314–31.

Gane, M. (1991) *Baudrillard: Critical and fatal theory*. Routledge: London.

Jameson, F. (1991) *Postmodernism, or the Cultural Logic of Late Capitalism.* Durham, NC: Duke University Press.

Kellner, D. (1989) *Jean Baudrillard: From Marxism to postmodernism and beyond.* Cambridge: Polity Press.

Levin, C. (1996) *Jean Baudrillard: A study in cultural metaphysics.* New York: Prentice Hall.

Luke, T. (1989) *Screens of Power: Ideology, domination, and resistance in informational society.* Urbana, IL: University of Illinois Press.

Ritzer, G. (1998) 'Introduction', in *The Consumer Society: Myths and structures*, by J. Baudrillard, pp. 1–23. London: Sage.

Stearns, W. and Chaloupka, W. (1992) *Jean Baudrillard: The disappearance of art and politics.* New York: St Martin's Press.

20
slavoj žižek

glyn daly

Slavoj Žižek was born in Slovenia in 1949. At the University of Ljubljana he studied philosophy and was later offered a position to study psychoanalysis with Lacan's disciple, J.-A. Miller, at the University of Paris VIII. On returning to Ljubljana he took up a research post and founded the Society for Theoretical Psychoanalysis. Žižek was very active in the Alternative Movement in Slovenia, and in 1990 stood for the presidency in the first multiparty elections.

Often described as a postmodern thinker (for example, Miklitsch, 1998), Žižek's interventions have been numerous – from cinema to cyberspace, cognitivism, theology, music and opera as well as social theory. Žižek, however, rejects postmodernism's preoccupation with *differentia specifica* in favour of philosophical transcendentalism and an ongoing commitment to political universalism.

Various works by the Essex School of discourse theory (for example, Stavrakakis, 1999; Torfing, 1999) have tended to link Žižek with the post-Marxist thought of Laclau and Mouffe and as an implicit supporter of radical democracy. In reality, Žižek gives only partial support for post-Marxist theory and has criticised the project of radical democracy on the grounds that, despite its emphasis on antagonism, it does not place enough stress on the fundamentals of economic power (Žižek in Butler et al., 2000, p. 319).

Something similar can be said about Žižek's position vis-à-vis cultural studies. As a brilliant cultural commentator, his texts have widely become required reading for courses in cultural studies. Yet Žižek discerns in some forms of cultural studies a certain complicity with global capitalist relations (Žižek, 1999, p. 218; 2001a, p. 226). The typical concern with 'pluralist' issues of race, gender, sexuality and so on, is viewed by Žižek as not only obfuscating the basic dimensions of power and exclusion but also underpinning the very forms of (liberal) discourse – the emphasis on difference, multiplicity, self-affirmation, and so on – through which contemporary capitalism is reproduced.

Kay (2003), by contrast, characterises Žižek as a philosopher of the Real. While this is reasonable, the temptation to be avoided is to argue that Žižek is limited to analysing the 'unreadable kernel' of the Real in our social existence and/or the way in which we attempt to resolve the radical inconsistencies of reality. In many respects we could say virtually the opposite: Žižek does *not* elevate the Real into an absolute horizon of impossibility about which we can do nothing. His position is rather one that may be said to reflect an explicit ethical commitment to the power of the miracle. Žižek's central point is that fundamental change can and does occur but that this means crucially assuming (rather than avoiding) the traumatic encounter with the Real itself (Žižek, 2001b, p. 84). For Žižek it is one of the great tragedies of our age that the miracle, and especially the political miracle, is not at present part of our (Western) imagination. Moreover this has created the very space in which today's forms of ideological cynicism and its more recent cousin, New Age obscurantism, continue to thrive.

This chapter focuses on what I take to be the main coordinates of Žižek's perspective. It then moves to a consideration of what is at stake in central ongoing debates with postmodern and post-Marxist positions. Finally it looks at the consequences of Žižek's thought for a more radical approach to politics; a politics of the Real.

all too inhuman

Following Kant, modern philosophical endeavour has tended to become less concerned with the 'object' and more with the latter's conditions of possibility. With Kant it is not so much the particular questions that are important – what is the nature of the soul? what is good? and so on – but what has to be generically presupposed in order to formulate these questions in the first place. Simplifying, the general problem for Kant is not so much *what* is the world but rather *how* do we arrive at such a notion as 'world' as an entity that can disclose information to us? on what type of transcendental *a priori* structure does it depend? This, of course, introduces the dimension of subjectivity to the world of objects and, in particular, the question of subjective engagement with that world.

From this point onwards what is rendered thematic in German idealism is an essential lack of fit between the human being and the world. We do not belong to any positive or predetermined order of Being and consequently our orientations are radically undecidable. We are thus *compelled* to ask (impossible) questions of ourselves in relation to the world precisely because of a fundamental asymmetry, an absence of any ecology of Being. As Trinity remarks to Neo in *The Matrix*, 'It's the question that drives us …' What is behind the question (of our place/Being in the world) is this basic condition of dislocation. This means that the *positivisation* of Being is something that can take place only through a transcendental logic of negativity. Thus what Kant speculatively refers to as diabolical evil – that is, an ethical commitment to evil along the lines of de Sade – is clearly possible (although Kant himself cannot countenance its existence). This is so precisely because of a constitutive negativity that, in principle, allows for an autonomy of Being and of disposition beyond any pregiven or naturalistic order (Žižek, 1993, p. 101). This self-relating negativity is made even more explicit in Hegel and his notion of the human being as an entity constituted in and through a transcendent 'night of the world': 'The human being is this night, this empty nothing, that contains everything in its simplicity – an unending wealth of many representations, images, of which none belongs to him – or which are not present' (Hegel, 'Jenaer Realphilosophie', cited in Žižek, 1999, p. 29).

Žižek affirms that psychoanalysis is the direct descendant of German idealism and that it articulates this dimension of self-relating negativity in terms of the idea of death drive (Žižek, 1999, pp. 65–6). Death drive is the existential consequence of the very gap in the order of Being identified in German idealism. It is neither a cancellation nor any kind of physical death but is rather a certain excessive impulse that persists beyond mere existence or biological life. As Žižek argues: 'Human life is never "just life", it is always sustained by an excess of life' (Žižek, 2001b, p. 104). The human being is precisely the entity that is sustained by a 'more than human'. It is that 'inhuman' excess – born of a fundamental alienation – which is the death drive and which is constitutive of humanity as such. Death drive is a constant impulse to resolve the gap, or heal the wound, in the order of Being; to overcome dislocation and establish the full presence of subjectivity by finding its ultimate name/place in the world.

In this context – and against the grain of standard postmodern thinking – Žižek insists on the validity of the notion of subject (Žižek, 1999, pp. 158–9). The subject is neither a positive entity nor an identifiable locus but is thoroughly desubstantialised – it is precisely 'this empty nothing' of which Hegel speaks. This is why the Lacanian mark for the subject is $ (S-barred, the empty place or void that cannot be filled out in an ultimate sense).

In the earlier works of Žižek, the subject is presented in terms of an inherent point of failure (the limit) in all forms of subjectivity – the bone stuck in the throat of signification – that shows the ontological gap of Being. The subject is the subject of the signifier precisely because of its status of void/impossibility that is the very condition of possibility for an infinitude of signification (Žižek, 1989, p. 175). Subject and subjectivity exist in a symbiotic and dynamic relationship. Subjectivity will be more or less stable according to context. Under the impact of a traumatic experience, however, we experience a certain 'night of the world' where coherence and cohesion become radically undermined – that is the condition of subject.

In later works, Žižek gives an added twist to the notion of subject. Thus the subject is not simply the gap/void in the order of Being, it is also 'the contingent-excessive gesture that constitutes the very universal order of Being' (1999, p. 160). As in Russell's paradoxical set of sets, the subject also functions as an excluded particularity that nonetheless generates the frame of universality as such. The frame of subjectivity is not constituted against an external force (the elimination of which would yield true subjectivity) but through an inherent blockage that is the subject (Žižek, 1999, p. 159). We might say that the subject gets caught in an impossible attempt to produce a framework of subjectivity (to find its name/place), but from which it is already ontologically excluded. In this sense, the subject marks the site where an irresolvable economy of lack and excess are played out.

This economy is perhaps best illustrated by the relationship between subject and its objects a (*objets petit a* – objects small Other). Lacan's object 'a' refers to the object-cause of desire: that which is in the object more than the object and which makes us desire it in the first place. It alludes to the originally lost object (the missing element that would resolve our drive and 'restore' fulfilment) and, at the same time, functions as an embodiment of lack; as a loss positivised (Žižek, 1997, p. 81; 1999, p. 107).

Object 'a' bears witness to an empty structure of desire – a structure that can never be filled out. Desire is always elsewhere and alludes to an absence whose central reference is a fundamental void around which drive constantly circulates and constantly misses its target. It is in this sense that Žižek refers to object 'a' in terms of a Kantian 'negative magnitude', something that acts as a stand-in for Nothingness (Žižek, 1999, p. 107). There exists a metonymy of lack whereby any empirical object can act as this stand-in. Object 'a' is doubly paradoxical in that it refers to an original 'lost' object (of completion/unity) that never existed, and also in that its own existence depends on its very unattainability.

The subject subsists in a kind of diabolical symmetry with its object(s) 'a' wherein the latter (partially) embodies the lack designated by the former; a lack that constantly strives to be recognised/resolved in positive terms but which can never be fully achieved – subject and object never coincide. A well known email circular is illustrative. A mock audit of staff morale is sent as an attachment in which the final exercise is one where you are asked to 'click here' if you want a bigger salary, better conditions, and so on. Of course, when you move your cursor to the relevant box, the 'click here' simply moves and pops up somewhere else on the screen no matter how quickly or stealthily you try to approach it. In this sense, fulfilment (the satisfaction of desire) is always just a click away; a promise that is sustained by the very lack/impossibility of (total) fulfilment.

The subject strives for a fullness in the object that it lacks. This accounts for the passionate attachment to certain objects and toward which people may risk everything. Tarantino's film *Pulp Fiction* is illustrative. In the boxer's story, the Bruce Willis character refuses to take a dive in a fixed fight and as a result falls foul of a local gangster. Instead of leaving town immediately, however, Bruce returns to his apartment to pick up his (dead) father's watch – thereby risking his life. Why do this? The answer is that this particular watch represents object 'a': a partial embodiment of the lost parent–child unity. It is this watch, and no other, that holds the promise of an ultimate reconciliation (to restore 'lost' unity) and, at the same time, underscores the fact that such reconciliation is always lacking – always a 'click' away. Every object 'a' is a reminder/remainder of a kind of pre-Big Bang consummate unity that has never existed. It is here that both lack (subject) and excess (identifications) – every 'pathological' gesture to positivise void – may be said to coincide (Žižek, 1999, p. 107).

The 'many' identifications and forms of collective objective life are made possible through the persistence of the 'one' of radical negativity. The infinitude of signification is the result ultimately of the one true signified … void. For Žižek this is the starting point of a new approach to politics. We are political animals not in the sense of Aristotle, who understood by this a certain capacity to recognise a pre-existing order of the good, but the opposite. It is precisely because there is no pre-existing order that we are *condemned* to be political animals. Without an ecology of Being, we are confronted with what Žižek, in his discussion of Schelling (Žižek, 1997), calls an unbridgeable abyss of freedom – an abyss that is simultaneously the source of universal rights and ethnic cleansing.

the touch of the real

The persistence of radical negativity is what the later Lacan generically characterised as the Real: the ultimate 'signified' around which all signification is constituted and through which signification simultaneously finds its limitation and inexorable failure. As is well documented elsewhere (for example, Fink, 1995), the Real is inextricably linked with the registers of the Symbolic and the Imaginary, and together they form a basic triadic structure for all (human) Being. In general terms, both the Symbolic and the Imaginary may be said to belong to the order of signification. While the Symbolic refers to the (potentially) infinite uses of signification through language and symbols, the Imaginary refers to the particular ways in which signification becomes arrested around certain fundamental images of ourselves that offer a sense of coherence and place in the world. It is through the Imaginary that we achieve particular forms of identification and through which we are able to resolve the basic question(s) of who we are for the Other: we 'narrate' ourselves around certain basic images with which we identify and/or from which we institute projections.

The Real, on the other hand, not only does not belong (directly) to the order of signification but crucially represents its negation. The Real is rather the transcendental (and constitutive) dimension of resistance in every process of signification. This transcendental aspect is something that does not sit easily with the main trends in postmodern thought. According to Butler, for example, the idea of the Real, as something that cannot be integrated symbolically, is already logically inconsistent:

> [T]o claim that the real resists symbolization is still to symbolize the real as a kind of resistance. The former claim (the real resists symbolization) can only be true if the latter claim ('the real resists symbolization' is a symbolization) is true, but if the second claim is true, the first is necessarily false. (Butler, 1993, p. 207)

In other words, if you *posit* something as external to symbolisation you can only do so through symbolisation itself; you cannot signify anything beyond signification. But as Žižek points out, the Real should not be thought of as some kind of external entity (which would indeed invoke the *petitio principii* to which Butler alludes). The Real is rather strictly an *internal* point of failure, an inherent limit. Thus what we have is a paradox rather than a logical contradiction:

> The paradox ... is that Butler is right, in a way: yes, the Real *is* in fact internal/inherent to the Symbolic, not its external limit, *but for that very reason*, it cannot be symbolized. In other words, the paradox is that the Real as external, excluded from the Symbolic, is in fact a symbolic determination – what eludes symbolization is precisely the Real as the *inherent point of failure* of symbolization. (Žižek in Butler et al., 2000, p. 121)

The Real is experienced in terms of Symbolic (dis)functioning itself. We touch the Real through those points where symbolisation fails, through trauma, aversion, dislocation and all those markers of uncertainty where the Symbolic fails to deliver a consistent and coherent reality. While the Real cannot be directly represented – hence Lacan's dictum that nothing is lacking in the Real (lack can only be formulated through some form of symbolic endeavour as it has no meaning in relation to radical negativity) – it can nonetheless be *shown* in terms of symbolic failure and can be alluded to through figurative embodiments of horror-excess that threaten disintegration (monsters, forces of nature, disease/viruses, and so on).

Schumacher's *Flatliners* is illustrative. The film concerns a group of medical students who, in an almost Faustian way, attempt to penetrate the mysteries of death, and thereby our true nature, by stopping each other's hearts (flatlining them), and then, after a given period of time, resuscitating them. At the point of death, each student begins a fantasmatic journey that takes them to the very edge of their symbolic-imaginary universe. Once they reach that edge, what they find is not some ultimate truth but a particular marker of negation, an unbearable encounter that cannot be resolved/domesticated in their symbolic universe and from which they desperately try to escape, to 'awaken' back into reality. Far from yielding a positive secret or tangible breakthrough, what their constant probing brings them into confrontation with is a thoroughly intangible and unsurpassable horizon of radical negativity. This is the point where we might say that rationalist (Enlightenment-led) subjectivity fails and is drawn into traumatic proximity with the subject *qua* night of the world, where it meets the subject as *an answer of the Real* (see Žižek, 1989, pp. 178–82).

In his earlier work, Žižek tended to focus on the Real as a hard limit to signification. More recently, he has developed a more subtle reading of the Real. Following the triadic structure of the Lacanian registers, Žižek stresses that there are in fact three basic orders of the Real: the real Real, the symbolic Real, and the imaginary Real (Žižek, 2001b, pp. 82–3; 2002, p. xii; Žižek and Daly, 2003). The real Real is the hard limit that functions as the horrifying Thing (the Alien, Medusa's head, maelstrom, and so on) – a shattering force of negation. The symbolic Real refers to the anonymous symbols and codes (scientific formulae, digitalisation, empty signifiers ...) that function in an indifferent manner as the abstract 'texture' onto which, or out of which, reality is constituted. In *The Matrix*, for example, the symbolic Real is given expression at the point where Neo perceives 'reality' in terms of the abstract streams of digital output. In the contemporary world, Žižek argues that it is capital itself that provides this essential backdrop to our reality and as such represents the symbolic Real of our age (Žižek, 1999, pp. 222, 276).

With the imaginary Real we have precisely the (unsustainable) dimension of fantasmatic excess-negation that is explored in *Flatliners*. This is why cyberspace is such an ambiguous imaginary realm. At first sight it would appear to be totally impervious to the Real – a free-floating universe of infinite fantasising. Yet it is precisely through cyberspace that we can take that 'click' too far and be brought into unbearable proximity with our most intimate fears and anxieties: repugnance-fascination towards certain images/practices, morbid obsessions, an insufferable connection with Otherness ('Am I really like that/them?').

It is particularly this aspect of the Real that Žižek emphasises in relation to 9/11 (Žižek, 2001c). What happened there was not so much that (Real) reality intruded into the fantasy world of US harmony, but rather that a certain fantasmatic excess intruded into reality (Žižek, 2001c, p. 18). What was so shocking about the 9/11 attacks was this aspect of the imaginary Real – this nightmarish excess of apocalyptic destruction (already prefigured in numerous Hollywood blockbusters) – from which 'we' could not awaken, which we could not leave behind in the cinema. In this way, the traumatic impact of 9/11 could be said to have been doubly inscribed: as a terrible physical event and, even more intensely, as a trans-dimensional breach, a fundamental transgression of the subliminal injunction that the nightmare fantasy should 'stay there!' and not come after us.

The central point is that the Real is strictly inherent to reality. The relationship between the two is not spatial but dimensional, one of mutual contamination. As Žižek argues, while reality is produced through a certain 'grimace of the Real' – a constitutive impossibility that becomes distorted into reality (like the blinding Sun that generates illumination through being beyond illumination and whose outline can only be perceived by 'looking awry') – the Real itself is 'nothing but a grimace of reality' (Žižek, 2002, p. xvii), that which shines through the distorted perspective we call reality.

The Real is always that which is in reality more than reality. As with humanity itself, reality is sustained by an excess that cannot be incorporated within it (the indigestible bone in the throat). Returning to *The Matrix*, it is not that we have reality, on the one hand, and a potentially removable 'splinter in your mind' that distorts it on the other. Rather reality itself is *the very consequence* of a mind splinter. Distortions in reality are always possible because of the basic distortion that *is* reality, which means that it can never be identical to itself, can never achieve an ontological fullness but always remains instead a perspectival orientation towards that which sustains and exceeds it.

This perspective undercuts the standard criticisms of psychoanalysis as simply a product of its age (a symptom of Victorian/Viennese repression) and/or as something that may have some benefit in treating individuals but which has no bearing on the collective world. What Žižek demonstrates is that such criticisms already miss the (Kantian-Hegelian) transcendental turn of psychoanalysis whereby the individual/collective division no longer holds. As he puts it:

> The focus of psychoanalysis is entirely different: the Social, the field of social practices and socially held beliefs is not simply on a different level from individual experience, but something to which *the individual has to relate*, something which *the individual* has to experience as an order which is minimally 'reified', externalized. (Žižek, 2002, p. lxxii)

The question is rather, how does the 'objective world' have to be organised in order for something like 'subjectivity' to be possible (and vice versa)? The psychoanalytic response is that both subjective and objective should be considered as (unstable) dimensions of a continuum that is traversed by the impossible Real. The basic human condition is that both objectivity and subjectivity are lacking towards an excess and against which they try to achieve homeostasis and mutual reassurance. This means that we can never stand on neutral ground. We are always minimally engaged in some kind of orientation in respect of the Real, one that necessarily involves the repression/ exclusion of alternative potential orientations. To reiterate, the human being is a political animal precisely *because* there is no pregiven/substantialist reality and because it always has to be forged as a matter of delusional consistency. It is in the context of this essential delusional (in)consistency of reality that Žižek has developed a thoroughgoing critique of ideology.

ideology and impossibility

Žižek has been concerned crucially to demonstrate the way in which ideology serves to support reality as a concrete fully integrated totality – reality cannot be reproduced without initial ideological mystification. Ideology does not conceal or distort an underlying positivity (the way things really are), but quite the opposite. What ideology attempts to do is provide a certain positive consistency against the distorting and traumatising effects of the Real (Žižek, 1989, p. 45).

All ideology presents reality as a full ontological totality, and in this way it tries to repress the traumatic fact that the latter is ultimately a delusion; it tries to eliminate all traces of (Real) impossibility (Žižek, 1989, p. 49). The exemplary figure here is that of the cynic. The typical cynic is someone who is 'pragmatic', who distances him or herself from sincerely held beliefs, dismisses alternative visions of social existence as so much juvenile nonsense ... and who, for all that, relies even more deeply on some absolutist conception of an independent fully-formed reality.

The cynic is the very model of an ideological subjectivity insofar as s/he is radically dependent on the idea of an externally ratified reality ('human nature', 'the way it is', and so on). What the cynic fears most is that they might lose the support of this independent (Other) reality and consequently their sense of 'place' in the world. The cynic gets involved in a certain short-circuiting procedure that is, in fact, generic to all ideological functioning: he/she is cynical towards every kind of ideological belief *except* his/her own fundamentalist belief in objectivist reality.

The cynical attitude is more widely reflected in today's predominant inclination towards 'postmodern ironising'. The key philosopher is arguably Rorty, who wants a world where individuals are free 'to pursue private perfection in idiosyncratic ways' (Rorty, 1991, p. 19) and where the public realm is restricted to minimal functions and is essentially aesthetic in orientation (Rorty, 1989, p. 125). For Rorty the central obligation is to be sceptical towards any projects of substantial social engagement for fear that it might curtail individual pursuits of happiness and lead towards despotic forms of cruelty in the name of a higher (collective) Truth (see Daly, 1994). The basic inconsistency in Rorty's position is that 'we' should exercise an ironic distancing towards every sociopolitical project *except* the liberal one:

the one true reality whose (private/public) structuring of social relations represents 'the last *conceptual* revolution' (Rorty, 1989, p. 63) and effectively suspends history.

This is why so much of what passes for contemporary postmodern thought should be understood as strictly ideological in character. With all its ironic distancing, disavowals of the authentic gesture and so on, it relies even more heavily on the functioning of the existing order as if it were a naturalistic, or immaculate, Other – a kind of preservation of the ontological dream through symbolic mortification. In other words, it tends to involve the very form of ideological identification that is formulated along the lines of 'we know very well that there is no such thing as Reality but nonetheless we believe in it'.

So how does ideology deal with its immanent impossibility, with the fact that it cannot deliver a fully integrated social order? Žižek's answer is that ideology attempts to reify impossibility into some kind of external obstacle, to fantasmatically translate the impossibility of Society into the theft or sabotage of Society (see Daly, 1999). Transcendental impossibility is projected into some contingent historicised Other (for example, the figure of 'the Jew' in Nazi ideology) in such a way that the lost/stolen object (social harmony/purity) appears retrievable, an object which, of course, 'we' have never possessed. By synonymising the impossible-Real with a particular Other (Jews, Palestinians, Gypsies, immigrants ...), the fantasy of holistic fulfilment through the (imagined or otherwise) elimination/suppression of the Other is thereby sustained.

Žižek has recently given this perspective a further more radical twist. Thus ideology not only presents a certain ideal of holistic fulfilment (Plato's Republic of Reason, Habermas's transparent modernity, Rorty's liberal utopia, multiculturalist harmony, and so on), it also serves crucially to regulate a certain distance from it. The paradox of ideology is that it advances a particular fantasy of being reconciled with the Thing (of total fulfilment) but with the built-in proviso that we do not come too close to it. The psychoanalytic reason for this is clear: if you come too close to the Thing it either fragments irretrievably (like a digitally produced image) or, as in the Kantian sublime, produces unbearable anxiety and psychical disintegration.

The point is that ideology is always already engaged reflexively with its own impossibility. Impossibility is articulated through ideology and in such a way that it both structures reality and establishes the very sense of what is considered possible. Here we have a double inscription. First there is the basic operation of translating impossibility into an external obstacle (an Other). But second, there is a further deeper stage whereby the ideological objective itself is elevated to the status of impossibility precisely as a way of avoiding any direct encounter with it (see Žižek and Daly, 2003).

Ideology seeks to maintain a critical distance by keeping the Thing in focus but without coming so close that it begins to distort and fragment (see Daly, 1999, p. 235). The paradigmatic example is of someone who fantasises about an ideal object (a sexual scenario, a promotion, a public performance, and so on), and when they actually encounter the object, they are typically confronted with a de-idealisation of the object, a return of the Real. By keeping the object at a certain distance, however, ideology sustains the satisfaction derived from the fantasy of holistic fulfilment: 'if only I had *x* I could achieve my dream'. Ideology is the impossible dream, not simply in terms of overcoming impossibility, but of constructing the latter in an acceptable way, in a way that itself yields a certain satisfaction of both having and eating the cake. The idea of overcoming impossibility subsists as a deferred moment of realisation but without having to go through the pain of overcoming as such. Ideology regulates this fantasmatic distance as a way of avoiding the Real in the impossible – the trauma involved in any real change.

Let us take the case of Iraq and the so-called New World Order. With extensive military mobilisation, widespread social upheaval and a terrible human cost, the invasion of Iraq was undertaken precisely in order that the underlying structures of Western–US socioeconomic power can continue to function in a relatively undisturbed way. While the invasion was initially justified on the grounds of international security, this has, consequent on a profound lack of evidence, been largely rearticulated in terms of a project of emancipation. And it is here that we get the ideological twist: 'we are here to liberate/democratise Iraq ... while recognising that a full implementation of the latter is impossible under present (any) circumstances'. Thus the occupation of Iraq continues in full force. The message is: 'In principle (you can have liberation), yes; but in reality, no.'

It is this hidden clause of deferral that effectively prevents any real attempt to realise the publicly stated objective. Along the lines of Henry Ford's famous declaration ('You can have any colour you like, as long as it's black') we see the same kind of forced choice at play: 'The Iraqi people can have all the democracy they want, all the popular control over their oil and natural resources ... as long as it is modelled on US–Western liberal capitalism, as long as it does not undermine US–Western interests.'

With New World Order discourse we see a similar ideological process. Any genuine attempt to realise such an order would involve massive (traumatic) changes: power sharing, the eradication of poverty and systematic social exclusion, a globalisation of equal rights/participation, and so on, as integral reflexive elements. In reality, the New World Order is routinely conjured as an indefinite ideal that serves precisely to prevent any real movement towards it. The same type of ideological clause is secretly functioning: 'We are moving towards a New World Order that will not tolerate the Saddam Husseins of this world ... while recognising that a true implementation of such an order (one that would be intolerant of all the autocrats and corporate profiteers/dictatorships) is currently/always impossible.' In this way, the category of impossibility itself functions as an implicit-obscene ideological supplement in today's *Realpolitik*, in today's cynical assertion of the way things actually are.

real politics

Building on Laclau and Mouffe's compelling impossibility-of-Society thesis, Žižek's intervention is one that also stresses the importance of the converse: that is, the socialisation of impossibility. For Žižek the key question concerns not so much the fact of social impossibility, but *how* is society impossible, and *how* is it dealt with politically?

In the postmodern age, the category of impossibility is one that underpins today's paradigmatic language of 'provisionality', 'partiality', 'precariousness', and so on. To borrow an expression from Lyotard, there is widespread incredulity towards substantial forms of political engagement. Through a predominant culture of irony, ersatz and eternal deferral (Derrida's 'to-come'), such forms of engagement are typically disavowed as so much ideological nonsense. In our sincerely cynical times, the greatest taboo seems to be sincerity itself. The postmodern enthusiasm for impossibility is one that can all too readily feed into a type of politics that itself becomes overly partial and provisional, where political ambition is already limited by its own sense of limitation as such. It is a politics that tends to remain at the level of impossibility without ever seeking to possibilise the impossible, or in Lacanian terms, without ever passing to the act.

To some degree, postmodern culture may be viewed as a form of collective obsessive neurosis: that is, a culture that generates all kinds of concerns and different facilities for addressing problems, but only insofar as it is able to *avoid* any real substantial change. Thus with today's characteristic forms of Third Way-ism we get the semblance of politics, but without the pain of actual political confrontation/transformation. Here we see a certain mortification of politics in which the latter becomes consumed with problems of endless preparation, politically correct protocol, the creation of more and more focus groups and the idolatrising of consensus. In Gramsci's language, it is as if the contemporary logic of hegemony is already hegemonised – effectively subsumed within wars of position (or positioning), without ever proceeding to any substantial war of manoeuvre.

This is reflected in the culture of political correctness. Recently there was a debate in the British media as to whether unemployed people should be allowed to refuse to work for Ann Summers (a chain of sex shops). The 'politically correct' response was that diversity needs to be taken into account and that if people had moral, religious and/or cultural objections then alternatives should be found. What was not even questioned, however, was the underlying policy principle of forcing people to work in the first place, of compelling people to assume responsibility for their marginalisation in a liberal-capitalist economy that *of structural necessity* produces systematic unemployment, underemployment and widespread poverty. In this way, the latter are not viewed as the barbaric consequences of a political construction for which we are collectively responsible, but simply as features of the way things are.

Ideology functions in this way by absolving 'us' from ethico-political responsibility. This is exemplified in the contemporary 'ethical' approach to worldwide poverty and destitution. The predominant (Western) response is charity-led where there is this model tendency towards ideological absolution: we are, in fact, *not* ultimately ethically responsible. The increasingly popular 'adoption' schemes are emblematic of this and reflect an almost 'zoological' approach to ethics in terms of this very type of absolution/distancing. With wildlife charities it is possible to make regular donations and thereby to 'adopt' the animal of your choice: dolphin, elephant, gorilla, and so on. Similarly, with human charities (especially those dealing with Africa and Asia) you can now 'adopt' a grandmother and/or a child. In return for payment you receive personalised feedback – usually a photograph, a progress report and (in the case of the child) a minimum of two letters per year. Axial to this exchange is a certain type of gaze: the imagining of how the victim-Other perceives 'us' as elevated benefactors. We connect with the Other on the grounds that they keep their distance, that they do not demand from us or assert their Being, but rather play the role of abstract/grateful victim. The perverse (postmodern) libidinal pleasure is one of having a relationship but without the relationship as such, without the Real in the relationship. Little wonder that the emotionally stunted Jack Nicholson character in *About Schmidt* found it so much easier to communicate with his assigned adoptee, someone who exists for him only through letters and drawings and onto whom he can project all kinds of fantasies. In general then, we can have our 'ethical' relationship with the abject-Other and do so precisely in such a way that we are not ethically implicated in the system that produces abjection in the first place. Abjection is always something that happens elsewhere – the result of unfortunate circumstances, acts of God, a barbarous lack of civilisation, and so on – so that 'we' are not responsible. This is the basic ideological alibi.

Žižek is concerned to confront this alibi head-on and to oppose it with an ethics of the Real (see also Zupančič, 2000). This is an ethics in which we assume responsibility for our own actions and our inscription within the broader lifeworld up to and including the construction of socioeconomic reality. This is not to embrace any kind of *carte blanche* approach to reality. The point is rather that we should address the full implications of the way in which our reality is reproduced in human terms and not as a cosmic order. We cannot hide behind terms like 'globalisation', 'pragmatism', 'economic reality', 'rationality', and so on, as if they described a neutral ontological order. On the contrary, we are obliged to confront the way in which such terms attempt ideologically to disguise the artificial nature of reality (this grimace of the Real), and, on that very basis, to make real (Real) ethical decisions, that is, decisions that begin from the position that genuine transformation is always possible and always involves this traumatic dimension of the Real, this dimension of rupture with existing symbolic structures.

An ethics of the Real is not one of accepting impossibility in the sense of an indefinite ideal, but is rather one that entreats us to risk the impossible – to break out of the bonds of existing possibility. This opens the way for what Žižek refers to as *the act* and also for overcoming the symbolic mortification associated with the ideological-cynical attitude that revolves around a fetishised notion of absolute reality. The Third Way-ist perspective, for example, is largely stupefied by its master signifier 'globalisation' and is consequently unable to mount any real challenge to the basic power structures. Global (capitalist) reality is in place, so it is chiefly a question of adjustment and of adopting a mature-pragmatic attitude. Politics is reduced to a repetitive logic of deliberation rather than active resistance, a politics of conformism towards a determinate order of reality rather than a reconfiguration of that reality. Like Hamlet, Third Way-ism remains transfixed by the spectre of impossibility (the global Thing), and this renders it incapable of risking the impossible, of passing to the act.

Žižek's thought is crucially concerned to reactivate the dimension of the miraculous in political endeavour. For Žižek the miracle is that which coincides with trauma in the sense that it involves a fundamental moment of symbolic disintegration (2001b, p. 86). This is the mark of the act: a basic rupture in the weave of reality that opens up new possibilities and creates the space for a reconfiguration of reality itself. Like the miracle, the act is ultimately unsustainable – it cannot be reduced to, or incorporated directly within, the symbolic order. Yet it is through the act that we touch (and are touched by) the Real in such a way that the bonds of our symbolic universe are broken and an alternative construction is enabled – reality is transformed in a Real sense.

The Real is not simply a force of negation against which we are helpless. In contrast to standard criticisms, what psychoanalysis demonstrates is that we are *not* victims of either unconscious motives or an infrastructural logic of the Real. If reality is a constitutive distortion then the ultimate lesson of psychoanalysis is that we are responsible for its reproduction. Miracles can and do happen. We are capable of Real acts that give reality a new texture and direction, acts that reflect this gap in the order of Being, this abyss of freedom. If Freud – in his theory of the unconscious – affirms an essential autonomisation of the signifier, then what Žižek emphasises is an essential autonomisation of the act: a basic capacity to break out of existing structures/cycles of signification. Far from being constrained by the notion of impossibility, Žižek's perspective is sustained and energised by the ontological potential for achieving the 'impossible' through Real intervention. In this sense, Žižek's conception of the Real may be said to constitute both an inherent limit and an inherent opening/beginning – the radically negative dimension that is the condition of *creatio ex nihilo* and the political itself.

Žižek's perspective functions as a powerful antidote to the type of politics that, in terms of their symbolic mandate, becomes overly procedural and deliberative. At the same time, I do not think that such a sharp distinction between the latter and a politics of action can so easily be drawn. We do not act in an abstract or acontextual way. On the contrary, we find the capacity to act (at least in part) in and through procedural and deliberative encounter and strategy. The paradox is that while both finally negate each other, both are needed. The movement towards a more ambitious and democratic universalism, for example, is consequent on a subversion of existing forms of globalisation, on releasing the emancipatory potentials that already exist within these forms. We might say that it is consequent on developing politically what there is in globalisation that is more than globalisation.

Here I think we should rather speak of a *politics* of the Real (or a Real politics). While every form of political subversion must involve the dimension of the Real, the Real itself cannot dictate the nature or direction of subversion. Through a radical reading of psychoanalysis, Žižek cuts through the sterility of postmodern cynicism and charges us with the full (in)human capacity and responsibility to act. How we choose to act, however, cannot be answered by psychoanalysis alone. This will depend on political engagement. Žižek's perspective exhorts us to be passionate in this engagement.

further reading

Besides the listing in the References below, further key works by Žižek (all in paperback) include *Enjoy Your Symptom!* (Routledge, 1992), *Looking Awry* (MIT Press, 1991), *For They Know Not What They Do* (Verso, 1991), *The Metastases of Enjoyment* (Verso, 1994), *The Plague of Fantasies* (Verso, 1997), and *The Fright of Real Tears: Krzystof Kieślowski* (British Film Institute, 2001). A useful collection of Žižek's papers with commentary is provided in *The Žižek Reader*, ed. E. and E. Wright (Blackwell, 1999). For texts that engage with Žižek's perspective, see the following: J. Copjec, *Read My Desire* (MIT Press, 1994) and *Imagine There's no Woman* (Polity Press, 2003); G. Daly, 'Politics and the Impossible: Beyond Psychoanalysis and Deconstruction', *Theory Culture and Society* 16 (1999): 75–98, and J. Glynos, 'The Grip of Ideology', *Journal of Political Ideologies* 6 (2001): 191–214. For more critical appraisals of Žižek, see P. Dews, 'The Tremor of Reflection: Slavoj Žižek's Lacanian Dialectics', *Radical Philosophy* 72 (1995): 17–29; S. Homer, 'Psychoanalysis, Representation, Politics: On the (Im)possibility of a Psychoanalytic Theory of Ideology', *The Letter* 7 (1996): 97–109, and 'It's the Political Economy, Stupid! On Žižek's Marxism', *Radical Philosophy* 108 (2001): 7–16. For a demystification of Lacanian terminology, see D. Evans, *An Introductory Dictionary of Lacanian Psychoanalysis* (Routledge, 1996).

references

Butler, J. (1993) *Bodies that Matter*. New York: Routledge.
Butler, J., Laclau, E. and Žižek, S. (eds) (2000) *Contingency, Hegemony, Universality: Contemporary dialogues on the left*. London: Verso.

Daly, G. (1994) 'Post-metaphysical Culture and Politics: Richard Rorty and Laclau and Mouffe', *Economy and Society* 23: 173–200.

Daly, G. (1999) 'Ideology and its Paradoxes: Dimensions of Fantasy and Enjoyment', *Journal of Political Ideologies* 4: 219–38.

Fink, B. (1995) *The Lacanian Subject*. Princeton, NJ: Princeton University Press.

Kay, S. (2003) *Žižek: A Critical Introduction*. Cambridge: Polity Press.

Miklitsch, R. (1998) '"Going Through the Fantasy": Screening Slavoj Žižek', *South Atlantic Quarterly* 97: 475–507.

Rorty, R. (1989) *Contingency, Irony and Solidarity*. Cambridge: Cambridge University Press.

Rorty, R. (1991) 'Habermas, Derrida and the Functions of Philosophy'. Paper presented at the University of Essex, reproduced in R. Rorty, (1998), *Truth and Progress*. Cambridge: Cambridge University Press.

Stavrakakis, Y. (1999) *Lacan and the Political*. London: Routledge.

Torfing, J. (1999) *New Theories of Discourse: Laclau, Mouffe and Žižek*. Oxford: Blackwell.

Žižek, S. (1989) *The Sublime Object of Ideology*. London: Verso.

Žižek, S. (1993) *Tarrying With the Negative*. Durham, NC: Duke University Press.

Žižek, S. (1997) *The Abyss of Freedom*. Ann Arbor, MI: University of Michigan Press.

Žižek, S. (1999) *The Ticklish Subject*. London: Verso.

Žižek, S. (2001a) *Did Somebody Say Totalitarianism?* London: Verso.

Žižek, S. (2001b) *On Belief*. London: Routledge.

Žižek, S. (2001c) *Welcome to the Desert of the Real*. New York: Wooster Press.

Žižek, S. (2002) *For They Know Not What They Do*. London: Verso.

Žižek, S. and Daly, G. (2003) *Conversations with Žižek*. Cambridge: Polity Press.

Zupančič, A. (2000) *Ethics of the Real*. London: Verso.

notes on the editors and contributors

Dimitrios E. Akrivoulis has recently received his PhD in International Relations from the University of Kent at Canterbury. Drawing on Paul Ricoeur's hermeneutics of imagination, his thesis investigates the functions of opposing scientific metaphors in politics and the dialectical relationship between their social imaginaries. Parts of his work appear in *Politics at the Edge*, ed. C. Pierson and S. Tormey (Basingstoke and London: Macmillan, 2000), and in the forthcoming collection of essays on Paul Ricoeur, *Interpretation, Values, Action*, ed. Y.B. Raynova (Vienna: Vienna Institute for Axiological Research and Peter Lang Publishing Group). He is currently teaching Political Philosophy and International Relations Theory at the New York College and the University of Western Macedonia, Greece. He is also an attorney-at-law at the Law Bar of Thessaloniki and a co-founder of the Hellenic Association of Public International Law and International Relations.

Benjamin Arditi was recently Professor of Politics in the Faculty of Politics and Social Sciences of the National University of Mexico, where he taught political theory. He is the author (with Jeremy Valentine) of *Polemicization: The contingency of the commonplace* (Edinburgh University Press and New York University Press, 1999); *La Política en los Bordes del Liberalismo* (Buenos Aires, 2005). He is also the editor of *El Reverso de la Diferencia: Identidad y política* (Caracas, 2000) and *¿Democracia Postliberal? El espacio político de las asociaciones* (Barcelona, 2005). His recent publications include articles on identity politics, populism, the concept of revolution, resistances to globalism and post-liberal politics. He is the co-general editor of 'Taking on the Political', a book series on Continental Political Thought published by Edinburgh University Press.

Gordon A. Babst is Assistant Professor of Political Science at Chapman University in Orange, California, where he teaches political philosophy. He is the author of *Liberal Constitutionalism, Marriage, and Sexual Orientation: A contemporary case for disestablishment* (Peter Lang, 2002). His research focuses critical attention on the role of religion in modern liberal-democratic society, as well as contemporary issues of diversity, law, and toleration.

Andrew Barry is Reader in Sociology and Director of the Centre for the Study of Invention and Social Process at Goldsmiths College, University of London. He is the author of *Political Machines: Governing a technological society* (Athlone, 2001) and co-editor of *Foucault and Political Reason: Liberalism, neo-liberalism and rationalities of government* (UCL Press, 1996).

Anthony Burns is Senior Lecturer in Philosophy and Political Theory in the School of Politics at the University of Nottingham. He is the author of *Natural Law and Political Ideology in the Philosophy of Hegel* (Ashgate, 1996) and co-editor (with Ian Fraser) of *The Hegel–Marx Connection* (Palgrave, 2000). He has published articles in a variety of journals, including *History of Political Thought*, *Political Studies*, *Utopian Studies*, *History of the Human Sciences* and *The Sociological Review*.

Kirsten Campbell lectures in Sociology at Goldsmiths College, University of London. She has published work on psychoanalysis and law, human rights and feminist theory, and is author of *Jacques Lacan and Feminist Epistemology* (London and New York, 2004). She is editor of the *Journal of Lacanian Studies*.

Terrell Carver is Professor of Political Theory at the University of Bristol. His DPhil dissertation was on Marx's methodology and he has published extensively on Marx, Engels and Marxism, as well as on sex, gender and sexuality from a postmodern perspective. His most recent books are *The Postmodern Marx* (Manchester University Press, 1998) and *Men in Political Theory* (Manchester University Press, 2004).

Renato Cristi teaches political philosophy at the Department of Philosophy, Wilfrid Laurier University, Waterloo, Canada. He is the author of *Le libéralisme conservateur: Trois essaies sur Schmitt, Hayek et Hegel* (Paris: Kimé, 1993) and *Carl Schmitt and Authoritarian Liberalism: Strong state, free economy* (Cardiff: University of Wales Press, 1998). Some of his articles have appeared in the *Canadian Journal of Political Science*, *Political Theory*, and *History of Political Thought*.

Glyn Daly is Senior Lecturer in Politics in the Faculty of Arts and Social Sciences at University College, Northampton. He is author of *Conversations with Žižek* (Cambridge, 2003) and has published other work on Marxism and post-Marxism, and ideology and fantasy. His *Žižek: Ideology, the Real and the Subject* is in preparation.

Michael Dillon is Professor of Politics at the University of Lancaster. His books include *Dependence and Deterrence* (Gower, 1983); *Defence Decision Making: A comparative analysis* (Pinter, 1988); *The Falklands Politics and War* (Macmillan, 1989); *The Political Subject of Violence*, ed. with David Campbell (Manchester University Press, 1993), and *Politics of Security: Towards a political philosophy of continental thought* (Routledge, 1996). He has also written extensively on cultural and political theory for a wide variety of academic journals, and is co-editor of the *Journal for Cultural Research*. He is currently working on three related projects: *The Liberal Way of War* (with Julian Reid), *Governing Terror*, and *Divine Violence* (with Paul Fletcher). He would like to express his thanks to Mark Lacy, Cindy Weber, Paul Fletcher and Paolo Palladino for conversations in aid of his chapter on Derrida.

Timothy Hall is Lecturer in Politics at the University of East London. His main interests are German idealist political thought and critical social theory. He wrote his PhD (2002) on the social and political thought of Georg Lukács at the Department of Philosophy,

University of Essex. He is currently writing a book on Lukács and is also co-authoring a book entitled *The Modern State: Theories and ideologies* for Edinburgh University Press.

Timothy W. Luke is Professor of Political Science at Virginia Polytechnic Institute and State University and has written on postmodern themes for many years. His books include *Screens of Power: Ideology, domination and resistance in information society* (University of Illinois Press, 1989), *Social Theory and Modernity: Critique, dissent and revolution* (Sage, 1990), and *Capitalism, Democracy, and Ecology: Departing from Marx* (University of Illinois Press, 1999).

Bradley J. Macdonald is Associate Professor in the Department of Political Science at Colorado State University, where he teaches political theory. He is the author of *William Morris and the Aesthetic Constitution of Politics* (Lexington Books, 1999), editor (with R.L. Rutsky) of *Strategies for Theory: From Marx to Madonna* (SUNY Press, 2003), and co-founder/co-editor of the interdisciplinary theory journal, *Strategies: Journal of theory, culture, and politics*. He is also the author of essays/chapters in journals and books on issues associated with contemporary political theory, Western Marxism and cultural politics.

James Martin is Senior Lecturer in Politics at Goldsmiths College, University of London. His publications include *Gramsci's Political Analysis: A critical introduction* (Macmillan, 1998) and, as editor, *Antonio Gramsci: Critical assessments* (Routledge, 2002). He is the co-author (with Steve Bastow) of *Third Way Discourse* (Edinburgh University Press, 2003) and co-editor of *Marx's Eighteenth Brumaire: (Post)modern interpretations* (Pluto Press, 2002). He has also published articles on poststructuralist theory and Italian political thought.

Keith Spence is Lecturer in Security and Risk at the University of Leicester, Scarman Centre. His research interests include hermeneutical and poststructuralist theorisations of contemporary politics. He is the author of *Modernity, Freedom and Community: Charles Taylor and political philosophy* (University of Wales Press, forthcoming 2006).

Lasse Thomassen is Teaching Fellow in Political Theory in the Department of Government at the University of Essex. He is the author of articles, chapters and reviews on Habermas and poststructuralist theory, the co-editor (with Lars Tønder) of *Radical Democracy: Politics between abundance and lack* (2005), and the editor of *The Derrida–Habermas Reader* (forthcoming). He is currently working on a research monograph on *Habermas and Radical Democracy*.

Roy T. Tsao is Lecturer in the Humanities at Yale University, where he also teaches in the Program in Ethics, Politics and Economics. He has published articles on the work of Hannah Arendt in several scholarly journals and is completing a book-length study of her thought.

Nathan Widder is Lecturer in Political Theory at the University of Exeter. His research focuses on issues of identity, difference, power, and knowledge, worked out through engagements with contemporary Continental philosophy on the one hand, and with ancient and medieval philosophies, on the other. He is the author of *Genealogies of Difference* (University of Illinois Press, 2002), and he is currently working on two book-length projects: one on ontologies of time and their relation to politics, and the other on the philosophy of Gilles Deleuze.

Caroline Williams lectures in political theory at Queen Mary College, University of London, and is author of *Contemporary French Philosophy: Modernity and the persistence of the subject* (London, 2001). She has published research on Althusser, Spinoza, theories of ideology and the subject, and is currently preparing a monograph on Spinoza's writings.

Howard Williams is Professor in Political Theory at the University of Wales, Aberystwyth. He is the author of *Kant's Political Philosophy* (1983); *Concepts of Ideology* (1988); *Hegel, Heraclitus and Marx's Dialectic* (1989); *International Relations in Political Theory* (1991), and *International Relations and the Limits of Political Theory* (1996), and has edited volumes on *Kant's Political Philosophy* (1992) and *Political Thought and German Reunification* (2000). His most recent book is *Kant's Critique of Hobbes: Sovereignty and cosmopolitanism* (2003), and he is currently editor of the journal *Kantian Review*. In 2004 he was Visiting Scholar at Stanford University and the Jagellonian University, Krakow.

Edward Wingenbach is Associate Professor of Government at the University of Redlands in Redlands, California. His work focuses on democratic theory (particularly deliberative democracy, social choice theory and issues of representation) and on contemporary European social thought. His articles have appeared in a range of journals and books in political science, philosophy and political theory, including the *American Journal of Political Science*, *Strategies*, and *The Journal of Politics*. He is a member of the Founding Committee of the Association for Political Theory.

index